KING FAMILIES

HERITAGE BOOKS
AN IMPRINT OF HERITAGE BOOKS, INC.

Books, CDs, and more—Worldwide

For our listing of thousands of titles see our website
at
www.HeritageBooks.com

Published 2007 by
HERITAGE BOOKS, INC.
Publishing Division
65 East Main Street
Westminster, Maryland 21157-5026

International Standard Book Number: 978-0-7884-0716-3

Our Maryland Heritage

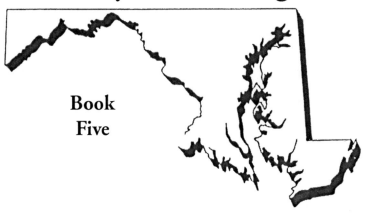

Book
Five

The
King
Families

William N. Hurley, Jr.

HERITAGE BOOKS
2007

ALSO BY W. N. HURLEY, JR.

Available from the publisher: Heritage Books, Inc.

Neikirk-Newkirk-Nikirk, Volume 1

Neikirk-Newkirk-Nikirk, Volume 2

Hurley Families in America, Volume 1

Hurley Families in America, Volume 2

John William Hines 1600, And His Descendants

Maddox, A Southern Maryland Family

Pratt Families of Virginia and Associated Families

Lowder Families in America

Our Maryland Heritage Series:

   Book One: The Fry Families

   Book Two: The Walker Families

   Book Three: The Fulks Families

   Book Four: The Watkins Families

INTRODUCTION

Among Montgomery County residents, the Kings need no introduction. They are well-known today, and have been throughout the history of the county. Primarily, they were farmers, but many of them served in political, professional and civic positions - and many of them became most successful in their endeavours. It is these King families that we have selected to study, providing the fifth book in the series devoted to a study of major families in Maryland, primarily in Montgomery County. There are Hurley connections among several of the families within the series, which is the underlying reason for the study. The author has now lived in Montgomery County for just over fifty years, and during that time, has become acquainted closely with a number of the members of these various families, often without realization of any familial connection.

This study, and those that have gone before, and others yet to be written, is but a gesture of friendship and respect to those families who have contributed so much to the growth and success of our county and state.

In 1985, the author produced a private printing entitled *The Ancestry of William Neal Hurley, III*, covering the major families found in his ancestry, including that of Hurley. This family had its American origins in Maryland, with the immigration of Daniel Hurley to Talbot County. According to *The Bristol Register of Servants Sent to Foreign Plantations 1654-1686*, by Peter Wilson Coldham, 1988, Daniel was, on September 19, 1676, bound to William Worrell for four years of service in Virginia, sailing on the *Maryland Merchant* out of Bristol, England.

In *Hurley Families in America, Volume 1*, 1995, Heritage Books, Inc., Bowie, Maryland, we have explained how Daniel's indenture was sold to one William Frige, and that he was actually transported to Talbot County, Maryland.

For nearly one hundred years thereafter, the Hurley family remained in Maryland. Finally, between 1766 and 1773, Edmond Hurley relocated with his family to North Carolina, where many of his descendants are found to this day in Montgomery, Moore, and other nearby counties of the State. Edmond was the grandson of the original immigrant, Daniel, and was born and lived the early years of his life in Prince George's County, Maryland. At the time of his departure for North Carolina, he left behind four brothers: Cornelius, William, Joseph and Thomas; all of whom remained in Maryland during their lifetime.

In *Hurley Families in America, Volume 1*, we have discussed the fact that Thomas Hurley, the youngest of the family, and the sole heir under his father's will, moved to Frederick County, and finally settled in the area of Clarksburg, Montgomery County. It is there that his children and grandchildren were to be found.

And they married members of the King family.

Order of Presentation

We begin our study with a brief look at the very earliest records of the King families in Maryland, originating in what was then Prince George's County after it was formed in 1695. In the first chapter, we discuss the family of John King, Sr., born c.1711, and his children.

One of his sons was Edward, born c.1740, who had at least eight children, one of whom was John Duckett King, born 1778, the subject of Chapter 2. In Chapters 3 through 15, we follow the descendants of the children of John Duckett; with the exception of only one, who died young; in both the male and female lineage, through eight generations. Each chapter devoted to a child of John Duckett King will be accompanied by a descendancy chart listing each child of that child. Within each of these chapters, the immediate family will first be presented, and following that, each child having issue will be discussed in detail.

In the final chapters, we present records of numerous members of the greater King family, who have not been identified in the main body of the study, but who are perhaps related to those with whom we are primarily concerned. It will be noted, however, that a large group of individuals bearing the King name have been found in Frederick County, who appear to the author to be of Germanic origin, with no apparent connection to the others studied. Frederick contains numerous families of German and Dutch extraction, having been widely settled by Pennsylvanian families moving to the west from the port of Philadelphia during the early years.

No effort has been made to follow the King families from Maryland to other states. In fact, few references have been found of family members having moved further west, which is a rather unusual circumstance for the period.

Throughout the text, there are numerous reports of marriages between distant cousins, with the record appearing under the name of both individuals. Their children, and further descendants, will be typically reported with the parent who appears first in the text, with a reference to that fact with the other spouse. Individuals having blood lineage through the King family appear in large numbers in the general area of the state of Maryland where the counties of Montgomery, Frederick, Carroll and Howard come together. From the time of the earliest settlement of the area, the names of King, Burdette, Duvall, Boyer, Waters, Purdum, Day, Mullinix, Walker, Baker, Pearce, Beall, Soper, Bowman, Poole, Browning, Davis, Fulks, Jones, Ward, Gloyd, Brown, Lawson, Watkins, Warfield, and many others, appeared in the public records. And they married each other, frequently. As the years passed, and later generations developed, distant cousins were married, and raised their families, often without even realizing that they carried some of the King blood from long ago.

A WORD OF CAUTION

The information included was derived from many sources, and is hoped to be as accurate as possible. However, as mentioned in the text on occasion, there have been some conflicting names, dates, and other data relative to some of the individuals described. We have personally toured the cemeteries where many members of the family are buried, researched the deeds, wills and settlements of estates in the local courthouses and at the State Hall of Records, but have relied on printed data and studies of other families relative to census and certain other information. Such is the way with any genealogical study; few of them are based entirely on original research.

Use the data as you wish, certain in the knowledge that an occasional error has crept in; and for that, let us apologize now.

AND A WORD OF THANKS

To Jane C. Sween, librarian of the Montgomery County Historical Society. Without her guidance, her knowledge of the county and its inhabitants, and her generous assistance, this work would have been woefully inadequate.

Jointly produced for the benefit of
future generations by:

William Neal Hurley, Jr.

&

Ann Paxton Brown

CONTENTS

CHAPTER 1

The King Families of Maryland

The King families with whom we will here be primarily concerned are found principally in Montgomery County, Maryland, descended from John Duckett King (1778) and his wife, Jemima Miles (1782). As will be seen, their descendants intermarried with many of the early families of the county, and many of their progeny often married distant cousins, perhaps without even realizing the relationships that existed. We will also discuss in more detail the fact that few members of this family, or those with whom they were allied, wandered far from Maryland. To the present day, they are found in large concentrations in the upper northern sections of Montgomery County, where their ancestors lived so many years before them and, indeed, often on the same properties.

Earlier members of the family are found in older records of Prince George's County, Maryland, and later in Montgomery and Frederick. From those records, we can identify the parents, and the paternal grandparents of our subject, John Duckett King. It should first be remembered that Prince George's was created in 1695 from parts of Charles and Calvert, both of which were original counties in the Maryland Province. As settlement moved further westward, and need for local government developed, Frederick was created from part of Baltimore County, but primarily from Prince George's. In 1776, two new counties were created from Frederick: Montgomery, between old Prince George's, and what remained of Frederick; and Washington, to the far west.

Formation of the Counties of Maryland

Name of County	Formed	Source County or Counties
Allegany	1789	Washington
Anne Arundel	1650	Original County
Baltimore	1660	Anne Arundel

1

County	Year	Formed From
Calvert	1654	Original County
Caroline	1773	Dorchester & Queen Anne's
Carroll	1837	Baltimore & Frederick
Cecil	1674	Baltimore & Kent
Charles	1658	Original County
Dorchester	1669	Somerset & Talbot
Frederick	1748	Prince George's & Baltimore
Garrett	1872	Allegany
Harford	1773	Baltimore
Howard	1851	Anne Arundel
Kent	1642	Original County
Montgomery	1776	Frederick
Prince George's	1695	Calvert & Charles
Queen Anne's	1706	Dorchester, Kent & Talbot
Somerset	1666	Original County
St. Mary's	1637	Original County
Talbot	1662	Original County
Washington	1776	Frederick
Wicomico	1867	Somerset & Worcester
Worcester	1742	Somerset

The census of 1776 for St. John's and St. George's Episcopal Parishes contains several references to King families, including:

Richard King, aged 85; five boys age 30, 16, 15, 13, 4, and 1; and Jane King, age 68; four girls age 43, 22, 18, and 6. The actual composition of this household is not known.

John King, age 38; one boy age 7. Eleanor King, age 33; six girls age 13, 12, 11, 9, 5 and 1.

John King, age 74. Mary King, age 29; two girls, 18 and 16.

Edward King, age 48; two boys age 5 and 1. Ann King, age 30; four girls age 13, 10, 6 and 3.

John King, age 25; two boys age 16 and 11. Kersey King, age 20; three girls age 14, 9 and 7. Obviously, from the ages, this is not a single household of parents and children.

The early King families were apparently found primarily in the Broad Creek area of Prince George's County, and many families in that area moved back and forth across the Potomac, owning land on both sides of the river. Presumably, the Kings did as well. The 1751 map of the area prepared by Colonel Joshua Fry and Peter Jefferson, clearly shows the Alexandria ferry across the Potomac not far upstream from the mouth of Broad Creek, making crossings with wagons and implements relatively easy.

John King, Sr.
1711-1790

One of the earliest records we find of the King family is in the will of one John King, filed in Will Book T-1, at page 286 in the records of Prince George's County, Maryland. Some sources suggest that he was born about 1711, and emigrated to Maryland about 1720, settling in what is now Prince George's County. Following the more or less standard beginning sentences relative to physical condition and requests for proper burial, he makes the following bequests in his will:

".....First, I will and bequeath unto Elizabeth Darcey and John King, my beloved daughter and son, all my goods and chattels now in the possession of my son Benjamin King, living near the Sugar Lands in Frederick County, viz, one mare, bridle and saddle, seven head of cattle, two large pewter dishes, and three basins, one bed and bed furniture, two bedsteads, two pots and one pair of pot hooks. Likewise all my moveable effects, also I will and bequeath unto the rest of my beloved sons and daughters in the manner and form following, unto my sons Edward King and William King I give and bequeath one shilling each. Likewise my daughter Mary Peacock and son Thomas King I will and bequeath one shilling each. I also will and bequeath unto my beloved son Benjamin King and my beloved daugher Rebeccah Vermillion one shilling sterling each. I likewise constitute make and ordain John Darcey and Elizabeth Darcey the sole executors of this my last will and testament .... this eighteenth day of December in the year of our Lord one thousand, seven hundred and eighty-nine."

The will was witnessed by Joseph Burgess, Josias Moore, and Jesse Moore, signed by John King, Sr., with his mark, and probated in the county, January 12, 1790.

3

The will does not name the wife of John King, Sr., but land entries in the county during 1792 suggest that she may have been Elizabeth Morris, born c.1711. Children included:
1. Elizabeth King, married to John Darcey.
2. John King.
3. Benjamin King.
4. Edward King, born c.1740, of whom more
5. William King, married to Letitia Duckett.
6. Thomas King.
7. Rebeccah King, married to Vermillion.
8. Mary King, married to Peacock.

Edward King
1740-1784

This son of John King, Sr. and Elizabeth Morris (1711), was born about 1740, probably in Prince George's County, Maryland, and died c.1784 in Montgomery County, Maryland. He appeared in the 1776 census in the Northwest Hundred, which is close to the present District of Columbia. He was married to Rebecca Duckett, born c.1742, daughter of John Duckett (1706) and Sarah Haddock Waring (1721), of Prince George's County. At some point Edward moved to what is now Montgomery County, where he lived in the area now known as King's Valley, near Damascus, although no record has been found of his ownership of land in the county. He appears to have moved between 1764; when his daughter, Sarah King, was born in Prince George's County; and 1769, when his daughter, Charity King, was born in what was then Frederick County, to become Montgomery in 1776. A check of deed records of Montgomery County prior to 1800 reveals no entry either as a grantor or grantee in the name of Edward King. There are several entries in those records for other members of the King family during that first twenty-five years or so of Montgomery County history, but none that can be identified with Edward King. Similarly, a check of the land records, will records and settlement of estates of Frederick County fails to disclose any reference to Edward King. Once again, there are other members of the King family referenced

4

in Frederick records in the early to mid-1700s. The census of 1776 provides names and births of most of the children of Edward King:
1. Elizabeth King, born 1763, probably Prince George's County
2. Sarah King, born 1764
3. Mary King, born 1767, perhaps in Frederick County
4. Charity King, born 1769, of whom more following
5. Benjamin King, born 1772; married November 1, 1804 to Nackey Penn.
6. Edward King, Jr., born 1774
7. Rececca King, born 1776
8. John Duckett King, born June 20, 1778, who, with his descendants, is the subject of our study, of whom more in Chapter 2

Charity King
1769-

This daughter of Edward King (1740) and Rebecca Duckett (1742), was born c.1769 in Frederick County, Maryland, in an area which became Montgomery in 1776. She was married April 30, 1803 to Thomas Watkins, son of Jeremiah Watkins and Elizabeth Waugh. They apparently lived in the Purdum area of Montgomery County, and were ancestors of large numbers of the Watkins family still living in the county. Their children included:
1. Alpha Watkins, born c.1803, of whom more following.
2. Elizabeth A. Watkins, born c.1805
3. Lorenzo Dow Watkins, born c.1807; married in Frederick County, Maryland, July 8, 1837, to Ara Ann Watkins, born 1814. They had children:
   a. Charity A. Watkins, born c.1838
   b. Martha T. Watkins, born c.1839; married to Luther M. Watkins, a cousin, born March 2, 1831, the son of Alpha Watkins (1803) and Harriet Ann Lewis (1805). A child:
      (1) Laura V. Watkins, born c.1859, and perhaps died young
   c. Evelina Watkins, born c.1846
   d. Mary C. Watkins, born c.1848

5

Alpha Watkins
1803-1880

This son of Thomas Watkins and Charity King (1769) was born c.1803, probably on the family farm near Cedar Grove, in Montgomery County, Maryland, and died c.1880. He was married to Harriet Ann Lewis, born c.1805. The family appears in the 1850 and 1860 census of Montgomery County, providing names of the children:

1. Oliver T. Watkins, born c.1828, and died August 26, 1894. Married December 23, 1851 in Montgomery County to Eleanor Jane Brewer, who died February 5, 1913, the daughter of Vincent Brewer and Catherine Lewis. Oliver and his wife were first cousins, and are buried together at the Upper Seneca Baptist Church in Cedar Grove, Maryland. They had children:

   a. Christopher E. Watkins, born June 10, 1854; died April 7, 1915. Married to Emma Jane Lewis, born July 12, 1857; died June 3, 1900. Children:
      (1) Melvin E. Watkins, born May 24, 1879; died 1945. Married Myrtle M. Stull.
      (2) Jesse Watkins, born February 10, 1893; died November 1912.
      (3) McKinley Watkins, born November 14, 1896 and died October 10, 1918.
      (4) Alpha Watkins, born March 21, 1900 and died June 10, 1919.
   b. Laura V. Watkins, born c.1857
   c. John Oliver Thomas Watkins, born November 3, 1860; died January 11, 1928. Married Eva Lee King, born August 31, 1864 and died January 11, 1928. She also appears in some records as Eveline Lee King, and was the daughter of Edward J. King (1821) and Mary Jane Burdette (1825). They had twelve children, discussed under their mother's name in Chapter 13, dealing with descendants of Edward J. King (1821), which see.

d. Ella Watkins, born after 1861; married March 29, 1893 in Cedar Grove, to Frederick Tschiffely. Both she and her husband were deaf mute.

e. Ida C. Watkins, born June 10, 1872; died May 17, 1942, and married to Bradley J. Riggs, born September 30, 1869, died February 9, 1920, son of William E. Riggs (1839) and Mary Ellen King (1843).

2. Mary P. Watkins, born c.1829, and married John Rufus Purdum.

3. Luther M. Watkins, born March 2, 1831; died April 15, 1900. He was married twice; first to his cousin, Martha T. Watkins (1839), daughter of Lorenzo Dow Watkins (1807) and Ara Ann Watkins (1814). They had a daughter, and he married second Mary Catherine Darby. The child was:

a. Laura V. Watkins, born 1859; perhaps died young.

4. William Watkins, born c.1832; married to Rachel A. Hobbs, but had no children.

5. Rebecca Watkins, born c.1834; married in Montgomery County, Maryland, December 9, 1852, to William Miller; and second May 29, 1867 to William Waters

6. Lorenzo Dallas Watkins, born August 28, 1835, died November 26, 1920. Married October 11, 1859 to Jane Dorsey Purdum, born May 12, 1840, died July 14, 1916, daughter of Charles Riggs Purdum (1807) and Mary Shaw (1803), (or Margaret Hobbs). Lorenzo and his wife are buried at Upper Seneca Baptist Church in Cedar Grove. They appear alone in the 1860 census for Damascus District of Montgomery County. In the 1880 census for Clarksburg District, they have seven children in the household. Accounting of the estate of Jane D. Watkins was made by her husband, Lorenzo D., dated November 22, 1916 and recorded in liber HCA 2 at folio 184 in the wills office of Montgomery County. Her husband receives one third of the estate, and the remainder is divided between the eight children then living, all listed by name. There is also a small bequest to Russell B. Lewis and Elva Lewis. The will of Lorenzo Dallas Watkins was dated August 22, 1819 and filed for probate December 21, 1920 in liber HCA 22 at folio 442 of the will records of Montgomery

7

County, Maryland. He makes a specific bequest of his watch and chain to his son, Joseph Dallas Watkins. He then provides that seven eighths of his estate is to be divided between his seven children, all named. The other one eighth is divided into two parts: one part goes to his grandson, Russell V. Lewis, and the other half in trust to his great granddaughter Elva Lewis, daughter of his late grandson, Grover Lewis. Joseph Dallas Watkins is named executor. They had children, not necessarily in this order:

a. Mary B. Watkins, born c.1861, apparently died young; not mentioned in the division of estate of her mother.

b. Margaret Florence Watkins, born December 7, 1862. Married April 24, 1882 to Crittenden King, born August 31, 1857, died January 13, 1918, son of Charles Miles King (1814). Their descendants are treated under the section dealing with their father in Chapter 10, which see.

c. Charles Lee Watkins, in his father's will, Charles J. L. Watkins; born c.1865. Married February 20, 1889 Minnie King. In other records, he is found as Charles Jefferson Lee Watkins, which appears to be correct. She is also found in some records as Amanda Cornelius King, born February 17, 1870; died November 4, 1946, the daughter of Edward J. King (1821) and Mary Jane Burdette (1825). She is buried at Upper Seneca Baptist Church, at Cedar Grove, Montgomery County. Her father's will lists her as Minnie; church records list her as Minnie A. Her will, dated April 10, 1942, was probated December 18, 1946 and filed in Liber OWR 21 at folio 135 in Montgomery County. She there lists eleven children, and three of her grandchildren, all following. Charles Lee is also buried at Upper Seneca Baptist, born 1864 and died 1937. They had at least these children:

(1) Charles Jefferson Lee Watkins, Jr., married September 14, 1916 at Upper Seneca Baptist Church, Cedar Grove, to Rose Mae Johnson, daughter of James W. Johnson of Clarksburg. At least one daughter:

(a) Margaret E. Watkins, born April 18, 1917; died December 27, 1995. She is perhaps Margaret Ellen Watkins, who was married June 19, 1943 to Samuel Sylvester Gloyd, born October 12, 1914, son of Henry Dorsey Gloyd (1879) and Margaret Lavina Arnold (1876).

(2) Talmadge Lodge Watkins, born 1891, died 1975; married Myrtle Bryan Burns, born June 25, 1896, and died 1979; daughter of Nicholas Edward Burns (1865) and Laura Gertrude King (1873). Talmadge and his wife are buried in the cemetery of Upper Seneca Baptist Church at Cedar Grove, Montgomery County, Maryland. Nearby are the graves of two of their sons:

(a) Charles Edward Watkins, born May 24, 1914 and died March 2, 1975. Married to Mary Belle Hawkins, born May 6, 1915, daughter of James Bradley Hawkins (1886) and Hattie Mae King (1893). Children:

1. Joanne Marie Watkins, born 1939. Married James Edward Musson, born 1936. A son: Larry Edward Musson; born June 22, 1966

2. Charles Edward Watkins, Jr., born 1940, known as Bucky. Married Barbara Joan Beall, born 1943. One daughter: Cynthia Elaine Watkins: born November 5, 1962. Married Dexter Gordon Mathis, and had children: Sarah Diane Mathis, born 1984 and Jason Kyle Mathis, born 1987

3. Carol Lee Watkins, born 1953. Married Richard Harold Collins, born 1945.

(b) Royce T. Watkins, born 1918, died March, 1972. Buried Upper Seneca Baptist Church. Married to Agnes S., born 1919. Children:

1. Mary Jo Watkins, married Mayer; a child: John Talmadge Mayer.

2. Jane W. Watkins, married Gartner; a child: David Wayne Gartner.
- (c) Gertrude Watkins, married Duvall.
- (3) Gladys D. Watkins, born 1894, died 1897.
- (4) Mary E. Watkins, married Johnson. Children:
  - (a) Bettie Bell Johnson.
  - (b) Charles Thomas Johnson.
  - (c) Paul Curtis Johnson.
- (5) Margaret J. Watkins, married Howes.
- (6) Clayton K. Watkins, born September 1, 1890. The author knew and respected this member of the family. He was, for many years, Clerk of the Circuit Court for Montgomery County. As such, there are hundreds of land record books bearing the initials, CKW, with a following numeral. That is the system of book numbering used by the county, rather than starting from book one and running into the thousands. Each clerk of the court during his tenure begins the next set of books with his initials, and continues that series during his term of office. Clayton was born August 30, 1890, and married January 31, 1917 at Upper Seneca Baptist Church at Cedar Grove, to Addie Belle Hawkins, daughter of James B. Hawkins of Woodfield. She was born October 25, 1898 and died October 12, 1961. They are buried in the Forest Oak Cemetery at Gaithersburg, Maryland.
- (7) Claudia Lucille Watkins, born August 20, 1894. Married to Howard.
- (8) Belle P. Watkins, married Hawkins.
- (9) Bessie K. Watkins, married Howes.
- (10) M. Hazel Watkins, married Allnutt.
- (11) Celeste P. Watkins, married Beall.
- (12) Lorraine E. Watkins, born September 30, 1906, died March 19, 1972. Married William Ralph Walker, born September 16, 1905, died February 13, 1995, the son of McKendree Walker (1870) and Rachel Corrine Holland (1878). No children.

10

d. Lizzie J. Watkins, born c.1867; married Charles W. Johnson (or Charles T. Johnson). Listed as Jennie E. Johnson in the settlement of estate of her mother.

e. Joseph Dallas Watkins, born c.1870 and died June 20, 1935 in Johns Hopkins University Hospital, Baltimore. Married at the Upper Seneca Baptist Church at Cedar Grove, November 16, 1893 to Ida V. Day, born 1872, died 1934; both are buried there. They had two sons and a daughter who survived him:

(1) Guy D. Watkins, born c.1908 at Cedar Grove, Maryland, and died May 30, 1988 at the Friends Nursing Home in Sandy Spring, Maryland. Buried at Upper Seneca Baptist Church, Cedar Grove. He served for 45 years as chief judge in the 12th Election District, and was a member of the Lions Club since 1947. He was a player and a coach of baseball. He was survived by his wife, Fannie E., born 1913, a niece and a nephew.

(2) Wilbur Day Watkins, born January 23, 1900 at Cedar Grove, of whom more following.

(3) Blanche Watkins married Carson Nicholson of Baltimore.

f. Henry L. Watkins, called Harry L. in his father's will, in the division of his mother's estate, and in the 1880 census. Born 1872, died October 30, 1950. Married August 27, 1897 in Montgomery County to Annie E. Hall, born 1873, died 1943. Harry's will, dated January 18, 1950, was probated November 8, 1950, and filed in Liber WCC 18 at folio 408 in the will records of the county. He identifies his father as being Lorenzo D. Watkins, providing funds for the maintenance of his father's grave, as well as his own. He also menions one son. Harry and his wife are buried at Upper Seneca Baptist Church cemetery, Cedar Grove, with stone marked "father" and "mother." Also in the cemetery is the grave of another individual who is probably their son, based on his name:

11

(1)   Harold Hall Watkins, born 1901, died August 6, 1920 by drowning at Great Falls on the Potomac River.

(2)   Philip Charles Watkins, born 1905, died January 2, 1966; who received the family farm at Cedar Grove. Married July 1, 1931 in Friendship, Anne Arundel County, Maryland, to Nettie Dorsey Etchison, born 1913. She was a daughter of Dr. and Mrs. Garnett Waters Etchison of Gaithersburg. Philip and his wife are also buried at the Upper Seneca Baptist Church in Cedar Grove. His will, dated November 8, 1950, was probated January 28, 1966 and filed in will book VMB 199 at folio 504 in Montgomery County. He names his wife, and provides that after her death, his estate is to be divided between his six children, who are not named.

g.   Cornelius A. Watkins; apparently the same who is buried at the Upper Seneca Baptist Church cemetery, in Cedar Grove, Maryland. He was born May 15, 1875, and died December 20, 1946. Marriage records of the county, and the *Sentinel* newspaper, report his marriage April 12, 1905 at the Upper Seneca Baptist Church, Cedar Grove, to Rebecca Woodfield, daughter of J. R. Woodfield; and that the couple plan to reside at 1927 Edmondson Avenue, Baltimore. She is perhaps Laura Rebecca Woodfield; and the mother of his children:

(1)   Alfred Woodfield Watkins, born June 18, 1906, died November 22, 1907, buried with his parents.

(2)   Cornelius R. Watkins.

h.   Pearl B. Watkins, who was married to George Otis Henderson of Germantown.

i.   May Watkins, not mentioned in the will, nor the division of the estate of her mother.

j.   Jennie Watkins, not mentioned in the will, nor the division of the estate of her mother.

7.   Edward King Watkins, born May 31, 1837; died January 21, 1913. Married September 19, 1861 in Ellicott City, Maryland,

Sophronia R. Phelps; daughter of a neighbor; born October 1, 1846 and died January 9, 1924; who became fifteen years of age just two weeks after her marriage. They had nine children:

a. George Orlando Watkins, born March 19, 1864, and died November 15, 1940; single.

b. Walter Wilson Watkins, born June 2, 1866, and died May 21, 1927. Married on November 11, 1891 to Rosa L. Mathews, (or Mathers) at Upper Seneca Baptist Church, Cedar Grove, Maryland. She was born July 21, 1870, according to the stone at Salem United Methodist Church, Cedar Grove, where both are buried. They had at least one daughter:

    (1) Marie Columbia Watkins, died January 15, 1951. Married to Felty and had at least one son:
        (a) Walter Thomas Felty.

c. Alonzo Claggett Watkins, born July 28, 1867, and died January 25, 1946. Married July 27, 1893 to Mary Luana Boyer, born March 9, 1870, died June 28, 1945, daughter of Milton Boyer (1834) and Elizabeth Washington Purdum (1840), and had six children:

    (1) Faye Huntington Watkins, born July 18, 1894, died May 14, 1962. Married October 28, 1915 to Oliver Morgan Duvall, born March 22, 1889, died June 12, 1964 at Damascus. She married second to Frederick T. Glaze, born November 16, 1882, died February 20, 1946. Children first marriage only:
        (a) Mary Virginia Duvall, married Ray Deitz.
        (b) Paul Duvall, married to Margaret Mussetter.
        (c) Edward Boyer Duvall, born December 11, 1925 in Damascus, died January 4, 1996, and buried Damscus Methodist Church cemetery. He was a Navy veteran of the second world war, and active in numerous organizations in his retirement. For years he was customer service manager for Kettler Brothers, Inc., builders of Montgomery Village and other communities. Married Ruth Olin, and was the father of six children:

1. Linda Duvall, married Barry Phelps.
2. Allen Duvall, married Hilda.
3. Stephen Duvall, of Damascus.
4. Deborah Duvall, married to James Popp of Monrovia.
5. Karen Duvall, married John Jordan of Adamstown.
6. Tim Duvall, married Kim.
(d) Gerald L. Duvall.
(e) Rodney H. Duvall, married Margaret Wygant.
(f) Shirley J. Duvall, who was married to John Trega Zimmerman
(g) William C. Duvall, married Shirley Johnson.
(h) Robert M. Duvall, of Dover, New Hampshire.
(i) Jane Duvall, died young.
(j) Rose Eleanor Duvall, died young.
(2) Paul W. Watkins, born November 22, 1897, died August 6, 1979. Married Rose Mullinix. Children:
(a) Kenneth Watkins.
(b) Walter Lee Watkins.
(3) Dorothy Elizabeth Watkins, born April 28, 1900 and died September 28, 1970. Married July 14, 1932 Raymond Lafayette Warfield, son of Basil T. Warfield (1859) and Alice Flavilla Mullinix (1867). He was first married to Bessie Allnutt, by whom he had two children. Children born to Dorothy Elizabeth included:
(a) Raymond Lafayette Warfield, Jr.
(b) Dorothy Warfield.
(c) Ellis Warfield, died at six months.
(4) Ralph W. Watkins, born 1901, and married to Nona M. Burdette, born 1904. Two children:
(a) Lula Mae Watkins married Edward Coolidge.
(b) Clara Watkins, married Gerald Johnson.
(5) Irma Watkins, born March 29, 1903. Married to Miel Wright Linthicum, son of Miel E. Linthicum (1865) and Mary L. Purdum (1866). The family is

discussed under the father's name in Chapter 5, dealing with the descendants of Jemima King (1805), which see.

(6) Annie Loree Watkins, born June 11, 1906, died May 20, 1975. Married William Kenneth Layton, born July 28, 1908 and died December 28, 1959 at Damascus. They had children:
(a) William Kenneth Layton, Jr.; married Emma.

d. Fannie Frank Watkins, born February 16, 1869; died April 18, 1869.

e. Florence Edward Watkins, born April 29, 1870, and married January 26, 1888 to Reuben M. Nicholson. The 1870 census lists her name as Frances E. Watkins, one month old at the time the census was taken. She and Reuben had children:
(1) Clifford Newman Nicholson, born November 13, 1888, apparently the father of:
(a) Dorothy Beatrice Nicholson.
(2) Carson Edward Nicholson.
(3) Jessie Randolph Nicholson.
(4) Walter Wilson Nicholson.
(5) Harriet Roberta Watkins, born March 3, 1872; died October 2, 1944. Married October 26, 1898 to Franklin Waters.

f. Harriet Roberta Watkins, born March 3, 1872; died October 2, 1944. Married October 26, 1898 Franklin Waters. The 1880 census reports a child born c.1872, named Alberta, which is probably this child, improperly reported by the census taker.

g. Addie Sophronia Watkins, born October 15, 1875, died December 21, 1970. Married to Jones. The 1880 census record for this child, while hard to read, appears to report Ada L. Watkins. Final accounts of her father's estate clearly read Addie S. Jones, confirming the name we report here, and the marriage, although some reports state that she was single. No reported children.

h. Samuel Watkins, born March 6, 1877; infant death

i. Nellie Watkins, born November 5, 1878; infant death

8. Levi Lewis Watkins, born c.1839, died 1913; married to Elizabeth Jane Buxton. Children, including:
   a. Grover Cleveland Watkins. Married, children:
      (1) Stanley Watkins
      (2) Philip Lewis Watkins
   b. Mary Watkins
   c. Blanche Watkins
   d. Alverta Watkins
   e. Helen Watkins
   f. William Watkins
   g. Edgar M. Watkins, born 1868; died 1900. Buried at the Neelsville Presbyterian Church cemetery.
9. Elizabeth A. Watkins, born 1841; married John Leamon.
10. Harriet Watkins, born c.1843; married John Boyer. They are both buried in Baltimore, at Louden Park Cemetery. Children:
    a. John Spencer Boyer
    b. Mollie Boyer; died 1918, single.
    c. Harry Boyer.
11. Benjamin Franklin Watkins, born December 20, 1844 in Cedar Grove, Montgomery County; died January 23, 1929, perhaps in Carroll County. Married November 11, 1868 Sarah Jane Benson, born March 2, 1849, and died January 7, 1931; the daughter of William H. Benson and Catherine Crawford. Buried with her husband in Forest Oak Cemetery at Gaithersburg. Children, perhaps all born near Middlebrook, Montgomery County; many are also buried at Forest Oak:
    a. Wesley W. Watkins, born May 2, 1871; died January 24, 1893 at Middlebrook, Montgomery County. Single.
    b. William Clarence Watkins, born April 26, 1873, died December 27, 1899. Single.
    c. Lillian May Watkins, born April 23, 1875; died July 3, 1963 in Montgomery County, Maryland. Married to James E. L. Sibley, born April 18, 1866; died June 4, 1949. Both buried at Forest Oak cemetery, Gaithersburg. Children:
       (1) Joseph Russell Sibley, born August 9, 1901, married Flora Elizabeth Watkins, born May 1, 1900, daughter of Maurice Watkins (1867) and Martha

16

Rebecca King (1874). Married second Hettie. One child from each marriage:

(a) Flora Elizabeth Sibley, born February 2, 1935, and married first to Vickroy, by whom she had a child. Married second to Martin Alexander Case, born October 18, 1932, and had a son. Children:
   1. Donna Lynn Vickroy: August 1, 1958
   2. David Martin Case: May 4, 1964

(b) Mary Sibley; married Norton. At least a son:
   1. Wayne Norton.

(2) Irene Sibley; married Roy Arnold.

(3) Edward Arnold Montgomery Sibley, born April 3, 1897 at Germantown, Montgomery County. Died November 19, 1991; single.

d. Bradley G. Watkins, born March 26, 1877, and died November 24, 1899.

e. Walter Howard Watkins, born May 5, 1879, and died February 8, 1881.

f. Harvey C. Watkins, born March 1, 1881; died November 30, 1916. Married March 29, 1904 at Germantown to Grace Violet Diffenderffer.

g. Virgie Lee Watkins, born January 9, 1882, and died November 8, 1931 in Montgomery County, Maryland. Married December 14, 1905 in Grace Methodist Church to Albert Franklin Thompson, born May 24, 1877; died February 5, 1951; son of John Thompson and Eliza Virginia Rabbitt. Husband and wife are buried in Forest Oak cemetery, Gaithersburg, Maryland. Children, born in Montgomery County:
   (1) Mabel Jane Thompson, born September 12, 1906; married to James Stephen Frendach, and had a son:
      (a) Paul Franklin Frendach, born July 28, 1941, married February 20, 1965 in Washington to Teresa Catherine Barnard, and had children:
         1. Eric Barnard Frendach: October 2, 1965
         2. Angela Christine Frendach, born December 27, 1966

17

3. Stephen Frank Frendach, born February 1, 1973

4. Katy Frendach, born after 1974

(2) John Franklin Thompson, born January 17, 1909; died March 14, 1993 in Washington Grove, Maryland. Married June 17, 1932 at Friendship, Anne Arundel County, Maryland, to Gladys Mae Fraley, born May 17, 1911 at Claysville, and died February 2, 1995; daughter of Ernest Lee Fenton Fraley and Daisy Belle Allnutt. Both are buried at Forest Oak cemetery, Gaithersburg. John Franklin was a farmer and a horseman; he and his wife were members of the Goshen and Redland Hunt Clubs, and won a number of trophies for their show horses. They owned the horse named "Black Caddy" which later became a world champion show horse, breaking several jumping records. Four children, first three born in Montgomery County, the fourth in Washington, D. C.:

(a) Janet Dale Thompson, born October 3, 1935; married October 15, 1955 Lovie Lee "Buck" Manuel, born September 14, 1930 Compton, Virginia, son of John Thomas Manuel and Linda Mae Hill. Two children:

1. Donna Lee Manuel, born April 11, 1957; married June 27, 1987 in Frederick, Maryland, David Allen Schultz, born there June 17, 1956, who was the son of David Kieffer Schultz and Avis Bondena Kepler. Children, born in Frederick:

a. Megan Elizabeth Schultz, born March 1, 1989

b. Matthew David Schultz, born December 16, 1991

2. Darin Thomas Manuel, born October 16, 1963, single, a musician and composer.

(b) Beverly Ann Thompson, born November 23, 1936, and married first November 26, 1951 at

18

Rockville, John Michael Eader, Jr., born May 20, 1931, son of John Michael Eader and Alice E. Whalen; three children. Married second at Grace Church in Gaithersburg, Joseph Mackin Ganley, born February 12, 1927. The children were:

1. Brenda Kay Eader, born September 22, 1951, and married first March 8, 1977 in Rockville, to Edward Franklin Knight, born October 24, 1948 in Charlestown, West Virginia, the son of Edward Franklin Knight and Daphne Carson Lawson; one son. She married second October 22, 1994 in Howard County, Maryland, David Richards.
   a. Steven Carson Knight, born December 23, 1979.

2. John Michael Eader, born February 10, 1960, and married October 14, 1989 at Germantown, to Brenda Lee Whitworth, born October 1, 1964, the daughter of George Irwin Whitworth and Wilma Elizabeth Fitzwater.

3. Carol Ann Eader, born February 8, 1962. Married first June 22, 1985 Edward Stephen Caglione, born June 20, 1963, son of Edward S. and Valeta Caglione. Married second September 7, 1991 to Clark Matthew Wagner, born April 30, 1961 in Casper, Wyoming, son of James Francis Wagner and Kathryn Jo Atwood. Two children, born to the second marriage; Montgomery County:
   a. Shannon Wagner, born September 6, 1993
   b. Matthew Wagner: March 12, 1995

(c) Nancy Jeanne Thompson, born May 2, 1940; married first June 8, 1957 at Rockville to

19

Louis William Carr, the son of William Harold and Helen Carr. Married second May 25, 1961 in Ellicott City, Maryland, to William Stone, born May 15, 1938 Rainelle, West Virginia, the son of William Stone and Dolly Mae Brown. She had two children from the first marriage, and one from the second:

1. William Dean Carr: October 8, 1957
2. Kenneth Paul Carr, born August 17, 1959; married January 21, 1989 in Boyds, Maryland, to Robin Kathleen Arnold, born September 2, 1964 at Silver City, New Mexico, the daughter of Walter Claude Arnold and Mary Lee Wilson. One child:
   a. Krysten Daniele Carr, born April 20, 1991
3. Robert Jay Stone, born March 19, 1962; married June 11, 1988 at Rockville, Maryland, to Holly Joy Lebowitz, born February 13, 1962 Bridgeville, Pa., the daughter of Alan Harvey Lebowitz and Shirley Cohen. Two children, born in Montgomery County, Maryland:
   a. Daniel Evan Stone: April 6, 1990
   b. Jena Renee Stone: March 6, 1993

(d) Joseph Franklin Thompson, born May 16, 1946; married first December 28, 1968 in Silver Spring, Maryland, to Kathleen McGuire, born May 17, 1947 in Takoma Park, Maryland, daughter of Martin Duane McGuire and Annetta Maline. Married second May 18, 1991 in Frederick, to Sarah Jane Tipton, born March 16, 1959 in Washington, daughter of Wellstood White Tipton and Elizabeth Ann Field. Two children, from the first marriage, Montgomery County:

1. Jeffrey Thompson: June 27, 1969

20

2. Katrina Lynn Thompson: July 8, 1973
(3) Myrtle Lee Thompson, born May 10, 1911
(4) Albert Thompson, born January 13, 1918; died January 17, 1918
(5) Judson Collins Thompson, born September 11, 1923; married November 18, 1945 to Miriam Groves Groves. One child:
   (a) Collins Groves Thompson, born October 12, 1946; married before 1973 Janet, and second before 1976 Mary Elizabeth Mack, by whom he had two children:
      1. Ann Marie Thompson: August 18, 1976
      2. Sarah Elizabeth Thompson, born July 18, 1978
h. Clara Blanche Watkins, born November 11, 1886. Married April 30, 1913 Thomas G. Hilton. Children:
   (1) Thomas Stinson Hilton, born March 31, 1914, and died February 7, 1955. Married February 28, 1933 to Annie Phillips.
   (2) Elizabeth Jane Hilton, born January 14, 1918; married October 10, 1947 Arthur John Lear.
(i) Bessie Myrtle Watkins, born September 8, 1888; died August 13, 1889. Single.
12. Noah Watkins, born August 23, 1846; died December 8, 1929. Married Julia Ann Linthicum, born October 21, 1850, and died December 27, 1931, daughter of John Hamilton Smith Linthicum and Julia Ann Garrett. Noah and wife are buried at Salem United Methodist Church at Cedar Grove, Montgomery County, Maryland. Children:
a. Garrett Webster Watkins, born 1872; died 1947. Married to Vertie A. Mullinix, born 1873, and died 1959. At least one daughter and a son:
   (1) Mabel A. Watkins, born April 8, 1909 at Cedar Grove and died July 6, 1996 at Shady Grove Hospital. Married John M. Tregoning; four grandchildren, five great grandchildren, and one son:
      (a) Robert Tregoning.

21

(2) Ray, or Roy, Watkins. Married Bessie King, daughter of Holady Hix King (1857). Children:
   (a) Lois Watkins, married to Charles King Burdette, born December 10, 1917, son of Claude H. Burdette (1872) and Sarah Rebecca Boyer (1874); no children.
   (b) Grace Watkins.
   (c) William Watkins, married a daughter of Joe Abrams.
b. Leah Jane Watkins, born 1874; married W. G. Iglehart.
c. Herbert Hamilton Watkins, born April, 1876; died October 6, 1880.
d. Mary Avondale Watkins, born February 25, 1878, and died February 15, 1958. Married June 8, 1898 at Cedar Grove Methodist Church to Franklin Monroe King, born January 5, 1876 and died June 9, 1932, son of Singleton Lewis King and Mary Rachel Elizabeth Burdette. Mary and Franklin are buried at the Wesley Grove Methodist Church cemetery. Descendants are discussed in Chapter 8, dealing with the family of Singleton King (1810), which see.
e. Nora Watkins, born January 9, 1880; married Charles Barber.
f. Bessie Watkins: January 9, 1880 to June 10, 1880.
g. John Lester Clark Watkins, born December 25, 1881; died March 25, 1966. Married to Bessie T. Wallach, born May 13, 1892; died April 20, 1967. Buried at Salem United Methodist Church, Cedar Grove.
h. Clinton Cleveland Watkins, born October 29, 1883; died December 12, 1911
i. Arthur Linthicum Watkins, born April 5, 1885; died March 16, 1957. Married c.1909 in Rockville to Esther Pearl Luhn, daughter of Randolph and Sarah Elizabeth Luhn, and had children:
   (1) Oliver Watkins.
   (2) Herbert Watkins; married Mary Mae Barnes.
   (3) Elizabeth Watkins.
   (4) Virginia Watkins.

22

(5) Lillian Watkins.

(6) Noah Luhn Watkins, born March 4, 1910; died July 26, 1910; buried at Salem Methodist Church

(7) Arthur Linthicum Watkins, Jr., born March 22, 1912; married first Ethel B. Gue, and second Hilda Hyatt Roekle.

j. Maude Ethel Watkins, born 1886; married Edgar Davis.

k. Raymond Ridgely Watkins, born December 26, 1888; died August 16, 1913. Married Nellie Cosgrove.

l. Grace Louise Watkins, born 1891; married Ralph Butterwick.

m. Frances Marian Watkins, born 1895 Cedar Grove, Maryland. Married July 20, 1914 to Filmore Cleveland Brown, born October 12, 1893 near Purdum, Maryland, son of John Wesley Brown (1850) and Frances America Cornelia Burdette (1857). Their family is discussed under the father's name in Chapter 6, dealing with the descendants of Harriet Ann King (1807), which see.

13. James Willard Watkins, born c.1849, and died November 29, 1928 at Cedar Grove, Maryland. Married Charlotte J. Williams, and had children:

a. Ola Watkins, married Englehart and McAtee

b. Daughter Watkins, married Harry King. This may be Manona E. Watkins, born 1873 and died 1958, who was married April 16, 1896 to Harry J. King, born 1867 and died 1949. Both are buried at Salem United Methodist Church at Cedar Grove, Maryland.

c. William Watkins.

d. Olive Watkins; married Windsor.

e. Haller Watkins.

f. Jessie Watkins, married Charles Tabler.

g. Daughter Watkins, married Charles Barber.

h. Maynard D. Watkins, born May 30, 1891 at Cedar Grove, and died January 13, 1981. Married November 22, 1911 to Laura Jane Soper, born c.1893; died 1967, daughter of William Wooten Soper (1850) and Catherine Jemima King (1854). Their children are discussed under

23

their mother's name in Chapter 3, dealing with the descendants of Middleton King (1801), which see.

Wilbur Day Watkins
1900-1969

This son of Joseph Dallas Watkins (1870) was born January 23, 1900 at Cedar Grove, and died March 21, 1969 in Sebring Ridge, Florida. He was a brother of Guy D. Watkins (1908) and Mrs. Blanche Nicholson. He owned and operated Watkins Sheet Metal before retiring and moving to Florida. Buried at Upper Seneca Baptist Church, Cedar Grove. Married December 26, 1922 in Kemptown to Ruth Selby King, born there June 6, 1904, daughter of Reginald Windsor King (1878) and Ida Mae Grimes (1876). They had children:

1. Wilbur Day Watkins, Jr., known as Buster, born September 27, 1923 at Cedar Grove, owned Watkins Cabinet Company at Barnesville. Married June 23, 1948 to Agnes Jeanette Walter, born January 2, 1930 at Redland. Seven children:
   a. Joan Marie Watkins, born December 26, 1949 in Frederick. Married first June 5, 1969 to Mark Harman Schendledecker, born March 8, 1947 in Baltimore, and had two daughters. Married second June 29, 1985 in Frederick to Gilmore Wayne House, born April 30, 1942, who had two children by a prior marriage. Joan's daughters were:
      (1) Judith Marie Schendledecker, born April 10, 1970 in Boston, Massachusetts
      (2) Joy Marie Schendledecker, born April 19, 1975 in Framingham, Massachusetts
   b. Kenneth Leroy Watkins, born December 13, 1950; married December 12, 1970 to Kathryn Ann Vandorf, born May 15, 1951 in Watertown, Wisconsin. Children:
      (1) Stephanie Ann Watkins, born July 11, 1971 at the Andrews Air Force Hospital, Camp Springs, Md.
      (2) Kristina Marie Watkins, born December 8, 1973 in Olney, Maryland

c.   Nancy Louise Watkins, born October 1, 1952 in Olney; married February 28, 1976 Michael Walter Lloyd, born September 28, 1952 in Leonardtown, Maryland, a cabinetmaker. They had four children, the first three born in Olney; the last in Frederick, Maryland:
   (1)   Emilie Auge Lloyd, born March 10, 1978
   (2)   Martin Webster Lloyd, born March 20, 1979
   (3)   Erich William Lloyd, born October 24, 1980
   (4)   Karin Reine Lloyd, born September 2, 1982
d.   Sue Ann Watkins, born July 4, 1955 in Olney; married April 6, 1973 Eben LaMonte Conner, III, born February 15, 1955 in Yakima, Washington. He is a cabinetmaker, owner of the Maugansville Planing Mill. They have children, the first born in Olney, the second in Washington, D. C., and the last four in Hagerstown, Maryland:
   (1)   AnnaMaria Conner, born January 21, 1974
   (2)   Elisabeth Marie Conner: September 26, 1975
   (3)   Deborah Sue Conner, born February 5, 1978
   (4)   Joanna Ruth Conner, born July 18, 1980
   (5)   Sarah Grace Conner, born February 21, 1982
   (6)   Rachel Jeannette Conner, born July 3, 1984
e.   Georgia May Watkins, born May 13, 1957 in Olney; married June 24, 1976 Arby Ryan Ray, born June 29, 1957 at Jordan, New York. Children, born at Fayetteville, North Carolina:
   (1)   Jennifer Marie Ray, born October 4, 1977
   (2)   Andrew Ryan Ray, born October 15, 1978
f.   Franklin Wilbur Watkins, born February 16, 1959 in Olney, Maryland; married first March 18, 1978 to Teresa Ann Jackson, and had three children; divorced. Married second April 26, 1985 to Marie Frances Eaton, born January 18, 1959 in Washington, D. C. Children were:
   (1)   Franklin Wilbur Watkins, Jr., born August 15, 1978 in Takoma Park
   (2)   Nicholas O'Bryan Watkins, born September 14, 1979 in Silver Spring; lived eleven days; buried in St. Mary's Cemetery, Barnesville, Maryland

(3) Joshua Stephen Watkins, born October 21, 1980 in Johns Hopkins Hospital, Baltimore

g. Gerrianne Watkins, born December 28, 1961 in Olney; married October 6, 1979 to James Owen Conway, born December 15, 1960 in Philadelphia, and had children:

(1) Mathew Brian Conway, born September 1, 1980 in Olney, Maryland

(2) James Paul Conway, born March 23, 1982 in Martinsburg, West Virginia

(3) Amanda Margaret Conway, born July 16, 1984 in Frederick, Maryland

2. Ida Louise Watkins, born January 22, 1925 at Cedar Grove; married December 11, 1944 in Frederick, Maryland, Charles Franklin Bartgis, born June 4, 1921. Divorced December 22, 1950. No children; moved to Florida.

Edward King
1740-1784
*

*

John Duckett King
1778-1858
*

*

* * * * *

*

* * Middleton King 1801-1872

*

* * Elizabeth Miles King 1802-

*

* * Jemima King 1805-1892

*

* * Harriet Ann King 1807-?

*

* * John A. King 1808-1888

*

* * Singleton King 1810-1897

*

* * Mary Ann T. King 1813-1894

*

* * Charles Miles King 1814-1886

*

* * Rufus King 1816-1899

*

* * Sarah Rebecca King 1818-1902

*

* * Edward J. King 1821-1899

*

* * Mary King 1822-

*

* * Luther Green King 1825-1909

*

* * Eveline King 1828-1899

28

CHAPTER 2

John Duckett King
1778-1858

This son of Edward King (1740) and Rebecca Duckett (1742), was born June 20, 1778, in Montgomery County, Maryland, created from Frederick in 1776, and died May 14, 1858 at Clarksburg, in Montgomery. He is buried in the King cemetery on the Leslie King farm, locally known as Kingstead Farms, which has been in the family for several generations. Married December 16, 1800 at Rockville, the county seat of Montgomery County, Maryland, to Jemima Miles, daughter of Charles Miles and Elizabeth Beall Miles. Cemetery records in the library of the Montgomery County Historical Society at Rockville report that Jemima was born March 8, 1782 at Clarksburg, and died October 30, 1861 at the age of 79 years, 6 months and 22 days, and is buried in the Kingstead Farm cemetery. They had a number of children, probably all born in Montgomery County. The census of 1850 for the Clarksburg District carries the couple, with two of their children. Note that a number of the children were married in Frederick, Maryland. It does not necessarily follow that they lived in Frederick County. Even to modern days, residents of the upper areas of Montgomery County are more oriented to Frederick for shopping and other business than to the county seat at Rockville.

His will, dated April 24, 1857, was entered for record May 18, 1858 in Liber JWS 1 at folio 5, in the will records of Montgomery County, Maryland. He was a slave owner, leaving to his wife the negro woman, Matilda Green, and her son, Ignatius Green. For some reason, he specifically stated that his daughter, Harriet Ann, and his son, John A., were to each receive the sum of one dollar, and no more of his estate. The daughter, Mary, that we list following, was not named in the estate, having predeceased her father, if indeed, she was a part of this family. He mentioned the fact that he had previously given one negro girl to each of his other five daughters, placing a value of one or two hundred dollars on each of them, for purposes of equalizing their shares of his estate. Those five girls received all the personal property, other than real estate, and including two negro men (Jeremiah Mason and Samuel Mason), share and share alike. To his remaining six sons (other than John A.), he left his lands, totalling 217 acres, to share jointly, as well as two negro men, Jeremiah Mason and Samuel Mason. The children were:

1. Middleton King, born 1801; see Chapter 3
2. Elizabeth Miles King, born c.1802; see Chapter 4
3. Jemima King, born April 11, 1805; see Chapter 5
4. Harriet Ann King, born 1807; see Chapter 6
5. John A. King, born October 1, 1808, see Chapter 7
6. Singleton King, born October 21, 1810, see Chapter 8
7. Mary Ann T. King, born March 20, 1813; see Chapter 9
8. Charles Miles King, born April 5, 1814; see Chapter 10
9. Rufus King, born January 25, 1816; see Chapter 11
10. Sarah Rebecca King, born March 6, 1818; see Chapter 12.
11. Edward J. King, born January 10, 1821; see Chapter 13.
12. Mary King, born c.1822, of whom nothing more is known, although family stories report that she fell into a fire at an early age, and died from those injuries. There is no mention of her in her father's will.
13. Luther Green King, born March 11, 1825; see Chapter 14
14. Eveline King, born July 4, 1828; died July 5, 1899. Married July 27, 1848 to Nathan James Walker, born October 27, 1824 and died May 4, 1913. (The will of her father states that she was the wife of Ignatius Walker, which is incorrect). Their descendants are treated in Chapter 15, which see.

Edward King
1740-1784
*

*

John Duckett King
1778-1858
*

*

**Middleton King
1801-1872**
*

*

* * * * * *

*

* * Walter James King 1823-1912

*

* * Jemima P. King 1826-?

*

* * John Middleton King 1830-1919

*

* * William P. King 1832-?

*

* * George Edward King 1835-1876

*

* * Mahala Ann Rebecca King 1836-1872

*

* * Zadoc Summers King 1839-1898

*

* * Mary Ellen King 1843-1913

CHAPTER 3

Middleton King
1801-1872

This son of John Duckett King (1778) and Jemima Miles (1782) was born 1801, and died November 6, 1872. Married May 17, 1822 at Rockville to Mahala E. Summers, born July 28, 1798 in Frederick County; died February 16, 1878 in Purdum, Maryland; daughter of Walter and Ursula Summers. The family appears in the 1850 census for the Clarksburg District of Montgomery County, Maryland, at which time six of their children were living at home, as well as one George Jackson, born c.1777 in England. In the 1860 census, only three of the children were listed, and there was one Matilda Anders, born c.1825, living in the household, perhaps as a domestic. The will of Middleton King, dated November 6, 1872, was entered for record January 14, 1873, recorded in Liber RWC 6 at folio 10, in the probate records of Montgomery County, Maryland. He names his wife and various children, with specific bequests to most of them. He mentions also his grandsons, Middleton N. King and George W. King. In Inventories, Sales, Debts and Accounts, Liber RWC 10, at folio 102, dated October 1, 1877, we find the First and Final Accounts of the estate of Middleton King. The heirs are listed there, including the first child listed following, who was excluded from participation in the estate by the terms of the will of his father, probably having received substantially during his lifetime. They had children, each of whom will be discussed in sequence following the family listing:

1. Walter James King, born March 24, 1823
2. Jemima P. King, born c.1826
3. John Middleton King, born February 1, 1830
4. William P. King, born c.1832
5. George Edward King, born c.1835
6. Mahala Ann Rebecca King, born October 9, 1836
7. Zadoc Summers King, born March 9, 1839
8. Mary Ellen King, born April 2, 1843

CHILD 1

Walter James King
1823-1912

The eldest son of Middleton King (1801) and Mahala E. Summers (1798), was born March 24, 1823 at Purdum, in Montgomery County, Maryland, died June 14, 1912 at his granddaughter's home at Middlebrook, and is buried at Sugarloaf Mountain Chapel on Old Hundred Road (Route 109), between Hyattstown and Comus. Married in Frederick County, July 11, 1843 to Caroline Windsor. She was born April 17, 1814 and died September 28, 1882, daughter of Zadoc and Jane Windsor. They had three sons and four daughters. He was married secondly to Emeline Price Pyles, widow of William W. Pyles. She was born December 20, 1837 and died June 18, 1898; buried at Mt. Ephraim cemetery in Dickerson. At the time of his death, Walter James reportedly had 27 grandchildren and 40 great grandchildren. He had seven children, all born in Frederick County, each of whom had multiple names:

1. Zadock Henson Windsor King, born July 8, 1844; died October 8, 1852.
2. John Edward Howard King, born November 18, 1845, and died June 19, 1908; buried in Providence Methodist Church cemetery at Kemptown, Frederick County. He was a farmer and a carpenter; married in Frederick County, Maryland, April 29, 1873 to Martha Elizabeth Linthicum, born February 18, 1844, died March 14, 1916, daughter of John Hamilton Smith Linthicum and Julia Ann Garrott. Martha Elizabeth is buried with her husband. Children:
   a. Julia Helen King, born July 4, 1875, and died 1943; buried in Upper Seneca Baptist Church cemetery at Cedar Grove. Married December 31, 1902 at Providence Methodist Church in Kemptown to William Upton Bowman, born 1865 and died 1935, son of Francis Asbury Bowman and Melissa D. Riggs, and had children:
      (1) Elizabeth Bowman, married to Ray Fox, and was killed in an automobile accident after they had moved to California. Three children:

(a) Shirleyjean Fox, married Clifford Gilbert, and lives in California

(b) Thomas Fox, married; lives in Pennsylvania

(c) Ann Fox, married Jeffries; lives in California

(2) Julian U. Bowman, born May 6, 1907, and died September 19, 1945 at Hyattsville. An engineer working for the Washington Suburban Sanitary Commission. Married Blanch, born in Pennsylvania; no children. He is buried at Upper Seneca Baptist Church cemetery in Cedar Grove; she is buried in Pennsylvania.

(3) John Sterling Bowman, born March 8, 1911 in Germantown, died November 6, 1956. His father and two uncles founded Bowman Brothers Mill about 1888 at Germantown, moving the business to Gaithersburg some time later. Sterling and his wife bought the mill in 1948, and operated it. Married Helen Douel Butts, born April 12, 1915 at Germantown, daughter of John Thomas Butts and Douel Thrift Gloyd. She was a school teacher and, after her husband's death, operated the mill full time until it was destroyed by fire. Three sons:

(a) John Upton Bowman, born July 19, 1937

(b) Thomas Sterling Bowman, born December 27, 1941, married to Carolyn Eckhardt, born December 27, 1947. Two daughters, and moved to the Seattle area in Washington state.

(c) James Marlin Bowman, born March 8, 1945; married first Sandra Fullerton and had three children. Married second Robin Monroe and had a son:

1. Anthony Sterling Bowman.
2. William Craig Bowman.
3. Kimberly Renee Bowman.
4. Tyson Michael Bowman.

b. Carrie Frances King, born May 30, 1876; died August 29, 1943; buried at Kemptown. Married June 7, 1898 at Kemptown to Reverdy Mason Purdum, born December

19, 1868, died January 27, 1937, son of John Dorsey Purdum (1830) and Sarah A. Baker. One surviving child:

(1)   Mary Purdum, married Albert Easter or Castir.

c.   Reginald Windsor King, born February 13, 1878, and of whom more following.

d.   Mary Lurena King, born October 13, 1880, died May 1, 1964 in Cincinnati, Ohio. Married first c.1899 to Luther Green King, her second great uncle, a widower, born March 11, 1825, died March 7, 1909. He was a son of John Duckett King (1778) and Jemima Miles King (1782). One child, listed first following. Married second December 1, 1909 to Charles A. Heagy at Kemptown, and was divorced in 1912. Married third October 1, 1912 at Kemptown to Herbert Clayton Smith, born November 9, 1886 in Miamisburg, Ohio; died March 15, 1952 at Dayton, Ohio. They had two children, the second and third listed:

(1)   Edna Estelle King, born July 13, 1905 in Kings Valley, Montgomery County. Married October 31, 1925 at Ann Arbor, Michigan, to Bennie Emanuel Brierton, born July 16, 1901 in Arkansas, died August 1, 1988 in Miami, Florida, son of Frank and Maude Brierton; divorced. Her descendants are discussed under her name in Chapter 14 of this study, devoted to descendants of Luther Green King (1825), which see.

(2)   John Woodrow Smith, born July 16, 1915 at Dayton, Ohio. Married June 10, 1938 in Cincinnati to Mary Alma Downing, born there October 26, 1914. Children:

(a)   Edwin Townsend Smith, born January 26, 1940 in Dayton, Ohio; married August 11, 1962 in Cincinnati to Betty Carol Hennjes, born November 28, 1940 in Dayton. Children, first third and fourth born at Cincinnati, Ohio; the second in Knob Noster, Missouri:

1.   Susan Lynn Smith: February 6, 1966

2.   Douglas Edwin Smith: February 6, 1968

3. Ceara Rene Smith: born April 30, 1975

4. Allison Leigh Smith September 17, 1976

    (b) Diane Lynn Smith, a teacher, born March 27, 1947 Cincinnati, Ohio; married there March 21, 1970 Eric Christian Schlanser, a dentist, born there March 11, 1947. Children:

        1. Jenny Marie Schlanser: June 15, 1978.

  (3) Mary Elizabeth Smith, born March 12, 1918 in Dayton, Ohio, died March 27, 1974 in Erie, Ohio. Married December 30, 1939 Newport, Kentucky, to Donald Edward Sheeran, born September 21, 1914 in Dayton, Ohio. Four children:

    (a) John Edward Sheeran, born November 7, 1940 in Tela, Honduras; disabled.

    (b) Mary Elizabeth Sheeran, born September 14, 1942 in Dayton, Ohio; lived two days

    (c) Donna Ellen Sheeran, born February 26, 1949 in Opa Locka, Florida

    (d) Thomas Donald Sheeran, born February 17, 1955 at Chillicothe, Ohio

e. Myrtle Estelle King, born May 13, 1883, died January 6, 1964 and buried at Browningsville, Maryland. Married February 3, 1909 in her home at Kemptown to William Ernest Watkins, born September 14, 1881; died January 6, 1915. They had three children, two of whom were:

  (1) William Ernest Watkins, Jr., born December 20, 1909 at Kemptown

  (2) Margaret Elizabeth Watkins, born July 5, 1911

f. Edna Maude King, born October 29, 1885; died June 16, 1950. Married Joseph Felix Aycock and had four children, two of them apparently infant deaths:

  (1) Edna King Aycock, born November 18, 1919

  (2) Lillian Ruth Aycock, born February 16, 1921

3. Arnold Rufus Franklin King, born June 1, 1848; died January 8, 1939 in Baltimore, while living at 1821 Guilford Avenue. Married first April 14, 1874 in Frederick County to Virginia E. Crawford, born March 8, 1850 and died August 16, 1886, daughter of Reverend James Henson Crawford and Caroline

Elizabeth Thompson. Arnold and Virginia are buried at the Urbana Methodist Church in Frederick County, and had two children. Married second after 1886 to Julia M. Bowen of Frederick County. The two children of the first marriage were:

a. Mertie Estelle King, born May 3, 1884; married Carey.
b. Charles King, married Jean.

4. Anna Frances Maryum King, born June 7, 1849, died December 18, 1929 at Glenmont, in Montgomery County, Maryland; buried at Mountain Chapel near Comus, Maryland. Married September 22, 1868 in Frederick County to Thomas Jefferson Connelly, born May 12, 1846 and died September 11, 1903 at their home near Laytonsville; buried at Mountain Chapel. He was a son of Michael Connelly and Lucinda Jones. They had twelve children:

a. Lucinda Roberta Connelly, born July 13, 1869 in Frederick County; died 1938 in Cabin John, Maryland. Married c.1887 to John William Lynch, born January 2, 1863, died April 26, 1929, the son of William Thomas Lynch and Mary Agnes Tarman; buried at St. Mary's Cemetery in Rockville. Children, all born on the family farm at Potomac, Maryland:

(1) John William Lynch, Jr., born November 28, 1886, and died December 28, 1892. Buried St. Gabriel Catholic Cemetery.

(2) Oley Irene Lynch, born October 30, 1888 in Cabin John, Maryland, died January 25, 1969. Married November 26, 1913 to Maurice Aloysius Collins, born September 14, 1884 in Washington, D. C., and died July 17, 1973. Two children:

(a) Mary Roberta Collins, born April 6, 1915 in Washington; married Robert Lee Millard.

(b) Evelyn Rita Collins, born July 5, 1920 in the city of Washington, D. C.; married June 4, 1940 Herbert Lester Houser, born November 1, 1917, and had children:

1. Herbert Joseph Houser: March 19, 1941
2. Richard Michael Houser: November 23, 1942

3. Sally Irene Houser: January 29, 1944

4. Elizabeth Ann Houser: May 28, 1947

(3) James Mackin Lynch, born December 8, 1889; died April 18, 1956; single. Buried St. Gabriel Catholic Cemetery.

(4) Mary Frances Lynch, born May 12, 1891 in Cabin John, Maryland, and died October 28, 1972 in Washington, D. C. Married December 11, 1922 Charles Nicholas Whelan, Jr., born February 11, 1891; died May 8, 1933, the son of Charles Nicholas Whelan and Kathryn Dalton. Two sons:

(a) Charles Nicholas Whelan, III, born February 7, 1923 and married October 2, 1948 to Anna June Hodtwalker, born January 10, 1926 in Crete, Nebraska, died May 28, 1991 in Washington, D. C., the daughter of Frederick Wilhelm Theodor Hodtwalker and Mary Luella Park. Children:

1. Charles Nicholas Whelan, IV: March 15, 1955

2. Mary Catherine Whelan, a twin, born August 8, 1961 in Bethesda; married November 24, 1990 in Potomac to Gordon David Smith, born January 3, 1961 in New Jersey. Children, born in Annapolis, Maryland:

   a. Katherine June Smith, born August 12, 1991

   b. Meghan Leslie Smith, born December 14, 1992

3. John Theodore Whelan, a twin, born August 8, 1961 Bethesda; married April 17, 1993 in Prince Frederick, Maryland, to Deborah Buckler, born January 15, 1959 Calvert County, Maryland.

(b) Robert Dalton Whelan, born January 22, 1926 in the city of Washington, D. C., and died October 10, 1985 in Brooksville, Florida; married Gladys Spaur, and had two children:

1. Thomas Dalton Whelan, born March 1, 1949 in Washington, D. C.; married during 1972 in Charlottesville, Virginia, to Mary Kay Zaiser, born December 18, 1949 in Minneapolis, Minnesota, and had children, born Richlands, Tazewell County, Virginia:

    a. Brandon Dalton Whelan, born August 25, 1977
    b. Lynn Alexandria Whelan, born on November 13, 1979

2. Lauren Kimberley Whelan, born March 28, 1955 in Arlington, Virginia; married in Falls Church to George Edward Morrison, IV, born August 1, 1947 in Woodstock, Virginia. Children:

    a. George Edward Morrison, V, born December 24, 1986 in Radford, Virginia
    b. Christopher Robert Morrison, born January 12, 1990 in Newport News, Virginia

(5) Martha Agnes Lynch, born August 2, 1896 in Cabin John, Maryland, died c.1974. Married to Allan Gathright and had at least two children:

(a) Alan Joseph Gathright, married August 19, 1947 to Wilma Sherri Moore and died in California c.1988

(b) Martha Ann Gathright, married April 19, 1956 to Richard J. Winterhalter

(6) Laura Elizabeth Lynch, born July 19, 1898; married to J. Leo Pope. No children.

(7) Emily Roberta Lynch, born August 14, 1901; married September 8, 1928 to Walt Mandry; no children.

(8) Ethel Catherine Lynch, born September 2, 1908 in Cabin John, Maryland, died 1983 in Olney. Married to Clinton W. Phillips, and had children:
    (a) James Phillips.
    (b) Steve Phillips.
(9) John Edgar Lynch, born July 21, 1911, died 1944 in Honolulu, Hawaii, buried at Arlington National Cemetery.

b. Caroline Delaware Connelly, born February 19, 1871, and died October 15, 1938, single.

c. Harry Elijah Connelly, born September 23, 1872; died March 15, 1917. Married July 12, 1899 Lottie Anne VanHorn, born April 19, 1876; died January 23, 1957. The wedding announcement gives her name as Charlotte VanHorn; Lottie appears to be a contraction. They appear to have had at least one daughter:

    (1) Myrtle Louise Connelly, born March 15, 1907; died August 17, 1963. Married November 6, 1924 Lynn Eugene Norman, born October 14, 1900; four children:

        (a) Doris Louise Norman, born August 14, 1926; married March 17, 1945 Alvin Samuel Insley, born October 25, 1924, and had two children:
            1. Geary Paul Insley: November 18, 1947
            2. Steven Dennis Insley: June 29, 1950

        (b) Alma Anne Norman, born October 30, 1931, and married August 30, 1952 Edward Weeks Brand, born October 25, 1928; children:
            1. Carol Anne Brand: September 30, 1953
            2. Douglas Edward Brand: May 6, 1956
            3. Gregory Michael Brand: June 7, 1961

        (c) Helen Ruth Norman, born November 18, 1933. Married December 26, 1960 to William Frederick Archbold.

        (d) Lynn David Norman, born April 16, 1942

d. Martha Mary Connelly, known as Mattie May, born April 10, 1874, died June 24, 1945. Married November 25, 1897 Geary Aloysius Fisher, born February 7, 1873 and died September 13, 1924, son of Millard Clay Fisher and Mary Elizabeth Boswell. Eleven children:

(1)　Helen Agatha Fisher, born August 11, 1898; died May 14, 1983. Married May 17, 1923 to Joseph Oscar Matthews, born March 17, 1901; died July 30, 1970. Four children:

- (a)　Mary Claire Matthews, born July 28, 1924. Married Yves Joseph Ogaard, born October 1, 1920; children:
  1. Elizabeth Jeanne Ogaard, born February 11, 1951
  2. Helen Cecilia Ogaard, born November 9, 1953
  3. Anthony Ogaard, born 1954 infant death
  4. Mary Caron Anne Ogaard born September 4, 1956
- (b)　Joseph Oscar Matthews, Jr., infant death December 26, 1925
- (c)　Joseph Oscar Matthews, Jr.: March 1, 1929
- (d)　Barbara Anne Matthews, born August 8, 1931, married April 8, 1955 George Joseph Hranicky. Children:
  1. Teresa Anne Hranicky, born February 15, 1956, died May 6, 1979 in Silver Spring, Maryland
  2. Justine Claire Hranicky: June 30, 1957
  3. Thomas Jerome Hranicky: November 1, 1958
  4. Kenneth Bede Hranicky: July 27, 1961
- (e)　John Barry Matthews, born September 6, 1933. Married September 1, 1956 Margaret Kennedy Keane, born September 13, 1934. They had children:
  1. John Barry Matthews, Jr., born August 26, 1957
  2. Margaret Keane Matthews, born October 5, 1958

3. Susan Fisher Matthews, born October 17, 1959
4. Steven Kennedy Matthews.

(2) Mary Caroline Fisher, born August, 1900, an infant death

(3) Evelyn Aloysius Fisher, born February 24, 1902; died November 10, 1959. Married February 11, 1929 to Roy Charles Arehart, born August 27, 1905; died January 8, 1986. At least one son:
 (a) Thomas Mitchell Arehart, born August 8, 1930. Married August 31, 1951 to Lucille Yvonne O'Neal, born 1936; and had children:
  1. Patricia Michelle Arehart: May 30, 1957
  2. Charles Michael Arehart: June 4, 1962
  3. Tracey Ann Arehart: June 1, 1963

(4) Lawrence Prescott Fisher, born March 18, 1903, died February 1, 1958 in Rockville. Married April 24, 1934 to Rose Camille Kirkland, born October 29, 1902. One son:
 (a) Geary Lawrence Fisher, born December 4, 1940; perhaps the father of twins:
  1. Patrick Geary Fisher.
  2. William Michael Fisher.

(5) Andrew Geary Fisher, born April 6, 1904; died December 22, 1983. Married April, 1929 Sarah Bridget Costello, born September 2, 1903, and died October 4, 1967. One daughter, adopted:
 (a) Mary Elsa Fisher.

(6) Joseph Milton Fisher, born August 18, 1905; died March 18, 1981. Married October 21, 1933 at St. Mary's Church Rockville, Janet Faville Armstrong, born June 28, 1910, daughter of Hugh Armstrong, and had children:
 (a) Lawrence Gregory Fisher, born March 4, 1936. Married April 30, 1968 Louisa Elko, born January 21, 1939
 (b) Robert Edward Fisher: October 21, 1940
 (c) Stanley Albert Fisher: November 12, 1944

43

(d) Douglas Vincent Fisher: October 17, 1947

(7) Jessie Theckla Fisher, born August 22, 1907; died December 14, 1972. Married October 8, 1942 to Forest Milburn George, born 1903 and died July, 1952. Children:
- (a) Michael Clair George, born July 16, 1943
- (b) Sarah Gail George, born October 9, 1945
- (c) Elizabeth Ann George, born May 2, 1947

(8) John Norman Fisher, born March 31, 1909; died March 26, 1950. Married November 11, 1939 Anna Marie Fannon, born 1912. Children:
- (a) John Norman Fisher, Jr., born October 3, 1941; perhaps the father of two children:
  1. Allison Fisher.
  2. John Warren Fisher.
- (b) Linda Anne Fisher, born May 18, 1946
- (c) Mary Constance Fisher: October 1, 1949

(9) Philip Adrian Fisher, born April 1, 1912; died December 24, 1982. Married Celestine Domin-owski, born November 3, 1923, and had children:
- (a) Leslie Ann Fisher, born May 21, 1952
- (b) Michael Alan Fisher, born August 19, 1954
- (c) Nancy Lee Fisher.

(10) Mary Edna Fisher, known as "Nook", born July 13, 1913. Married October 21, 1939 to Frank John Nivert, born October 18, 1915, and had children:
- (a) Frank John Nivert, Jr., born May 21, 1942
- (b) Mary Catherine Nivert, born October 25, 1944. Married February 27, 1972 William Thomas Danoff and had children:
  1. Emma Seton Danoff: October 26, 1975
  2. Lucy Caroline Danoff: January 26, 1979
- (c) Edward Joseph Nivert, born January 5, 1947

(11) Thomas Warren Fisher, born August 22, 1921; married 1948 to Lois Jean Foster, born April 14, 1926 and died January 24, 1964, and had the first three children listed. Married second February 2,

1966 Sheila Ann Marie Hall, born January 30, 1943, and had the last daughter:
(a) Lois Ann Fisher, born May 10, 1949; married Covati and had children:
    1. Stephanie Amber Covati.
    2. Matthew Warren Covati.
(b) Christine Lee Fisher, born April 17, 1951
(c) Patricia Marie Fisher, born June 27, 1955; married John Patrick Morris, born September 29, 1954, son of Harold Clayton Morris (1923) and Jean Evelyn Burdette (1927); and had children:
    1. Joseph Guy Morris, born 1989
    2. Andrew Madison Morris, born 1991
(d) Elizabeth Catherine Fisher.
e. Sarah Thomas Connelly, born October 24, 1877 at Travilah, died March 30, 1955 at Glenmont, Maryland. Married November 25, 1897 at St. Mary's Catholic Church in Rockville to William George Thomas Carroll, born January 2, 1867; died April 7, 1948, son of Joseph L. Carroll and Catherine Ellen Rabbitt. Three children:
(1) Annie Irma Ellen Carroll, born February 20, 1900; died June 28, 1954. Married August 24, 1924 to William Talmadge Miller, born April 18, 1887 and died February 13, 1939. He was a son of William Preston Miller and Lyda Hobbs, and is buried at Arlington National Cemetery. One daughter:
    (a) Lyda Carroll Miller, born July 4, 1925. Married August 24, 1946 to Thomas Addison Walker, (or Thomas Allison), born August 25, 1925, and had children:
        1. Lynda Carroll Walker, born July 6, 1948; married April 18, 1970 to Jeffrey Eugene Beach, born July 2, 1941, and had children:
            a. Jessica Anne Beach: July 6, 1974
            b. Joshua Edward Beach, born April 23, 1976

   c. Brittany Carroll Beach, born April 18, 1987

  2. Mary Christine Walker, born March 1, 1953; married July 26, 1975 Nolan Miller and had a son:

   a. Russell Ellis Miller, born January 26, 1979

  3. Patricia Alana Walker, born December 7, 1957/59

  4. Nancy Lou Walker, born May 9, 1961

(2) Margaret Elizabeth Carroll, born August 22, 1907; married June 2, 1934 Charles Rosensteel Smith, born June 20, 1905. No children.

(3) William George Thomas Carroll, Jr., born July 30, 1913, died January 12, 1966. Married July 29, 1939 at Manassas, Virginia, to Lenora Lonas Hausenfluck, born June 23, 1914 in Shenandoah County, Virginia, and died July 26, 1964. They had children:

 (a) Joan Marsha Carroll, born December 17, 1942; married June 20, 1964 to Austin Dais Banda, born January 22, 1937.

 (b) John Robert Carroll: September 16, 1945

f. Mary Augusta Connelly, born December 23, 1878; died August 11, 1957. Married May 18, 1911 to Daniel Boone Parsley, born March 7, 1885; died May 26, 1911, just eight days after their marriage. No children. She married second March 1, 1930 Jacob Louis Nuber, born March 1, 1863; died December 16, 1944, a widower with three children. No children.

g. Thomas Walter Connelly, born August 27, 1880; died January 9, 1905 from a fall while working in a stone quarry; single. He is buried at Mountain Chapel cemetery in Frederick County.

h. Spencer Brown Connelly, born April 7, 1884; died 1934. Married first to Beatrice Fisher, and second to Clara. No children born to either marriage.

i. Jessie Ada Connelly, born August 14, 1887; died June 3, 1897. She was apparently accidentally shot and killed by a neighbor's son, who was playing with his father's pistol.
j. Arnold Lewis Connelly, born c.1889, an infant death.
k. Dorsey Meshack Connelly, born c.1891; an infant death.
l. Everett Paul Connelly, born November 5, 1892; died September 24, 1956 at Cabin John, Maryland; single.

5. Mahala Jane Victory King, born July 26, 1853; died February 19, 1887, probably as a result of childbirth with her second child. Buried at Salem United Methodist Church. Married John Richard Silance, who died c1905, and had children:
   a. William Walter Silance, born September 19, 1881; died December 24, 1913
   b. Nannye Mae Silance, born January 9, 1887; married July 20, 1914 Julian A. Koelkebeck and second July 10, 1931 to Charles Wesley Moore. Daughter from first marriage:
      (1) Maxine Mahala Koelkebeck, born August 11, 1915; also found as Catherine Mahala. Married November 19, 1933 Robert M. Irwin, who died June 2, 1952. A son:
         (a) Robert M. Irwin, Jr., born August 2, 1934, and died June 2, 1952
6. Mary Catherine Eunice King, born February 6, 1855 of whom more following
7. Jemima Drucilla James Ellen King, born November 18, 1859, and of whom more following

Reginald Windsor King
1878-1952

This son of John Edward Howard King (1845) was born February 13, 1878, and died August 10, 1952; buried in the Providence Methodist Church cemetery at Kemptown, in Frederick County. Married December 26, 1899 at Bethel Methodist Church in Frederick County, to Ida Mae Grimes, born December 7, 1876; died April 18, 1930, daughter of John E. Grimes. Married second August 12, 1935 in Frederick to Frances Elinor Grimes Browning, a widow, born November 3, 1892, died November 3, 1971 at Gaithersburg. Nine children from the first marriage:

1. Lorena Maye King, born December 11, 1900, at Clarksburg, and died August 12, 1985; buried in Providence Methodist Church cemetary at Kemptown. Married April 14, 1920 in Frederick to Allan Philip Sadtler, born May 31, 1892 in Harford County, Maryland, and died March 9, 1977 at Martinsburg, West Virginia; buried in Pine Grove cemetery at Mt. Airy, Maryland. He was a son of Philip Benjamin and Jennie Mariald Sadtler. Allan Philip and Lorena Maye had children, and were divorced:

   a. Helen Maye Sadtler, born May 10, 1922, at Kemptown; married May 13, 1939 in Winchester, Virginia, to Dorsey Clements Griffith, born November 21, 1914, son of Worthington Griffith and Lena Gertrude Gloyd. Helen was the second of his three wives, and she divorced Dorsey April 22, 1946, after having two children. She was married second May 3, 1946 at Frederick, to Elmer Augustus Horman, Jr., born June 30, 1923, the son of Elmer Augustus Horman, Sr. and Mildred Virginia Price, and had one child:

      (1) James Dorsey Griffith, born February 7, 1940. His birth name was Neal Leon Griffith, changed when he was adopted by his uncle and aunt, Douglas Augustine and Opal Griffith. He was married to Cynthia Ann Voight, and had children:
         (a) Cynthia Lynn Griffith, born April 19, 1960
         (b) James Douglas Griffith, born March 30, 1961
         (c) Michael Dorsey Griffith, born August 7, 1962
         (d) William Earl Griffith, born July 29, 1963
         (e) Joseph Milligan Worthington Griffith, born September 12, 1964

      (2) Joyce Jean Griffith, born January 21, 1942, and married February 1, 1959 to Paul Xavier Reid, Jr., born July 3, 1940; they had two children. Married second Halbert Davidson, and had four children:

(a) Anthony Eugene Reid, born September 13, 1959. Married Kimberly Weber; children:
1. Lisa Reid, born March 30, 1981
2. Jacquelyn Reid, born May 2, 1982
(b) Paul Xavier Reid, III, born February 7, 1963
(c) Timothy Davidson, born January 19, 1965; married to Shelley Burkett
(d) Salina Marie Davidson: October 12, 1966
(e) Ronald Davidson, born December 5, 1968
(f) Lorena Mae Davidson, born July 16, 1970
(3) Jerry Augustus Horman, born September 25, 1949. Married first Bonnie Lee Baker and had two children. Married second Nancy Hunt; no children. Children from first marriage were:
(a) Duane Horman, born March 21, 1971
(b) Aaron Horman, born August 4, 1978
b. Allan Philip Sadtler, Jr., born September 18, 1923 at Monrovia, Maryland. Married February 12, 1949 in Gaithersburg, Edna Lorraine Walter, born April 28, 1923 at Derwood, Maryland, the daughter of George Cloudsley Walter and Ethel May Zimmerman. Four children:
(1) Kay Valerie Sadtler, born October 5, 1950 in Takoma Park; married first May 6, 1972 Damas-cus to John Richard Fadely. Lived in Boonesboro and had two children, born in Charlestown, West Virginia, listed following. Married second May 14, 1988 Thomas Minnick. Children were:
(a) Dawn Marie Fadely, born August 12, 1975
(b) John Shane Fadely, born May 3, 1977
(2) Carol Leslie Sadtler, born April 12, 1952 in Bethesda; married first April 3, 1971 to Virgil McClendon, divorced in 1974; no children. Married second 1976 to John Pearson, and had a child; divorced in 1978. Married third June 13, 1981 in Creagerstown, Frederick County, to Edward F. Whipp, who adopted the child, changing her last name from Pearson to Whipp. She was:

49

        (a)   Erica Lorraine (Pearson) Whipp: November 27, 1977

    (3)   Brian Allan Sadtler, born December 2, 1957 in Bethesda; married May 26, 1979 in Mt. Airy, Maryland, to Melissa Mae Boller. Children:

        (a)   Rachel Christine Sadtler, born January 22, 1987 in Washington, D. C.

        (b)   Daniel Allan Sadtler: September 25, 1989

    (4)   Ronald Philip Sadtler, born January 5, 1963 at Bethesda, Maryland, and married December 2, 1990 to Kimberly Thompson at Rocks State Park. Living at Bel Aire, Md.

c.. John Edward Sadtler, born August 1, 1925 at Cabin John, and married first on June 22, 1945 in Glenwood City, Wisconsin, Patricia Lou Daggett, born September 27, 1926, daughter of Bruce and Ramona Daggett, had four children; divorced. Married second October 6, 1971 in Florida to Patricia Ann Bailey, born December 10, 1933; no children. Children were:

    (1)   John Allan Sadtler, born January 14, 1946; married Rita in Wisconsin, and had children:

        (a)   Jackie Ray Sadtler: November 9, 1975

        (b)   Shiloh Raelene Sadtler: February 9, 1979

    (2)   Colleen Ann Sadtler, born July 31, 1949; married Thomas Bremer in Minnesota, and had children:

        (a)   Sarah Ingrid Bremer: June 20, 1978

        (b)   Douglas Dakota Bremer: November 16, 1979

        (c)   Marshall Thomas Bremer: September 8, 1982

    (3)   Deborah Lou Sadtler, born October 29, 1954 in Wisconsin

    (4)   Kevin Bruce Sadtler: May 4, 1956, Wisconsin

d. Beverly King Sadtler, born February 12, 1928 at Cabin John. Married November 11, 1944 in Washington Grove, Donald Preston Rau, born July 1, 1921, died November 24, 1969; buried at Upper Seneca Baptist Church cemetery in Cedar Grove, Maryland. They had children:

    (1)   Donald Preston Rau, Jr., born December 5, 1945

(2)   Richard Eugene Rau, born May 2, 1947 in Bethesda; married June, 1973 in Alliance, Nebraska to Barbara J. Ditsch, and had children:
       (a)   Robert Preston Rau, born October 5, 1973
       (b)   Dawn Rene Rau, born December 10, 1975
(3)   Roger Dale Rau, born August 2, 1949 Frederick; married May 31, 1970 in Rockville to Katherine Marie Ditsch, and had children:
       (a)   Roger Dale Rau, Jr.: March 23, 1971
       (b)   Beverly Elizabeth Rau: February 2, 1973
(4)   Charles Keith Rau, born November 23, 1953 in Olney. Married Alice Marie Lane, two children. Married second May 2, 1983 to Dana Hill in Rockville. Children by his first wife were:
       (a)   Phyllis Lorraine Rau: September 25, 1973
       (b)   Angela Marie Rau: April 2, 1975

e.   Charles Emile Sadtler, born November 7, 1929 at Cabin John. Married first July 1, 1949 at Derwood, Maryland, to Betty Jane Butt, born January 4, 1931, died November 10, 1988 at Baltimore; daughter of Raymond O. and Ethel L. Butt. They had children. He was married second to Jean; no children. She was married second to William J. Monteith. Children were:
(1)   Charles Michael Sadtler, born May 1, 1950; married first Betty Lou Schaefer; no children. Married second to Carla Fleenor.
(2)   Stephen Gary Sadtler, born May 1, 1953; married Cathi Barrick, and had children:
       (a)   Brittani Sadtler, born December 20, 1975
       (b)   Seth Stephen Sadtler, born March 6, 1979
(3)   Robert Allen Sadtler, born April 17, 1954; married to Cynthia Bennett, daughter of Harold T. Bennett and Helen Carolyn Woodfield, and had children, probably born in Mt. Airy, Maryland:
       (a)   Angela Sadtler, born March 24, 1979
       (b)   Kelly Sadtler, born January 8, 1981
       (c)   Amanda Sadtler, born March 3, 1984

(4)   David Ray Sadtler, born June 10, 1955; married to Carol Schultz.

f.   Jennie Ida Maye Sadtler, born October 1, 1931 at Cabin John, Maryland; married September 2, 1950 to William Alfred Cruickshank. He was born August 19, 1927, son of William Cruickshank and Dorothy Veirbuchen, and had children:

(1)   Donna Lynn Cruickshank, born March 12, 1953 in Olney; married October 14, 1978 in Gaithersburg, to Harry Lewis Marmer, and had a daughter:

(a)   Lindsay Michelle Marmer, born September 16, 1982

(2)   Barbara Lee Cruickshank, born December 3, 1954, and married June 24, 1972 in Gaithersburg, to Lawrence Edward Whatman. Two children:

(a)   Wesley Ryan Whatman, born June 28, 1979

(b)   Stephanie Leigh Whatman, born June 7, 1982

(3)   David Randall Cruickshank: October 17, 1966

g.   Neal Benjamin Sadtler, born June 19, 1933, died December, 1993 in Clearwater, Florida. Married January 28, 1960 in Bethesda, Maryland, to Nola Mae Hopkins, born December 5, 1943; divorced, and had children:

(1)   Ralph Allan Sadtler, born July 28, 1961

(2)   Early Luke Sadtler, born June 15, 1962. Married; at least a son.

(3)   April Marie Sadtler, born August 9, 1963

2.   Violet Elizabeth King, born July 23, 1902, Frederick County; died November 7, 1977 at Sebring Ridge, Florida, and buried there. Married June 15, 1921 at her family's Kemptown home to Robert Eugene Davis, born June 15, 1898. Children:

a.   James Windsor Davis, born April 2, 1922; died before August 1, 1993. Married June 25, 1949 Inez Christensen. No children.

b.   Roberta Elizabeth Davis, born December 1, 1923; married August 25, 1941 at the Trinity parsonage, in Frederick County to Donald Dexter Blood, born August 20, 1920 in Washington, D. C., died June 20, 1978, and had six children. Donald was a jeweler in the town of Gaith-

ersburg from the late 1940s until 1976, with his shop located in part of what is now *Chris' Steak House* on Diamond Avenue. The children were:
- (1) Roland Dexter Blood, born December 31, 1942
- (2) Lester Eugene Blood, born October 20, 1946
- (3) Karen Ann Blood, born May 25, 1948, and married Malone
- (4) Jane Elizabeth Blood, born January 4, 1951, and married to Ernst
- (5) George Francis Blood, born February 18, 1959
- (6) Tracy Allen Blood, born May 14, 1963

c. Reginald Hugh Davis, born October 12, 1925; married March 17, 1945 to Daisy Belle Fraley, born October, 1926. They had one child and were divorced, and he was married second September 3, 1949 to Mary Frances Mullican, born June 9, 1928, and had a child. Hugh is remembered as one of the better duckpin bowlers of the area in the late 1940s and early 1950s. His children were:
- (1) Bonita Faye Davis, born November 25, 1946; adopted by a family named English.
- (2) Robert Francis Davis, born August 17, 1954

3. Ruth Selby King, born June 6, 1904 in Kemptown, Maryland. Married December 26, 1922 in Kemptown to Wilbur Day Watkins, born January 23, 1900 at Cedar Grove; died March 21, 1969 in Sebring Ridge, Florida. He owned and operated Watkins Sheet Metal before retiring and moving to Florida. They had children:
a. Wilbur Day Watkins, Jr., known as Buster, born September 27, 1923 at Cedar Grove, owned Watkins Cabinet Company at Barnesville. Married June 23, 1948 to Agnes Jeanette Walter, born January 2, 1930 at Redland. Seven children:
- (1) Joan Marie Watkins, born December 26, 1949 in Frederick. Married first June 5, 1969 to Mark Harman Schendledecker, born March 8, 1947 in Baltimore, and had two daughters. Married second June 29, 1985 in Frederick to Gilmore Wayne

House, born April 30, 1942, who had two children by a prior marriage. Joan's daughters were:

(a) Judith Marie Schendledecker, born April 10, 1970 in Boston, Massachusetts

(b) Joy Marie Schendledecker, born April 19, 1975 in Framingham, Massachusetts

(2) Kenneth Leroy Watkins, born December 13, 1950; married December 12, 1970 to Kathryn Ann Vandorf, born May 15, 1951 in Watertown, Wisconsin. Children:

(a) Stephanie Ann Watkins, born July 11, 1971 at the Andrews Air Force Base Hospital, in Camp Springs, Maryland

(b) Kristina Marie Watkins, born December 8, 1973 in Olney, Maryland

(3) Nancy Louise Watkins, born October 1, 1952 in Olney; married February 28, 1976 Michael Walter Lloyd, born September 28, 1952 in Leonardtown, Maryland, a cabinetmaker. They had four children, the first three born in Olney; the last in Frederick, Maryland:

(a) Emilie Auge Lloyd, born March 10, 1978

(b) Martin Webster Lloyd, born March 20, 1979

(c) Erich William Lloyd, born October 24, 1980

(d) Karin Reine Lloyd, born September 2, 1982

(4) Sue Ann Watkins, born July 4, 1955 in Olney; married April 6, 1973 Eben LaMonte Conner, III, born February 15, 1955 in Yakima, Washington. He is a cabinetmaker, owner of the Maugansville Planing Mill. They have children, the first born in Olney, the second in Washington, D. C., and the last four in Hagerstown, Maryland:

(a) AnnaMaria Conner, born January 21, 1974

(b) Elisabeth Marie Conner: September 26, 1975

(c) Deborah Sue Conner, born February 5, 1978

(d) Joanna Ruth Conner, born July 18, 1980

(e) Sarah Grace Conner, born February 21, 1982

(f) Rachel Jeannette Conner, born July 3, 1984

(5) Georgia May Watkins, born May 13, 1957 in Olney; married June 24, 1976 Arby Ryan Ray, born June 29, 1957 at Jordan, New York. Children, born in Fayetteville, North Carolina:
  (a) Jennifer Marie Ray, born October 4, 1977
  (b) Andrew Ryan Ray, born October 15, 1978
(6) Franklin Wilbur Watkins, born February 16, 1959 in Olney, Maryland; married first March 18, 1978 to Teresa Ann Jackson, and had three children; divorced. Married second April 26, 1985 to Marie Frances Eaton, born January 18, 1959 in Washington, D. C. Children were:
  (a) Franklin Wilbur Watkins, Jr., born August 15, 1978 in Takoma Park
  (b) Nicholas O'Bryan Watkins, born September 14, 1979 in Silver Spring; lived eleven days; buried in St. Mary's Cemetery, Barnesville, Maryland
  (c) Joshua Stephen Watkins, born October 21, 1980 in Johns Hopkins Hospital, Baltimore
(7) Gerrianne Watkins, born December 28, 1961 in Olney; married October 6, 1979 to James Owen Conway, born December 15, 1960 in Philadelphia, and had children:
  (a) Mathew Brian Conway, born September 1, 1980 in Olney, Maryland
  (b) James Paul Conway, born March 23, 1982 in Martinsburg, West Virginia
  (c) Amanda Margaret Conway, born July 16, 1984 in Frederick, Maryland
b. Ida Louise Watkins, born January 22, 1925 at Cedar Grove; married December 11, 1944 in Frederick, Maryland, Charles Franklin Bartgis, born June 4, 1921. Divorced December 22, 1950. No children; lived in Florida.
4. Claudia Estelle King, born December 9, 1906, and married September 13, 1923 at Clarksburg to Walter Grimes.
5. Helen Jane King, born November 9, 1908, died November 11, 1910

6. John Edward King, born September 13, 1910, and died April 9, 1980. Buried at the Bethesda United Methodist Church cemetery at Browningsville, Montgomery County, Maryland. Married February 15, 1934 to Claudia Marie Mullinix, born June 9, 1905, died April 18, 1992 at Shady Grove Hospital, daughter of Resin Thomas Mullinix and Julia E. Cutsail. They had four children and, at the time of the death of Claudia, eleven grandchildren and sixteen great grandchildren. The children were:

    a. Betty Jean King, born November 4, 1934; married June 30, 1956 to Garland Roland Beard, born September 12, 1931 and had two children:
        (1) William John Beard, born March 7, 1957
        (2) Donna Jean Beard, born April 24, 1959
    b. Ruth Carolyn King, born September 27, 1938; married September 29, 1956 at Buckeystown to David Carlson Gardiner, born May 28, 1934; four children:
        (1) Teresa Ann Gardiner, born October 4, 1957
        (2) David Wayne Gardiner, born September 13, 1959
        (3) Janet Sue Gardiner, born December 26, 1960
        (4) Randy Lee Gardiner, born November 10, 1961
    c. Ida May Kind, born March 27, 1942, died December 30, 1993 in Olney, Maryland; buried at Browningsville. Married February 11, 1961 to John Edward Grimes, born October 28, 1941, and had children:
        (1) Deborah Ann Grimes, born October 23, 1962; married to Sickmen, and had children:
            (a) Stephen Sickmen.
            (b) Matthew Sickmen.
        (2) Eddie Grimes, born c.1964
    d. Joan Elane King, born February 23, 1945, and married to Golliday

7. William Howard King, born May 19, 1912 at Camptown, died December 5, 1982 in North Fort Myers, Florida. Married January 20, 1934 Frederick, Maryland, Bessie Love Geisbert, born September 30, 1914. Eight children:

a. Reginald Windsor King, born December 21, 1934, and married August 30, 1956 Evelyn Virginia Smith, born January 28, 1938. They had children:
   (1)   Sandra Gail King, born July 29, 1958
   (2)   Jo Ann King, born December 13, 1959
   (3)   Susan Virginia King, born November 18, 1960
   (4)   Reginald Windsor King, Jr., born April 6, 1962
   (5)   Howard James King, born October 9, 1964

b. Joseph Austin King, born January 6, 1936; married September 4, 1962 to Linda Louise Batty, born October 21, 1942 and had children:
   (1)   Melissa Ann King, born March 13, 1963
   (2)   William Harold King, born July 13, 1964
   (3)   Anita Renee King, born April 20, 1966

c. William Howard King, Jr., born February 16, 1937; married November 14, 1959 to Helen Elizabeth Repass, born September 21, 1942. Divorced May, 1963. Married second October 16, 1964 to Gloria Jean Kave, born August 3, 1945, and had children:
   (1)   John Edward King, born April 30, 1967
   (2)   Tina Louise King, born August 1, 1969

d. Lee Albert King, born August 12, 1938; married November 20, 1960 to Jane Elizabeth Trigger, born September 27, 1943 at Redland, Montgomery County, Maryland. Four children, the first born at Ft. Smith, Arkansas; the last three Bethesda, Maryland:
   (1)   Lee Albert King, Jr., born June 21, 1962; married to Annette Faye Sargent, born September 13, 1963, the daughter of Joseph Graham Sargent and Brenda Ilene Radford. She was first married to Willie Burns, and had one child; a second to Lee Albert, Jr.:
      (a)   Sabrina Marie Burns, born October 6, 1986 at Gaithersburg, Maryland
      (b)   Joseph Lee King, born November 29, 1994 at Gaithersburg.

(2) Steven Todd King, born January 13, 1964; married September 10, 1988 Kelley Chapman. Children:
    (a) Ashley Nicole King.
    (b) Steven Todd King, Jr.
(3) Kimberly Sue King, a twin, born April 23, 1968; married in Frederick, to Larry Dwayne McConnell, who was born in Nebraska.
(4) Kevin Scott King, a twin, born April 23, 1968; married October 2, 1993 to Laurie Michelle Luck.

e. Roger Hood King, born January 15, 1940; married June 17, 1960 Beverly Ellen Tate, born April 20, 1940, died July 7, 1986 in Baltimore, a daughter of Charles and Pearl Tate. Married second Loretta, her second marriage also. Children from the first marriage only:
(1) Karen Louise Tate King, born August 7, 1963
(2) Roger Hood King, Jr., born December 8, 1967

f. Walter Ross King, born June 2, 1941; married to Judith Marie Jones, born March 19, 1944. She was first married to Thomas, and had a daughter by that marriage; Ann Frances, born April 21, 1963. Walter Ross had one child:
(1) Margaret Ellen King, born January 24, 1968

g. Ruth Ann King, born February 1, 1946, and married February 18, 1967 Michael Lawrence Swaney, born May 3, 1946 and had children:
(1) Sean Michael Swaney, born September 24, 1968
(2) Kevin Lawrence Swaney, born December 13, 1971
(3) Kathleen Anne Swaney, born October 5, 1976

h. Sarah Elizabeth King, born December 25, 1950; married April 22, 1970 James Vincent Thompson, born November 11, 1946. They divorced after one daughter. Married second November 7, 1976 to Mike Smith, and had a son:
(1) Stephanie Suzanne Thompson, born May 25, 1971
(2) Maxwell Eli Smith, born November 20, 1979

8. Julia Maude King, born February 28, 1915; married February 24, 1934 at Germantown to Carl Elmer Moyer, a twin, born February 22, 1912, the son of George D. Moyer and Anna Gertrude Gilliss; divorced, no children. She married second

September 22, 1943 to George Anthony Stanley, born 1915, and divorced; no children. Married third July 11, 1950 to Guiseppe Simone, born July 30, 1903, Divorced October 6, 1960, no children. Married fourth August 15, 1976 to Oney T. Creech, born in Troy, Missouri and died there June 19, 1985; no children.

9. Sarah Jane King, born May 24, 1916 at Kemptown, in Frederick County, and died December 16, 1988 in North Fort Myers, Florida; buried at Upper Seneca Baptist Church cemetery, in Cedar Grove, Maryland. She was married January 22, 1934 at Rockville, to Thomas Dorsey Woodfield, born January 22, 1915 at Woodfield, died September 16, 1990 at Olney, Maryland; son of John Dorsey Woodfield and Mazie Marie Watkins. He owned and operated the Thomas D. Woodfield and Sons electrical contracting business in Damascus. They had children:

a. Robert Dorsey Woodfield, born February 28, 1936 in Damascus and died August 21, 1992 at Shady Grove Hospital; buried Upper Seneca Baptist Church cemetery, in Cedar Grove. He was the historian of the Sugarloaf Mountain Region, member of the Izaac Walton League, and the Antique Automobile Club of America. Married September 16, 1955 to Catherine Irene Dillahay, born November 3, 1935. Children, born at Olney, Maryland:

(1) Deborah Sue Woodfield, born February 20, 1957. Married Harry Martin Paulsgrove. There is a Harry Martin Paulsgrove buried at the Clarksburg United Methodist Church. He was born April 26, 1914 and died February 22, 1982; perhaps this individual, or his father.

(2) Bryan Dorsey Woodfield, born November 2, 1959

b. June Marie Woodfield, born January 21, 1938 at Damascus; married October 15, 1960 to Dana Roosevelt Jordan, born March 13, 1934 in Webster County, West Virginia, son of Roy Sullivan Jordan and Lizzie Carpenter. One daughter:

(1)   Bonita Fay Jordan, born July 20, 1963 in Olney; married September 8, 1990 Upper Seneca Baptist Church in Cedar Grove, to Sean Patrick Bennett.

c.   Thomas Leslie Woodfield, born June 20, 1939 in Damascus; and married August 9, 1957 to Mary Eloise Haney, born June 28, 1940 at Clarksburg, daughter of Forrest N. Haney (born October 27, 1918, died September 4, 1981) and Mary Esther King, born July 3, 1919. Children:

(1)   Alethia Kae Woodfield, born March 9, 1961; married in Clarksburg to Michael Craig Watkins, born June 17, 1964, a son of Donald Watkins and Barbara Wright, and had a child:

(a)   Kelsey Lynn Watkins, born May 17, 1992

(2)   Tara Lee Woodfield, born July 19, 1966, and married November 6, 1993 at Gaithersburg to Kevin Michael Pumphrey, son of Frank Pumphrey of Damascus and Anne Smiley of Clarksburg. Tarra was named Maryland Dairy Princess for 1984-1985.

d.   Jacqueline Marie Woodfield, adopted, born August 3, 1957. Married first Stephen Carlson and had a daughter. Married second to Kevin Grantham at Long Corner, Maryland, born August 3, 1955, with two children from a prior marriage. Jackie's one child was:

(1)   Jill Marie Carlson, born June 13, 1982

Mary Catherine Eunice King
1855-1889

This daughter of Walter James King (1823) and his wife, Caroline Windsor (1814), was born February 10, 1855, and died August 9, 1889, probably as a result of childbirth of her sixth child. Married April 1, 1875 George Thomas Mullican, born September 8, 1850, died January 31, 1922 at Browningsville. He was married second January 19, 1905 to Annie Belle Norwood, born 1871. Children born to Mary Catherine Eunice were:

1.   Clarence Mayfield Mullican, born April 12, 1876. Married 1910 to Margaret Rebecca Klinefelter, born March 17, 1874

60

and died February 12, 1951. He married second December 15, 1951 Marguerite Callis, born April 26, 1882; no children. Children, born to his first marriage only:

a. Clarence Mayfield Mullican, Jr., born September 15, 1911. Married February 2, 1934 to his second cousin, Elizabeth Naomi Willett, born June 3, 1914, the daughter of Clifford Willett and Esther Mazenar Peters. Children:

    (1) Patricia Lee Mullican, born November 3, 1934; married February 25, 1956 Thomas Edward Davis born June 2, 1929, and had children:

        (a) George Edward Davis, born August 10, 1957

        (b) Mark Stanley Davis, born July 16, 1960

    (2) Jacqueline Willett Mullican, born December 31, 1935; married September 7, 1956 Walter Franklin Lusby, Jr., born September 26, 1932. Children:

        (a) Walter Kevin Lusby, born May 26, 1957

        (b) David Franklin Lusby, born October 3, 1958

        (c) Sharon Willett Lusby, born June 9, 1963

b. Gene Francis Mullican, born December 28, 1912. Married April 4, 1936 to Maxine Clara Rice, born September 6, 1913, his first cousin, once removed, daughter of Douglas Dutrow Rice and Ollie May Peters. Children:

    (1) James Rice Mullican, born August 11, 1938; married January 28, 1961 to Mary Eunice Mann, born November 20, 1939

    (2) Jean Frances Mullican, born April 27, 1940; married June 9, 1962 to Gerald Leo Rooney

    (3) Jerald Anthony Mullican, (or Gerard Anthony), born August 18, 1943

    (4) Judith Maxene Mullican, born December 31, 1945

    (5) Jo Ann Margaret Mullican, born July 26, 1947

    (6) Jeffrey David Mullican, born May 12, 1954

2. Edith Helen Mullican, born October 18, 1878; died August 24, 1935; buried Clarksburg Methodist Church. Married at Hyattstown Christian Church, December 28, 1899 to Herbert Plummer Price, born February 17, 1878 and died October 20, 1955. He was married second February 28, 1948 to Lavinia Baker Butts. Edith Helen had children:

a. Bessie Helen Price, born September 24, 1900; died January 12, 1919. Buried Clarksburg Methodist Church
b. Arnold Sylvester Price, born July 10, 1904, and died on December 10, 1974. Buried at Hyattstown Methodist Church cemetery. Married September 28, 1927 Frances Helen Nicholson, born February 26, 1904, and died September 19, 1983; buried with her husband. Children:
   (1) Mildred Helen Price, born December 2, 1928; married July 19, 1948 to Kenneth Eugene Smith, born July 29, 1931, and had a daughter:
      (a) Virginia Kay Smith, born August 7, 1949
   (2) Mary Edith Price, born July 27, 1933; married December 2, 1954 to Wilfred Connly Murphy, born April 30, 1929, and had children. He was a dairy farmer and they moved to Pennsylvania. Children:
      (a) Connly Loretta Murphy: March 18, 1956
      (b) Linda Marie Murphy, born October 21, 1957
      (c) Wilfred Connly Murphy, Jr., born December 16, 1959
   (3) Frances Virginia Price, born January 3, 1941; married October 17, 1952 Luther Franklin Staub, II, born August 4, 1940.
3. Earnest Walter Mullican, born June 19, 1881; died March 30, 1935. Married Laura Webb and second to Etta Kinna Kenny, born 1884 and died 1957. Two children born to the first marriage, and one to the second:
a. Margaret Mildred Mullican, born February 11, 1911. Married August 20, 1932 to Edgar Nolan Edwards, born October 26, 1904, and had children:
   (1) Nolan Wayne Edwards, born November 7, 1935, and married November 4, 1961 to Nancy Carol George, born November 9, 1941.
   (2) Gerald Webb Edwards, born August 1, 1937; married February 24, 1957 to Irene Kastner, born July 16, 1937, and had children:
      (a) Glenn Webb Edwards: December 13, 1957
      (b) Dean Evan Edwards: December 30, 1961
   (3) Jeanette Louise Edwards, born June 13, 1944

b. Marcel Maryland Mullican, born January 14, 1917. Married March 22, 1939 to Rudolph Oscar Bloomquist, born December 23, 1907, and had children:
  (1) Kenneth Warner Bloomquist, born November 23, 1939, and married June 11, 1958 to Barbara Dahl, born July 27, 1939, and had children:
    (a) DeLyle Wade Bloomquist: March 24, 1959
    (b) Renel Bloomquist, born November 29, 1960
    (c) Virgil Rudolph Bloomquist, born September 17, 1961
  (2) Joan Marilyn Bloomquist, born March 7, 1941; married May 7, 1960 Bradley Lester Finley, born July 12, 1934, and had a child:
    (a) Pamela Marcel Finley: February 17, 1961
  (3) Robert Bloomquist, born November 9, 1942
c. Gail Ernestine Mullican, born February 21, 1921. Married November 27, 1939 to Paul Cordell Kelley, born October 11, 1909; died December 3, 1954; buried at Hyattstown Methodist Church. They had the first three children listed. She married second March 22, 1941 to Carl Montgomery Lickner, born May 27, 1911 and had the last two children:
  (1) Rita Diane Kelley, born August 4, 1940; married July 7, 1958 to Frank Verlin Williams, born September 27, 1937, and had children:
    (a) Karen Lynn Williams, born February 3, 1959
    (b) Yvonne Carol Williams, born March 7, 1960
    (c) Renee Lorraine, born December 29, 1961
  (2) Sylvia Jeanette Kelley, born February 8, 1942; married July 6, 1961 Oliver David Seymour, born September 13, 1937; a child:
    (a) Daniel Lee Seymour, born August 12, 1962
  (3) Ernest Cordell Kelley, born October 5, 1948
  (4) Craig Allen Lickner, born December 16, 1951
  (5) Carol Ann Lickner, born February 6, 1956
4. Theodore Elmer Mullican, born December 6, 1883; died July 12, 1962. Married September 10, 1910 Elizabeth Ellen Daly, born September 14, 1883; died 1951. A daughter:

a. Mary Agnes Mullican.
5. Oscar Thomas Mullican, born September 15, 1886; married to Cordelia B. Mullinix Watkins, born January 23, 1870 and died May 30, 1937, daughter of Robert T. Mullinix and Mary E. Davis. She had four children from her first marriage to Edward E. Watkins (1861-1895), and four were born to the marriage of Oscar Thomas and Cordelia. He married second May 11, 1940 to Helen Elizabeth (Hull) Bayne, born June 21, 1891 and died November 22, 1962, who also had a child from a prior marriage. The four children of Oscar were:
a. Carl Oscar Mullican, born June 22, 1906, died 1978. Married October 20, 1927 in Frederick, Maryland, to Helen Mildred Day, born June 8, 1909 at Browningsville, daughter of James Start Day and Laura Helen Davis. Carl Oscar was the father of:
   (1) Oscar Ray Mullican, born September 13, 1928 in Lewisdale, Montgomery County, Maryland, and married September 11, 1954 in Frederick to Olive Elizabeth Rice, born June 12, 1937. Children, born at Lewisdale, in Montgomery County:
      (a) Danny Lee Mullican, born May 26, 1959
      (b) David Scot Mullican, born April 26, 1960
      (c) Dennis Ray Mullican, born March 10, 1965
   (2) Robert Day Mullican, born August 6, 1932 at Lewisdale; married March 22, 1952 Delores Ann Burdette, born August 17, 1934; twins, born at Olney, Montgomery County, Maryland:
      (a) Deborah Lynn Mullican, born 1952; married to S. Darron Long, son of Irvin Long and Betty Burdette.
      (b) Marcia Ann Mullican, born 1952; married May 19, 1972 in Damascus to James Stephen Robertson, son of Robert L. Robertson.
   (3) Carroll Lee Mullican, born May 21, 1943 in Lewisdale and died that same day
b. Herbert Eugene Mullican, born July 22, 1908, died July 24, 1979, buried at Browningsville. Married to Shirley Wilcox. No children.

c. George Robert Mullican, born May 7, 1910. Married twice; first to Elizabeth Insley, and second Lena Thomas. One child born to each marriage:
   (1) Wayne Mullican, born April 5, 1939
   (2) Suzanne Mullican, adopted, born August 20, 1947, married to Carra.
d. Mary Cordelia Mullican, born January 12, 1912; married to Robert Carroll.
6. Mary Catharine Mullican, born August 4, 1889; lived thirteen days and died August 17, 1889.

Jemima Drucilla James Ellen King
1859-1932

This daughter of Walter James King (1823) and his wife, Caroline Windsor (1814), was born November 18, 1859 in Montgomery County, Maryland, and died there March 15, 1932. Married December 7, 1880 in Frederick County to Horace Thomas Peters, born December 20, 1851; died July 28, 1923. He was a blacksmith and a merchant; and the son of John Peters (1818), a wheelwright at Thurston near Urbana, and Cassandra Nicholson (1822). The grandfather of Horace was also named John Peters, who served as a Major in the Revolution, was married to Ellen Bassford, and had six children. Horace was a wheelwright and a blacksmith, in which business he was engaged for several years. He later ran a store at Comus, Maryland, for one year, before moving back to the Thurston area. In 1889, he purchased the *Forge Farm* of some 120 acres, on the road between Urbana and Park Mills, where they made their home. They had children:
1. Ollie May Peters, born August 16, 1882 at Thurston, Frederick County, Maryland. Married first December 28, 1909 Douglas Dutrow Rice, born January 28, 1882 and died February 2, 1944. They had two children, and Ollie May married second May 22, 1956 Francis Garland Kessler, born February 16, 1883; no children. The children were:
   a. Lillian Glenda Rice, born August 24, 1912; married June 8, 1957 to Arthur B. Maton.

65

b. Maxine Clara Rice, born September 6, 1913; married April 4, 1936 to her cousin, Gene Francis Mullican, born December 28, 1912, son of Clarence Mayfield Mullican and Margaret Rebecca Klinefelter, which see previously.

2. Esther Mazenar Peters, born February 29, 1884. Married August 15, 1905 to Clifford Willett, born December 14, 1874; died December 25, 1924 and had children. Married second January 21, 1926 John Wesley Ward born June 10, 1883; no children. The Willett children were:

a. Elton Clifford Thomas Willett, born September 3, 1906; married September 6, 1930 Katherine Evelyn Gerstmyer, born February 21, 1910. Children:

(1) Nancy Joan Willett, born December 29, 1931; married June 6, 1953 to Walter Emanuel Johnson, Jr., born November 25, 1931, and had children:
(a) Pamela Gail Johnson: September 12, 1954
(b) Jennifer Lynn Johnson, born June 21, 1960

(2) Thomas Elton Willett, born August 4, 1937, and married September 17, 1960 to Carol Sue Kale, born November 25, 1939; a child:
(a) Cynthia Willett, born August 29, 1961

(3) Richard Bruce Willett, born September 3, 1944; married October 20, 1962 to Judith Jean Parks, and had a son:
(a) Donald Bruce Willett, born May 11, 1963

b. Clifford Mazenar Willett, born September 9, 1910; married October 20, 1932 Madeline Nina Owens, born September 23, 1907

c. Elizabeth Naomi Willett, born June 3, 1914; married February 2, 1934 to her cousin, Clarence Mayfield Mullican, Jr., born September 15, 1911, which see.

3. Mary Ellen Peters, or Mary Virginia, born June, 1885, and died in infancy

4. Zora Viola Peters, born October 28, 1887, died March 2, 1975, buried in Monocacy cemetery at Beallsville, Maryland. Married at Bloomsburg, in Frederick County, April 11, 1907 to Eberly Thomas Dixon, born February 17, 1871; died October 14, 1953; buried at Monocacy cemetery. Children:

a. Agnes Virginia Dixon, born October 6, 1908; married February 15, 1930 to Stonestreet Wilson Luhn, born October 17, 1908, died September 23, 1966; buried at Monocacy cemetery in Beallsville, Montgomery County. They had a son:
   (1) Wilson Stonestreet Luhn, born December 5, 1930; married September 1, 1951 to Elsie Beahm, born January 20, 1930, and had a daughter:
      (a) Teresa Diane Luhn, born December 23, 1954
b. Herbert Thomas Dixon, born October 14, 1913
c. Evelyn Dixon, born October 22, 1920; married January 8, 1941 to Hubert Wilson Matthews, born January 9, 1920, and perhaps had children, including:
   (1) Hubert Wilson Matthews, Jr.: October 14, 1941
   (2) Nancy Jean Matthews: July 29, 1951
5. John Thomas Peters, born January 12, 1894; died October 19, 1927. Buried in Sugarloaf Mountain cemetery. Married in Frederick June 20, 1912 Nannie Axie Thompson, born July 16, 1894, and had children:
   a. Andrew Thomas Peters.
   b. Louise Ellen Peters, born January 27, 1926; married August 10, 1945 to Nelson Edward Trout, born November 26, 1924, and had children:
      (1) Susan Cheryl Trout, born February 25, 1947
      (2) Jerry Lamar Trout, born June 4, 1949
      (3) Robert Nelson Trout, born May 24, 1950
      (4) Ralph Thomas Trout, born January 7, 1952
      (5) John Cleve Trout, born August 18, 1954
      (6) Donald Eugene Trout, born December 30, 1955
      (7) Rebecca Louise Trout, born February 8, 1957
      (8) Steven Paul Trout, born May 8, 1958
      (9) Andrew Peters Trout, born November 30, 1960
   c. John Horace Peters, born December, 1929. Note that this date is in conflict with the reported death date of his father. One of them is obviously incorrect.
6. Caroline Frances Peters, born March 8, 1899; married Joseph E. Roberts and had children:

a. Frances Maryland Roberts, born December 1, 1912, and died October 13, 1913
b. Madeline Roberts, born October 16, 1914, and married Albert Edward Young, born February 29, 1908, died September 27, 1973 in Monocacy cemetery at Beallsville. A daughter:
   (1) Frances Louise Young, born February 7, 1932; married September 13, 1952 to Merle Ray Mills.
c. Anne H. Roberts, born April 14, 1918; died April 18, 1918
d. Windsor Roberts.

CHILD 2

Jemima P. King
1826-?

This daughter of Middleton King (1801) and Mahala E. Summers (1798), was born c.1826, and married January 30, 1850 to Reuben Brown. In the Accounts, her last name is stated as being Ball, from her second marriage. At least two children:

1. Reuben Middleton Brown, born June 9, 1851 and died March 6, 1927. He lived in the District of Columbia, where he operated a paint store on Seventh Street. Married December 10, 1872 to Anna Gertrude King, born April 19, 1856, died March 25, 1934, daughter of Rufus King (1816). Their descendants are discussed in Chapter 11, dealing with the family of Rufus King (1816), which see.
2. Nellie Louise Brown, died November 26, 1920. Married to Henry B. Lain.

CHILD 3

John Middleton King
1830-1919

This son of Middleton King (1801) and Mahala E. Summers (1798), was born February 1, 1830 in Montgomery County, and died October 19, 1919. Under his father's will, he received a tract of land called *Trouble Enough*. He and his brother George Edward together got the lot adjoining the mill and distillery of Luther Green King, called *Clothes Tract*. He was married September 16, 1853 to Amy C. Brewer, born May 6, 1836 in Montgomery County, and died July 11, 1874, daughter of Vincent Brewer; by whom he had eight children. He was married second February 18, 1875 to Mary Keziah (Layton) Waters, by whom he had three children. She was a daughter of John Layton and Catherine Hinton, and was first married to Rufus Waters, by whom she had five children. She was born April 30, 1836 and died April 6, 1902. Both gravestones of the wives are marked "mother". They are all buried in Mountain View Methodist Church cemetery. He was married third September 24, 1903 at Lewisdale, to Cora Clark Burdette, daughter of Greenbury Burdette; no issue. He appears as head of household in the 1860 census for Clarksburg, Montgomery County, Maryland, with his wife, there spelled Emma, and three of their children. In the 1870 census, he is listed in Damascus, with several more of his children. In Bonds of Montgomery County, dated September 6, 1876 and filed in Liber RWC 9 at folio 43, a bond is filed by John M. (Middleton) King, with William W. Soper and Edward King as sureties, for guardianship of Elias Dorsey King, Mary T. King, Georgellen W. King, and James M. King, infant children, following the death of his wife, Amy Brewer. Children included:

1. Catherine Jemima King, born July 30, 1854, and died February 3, 1929. Married William Wooten Soper, born July 15, 1850 and died June 27, 1919, son of John T. Soper (1812); both buried at Upper Seneca Baptist Church, Cedar Grove, Maryland. The family appears in the 1880 census for Clarksburg District of Montgomery County, Maryland, with four of their children. Her will, dated August 28, 1922 and probated

March 18, 1929, is recorded in Liber PEW 14 at folio 190 in Montgomery County. She was residing in Washington, D. C. at the time. She names several of her children, and their descendants, which include:

a. Robert Percy Soper, born March 19, 1873, and died May 26, 1945. Married to Mary V. Benson, born January 12, 1875 and died June 7, 1960. Both buried at St. John's, Olney, Maryland. He was the father of:

(1) Robert Percy Soper, Jr., born c.1900, and married June 3, 1925 at Goshen, Alice Pearl Armstrong, born 1904, daughter of Laban B. and Minnie Armstrong of Laytonsville. They had children:

(a) Dorothy Louise Soper, born 1926, married November 9, 1949 to David Franklin Bready, born 1923. They had children:
1. Steven Franklin Bready, born 1951
2. Sandra Ellen Bready, born 1952

(b) Alice Estelle Soper, born 1929, married September 8, 1949 to Neil Gordon Corbett, born 1927. Children:
1. Patti Kaye Corbett, born 1952

(c) Robert Armstrong Soper, born 1934

(2) Mary Helen Soper, born August 2, 1902; married John W. Dillon, born March 13, 1897, died March 11, 1956, buried St. John's at Olney. Children:

(a) John Robert Dillon, born 1923; married Mary Jane Zimmerman, born 1925. Children:
1. John Robert Dillon, Jr., born 1943
2. John W. Dillon, II, born 1947
3. Thomas Preston Dillon, born 1950

(b) Mary Jane Dillon, born 1927; married James C. Bowman, born 1928, and had children:
1. James C. Bowman, Jr., born 1948
2. Mary Elizabeth Bowman, born 1949

(c) Margaret Helen Dillon, born December 15, 1928; and died December 12, 1929. Buried at St. John's in Olney, Maryland.

(d) Catherine Elizabeth Dillon, born 1931; married Franklin Vernon Leizear, born 1927, and had a child:
1. Sharon Patricia Leizear, born 1952
(3) Catherine Virginia Soper, born 1907; married June 20, 1929 to Charles W. Alderton of Layhill, born 1908. Children:
   (a) Charles W. Alderton, Jr., born 1931
   (b) Virginia Alderton, born 1932; married Dale Butler, born 1928.
(4) Annie Elizabeth Soper, born 1908; married June 20, 1934 DeWitt Hanse Tooks of Snow Hill, Maryland, born 1902
(5) Leroy Benson Soper, born 1913; married Lucille Nance, born 1907, and had children:
   (a) William L. Soper, born 1938
   (b) Robert Donald Marcus Soper, born February 24, 1943
(6) Elgar Clyde Soper, born 1914; married Audrey Ricketts, born 1927, and had a child:
   (a) David Stanley Soper, born 1950
b. William Oscar Soper, born June 6, 1877, died March 27, 1950; buried at Mt. Olivet in Frederick. He married Mary Somerville "Sommie" Duvall, born November 11, 1878, died June 28, 1958; buried at Mt. Olivet; daughter of William Frank Duvall, and had children:
(1) W. Franklin Soper, born 1905; married first December 24, 1930 at Clarksburg to Mary Belle Davis, born May 8, 1913, died February 11, 1940, daughter of Charles T. and Harriet M. Davis. She is buried at the Hyattstown Christian Church cemetery. Married second Mildred Allman, born c.1911. Children:
   (a) Harriet Elizabeth Soper, born 1931, and married to Billie Wayne Walker, Jr.
   (b) W. Franklin, Jr. Soper, born 1934
(2) Kathryn Soper, born 1907; married first Creighton Jones and second to Charles Crone.

71

(3) Bertie Bell Soper, born 1912; married Richard E. Thompson, born 1902, and had children:
  (a) Richard W. Thompson, born 1932
  (b) Kathryn Loraine Thompson, born 1937
c. Charles W. Soper, born c.1877, and died 1956. Married to Nellie Howse Benson, born 1879 and died 1969. Both are buried at Upper Seneca Baptist Church, Cedar Grove.
d. Spencer Jones Soper, born December, 1878 in Montgomery County; died 1938. Married September 4, 1900 to Dora Higgins, born 1862, and died 1943, daughter of Erie Higgins. Buried Upper Seneca Baptist Church in Cedar Grove. They had at least a son and a daughter:
  (1) Joseph Luther Soper, born November 22, 1901
  (2) Marguerite D. Soper, died January 12, 1902, an infant death, and buried at Upper Seneca Baptist Church, Cedar Grove
e. Effie May Soper, born c.1880, and married December 27, 1899 John Spencer Mullican, born 1877, died 1943; buried at Neelsville Presbyterian cemetery. He was a son of Archibald Mullican. Married second Frank Bannon, born 1883. She had children from her first marriage only:
  (1) Roscoe Mullican, born 1901; married Cora Wentz, born 1902.
  (2) Russell Mullican, born 1903 and died 1918
  (3) Edward Mullican, born 1904, and married to Rita Kremar, born 1914, and had children:
    (a) Dawn M. Mullican, born 1940
    (b) John E. Mullican, born 1945
  (4) Dora Mullican, born 1908; married Martin J. Coppinger, born 1903 and had children:
    (a) Joseph M. Coppinger, born 1925; married to Kay White, born 1924, and had children:
      1. Joseph M. Coppinger, Jr., born 1948
      2. John E. Coppinger, born 1948
      3. Cheryl A. Coppinger, born 1949
      4. James P. Coppinger, born 1951
    (b) Mary P. Coppinger, born 1949

(5) Irwin Mullican, born 1909, died 1951, and married Dorothy Elizabeth Adelle, and had a son:
    (a) J. Michael Mullican, born 1940
(6) Blanche Mullican, born 1911; died 1922; buried at Upper Seneca Baptist Church at Cedar Grove.
(7) Charles Mullican, born 1913; died 1944
(8) Thomas E. Mullican, born 1915; married Dorothy Fisher, born 1919, and had children:
    (a) Charles Thomas Mullican, born 1943
    (b) James Joseph Mullican, born 1946
    (c) Paul Emory Mullican, born 1951
(9) Robert B. Mullican, born 1917; married Helen Stotler, born 1918, and had children:
    (a) Robert E. Mullican, born 1939
    (b) Janice I. Mullican, born 1945
(10) Bertie Mullican, born 1919; married Scott Shaw, born 1909; and had at least one son:
    (a) Charles M. Shaw, born 1945
f. Mamie F. Soper, born August 19, 1883; died May 14, 1975. Buried at Damascus Methodist Church cemetery. Married October 12, 1910, as his second wife, to Samuel E. Reid, born June 7, 1858; died March 11, 1937. They had children:
(1) N. Eugene Reid, born 1917, and married to Marie Piquette. They had children:
    (a) Barbara Jean Reid.
    (b) Linda L. Reid, born 1949
(2) Harrington Reid, born 1918
(3) John Franklin Reid, born 1920
(4) Robert Earl Reid, born 1923
g. Carey Clark Soper, born c.1885, died January 4, 1919 of flu and pneumonia. Married November 3, 1909 to Sarah Jane Harris, born 1883 and died 1942. He had children:
(1) Mary Soper, born 1911; married J. Bradley Baker, born 1877, and had children:
    (a) J. Bradley Baker, Jr., born 1931
    (b) Thomas R. Baker, born 1933
    (c) John C. Baker, born 1935

(d) Donald E. Baker, born 1946
(2) Dorothy Soper, born December 24, 1914; married to Vincent Roddy, born 1898, and had children:
(a) Dorothy A. Roddy, born 1939
(b) Mary J. Roddy, born 1941
(c) Nancy L. Roddy, born 1943
(3) Thomas Llewellyn Soper, born August 16, 1917; died 1940.
h. Blanche Soper, born 1890; married to Wilson Cecil, born 1889. Children:
(1) Hazel Cecil, born 1915; married Stewart Carter, born 1916 and had a son:
(a) Richard Carter, born 1942
(2) James H. Cecil, born 1920; married Mildred Haley Dillon, born 1919, and had a son:
(a) Randolph Cecil, born 1947
(3) Dorothy L. Cecil, born 1924; married Robert E. Windam, born 1919, and had children:
(a) Robert C. Windham, born 1949
(b) George Cris Windham, born 1950
(4) Anna Mae Cecil, born 1927; married to Paul F. Burner, Jr., born 1926, and had children:
(a) Gary W. Burner, born 1950
(b) Kathleen M. Burner, born 1953
i. Laura Jane Soper, born c.1893; died 1967. Married November 22, 1911 Maynard D. Watkins, born May 30, 1891, died January 13, 1981, son of James Willard Watkins (1848) and Charlotte J. Watkins. Both buried at Upper Seneca Baptist Church at Cedar Grove. Children:
(1) Charlotte Watkins, born 1912; married Elroy Kaufman.
(2) William D. Watkins, born 1914; married Julia Norwood and had a child. Married second Frances Chandler. His child was:
(a) Shirley Watkins.
(3) E. Wheeler Watkins, born 1921. Married to Phyllis Thompson, born 1923, and had children:
(a) Dianne K. Watkins, born 1947

(b) Gail M. Watkins, born 1951

    (4)   Maynard D. Watkins, Jr., born 1928, and married to Mary Jane Mullinix.

2. Ursula Mahala King, born August 30, 1857; died December 2, 1940. Married to her cousin, Rufus Filmore King, born October 7, 1850 and died April 26, 1926, son of Luther Green King (1825). Both are buried in the Damascus Methodist cemetery. Their family is discussed under her husband's name in Chapter 14, dealing with the descendants of Luther Green King (1825), which see.

3. Elias Dorsey King, born 1863 and died February 26, 1947; buried at Mount Olivet Cemetery, Frederick, Maryland. He was married October 9, 1885 in Frederick County, to Hattie Gertrude Lawson, born 1865 and died December 16, 1935 in Montgomery County; buried with her husband. She was a daughter of James Uriah Lawson and Catherine Lawson of Frederick County. His will, dated August 1, 1940, is recorded in Liber OWR 21 at folio 219 in the will records of Montgomery County, and entered for record March 3, 1947. In the will, he requests that he be buried at Mt. Olivet Cemetery with his wife, and makes specific bequests to seven of his children, and one of his granddaughters. He mentions that there are ten children, but names only seven of them. The ten children, not necessarily in order, were:

a. Ivy C. King, born May 3, 1885, died October 7, 1972. Married to Joseph G. Howes, born November 15, 1880 and died July 4, 1967. Both are buried at the Neelsville Presbyterian Church cemetery, Montgomery County. Her name is listed here as it was found on her tombstone; it has also been reported as Iva C. King.

    (1)   Dorsey Howes, born July 28, 1914. Married Jane Bell, born November 28, 1919, died February 8, 1995, daughter of Garrison W. Bell and Janet W. Williams. Children and grandchildren.

    (2)   Catherine Howes, born July 29, 1916. Married Albert Clagett, Jr.

b. Lola Edna King, married December 26, 1905 to her second cousin, once removed, Albert Essex King, born 1876 and died 1948, son of James Harrison King (1841) and Mary Emma Essex (1845). She is believed to be buried at Mt. Olivet in Frederick. They reportedly had three children:

(1)　Gertrude King.

(2)　Francis King.

(3)　Margaret King.

c.　James Deets King, born February 4, 1889 on the family farm near Damascus, Montgomery County, and died January 10, 1958. He was president of Montgomery County Farm Bureau for ten years, and a director of the Maryland Farm Bureau for many years. In 1897, he moved with his parents to Frederick County, near Urbana, returning to Montgomery about 1905. He lived near Dawsonville, and was a president of the Montgomery County Soil Conservation District, and held numerous other offices related to agriculture. Married Macie Schaeffer, born April 19, 1893 in Frederick County, Maryland, and died at the age of 99 years, November 4, 1992, daughter of Allen Schaeffer. She and her husband are buried at Mount Olivet Cemetery in Frederick, with numerous other family members. She was first president of the Montgomery Farm Women's Market in Bethesda, and a co-founder, where, for many years, she sold vegetables grown on the family farm on Schaeffer Road, named for her family. She was a member of the Eastern Star and the DAR. At the time of her death, she had eight grandchildren, fourteen great grandchildren, and four great great grandchildren surviving, as well as her two daughters. His will, dated November 2, 1951, was probated January 29, 1958, and recorded in liber VMB 134 at folio 8, in the will records of Montgomery County. His principal asset was his farm at Old Germantown, and he names his wife, his son and his two daughters, providing legacies for each of them. He also names one grandson, James M. Mims, whom I have not yet identified. They had children:

(1) James Schaeffer King, born c.1913 and died February 20, 1987 at his home in Snow Hill, Maryland, to which he had retired. Married April 17, 1937 to Hilda Rebecca Walker, born February 6, 1917, the daughter of Nathan Walter Walker (1886). They had children:
   (a) Faith Virginia King, born November 7, 1946; married to Paul Duvall and had a son:
      1. Paul Duvall, Jr.
   (b) Sara Rebecca King, born November 14, 1949; married William Stark and had a son:
      1. James William Stark.
(2) Helen Gertrude King, married Thanksgiving Day, 1935, to Garner William Duvall of Gaithersburg. Children:
   (a) Barbara Duvall.
   (b) William Duvall.
   (c) Sharon Duvall.
(3) Irene King, married Clifford Weed of Hagerstown, Maryland, and had children.
d. Gabriel D. King, born c.1891, and died March 7, 1968 at Montgomery General Hospital. Married September 1, 1926 at Rockville, to Pearl Selby Clemente, who had been previously married, with at least one daughter. She was Regina, born July 3, 1914; died February 8, 1988. Regina was married at least three times, the last to Archie O. Hood, born April 7, 1919; died December 28, 1990. Regina and Archie are both buried at Clarksburg United Methodist Church cemetery. Gabriel D. had no children.
e. Forest King, born c.1894, and married August 30, 1916 at Laytonsville, Pearl Elizabeth Ray, who died February 13, 1970 in Rockville; daughter of George F. Ray of Laytonsville. At least one son:
   (1) Forest King, Jr., born c.1918; died of cancer January 26, 1982 at his home in Rockville. Married to Katherine, known to her friends as Kitty, and had children:
      (a) Forest Donald King, died April 5, 1993

    (b)   John R. King.

    (c)   Mark W. King.

    (d)   Patricia King, married Lee, and had children:
        1.   Laura Lee.
        2.   Keith Lee.

f.   William Lawson King, born November 21, 1897 at Urbana, Maryland; died April 12, 1985 at Gaithersburg, Montgomery County, Maryland. Baptized February 7, 1899 at Clarksburg United Methodist Church. Married June 24, 1920 at Gaithersburg, to Cordelia Elizabeth Fulks, born June 4, 1899, daughter of Thomas Iraneus Fulks (1870) and his wife, Frances Lois Williams. (Her name has also been found as Elizabeth Cordelia). She was known to many in Gaithersburg as "Miss Elizabeth" which is a southern colloquialism signifying great respect. Her husband, known by his middle name, Lawson, was justly called "Mr. Gaithersburg" by his many friends. Over time, he acquired ownership of a large portion of the older business district in the town, first operated King Pontiac there, and later relocated it to a part of his home farm, *Irvington Farms*, south of the town toward Rockville, raising purebred cattle, producing milk for the old Thompson's Dairy. He was widely known for his philanthropies and support of projects benefitting his community. He maintained his business office in the old part of Gaithersburg, on North Summit Avenue. It seems fitting that the address was Number One. He was active in politics, and known throughout the state of Maryland as well as locally. Parents of three children:

   (1)   William Irving King, born December 21, 1921. Billy operated the family farm after the death of his father, extensive commercial holdings in the City of Gaithersburg, and property in Georgia. He married first September 19, 1942 Mary Margaret Garrett, the daughter of Thomas Moore Garrett and Anna Braddock Hurley (1891). The author believes that a relationship exists between himself and Anna Braddock Hurley, as may be shown in

Hurley Families in America, Volume 1, published 1995 by Heritage Books, Inc. Two children, and divorced. Married second Anna Mae Moesinger, born May 5, 1926, and had one daughter. The children were:

(a) Thomas Irving King, born July 4, 1943
(b) Anne Garrett King, born October 30, 1945. Married August 22, 1965 to Phillip Lawrence Throne, born October 2, 1942
(c) Katherine Elizabeth King, born October 1, 1951, and married December 26, 1976 Richard Allan Berman, born March 4, 1951.

(2) Elizabeth Jeanne King, born December 6, 1927; married September 13, 1947 James Wriley Jacobs, born July 25, 1923, son of Norman Bliss Jacobs (1883) and Roberta Columbia King (1885). James Wriley and Betty Jeanne had children, born at Montgomery General Hospital, Olney, Maryland:

(a) Betsy Jeanne Jacobs, born October 24, 1949; married July 19, 1969 to David Edward Rippeon, born January 28, 1949. Children:
1. Jonathan David Rippeon: June 12, 1974
2. Michael Lawson Rippeon: November 27, 1975
(b) James Wriley Jacobs, Jr., born July 28, 1952; married June 22, 1973 Margaret Ann Rhodes, born March 11, 1952, and had children:
1. Brian Patrick Jacobs: November 9, 1982
2. Caroline Jeanne Jacobs, a twin, born March 29, 1985
3. John Wriley Jacobs: March 29, 1985; twin
(c) Jonathan Mark Jacobs, born November 12, 1957, and married June 18, 1983 Sally Jean Squire. Three children:
1. Courtney Elizabeth Jacobs, born August 29, 1984
2. Jessica Eileen Jacobs, born May 1, 1987

3. Tyler Michael Jacobs: October 28, 1989
(3) Fannie Lois King, born January 7, 1935; married September 22, 1952 to Conrad Victor Aschenbach, born September 28, 1932. Connie operates the original King Pontiac franchise, and has expanded in the auto field to include Lincoln, Mercury and Saturn lines. Children, all born at Gaithersburg:
(a) Robert Victor Aschenbach, born December 27, 1953; died September 1, 1983 in an accident. His parents have since endowed the Emergency Wing of Shady Grove Adventist Hospital in his name.
(b) William Henry Aschenbach, born July 6, 1955; married September 22, 1979 to Joanne Johnson; three children:
1. Conrad Robert Aschenbach: November 16, 1981
2. William Lawson Aschenbach: November 22, 1983, the 86th anniversary of the birth of his grandfather, for whom he was named.
3. Dustin Victor Aschenbach, born May 20, 1986
(c) Lois Marlene Aschenbach, born August 7, 1956; married July 15, 1978 to Richard Harlan Kelly. Four children:
1. Megan Elizabeth Kelly: May 20, 1980
2. Kristin Marlene Kelly, born February 23, 1982
3. Shannon Marie Kelly: August 14, 1984
4. Morgan Anne Kelly: May 27, 1986
(d) Conrad Lawson Aschenbach, born February 13, 1959; married August 3, 1984 Audrey Gianelli. Four children:
1. Jason Robert Aschenbach: February 18, 1985
2. Shaun Michael Aschenbach: November 5, 1986

80

3. Ryan Conrad Aschenbach: December 7, 1990
4. Brandon Victor Aschenbach: January 28, 1992
(e) Elizabeth Anne Aschenbach, born January 27, 1961; married October 24, 1987 Gary Mark Mendelson and had children:
1. Joshua Robert Mendelson May 13, 1991
2. Elizabeth Marlene Mendelson: March 31, 1993
g. Fannie Thelma King, born September 23, 1899; married October 25, 1925 at *Maple Grove*, the family home near Germantown, to Howard Watson Leese, born April 26, 1900. One son:
(1) Watson King Leese, born February 9, 1933; married December 24, 1960 to Ida Olivia Mullins, born April 22, 1935 and had three children:
(a) William Craig Leese, born January 6, 1962; married July 9, 1988 to Kristin Lee Kerwin, born June 14, 1965
(b) Joan Olivia Leese, born September 5, 1964, and married February 16, 1991 to Steven Samuel, born July 20, 1956. One child:
1. Ashley Olivia Samuel, born September 29, 1992
(c) David Watson Leese: September 16, 1970
h. Merhle Uriah King, born July 11, 1901 at Urbana, Maryland; died Saturday, August 25, 1979. He was married to Elizabeth Birgfield, and had three children:
(1) Merhle Alan King, married to Margaret Watkins King, widow of his uncle, Parke Leo King, and had a daughter.
(2) Cecile Janet King (middle initial S. shown in her grandfather's will, under which she inherited his piano); married first Lanier Floyd, and second Max S. Jones.
(3) Mary E. King; married to Purkey.

i. Virginia Gertrude King, born December 31, 1904 and died March 6, 1996. Married to Martin William Porrey, born December 6, 1899 and died February 14, 1987. They had no children.

j. Parke Leo King, born 1912; died 1943, and buried at Mount Olivet Cemetery in Frederick. The first codicil to the will of his father, dated April 11, 1944, states that this son is then deceased. He was married to Margaret Watkins, who, after his death, was married secondly to Merhle Alan King (above).

4. William King, born c.1859, perhaps died young
5. Nellie King.
6. Mary T. King, born c.1865; married Phillip Lawson, also reported as William Filmore Lawson, and had children:

a. Marie D. Lawson, married Merhle Staley.
b. Cleveland F. Lawson.
c. Evie Lawson, married Burdette.
d. Margaret or Maggie Lawson, married Burdette.
e. John Lawson.
f. Uriah Lawson.
g. Amy Lawson, married Beall.
h. Dorsey E. Lawson.
i. Spencer Lawson.

7. Georgia Ellen Waters King, born June 3, 1867, died October 5, 1931 at her home near Damascus. Married February 25, 1886 to Abraham Lincoln Burdette, a lifelong farmer in the Damascus district, born November 17, 1864 and died March 24, 1931 at his home near Purdum, of paralysis. He was a son of Robert Emory Burdette and Eveline Webster Purdum. Georgia Ellen ahd Abraham had children:

a. Infant death, January 18, 1887
b. Mary Adella Burdette, born February 2, 1888, died March 8, 1951. Married to Emory Dorsey Moxley, born April 20, 1888, died June 20, 1968; buried Montgomery Chapel, Claggettsville; son of Cornelius Edward Moxley and Florence E. Poole. No children.
c. Emory Whitehead Burdette, born July 30, 1890, and died July 30, 1953. Married Susie Elizabeth Layton, born

October 28, 1886, died April 6, 1957 at her home in Damascus, daughter of Charles F. Layton and Sarah E. Warfield. Emory and Susie are both buried at the Bethesda United Methodist Church cemetery near Browningsville. They had children:

(1) Roger Franklin Burdette, born May 20, 1909, died July or August, 1989. Married August 5, 1933 to Isla Lorraine Baker, born April 4, 1909, daughter of William Andrew Baker (1880). Children:

(a) Natalie Ann Burdette, born September 9, 1938 at Takoma Park, Maryland. A school teacher, she died August 20, 1966, single.

(b) Carol Baker Burdette, born January 5, 1942 at Takoma Park. Married February 19, 1960 to George Edgar Calahan, born December 21, 1937 at Miami, Arizona, a mining superintendent. Children, born at Tucson, Arizona:

1. Kenneth Roger Calahan, born December 9, 1960

2. Rebecca Lynn Calahan, born September 9, 1962

(2) George Robert Burdette, born March 11, 1913 and died September, 1968; buried Parklawn Cemetery, Baltimore. Married Gladys Markley, born 1913, died July, 1964. They had one child:

(a) Robert Burdette.

(3) Sarah Evelyn Burdette, born July 31, 1915, and married September 2, 1933 at the Methodist parsonage in Ridgeville, to Silas Cronin Beall, born September 10, 1906, son of Cronin Beall and Sally Lawson. Children:

(a) Shirley Ann Beall, born April 27, 1937, and married Reverend Raymond Bryant.

(b) Sally Louise Beall, born December 24, 1940. Married Robert Runkles.

(c) David Emory Beall, born May 20, 1946 and married Barbara Buxton.

(d) Daniel Beall, married Joyce.

(4) Nellie Laura Burdette, born May 14, 1917. Married William M. Browning, born January 22, 1914, and had children:
  (a) William M. Browning, Jr., born July 15, 1948; married Paula Yoft.
  (b) Susan Browning: April 29, 1950
  (c) Brenda Kay Browning: October 11, 1951

(5) Emory Warfield Burdette, born July 19, 1919. Married Dorothy Linton, born December 25, 1915 and had children. Married second to Pauline Seir; no children. His children from first marriage were:
  (a) Betty Lou Burdette, born November 2, 1936. Married Rex Keesee, born March 13, 1937, and had children:
    1. Rex Keesee, Jr., born December 9, 1957
    2. Dale Keesee, born March 26, 1959
    3. Lisa Lynn Keesee, born July 9, 1968
    4. Betty Ann Keesee, born July 13, 1969
  (b) Robert Emory Burdette, born January 31, 1938. Married to Libby Griffith and had a child. He married second Mary and had two more children. He married third Bonnie Myler and had two more children. The first five children listed are from the three marriages of Robert Emory Burdette; the last two are children of Bonnie Myler by prior marriage, whom he adopted:
    1. Randy Burdette, born November 6, 1960
    2. Sheryl Burdette: December 26, 1962
    3. Robert Burdette: May 8, 1964
    4. Kelly Burdette, born November 7, 1973
    5. Shane Marie Burdette, born December 20, 1974
    6. Kaye Burdette, born December 31, 1963
    7. Sherry Burdette: September 18, 1967.
  (c) Nancy Elizabeth Burdette, a twin, born March 12, 1945. Married Richard Myers, and had children:

1. Thomas Emory Myers: July 11, 1961
2. Judy Ann Myers: November 3, 1964
(d) Florence Patricia Burdette, a twin, born March 12, 1945. Married Charles Diller, Jr., born April 4, 1945. Children:
   1. Patty Ann Diller, born June 1, 1965
   2. Charles Diller, born April 13, 1968
(e) James Richard Burdette, born April 20, 1947. Married to Dorothy Louise Deihl. Children:
   1. Richard E. Burdette: February 22, 1971
   2. James Jeffry Burdette: March 16, 1972
(f) Jo Ann Burdette, born August 10, 1958, died September 10, 1958. Buried Pine Grove Cemetery at Mt. Airy, Maryland
(6) Betty Jane Burdette, born October 2, 1922. Married Charles Elon Reed, born September 9, 1919. Children:
   (a) Allen Elon Reed, born December 17, 1939. Married to Marie Ventresca.
   (b) William Lloyd Reed, born December 10, 1940. Married Barbara Woodfield.
   (c) Charles Francis Reed, born July 13, 1942, and married to Lillian Holt.
   (d) James Edward Reed, born April 5, 1944
   (e) Betty Jane Reed, born December 10, 1946, and married Harold Louis Jones.
(7) Georgetta Burdette, born May 22, 1924. Married Paul Kelly, who died in 1967. One daughter:
   (a) Kathleen Kelly.
(8) Ira Layton Burdette, born April 28, 1926 in Schaueffersville, Maryland, and died June 14, 1984 of a heart attack at his home in Selbyville, Delaware. Buried at the Howard Chapel United Methodist Church, Long Corner Road, Mt. Airy. The place of his birth is as it was reported in his obituary, although it is not to be found in the Postal Zip Code nor in the Rand McNally maps. Married to Mildred M. Gue, and had children. The

places of their residence is as reported in their father's obituary in 1984:

    (a)   Ira Layton Burdette, Jr., born July 25, 1945, of Union Bridge, Carroll County, Maryland. Married Clem Darr, born June 25, 1944 and had children:

        1.   Kimberly Burdette: November 30, 1968

        2.   Brenda Burdette: September 4, 1971

    (b)   Mildred Ann Burdette, of Silver Run (state ?); married James Fritz.

    (c)   David L. Burdette, of Walkersville, Maryland

    (d)   Kevin E. Burdette, of Seaford, Delaware

    (e)   Joyce A. Burdette; Bishopville, in Worcester County, Maryland; married Tubbs.

(9)   John Nathan Burdette, born November 28, 1927. Married to Velma Martin; no children.

(10)   Margaret Enolia Burdette, born August 22, 1929. Married Eldon Sylvanes Dayhoff, born November 11, 1926. Children:

    (a)   Margaret Ann Dayhoff, born July 16, 1949

    (b)   Allen Milton Dayhoff, born April 4, 1951

d.   Pomona Burdette, born December 22, 1894, died January 1, 1967. Married about 1912 to Thurston B. King, born December 28, 1889, died September 14, 1972, son of Holady Hix King (1857). Their descendants are discussed under her husbands name in Chapter 13, devoted to the descendants of Edward J. King (1821), which see.

e.   George Lincoln Burdette, born July 9, 1897, died January 25, 1918 of lobar pneumonia at home near Browningsville, Montgomery County, Maryland. Buried there at the Bethesda United Methodist Church cemetery. Married Roberta E. Watkins, born 1901, died 1961, the daughter of Bradley Watkins and Rebecca Zerah Burdette. No children. After the death of her husband, Roberta married second Charles F. Burdette, born 1898, died 1947, and third Tightus E. Brown, born 1880, died June 11, 1966.

f.   Ira Lansdale Burdette, born January 5, 1900, died April 11, 1970; buried at Bethesda United Methodist Church near Browningsville, where he had been a Trustee since the age of eighteen, and a former superintendent of the Sunday School. Married December, 1917 to Fannie C. Cutsail, born there and died April 26, 1977 at the Frederick Nursing Center; buried with her husband. She was daughter of George H. Cutsail and Rosetta Watkins. Ira and Fannie had one daughter:

  (1) Olive Virginia Burdette, born January 3, 1919, died April 16, 1995 at home in Damascus. Married September 2, 1939 to Glenwood Dawson King, who died in 1996, and was son of R. Delaney King (1874) and Mary Sybil Ward (1880). Glenwood and Virginia had children, who are discussed under their father's name in Chapter 7, dealing with the descendants of John A. King (1808), which see.

  g. Mima Burdette, died September 14, 1902
  h. Ernest Vincent Burdette, born June 30, 1908, died March 20, 1970. Married to Mary Catherine Laname. Children:
    (1) Mary Ellen Burdette.
    (2) Ernest Vincent Burdette, Jr.
    (3) Donald F. Burdette.

8. James M. King, born c.1871; died September 27, 1889
9. Ernest King, born 1875, died 1950, buried Mt. Olivet cemetery in the City of Frederick. Married December 2, 1897 at Mountain View Church to Lola May Lawson, born 1873, died 1935; the daughter of James Uriah Lawson and Keziah Turner. Children:
  a. Hugh Francis King, born September 6, 1899, died 1952. Buried at Mount Olivet with his parents, single.

10. Altie Everett King, born November 30, 1876; died March 15, 1957. Married July 11, 1900 at Purdum to Samuel Webster Beall, born February 16, 1877, died June 28, 1953, son of Caleb Beall and Lucinda Watkins. Both are buried at Mt. Olivet in Frederick. They had twin daughters:
  a. Hilda L. Beall, born August 10, 1901; married October 26, 1922 to Tightus Deets Day, son of Tightus Wilkison Day and Rosa Belle King (1867). They had children, who are discussed under their father's name in Chapter 3,

87

dealing with the descendants of Middleton King (1801), which see.

b. Helena Beall, born August 10, 1901; married October 23, 1919 to Dorsey Lewis. No children.

11. Pearl Clark King, born June 12, 1879; died October 14, 1954. Married March 5, 1902 Alice E. Price, born September 13, 1866 and died October 4, 1926. Both buried at Hyattstown Christian Church. Married second to Ruth Darner Rice, born July 28, 1899, died March 24, 1987, daughter of Joseph William and Alice Elizabeth Himes Darner. She had been previously married to Millard Fillmore Rice, by whom she had children. The children of Pearl Clark King, born to his first marriage, were:

a. Ira King, born May 6, 1902; died August 27, 1932, after being struck by an automobile. Married November 27, 1926 at Kings Valley to Lucille Clara King, born July 3, 1908; died October 26, 1970 daughter of Luther N. King (1850) and Clara Mullineaux (1872). She was married second to Jacobs; third to Gavin L. Brown. No children.

b. Earl Virginia King, born July 24, 1904, and died February 23, 1967, and is buried at Mountain View Cemetery. Married first September 28, 1929 at Frederick, Maryland, to Fannie Montgomery, daughter of George W. Montgomery. She was born c.1899 and died in childbirth September 11, 1931, with her infant child. He was married second June 18, 1938 to Mildred Frances Brown, born November 23, 1919 and died November 10, 1953, daughter of Willard Harrison Brown and Sarah Elizabeth King. Buried with her is an infant due to have been born about December 10. There were ten children:

(1) Betty Mae King, born May 2, 1940 at Purdum, Maryland. Married August 12, 1961 at Bethesda Methodist Church, Browningsville, Maryland, to Aubrey Gene Barton, born July 3, 1940. He was the son of Charles William Barton and Gladys Irene Hammond, and had children:

(a) Bonnie Jean Barton, born February 14, 1966 at Montgomery General Hospital, Olney

(b) Roger Earl Barton, born April 25, 1968 at Montgomery General Hospital, Olney.

(2) Joan Alice King, born November 28, 1941 at Purdum, single.

(3) Lola Virginia King, born November 28, 1942 near Purdum; married June 30, 1963 at Mountain View Methodist Church at Purdum, Maryland, to James Harry Haupt, born January 17, 1940 at Middletown, son of Harry Jacob Haupt and Ethel Blanche Moser (1907) of Middletown, Maryland. Children:

    (a) Kathy Lynn Haupt, born January 24, 1964 in Frederick, married April 25, 1987 at Middletown to James Glen Bliss, son of James W. and Bonnie Wood. Divorced; no children.

    (b) Julie Marie Haupt, born January 5, 1966; married July 1, 1989 at Middletown to John Timothy Salmon, born October 13, 1964 at Frederick, son of Reverend A. D. Salmon. At least one daughter, born there:

        1. Logan Marie Salmon, born September 14, 1991

(4) Frances Elizabeth King, born May 28, 1944 at Purdum. Married June 28, 1964 at Purdum to Gerald Richard Flook, born July 8, 1941 at Myersville, son of Albert D. Flook, Jr., and Edna Virginia Main. A daughter, born at Olney:

    (a) Sharon Marie Flook: December 24, 1969

(5) Kenneth Earl King, born July 23, 1945 at Purdum; married June 3, 1978 at Hagerstown to Kathy Annette Snyder, daughter of Thomas Harwood Snyder. At least one daughter:

    (a) Kimberly Ann King, born c.1981

(6) Daughter King, premature stillbirth

(7) Ruth Ann King, born November 27, 1947 in Frederick; married first May 30, 1970 at Mountain View Church, to Joseph Edward Spates, born January 12, 1948, son of George Edward Spates and Dorothy Ruth Fox; divorced after having a

daughter. Married second July 3, 1981 to Richard Burton Duvall, born December 9, 1941, son of Paul Burton Duvall and Margaret Musgrove. He was previously married to Mary Ray, and had two daughters from that marriage. Richard and Ruth Ann had no children. Her daughter was:

(a) Dorothy Ann Spates, married May 14, 1994 Thomas Ervin Carbo, Jr. at Mountain View. At least one child:

    1.   Jacqueline Ann Carbo, born premature May, 1995

(8)   Fairy Fay King, born August 20, 1949 at Purdum; married first April 30, 1965 to Jason Dennis Pearre, born November 24, 1947 at Frederick, and had two children. He was a son of Emmet Ray Pearre and Lucille V. Hawkins. She was married second December 11, 1992 to Richard Dressell. Children were:

(a) Lisa Lynn Pearre, born September 26, 1965 at Olney; married June 19, 1994 at Comus, Maryland James Arthur Ladson. A son:

    1.   Zachary Ladson, born c.1994

(b) Dennis Lee Pearre, born January 12, 1967 at Olney, and known as Jody, married August 29, 1992 Herndon, Virginia, Michelle Marie Pryor, daughter of Harvey Edward Pryor.

(9)   Joyce Marilyn King, born November 11, 1950 at Purdum; married December 9, 1972 at Damascus, to Robert Dennis Hummer, the son of J. Ellwood Hummer and Bernadine L. Douglas Hummer of Woodsboro, and had a daughter:

(a) Jan Elizabeth Hummer, born May 25, 1980 in Silver Spring

(10) Bonnie Jean King, born June 27, 1952, and died January 3, 1961 Purdum, Maryland. She suffered spina bifda with meningiseal at birth, and was not expected to live past twelve years.

c. Jesse P. King, born May 14, 1908, died of cancer, October 10, 1944; buried at Mountain View cemetery. Married to Edna P. Brashears, and had children:

(1) Jesse P. King, Jr., single.

(2) Ira Leroy King, married and divorced; no children. Employed by Hawkins Floor Company.

(3) Mary Ellen King; married to Smith, with children.

CHILD 4

William P. King
1832-

This son of Middleton King (1801) and Mahala E. Summers (1798), was born c.1832, but not mentioned in the Accounts of the settlement of his father's estate, and was perhaps an early death.

CHILD 5

George Edward King
1835-1876

This son of Middleton King (1801) and Mahala E. Summers (1798), was born c.1835, and died May 27, 1876. He received the home farm under his father's will, and was married January 24, 1862 to Julia Ann Burdette, born August 10, 1837; died October 22, 1916 at Purdum; daughter of Hazel Burdette and Elizabeth Miles. As can be seen, he was deceased by the time of Final Accounts of his father's estate, and his heirs were there mentioned, without naming them. Her Bond as Administrator of his estate is found in Liber RWC 9 at folio 25 in the office of the Register of Wills of Montgomery County, Maryland, dated June 13, 1876; there is no information there of genealogical value. However, there is also Equity No. 1139 filed October, 1893, relative to the estate of George Edward King, deceased. The case was brought by his five children, filed against their mother, and her second husband, Zadoc Summers King (brother of their deceased father). The petition states that the father is deceased, and that he died intestate, possessed of large and valuable real estate in the county. The petitioners request that the widow's dower be laid off, and the remainder distributed to the five children, his legal heirs. They are all named there, as well as two of the spouses. As noted following, Julia Ann was married secondly to Zadoc Summers King, the brother of her deceased husband. Julia Ann and George Edward had children:

1. Middleton Newton King, born February 19, 1863 near Clarksburg, and died January 2, 1938. After the death of his father, his mother was married secondly to Zadoc Summers King (1839), who had also been married before, and had two children from that marriage. As discussed above, Middleton and his siblings were raised by his stepfather (in reality, his uncle). He was married January 4, 1886 to Rufus Francis Waters, born March 6, 1864 and died May 2, 1953. According to all records, her name is actually intended to be spelled as customarily found for a man. She was the daughter of Rufus Waters and Mary Layton (1836). His obituary states that he was survived by his widow, four daughters, two sons, two brothers, and a sister. They are buried at Mountain View cemetery, with three of their children. There were more, apparently all born at Purdum:

   a. Georgia Blanche King, born December 1, 1886, and died December, 1944. Married May 17, 1905 to Columbus W. "Lum" Windsor, born 1875; died May 18, 1944 at Ridgeville, son of Harry Winfield Windsor and Sophia Catharine Cain. A son:

      (1) Jackson E. Windsor, born February 7, 1906, and died February 24, 1920; buried at Claggettsville

   b. Sarah Elizabeth King, born August 16, 1888 at Purdum, Maryland, died January 25, 1952 at Olney, Maryland. Married June 4, 1917 to Willard Harrison Brown, born August 29, 1888 at Purdum, and died there March 28, 1969. He was a son of John Wesley Brown (1850) and Frances America Cornelia Burdette (1857). He was a farmer all of his life, and they had children:

      (1) An infant death, premature, c.1917

92

(2)   Mildred Frances Brown, born November 23, 1919 at Clarksburg; and died November 10, 1953 at Purdum. Her death was caused by a goiter in her throat, which choked her as she and her husband were riding in their car, taking the children to the school bus stop. Her eleventh child died with her. She was married June 18, 1938 in Kemptown to Earl Virginia King, born July 24, 1904 at Purdum, and died February 23, 1967. Their descendants are treated under her husband's name, which see.

(3)   Winfred Willard Brown, born November 24, 1925 at Purdum, died October 20, 1985 at Olney, Maryland. Married December 6, 1946 Clarksburg, to Ann Elizabeth Paxton, born May 11, 1926 at Wilmington, Delaware. She has furnished much of the material on this family; is a dedicated family historian, and a lovely lady. Two children:

(a)   Verna Mae Brown, born January 13, 1948 at Bethesda. Married April 10, 1971 Damascus to Richard Dennis Hines, son of Richard G. Hines. Children:

1.   Richard Ryan Hines, born October 23, 1976 at Frederick, Maryland. Adopted during March, 1977.

2.   Jeffry Dennis Hines, born January 12, 1980 in Alleghany County, Maryland; adopted during September, 1981.

(b)   Sherry Sue Brown, born May 26, 1950 in Bethesda and died there June 2, 1982, single. She was a graduate of the University of Maryland, and employed as travel agent.

(4)   Edward Middleton Brown, born February 29, 1928 at Purdum. Married February 10, 1951 at Damascus, to Betty Estelle Brandenburg, born there July 23, 1929. One child:

(a)   Glenwood Middleton Brown, born January 11, 1952 Olney, Maryland. Married August 30, 1974 to Barbara Duvall, and had a son:

1. Jeffry Brown, born November 19, 1984
c. Harvey Webster King, born May 25, 1890; died August 7, 1964. Married April 8, 1912 to Martha Pauline Burdette, born August 12, 1893, and died January 26, 1986, daughter of Webster Burdette and Mary Catharine Tabler. Both are buried at Mountain View Cemetery. Children, born at Purdum:
(1) Stillbirth son, August 18, 1913
(2) Marjorie Belle King, born April 28, 1915, died June 8, 1994 at Avalon Manor Nursing Home in Hagerstown. Married September 26, 1940 at Hyattstown Eldridge Simpers Barber, born April 1, 1916 and died 1983. Her obituary states that she was survived by her son (listed below), two foster daughters: Betty Jo Harris of Gaithersburg, and Norma Jeanne Savage of Oakland; and other family members. Her son was:
(a) James Webster Barber, born November 25, 1942; married November 25, 1961 Neelsville to Dorothy Ware and had children:
1. Cheryl Pauline Barber, adopted
2. Diane Marie Barber, adopted
3. Susan Barber.
(3) Violet Louise King, born July 25, 1919; married January 26, 1939 at Mt. Airy, Horace Frizzell, and had children:
(a) Marjorie Eloise Frizzell, born January 30, 1941 and died January 2, 1943
(b) Elizabeth Louise Frizzell, born May 24, 1943, married June 24, 1961 Eugene Orrie Smith and had children:
1. Infant son, stillbirth May 4, 1962
2. Tammy Louise Smith: July 12, 1963
3. Horace Michael Smith: January 12, 1965
(c) Harry Webster Frizzell, born April 9, 1946. Married May 11, 1968 Diane Heltner, and had one son:

1. Kevin Scott Frizzell: August 2, 1970
(4) Franklin Webster "Chubby" King, born March 31, 1927; married June 29, 1946 at Mountain View to Dorothy Lillian Johnson of Purdum, born June 3, 1928, daughter of William Johnson and Gertrude Poole. Children, including:
    (a) Dorothy Ann King, born May 20, 1949, and married November 29, 1968 to Robert Lee Anderson, born December 8, 1948, the son of James William Anderson and Elizabeth E. Fox Anderson (1920); and had a daughter:
        1. Heide Lynn Anderson: October 5, 1969
    (b) Frank Robert King, born January 28, 1951; married twice, and had children.

d. Frances Belle King, born August 5, 1892; died August 26, 1910 from influenza

e. Delsie White King, born October 3, 1895, and married May 18, 1912 in Frederick County, Thomas Seymour Brown, born April 19, 1889; died November 16, 1945. They had children:
    (1) Hilbert S. Brown, born April 10, 1913; married 1934 to Betty Linthicum, and had children:
        (a) William Hilbert Brown.
        (b) David Thomas Brown.
        (c) Ruth Louise Brown.
        (d) James Sanford Brown.
    (2) Audrey Bernadine Brown, born November 27, 1922; married June 25, 1945 to Robert C. Dysland and had children:
        (a) John Thomas Dysland: November 14, 1953
        (b) Roland Phillip Dysland, born July 28, 1956

f. Infant death King, March 30, 1897

g. Mary Julia King, born December 1, 1898; died March 11, 1959. Married to Zachariah Thompson Windsor, born August 8, 1888; died June 30, 1958, buried at Montgomery Church, Kemptown, son of Harry Winfield Windsor and Sophia Catharine Cain. His brother, Columbus W. Windsor was married to his wife's sister,

Georgia Blanche King; two brothers married to two sisters. They had a daughter:

    (1)   Fannie Blanche Windsor, born July 28, 1930; married January 7, 1948 at Ridgeville to Stuart Davison, born October 20, 1916 in Washington, D. C., son of William Stuart Davison and Celia Anna Thompson Davison. They had two daughters and a son:

        (a) Stuart Davison, born December 5, 1948

        (b) Mary Louise Davison, born October 13, 1950

        (c) Frances Rebecca Davison, born May 15, 1953; married May 10, 1970.

h.   Clarence Middleton King, died April 3, 1901 infant death

i.   Willett Smith King, born June 8, 1904; died April 5, 1950. Married November 9, 1929 to Addie R. Beall, born June 25, 1900, and died May 16, 1952, daughter of Luther T. and Leathey P. Beall. They are buried at Mountain View cemetery, with other members of the family. They had at least one son:

    (1)   Willett Ray King, born November 21, 1930; married April 17, 1950 to Mary Esther Yowell, the daughter of Thaddeus Yowell. They had children:

        (a) David Ray King, born November 11, 1950

        (b) Crystal Paulette King, born March 23, 1952

        (c) Pamela Denise King, born March 6, 1953

        (d) Richard Willett King.

        (e) Kevin Lee King.

        (f) Jeffery Wayne King.

2.   Mahala E. King, born December 5, 1864, single; died August 20, 1900 at Hyattstown, Montgomery County, Maryland

3.   George William King, born October 13, 1867, and mentioned in his grandfather's will. He died single, August 4, 1948 in Montgomery County, having lived all his adult life in the city of Washington, where he worked in his cousin's paint store. His will, dated June 26, 1946, was entered for record August 17, 1948 in the will records of the county, recorded in liber WCC 3 at folio 373. He does not mention a wife, but names three cousins: Royce M. Riley; Reuben Middleton Brown; and

Ann G. Riley. Also a brother, Edward W. King; a sister, Gertrude Burns; Fannie King, widow of his late brother Middleton N. King; and Mary L. Riley, wife of Royce M. Riley, and their two children, William M. Riley and Dorothy L. Riley. These various individuals who bear the Riley name, all cousins of George William King, are members of the family of Anna Gertrude King (1856), sixth child of Rufus King (1816), all of which is discussed in Chapter 11, which see.

4. Edward Walter King, born December 3, 1869 near Purdum, Maryland, and died June 1, 1956. He is buried at Mountain View Cemetery, and there appear to be the stones of two wives nearby. One is Edith, born August 22, 1877 and died January 22, 1896. She is Edith C. Burns. The second is Fannie D., born September 21, 1876 and died March 7, 1942. She is Fannie D. Dutrow, daughter of William O. Dutrow and Amanda Browning. They were married December 27, 1898 at Hyattstown, Maryland. Edward was a member of the King's Valley Band from 1890 to its end in 1931, playing the euphonium, a baritone horn. He often played for friends at his farm home, and occasionally accompanied the choir at the Mountain View Church. He was survived by a sister, Mrs Gertrude Burns; two grandsons, George and James Watkins; and two great grandchildren. He had children:

a. John Dutrow King, born February 21, 1900 and died January 22, 1965, single. Buried with his parents at Mountain View. His will, dated June 3, 1964, was probated February 3, 1965 and recorded in liber VMB 185 at folio 783 in the will records of Montgomery County, Maryland. He mentions one brother and two sisters. To his brother, William Taft King, he leaves an antique muzzle-loading musket that was formerly owned by their grandfather Dutrow. He left a 20-guage shotgun to his nephew James Edward Watkins; and two 22 caliber rifles and fishing equipment to nephew George Lacy Watkins.

b. Amanda Marie King, born July 1, 1902; married Archer Brett Watkins, born July 16, 1895 at Cedar Grove, son of John Oliver Thomas Watkins (1860) and Eveline L. King (1864). They had children:

(1) George Lacy Watkins, born March 29, 1922 at Purdum, single. Injured at birth by forceps; worked for the U. S. Army in Washington, D. C.

(2) James Edward Watkins, born September 24, 1925 in Washington, D. C.; married June 6, 1947 to Barbara and had children:

    (a) Bruce Allen Watkins, born March 30, 1948, and married to Deborah Lynn Lewis.

    (b) Bradford Lee Watkins, born February 7, 1955, adopted

    (c) Marsha Lynn Watkins: October 22, 1958

    (d) Stacy Elizabeth Watkins: September 5, 1964

c. Nora Bell King, born July 7, 1907; married at Kemptown, May 18, 1940 to Wilbur Noah Watkins, born December 4, 1900 at Cedar Grove. No children.

d. Edward Ray King, born May 24, 1914; married to Hattie Lorraine King, and died of gunshot wound, March 29, 1954; no children. Hattie Lorraine apparently married second to Howard Tabler.

e. William Taft King, born March 24, 1909 at Purdum; died March 18, 1989, and buried at Mountain View. Married to Burnette E. Richter Taylor, born July 25, 1909 at Wheeling, West Virginia, the daughter of Philip and Pearl Welch Richter. She was a widow, with one daughter; William Taft had no children.

5. Laura Gertrude King, born March 17, 1873; married June 9, 1893 at Frederick, Maryland, to Nicholas Edward Burns, born January 24, 1865, died November 15, 1921 at his home near Purdum; he was the son of Sylvester Burns and Elizabeth A. Riggs Burns. They had children:

a. Linda King Burns, born September 18, 1894, died September 3, 1895; buried at Salem United Methodist Church in Cedar Grove, Maryland.

b. Myrtle Bryan Burns, born June 25, 1896; married to Talmadge Lodge "Doc" Watkins, born 1891, died 1975, the son of Charles Jefferson Lee Watkins (1864) and Amanda Cornelius King (1870). Talmadge and his wife are buried in the cemetery of Upper Seneca Baptist

98

Church at Cedar Grove, Montgomery County, Maryland. Nearby are the graves of two of their sons:

    (1)   Charles Edward Watkins, born May 24, 1914 and died March 2, 1975. Married to Mary Belle Hawkins, born May 6, 1915, daughter of James Bradley Hawkins (1886) and Hattie Mae King (1893). Children:

        (a)   Joanne Marie Watkins, born 1939. Married James Edward Musson, born 1936. A son:

            1.   Larry Edward Musson; June 22, 1966

        (b)   Charles Edward Watkins, Jr., born 1940, known as Bucky. Married Barbara Joan Beall, born 1943. One daughter:

            1.   Cynthia Elaine Watkins: November 5, 1962. Married to Dexter Gordon Mathis; children:

                a.   Sarah Diane Mathis, born 1984

                b.   Jason Kyle Mathis, born 1987

        (c)   Carol Lee Watkins, born 1953. Married Richard Harold Collins, born 1945.

    (2)   Royce T. Watkins, born 1918, died March, 1972. Buried Upper Seneca Baptist Church. Married to Agnes S., born 1919. Children:

        (a)   Mary Jo Watkins, married Mayer; a child:

            1.   John Talmadge Mayer.

        (b)   Jane W. Watkins, married Gartner; a child:

            1.   David Wayne Gartner.

    (3)   Gertrude Watkins, married Duvall.

c.   E. Minor Burns, born November 9, 1901; died March 4, 1968. Married to Ruth A. Stanley, born February 28, 1903, daughter of Harry Stanley and Fannie Gertrude Mount; and had children:

    (1)   Mary Mae Burns.

    (2)   Anna Mae Burns, married Mutt Burdette, son of Willie Lloyd Burdette; and had a son:

        (a)   Donald Burdette, who was married to Jeannette McDonough, daughter of Thomas C. McDonough and Lorraine Page.

d.   Ida Mae Burns, born March 16, 1904; died December 12,
     1972. Married Aubrey Mullineaux, born February 3,
     1899, and had children:
     (1)   Aubrey Mullineaux, Jr., married to Anna Lee
           Gladhill, daughter of Upton Gladhill of Damascus.
     (2)   Jane Mullineaux.
e.   George William Burns, born April 29, 1906; married and
     moved to West Virginia.

CHILD 6

Mahala Ann Rebecca King
1836-1872

This daughter of Middleton King (1801) and Mahala E. Summers (1798), was born October 9, 1836, and died September 4,
1872, while giving birth to twins, one of whom also died. Buried at
Hyattstown Methodist Church. Married October 16, 1857 to William Homer Orme, born about July 18, 1828 and died December
27, 1908; son of Jacob Benjamin Orme (1800-1863) and Eliza
Summers. An unidentified paper that we came across states that
Jacob Orme was a very wealthy man, owning thousands of acres of
land running from the Sugarloaf Mountain to the Monocacy River
valley. On one occasion, he travelled south and bought a train of
slaves to work his plantations, but when he arrived at the railroad
station in Frederick, Lincoln had just declared the slaves free, and
he lost everything. Reportedly, he hung himself in despair.
    William Homer Orme and Mahala Ann Rebecca King had
children, listed following. After his wife's death, he apparently
found foster homes for several of his children. There is, for example, a document entitled *Articles of Agreement*, dated July 17,
1874, between Caleb J. Burdette of Montgomery County, and William Homer Orme of Frederick County, in which Orme releases all
rights he has relative to two of his children, to Burdette, who agrees
to raise and properly care for them until they come of age, and at
that time to give William Hiram King Orme (the son) a horse, saddle and bridle; and to give Ella Independence Orme (the daughter),
the sum of fifty dollars. William Homer Orme was married second

to Hannah Dixon, born July 18, 1854 and died June 14, 1930, daughter of John W. Dixon and Leona Kohlenberg, and they had two children: McComas Orme, born 1880, died 1945; and Allen Orme, born January 10, 1887 and died August 27, 1921. Final accounts of the estate of the father of Mahala Ann Rebecca King Orme mention her heirs as beneficiaries of the estate, without naming them. She and her husband appear in the 1870 census of the Urbana District, Frederick County, with five of their ten children. The children included:

1. James Edward Orme, born August 7, 1858, died February 8, 1862.
2. Mary Frances Orme, born March 9, 1860, died January 18, 1862.
3. Jacob Middleton Orme, born October 31, 1861; died February 2, 1862.
4. Laura Mahala Orme, born November 9, 1862, and died May 3, 1919. Married April 17, 1881 to John McClellan Dixon, born July 21, 1863 at Flint Hill, Frederick County, died February 11, 1910, the son of John W. Dixon and Leona Koehmburg. Buried at Mt. Olivet, Frederick. Children, born at Flint Hill, Frederick County, and several are buried at Mt. Olivet:

   a. Stannie Mahala Dixon, born June 21, 1882; married June 29, 1903 at Frederick to John Henry Clark, born January 26, 1866; died March 13, 1948; buried Mt. Olivet. No children.

   b. Archie McClellan Dixon, born March 31, 1884, and died April 18, 1908; buried with his wife at Mt. Olivet, Frederick, Maryland. Married April 15, 1904 to Sadie R. Price, daughter of Daniel W. Price and Frances Hall. Children:

   (1) Eva Rebecca Dixon, born September 17, 1905; married December 24, 1923 Edward Thomas Riddle, born February 14, 1901. They lived in Sacramento, California; children:

   (a) Edward Stanley Riddle, born November 21, 1924, and married November 10, 1946 to Beulah Fay. Children:

1. Constance Eileen Riddle.
2. Edward Everett Riddle.
3. Stanley Douglas Riddle.
4. Thomas Eugene Riddle.
5. Deborah Sue Riddle.
6. Cynthia Louise Riddle.

(b) Richard Samuel Riddle, born January 22, 1926; married May 29, 1941 to Dorothy Pauline and had children:
   1. Mildred Rebecca Riddle, and married to Espanoza.

(c) Harry Lee Riddle, born January 29, 1927; married August 18, 1944 and divorced; three children. Married second Gloria Lee James, who had three children from a prior marriage. His children were:
   1. Harry Lee Riddle, Jr..
   2. Michael Thomas Riddle.
   3. Scharilyn Fay Riddle.

(d) William Russell Riddle, born February 22, 1928, and married to Marion. Children:
   1. David William Riddle.
   2. Stephen Russell Riddle.

(e) Leo Lionell Riddle, born February 22, 1933; married December 29, 1951 to Geraldine June and had children:
   1. Jerry Thomas Riddle.
   2. Dean Lee Riddle.

(f) Homer Donald Riddle, born April 15, 1938; married January 2, 1959 to Thelma Louise and had children:
   1. Deborah Sue Riddle.
   2. Eva Marie Riddle.
   3. Edward William Riddle.
   4. Donna Louise Riddle.

(g) Delores Louise Riddle, born April 19, 1942; married December 14, 1961 to Tindal and had children:

1. Helena Rebecca Tindal.
2. David Alan Tindal.
3. Jason Isaac Tindal.
4. Wanda Gayle Tindal.
5. Patricia Mealy Tindal.
(2) Dorothy Laurena Dixon, born September 11, 1908; married February 2, 1924 to John Thomas Harris, born June 26, 1899, died December 2, 1965. Last reported living in Alexandria, Virginia, with children:
(a) Shirley Ruth Harris, born June 5, 1925; married October 31, 1942 to Richard Winthrop Nelson, born September 18, 1923, and had three children. Married second May 6, 1976 to John Allison Frye, Jr., born December 24, 1930. Children from marriage to Nelson were:
1. Richard Winthrop Nelson, Jr.: December 23, 1946
2. Kathleen Ann Nelson, born November 4, 1948; married April 29, 1967 to Martin C. Arntzen, Jr., born February 28, 1942, and had children:
a. Michael David Arntzen: December 25, 1967
b. Karen Lynn Arntzen: July 31, 1969
c. Marcus Damaine Arntzen: January 27, 1976
3. Joyce Marie Nelson: November 8, 1957
(b) Christine Harris, born July 27, 1927, died December 9, 1976. Married May 3, 1946 to Llewellyn Powell Hurley, born August 18, 1922; died May 7, 1973. They had three children, and she married second April 4, 1975 to Charles Barclay Burch, Jr., born November 11, 1936; no children reported. Her children:
1. Llewellyn Powell Hurley, Jr., born March 25, 1947. Married June 2, 1967

to Linda Lee Hamlett, born October 22, 1948, and had children:

    a. Duane Edward Hurley: February 13, 1968

    b. James Eric Hurley: September 14, 1971

2. James Thomas Hurley, born April 26, 1948; married and had at least one child:

    a. Christine Lynn Hurley, born July 21, 1972

3. Dorothy Mae Hurley, born June 7, 1954. Married November 26, 1971 Paul Carl Gualdoni, born October 3, 1947, and had children:

    a. Paul Carl Gauldoni, Jr.: November 3, 1972

    b. John Michael Gauldoni: June 24, 1974

(c) James Edward Harris, born July 17, 1930; married June 18, 1954 to Mabel Irene Wolfender, born April 30, 1935, and had four children, listed following. Married second July 31, 1970 to Elaine Louise Campbell Cash, born October 3, 1927. No children. His children were:

1. James Edward Harris, Jr., born May 30, 1955; married December 25, 1976 to Jeanine Marie Campbell, born December 23, 1956.

2. Stephen Brian Harris: February 1, 1958

3. Gary Kevin Harris, born July 30, 1960

4. Sharon Lynn Harris: August 20, 1965

(d) Barbara Ann Harris, born August 31, 1934; married February 18, 1956 to E. Jay Zuspan, born July 26, 1935; children:

1. Barbara Jean Zuspan: June 11, 1957

2. E. Jay Zuspan, Jr.: July 14, 1959

(e) Linda Kay Harris, born April 16, 1947; married July 18, 1964 Stephen Walker Early, born May 1, 1945. Children:
   1. Susan Marie Early: February 19, 1965
   2. Thomas Michael Early: May 26, 1967

c. John Harrison Dixon, born July 21, 1886, died June 30, 1972 in Frederick County; buried Mt. Olivet. Married on April 13, 1921 to Mary May Morgan, born October 13, 1902 and died January 29, 1971. Children:

(1) Pauline Elizabeth Dixon, born February 3, 1925; married March 7, 1946 William Nelson Hoffman, born November 30, 1921. Live in Frederick; three children:
   (a) Darlene Frances Hoffman, born November 6, 1946; married to Richard E. Stockman, born September 1, 1942, and have children:
      1. Cindy Lynn Stockman, born September 8, 1971
      2. Cheryl Ann Stockman: May 10, 1973
   (b) Denise Darcel Hoffman, born May 29, 1953
   (c) Diane Carol Hoffman, born May 13, 1968

(2) Lillian Marie Dixon, born November 21, 1926; married December 19, 1945 to Austin Ralph Cramer, born July 17, 1926. Live at Liberty, and have children:
   (a) Austin Ralph Cramer, Jr., born July 28, 1946; married July 4, 1969 to Linda Ann Latham, born March 26, 1949 and had a daughter:
      1. Melissa Ann Cramer: March 14, 1972
   (b) John Harrison Cramer, born September 16, 1949; married January 20, 1968 to Barbara Jean Haller, born August 16, 1948. A son:
      1. John Harrison Cramer, Jr., born August 23, 1969
   (c) Ricky Dale Cramer, born March 29, 1955

> (d) Lisa Marie Cramer, born April 6, 1959; married September 19, 1976, Michael Robert Stup, born January 12, 1958.
>
> (e) Randy Allen Cramer, born July 1, 1962

(3) Melvin Harrison Dixon, born January 3, 1929; married to C. Virginia Garber, born September 30, 1927. Lives in Montgomery Village; children:

> (a) Roxie Lee Dixon, born August 8, 1954; married to Gary Wetzel, born November 4, 1950; divorced with one daughter:
>
> 1. Renee Wetzel, born January 13, 1972
>
> (b) Sherrie Lee Dixon, born August 15, 1962

d. Effie Johnson Dixon, born May 12, 1889, and died October 15, 1918 of the flu. Married Eugene Henry Dixon, born May 9, 1879 and died July 18, 1950, the son of William Dixon and Lizzie Nicholson. Children:

(1) Laura Elizabeth Dixon, born July 15, 1908; married Charles Hahn

(2) Milton Eugene Dixon, born February 19, 1911. He was a chauffer, and married Pauline Winpigler

(3) Myrtle Stannie Dixon, born February 22, 1912; died February 26, 1975. Married John Cramer.

(4) Mahala Effie Dixon, a twin, born September 20, 1915, Married Woodrow Wilson Main; children:

> (a) Charles Eugene Main, a minister
>
> (b) Robert Wilson Main.

(5) Marie Gertrude Dixon, a twin, born September 20, 1915, and married Norman Chester King, a machinist. Last reported living at Waynesboro, Pennsylvania, and had a daughter:

> (a) Carol Ann King.

(6) James Bradley Dixon, born March 6, 1918; lived three days.

e. Nola Florence Dixon, born September 24, 1891; married September 25, 1909 to Robert Leese Soper, born May 25, 1888, and died February 17, 1957. Buried at Mt. Olivet in Frederick. They had three children:

(1) Roy Roger Soper, born October 9, 1911. Married December 31, 1939 to Dorothy Lyle, born September 28, 1913, and had one daughter:
   (a) Sharon Soper, born July 25, 1947, and married to Walter Ronald Hiltner. Children:
      1. Wendy Hiltner, born July 7, 1966
      2. Walter Ronald Hiltner, Jr.: June 6, 1970
      3. Penny Hiltner, born December 7, 19 ?
(2) Archie Leo Soper, born January 4, 1914, single
(3) Dorothy Soper, born May 16, 1921; married May 3, 1946 Richard Calvin Tucker, Sr., born February 19, 1917; died July 13, 1975. Three children:
   (a) Judith Tucker, born November 26, 1947
   (b) Richard Calvin Tucker, Jr.: March 9, 1949
   (c) Thomas Jeffrey Tucker: September 16, 1957

f. William Herman Dixon, born July 31, 1893; died October 20, 1918 of influenza. Married July 17, 1917 to Phebe Humrick, and had a son:
   (1) William Herman Dixon, Jr., born January 17, 1918; married Bernice Miller, and had three children. He worked for the Chicago Iron and Bridge Company, and later lived in Wilmington, Delaware. Married second Marybell; his children, all married, lived in New Jersey:
      (a) Wayne Dixon.
      (b) Sheila Dixon.
      (c) William Dixon.
      (d) Betty Dixon.

g. Bradley Smith Dixon, born November 26, 1894; married September 6, 1937 to Helen Smith, born July 12, 1906 and died February 16, 1964. They had children:
   (1) Catherine Dixon, born August 15, 1942; married May 5, 1961 in Frederick to Richard Crutchley, born March 28, 1941, and had children:
      (a) Sandra L. Crutchley, born June 30, 1962
      (b) Richard W. Crutchley: November 6, 1964
      (c) Charles B. Crutchley, born May 26, 1973

107

h.   Earl Butler Dixon, born November 11, 1896; died August 27, 1965. Married to Daisy Virts and had a daughter:
    (1)   Helen Dixon; married Jenkins, both deceased.
i.   Forrest Milton Dixon, born June 12, 1899; died December 11, 1967/8. Married to Elsie M. Hall and had a daughter:
    (1)   Pauline Dixon, married at Ridgeville to Wallace Norris.
j.   Lillie Laura Dixon, born November 5, 1901, died February 6, 1973. Married July 10, 1919 to Vernon L. Rhoderick, born November 27, 1901; died December 18, 1973. No children.
k.   Roger James Dixon, born October 7, 1903, died October 28, 1972. Married first to Mildred Shelton, and second in 1925 to Viola Watt. Children from his second marriage:
    (1)   Jean Dixon, last reported living in Denver
    (2)   James Dixon, last reported Fredericksburg, Va.
l.   Merhle Emerson Dixon, born June 15, 1906, died September 26, 1907.

5.   Ella Independence Orme, born July 4, 1864, and married September 30, 1879 to Warner Seymore Poole. They had stillbirth twins, and the following children:
a.   Laura Poole; married John Gartner or Gardner.
b.   Nora Poole; married Johnson
c.   Rebecca Poole.
d.   Nettie Poole; married Henry Jacobs
e.   Ella Poole; married Charles Storm and second Hickman
f.   Virgil Poole; married Jennie Barry, and second to Kate.
g.   Lloyd Poole, died young, single
h.   Leland Stanford Poole, married Vera.
i.   Edgar Poole; married Hattie
j.   Warner Poole; married first Anna Dodd and second to Helen. Children from his second marriage:
    (1)   Bernard Poole.
    (2)   Verna Poole, married R. L. Grisby
k.   Motter Poole, married Bertha Lunsford.
l.   Margaret Ruth Poole, married to Angus Hayes and had two children, listed following. Married second Snyder:

108

        (1)   Edward Hayes.

        (2)   Catherine Hayes.

m.   Furman Poole, or Firmin Poole, born November 6, 1908; married March 2, 1932 to Pauline McDaniel, born November 8, 1908, and had children:

        (1)   Kenneth Poole, born April 27, 1933; married June 17, 1954 Pamela, born February 25, 1933, and had children:

               (a)   Randal Poole, born March 30, 1955

               (b)   Eugene Lee Poole, born May 24, 1956

               (c)   Stephen Poole, born March 6, 1959

               (d)   Naomi Poole, born September 27, 1960

               (e)   Karen Poole, born April 27, 1964

        (2)   Phyllis Lorraine Poole, born October 21, 1935; married Lee Thomas Degges, and had children:

               (a)   Pamela Degges, born September 1, 1960

               (b)   Lee Thomas Degges, Jr., born April 20, 1964

               (c)   Tromila Degges, born January 9, 1969

               (d)   Troy Degges, born October 27, 1970

6.   William Hiram King Orme, born September 22, 1866, and died October 11, 1956. Married Malinda Dixon, born January 1, 1866 and died November 15, 1922, daughter of John W. Dixon and Leona Kohlenberg. They had children:

a.   Ginga A. Orme, born 1889; died January 13, 1919

b.   Homer Baker Orme; died October, 1970

c.   Ella Orme; married Harry W. Merchant, and second Arthur Seidling. Two children born to the first marriage; three to the second:

        (1)   Dorothy Merchant, married Charles Plunkett

        (2)   Winford Merchant.

        (3)   Ruth Seidling, married Harry Gray, Sr.

        (4)   William Seidling, married Myrtle Wagner. A son:

               (a)   William Seidling, Jr.

        (5)   Edward Seidling, married Jerry, and had a son:

               (a)   William Seidling.

d.   Etta Orme; married Thomas Reed

e.   Ethel Orme, married Charles Easton

f. Erma Orme; married Jerome Shaffer, who died October 30, 1938, and married second Howard Taylor. Children born to Shaffer:
   (1) Helen Shaffer.
   (2) William Shaffer.
   (3) Robert Shaffer.
g. Gladys Orme, married Lewis Hildebrand. Children, including:
   (1) Dorothy Hildebrand, married Troxell
   (2) Mary Jane Hildebrand, married Wachter
h. Ernest McKinley Orme.
i. Cinca Orme, or Seneca Orme, married Nellie Hines and divorced.

7. Ursula M. Jemima Orme, born July 14, 1868, and died June 11, 1935. Married to Curtis A. Dixon, born April 15, 1865, and had children:
a. Lottie L. Dixon, born January 2, 1886, died May 31, 1951; buried at Mt. Olivet, Frederick. Married Luther Victor Cook, born August 29, 1881 and died December 28, 1961. Children:
   (1) Merhl C. Cook, born March 28, 1911; died December 2, 1974. Married to Elmira J., born September 13, 1913
   (2) Etta Mae Cook, died March 25, 1927
b. Exie M. Dixon, born February 19, 1889 at Park Mills; died August 4, 1971; buried at Mt. Olivet, Frederick. Married to John P. White, born February 22, 1873; died June 4, 1968. Lived near Buckeystown, Frederick County. Obituary in the *Frederick Post* does not mention any children.
c. Della Dixon; married Sheridan Cline, or Shareton Cline. They were divorced; she married secondly and was divorced, and she and Cline were remarried. No reported children.
d. Mervin M. Dixon; lived in California
e. William M. Dixon, born April 14, 1897; married 1920 to Ethel Lewis, born August 14, 1902; died October 16,

1958. They lived in Lewistown, Maryland; at least one
daughter:
    (1)   Lucille Dixon, born August 21, 1929; married No-
vember 10, 1959 to Daniel L. Putman, born September 20, 1928.
f.   Norman Dixon, born October 4, 1900; died February 28,
1974. Married in Frederick, Maryland, to Ethel A. Stine,
born April 1, 1901.
8.   Ida Rebecca Orme, born February 20, 1870; died June 4,
1870.
9.   Marietta Still Orme, a twin, born September 3, 1872, and died
November 2, 1959. Married December 29, 1891 to Frederick
Herman Koehler, born February 29, 1864, and died September
4, 1938. They had children:
a.   John Godfrey Koehler, born February 18, 1893; died July
14, 1893
b.   Minnie Rebecca Koehler, born December 15, 1894, and
died November 16, 1965. Married March 26, 1910 to
Thaddeus Hamilton Bussard, born February 28, 1883,
died April 14, 1974. Children:
    (1)   Minnie Evelyn Bussard, born March 5, 1911, and
died August 15, 1919.
    (2)   Thaddeus Arly Bussard, born July 18, 1913, and
died August 13, 1914.
    (3)   Dorothy Mary Ella Bussard, born August 25,
1915. Married November 25, 1939 to Harold
Nusbaum Devilbliss, born June 27, 1917, and had
children:
        (a)   Minnie Rebecca Devilbliss, born September
4, 1940
        (b)   Harold Nusbaum Devilbliss, Jr.: February 17,
1942
    (4)   Bertie Pauline Bussard, born June 20, 1920; mar-
ried April 5, 1942 to Glenn Abraham Brubaker,
born October 4, 1916. A daughter:
        (a)   Ruth Blanche Brubaker, born September 26,
1944; married August 22, 1965 Ronald David
Cline, born February 1, 1944. Children:

111

        1. Renee Michelle Cline: December 14, 1968
        2. Jason David Cline, born July 23, 1971
        3. Rhonda Mae Cline, born July 19, 1973
        4. Roni Amanda Cline, born April 8, 1977
    (b) Daisy Pauline Brubaker, born September 26, 1944 and died September 26, 1977
    (c) Julia Naomi Brubaker, born November 2, 1956, and married October 22, 1977 to Thomas W. Fleming, born July 4, 1956.
  (3) Ruthella Bussard, born May 2, 1924.

c. Etta Amelia Koehler: March 26, 1897; infant death.
d. Ella Mahala Koehler, born April 14, 1898; died April 25, 1917. Married Paul Z. Zimmerman, born February 21, 1898, and had children:
  (1) Jean Ella Zimmerman, born October 11, 1931; married April 17, 1954 to Eugene Trainor, born September 12, 1928. Children:
    (a) Sheryl Ann Trainor, born July 4, 1955
    (b) Susanne Patricia Trainor: December 24, 1957
    (c) Melissa Jean Trainor, born August 17, 1966
  (2) Paula Patricia Zimmerman, born July 13, 1934; married first January 8, 1956 to David Sudrabin, born September 13, 1931, and had two children. Married second January 7, 1973 to Gus Vazac, born September 25, 1930, and had a child:
    (a) David Sudrabin, born February 19, 1957
    (b) Steven Sudrabin, born January 29, 1959
    (c) Laura Vazac, born November 21, 1973
e. John G. Koehler, born c.1899, died August, 1903
f. Herman H. Koehler.
g. Annie Gertrude Koehler, born January 31, 1900, and died September 14, 1900.
h. Joseph Frederick Koehler, a twin, born February 1, 1901; died March 18, 1901.
i. William Herman Koehler, a twin, born February 1, 1901; died January 14, 1971. Married Lillian Swope, divorced;

married second December 1, 1934 to Marie Margaret Smith, born January 7, 1908, and had a son:
    (1)   William Herman Koehler, Jr., born July 2, 1936; died July 17, 1971. Married c.1955 to Dorothy Williams, and second in 1970 to Betsy. Two children, first marriage:
        (a)   Diane Marie Koehler: September 6, 1963
        (b)   Daphne Koehler, born April 4, 1967
    (2)   Wilhelmina Margaret Koehler, born June 22, 1942; married July 20, 1963 Vincent Hammell, born December 28, 1941, and had children:
        (a)   Vincent Steven Hammell, born March 4, 1965
        (b)   Mark Edwin Hammell, born May 8, 1967
        (c)   David Phillip Hammell, born April 3, 1969
        (d)   Heidi Christine Hammell: March 1, 1973
    (3)   John Godfrey Koehler, born August 6, 1944; married September 7, 1963 to Nancy Lee Zile, born October 23, 1946, and had children:
        (a)   John Godfrey Koehler, Jr.: February 2, 1964
        (b)   Michael Anthony Koehler: December 20, 1969

10. Stillbirth Orme, a twin, September 3, 1872, died with the mother and buried in her arms in the same casket at the Hyattstown cemetery.

CHILD 7

Zadoc Summers King
1839-1898

This son of Middleton King (1801) and Mahala E. Summers (1798), was born March 9, 1839, and died April 17, 1898. He was apparently married three times, as will be discussed following: first May 7, 1861 to Joanna Sibley; second September 20, 1872 to Mary E. Lewis; and third May 28, 1878 to Julia Ann Burdette King, widow of George Edward King (1835). The only information we have as to the second marriage are records of the marriage, where he was listed as being 32 years old, a huckster, and a widower; she was listed as being aged 18, thus born c.1854. He is buried at Mountain View Cemetery in Montgomery County, with "father" on his stone, near Julia A. King, born August 10, 1837 and died October 8, 1916, who was his wife. She was Julia Ann Burdette, having first been married to his brother, George Edward King (1835), by whom she had five children (see Chapter 3). All of them are listed in the household of Zadoc and Julia in the 1880 census of Damascus District, Montgomery County, where each is designated as a stepson or stepdaughter. At the Salem Methodist Church cemetery in Cedar Grove, there is the grave of Joanna King, born c.1840, and died May 6, 1872 at the age of 32 years, 8 months and 18 days. Her stone states that she is the wife of Zadoc S. King, being the first of three marriages of Zadoc Summers King. The 1850 census of Montgomery County includes the household of Jonathan Sibley, born 1797, with his wife, Harriett, born c.1804, and several children. Among them is Joanna, born c.1839, who is perhaps this individual. In addition to the children of his brother, whom he raised after marrying their mother, Zadoc and Julia A. also raised his two daughters from the first marriage to Joanna:

1. Rosa Belle King, born April 29, 1867. Married Tightus Wilkison Day, born August 9, 1861 near Clarksburg, died June 7, 1946. He was a son of James Wilkerson Day (1827) and and Sarah Wilson Beall (1830). The book, *James Day of Browningsville and his Descendants*, by Jackson H. Day, privately printed 1976, reports the husband of Rosa Belle as being Titus Washington Day. They had a son:

    a. Tightus Deets Day, born July 19, 1898, and died January 20, 1957, reported by Jackson H. Day as Titus Deets Day. Married first Mazie N., born 1899, died 1919 of influenza, no children. Married second October 26, 1922 to Hilda L. Beall, born August 10, 1901, daughter of Samuel Webster Beall (1877) and Altie Everett King (1876). Children:

        (1) Joyce Day, born May 3, 1925. Married to Rudell Beall and had children:

            (a) Robert Beall, born November 10, 1944. Married Mary Ann Linthicum, born December 8, 1944, and had at least one son:

114

1. Kevin Beall, born March 4, 1967
   (b) Clark Lee Beall, born September 15, 1947, and married Diane Ray Cooley.
   (2) Winfred Day, born July 27, 1934. Married June 25, 1955 Martha Ann Wilson. They lived on Price Distillery Road near Damascus, and had children:
      (a) Robert Gregory Day: November 30, 1958
      (b) Christopher Day: October 25, 1961
      (c) Timothy Day, born May 8, 1964
      (d) Domini Day, born December 4, 1965
2. Olive W. King, born c.1869; married William Bergman and had children:
   a. Alma Bergman.
   b. Ralph Bergman.

CHILD 8

Mary Ellen King
1843-1913

This daughter of Middleton King (1801) and Mahala E. Summers (1798), was born April 2, 1843, and died September 24, 1913; buried at Salem United Methodist Church at Cedar Grove. Married December 3, 1862 to William E. Riggs, born March 25, 1839; died January 14, 1914; buried at Cedar Grove. The Riggs family is discussed in great detail in *The Riggs Family of Maryland*, by John Beverley Riggs, which see for complete genealogical coverage. William E. was a son of Joshua Riggs (1811-1879) and Editha Lewis (1815). Also buried at Cedar Grove is one M. Iriedella Riggs, born c.1882; died December 30, 1883, who is not yet identified. Children:
1. Reuben M. Riggs, born September 19, 1863 in Montgomery County, Maryland, and died July 2, 1909. Married to Laura M. Young, born March 31, 1866, and died November 9, 1931. Buried at Cedar Grove. Children:
   a. Daisy Riggs, born August 10, 1884; died February 14, 1885.

115

b. William B. Riggs, born April 11, 1887, died May 3, 1887
2. Joshua L. Riggs, born c.1865; died 1938.
3. William Walter Riggs, born April 20, 1867; died December 9, 1869.
4. Bradley J. Riggs, born September 30, 1869, and died February 9, 1920. Married to Ida C. Watkins, born June 10, 1872 and died May 17, 1942, daughter of Oliver T. Watkins (1828) and Eleanor Jane Brewer.
5. Carroll C. Riggs, born March 12, 1875; died August 6, 1875

Edward King
1740-1784
*
*
John Duckett King
1778-1858
*
*
Elizabeth Miles King
1802-?
*
*
*   *   *   *   *   *
*
* *   Hamilton H. Browning 1825
*
* *   Charles T. Browning 1827
*
* *   Amanda P. Browning 1839

CHAPTER 4

Elizabeth Miles King
1802-

This daughter of John Duckett King (1778) and Jemima Miles (1782) was born c.1802, and married March 4, 1823 in Frederick, Maryland, to Perry Browning. He appears as head of the household in the 1850 and 1860 census for Damascus, Montgomery County, born c.1799. His wife was listed there as having been born c.1802. They had children:

1. Hamilton H. Browning, born c.1825; married January 21, 1861 in Frederick County, Susan E. Soper. No children.
2. Charles T. Browning, born June 9, 1827, and died February 11, 1885; buried Hyattstown Methodist Church cemetery. Married March 1, 1859 in Frederick County to his cousin, Mary Jane King, born May 20, 1838 and died January 4, 1905; the daughter of Singleton King (1810) and Jane Rebecca Lewis. Their family is discussed under the name of Mary Jane King in Chapter 8, devoted to the descendants of Singleton King (1810), which see.
3. Amanda P. Browning, born c.1839; married April 26, 1859 in Frederick County, to William Dutrow.

Edward King
1740-1784
*

*

John Duckett King
1778-1858
*

*

Jemima King
1805-1892
*

*

*   *   *   *   *   *

*

* * Rufus King Purdum 1827-1909

*

* * Sarah Rebecca Purdum 1829-1911

*

* * John Dorsey Purdum 1830-1896

*

* * Jemima King Purdum 1831-1886

*

* * Joshua Hinkle Purdum 1833-1874

*

* * Rachel Browning Purdum 1835-1910

*

* * Mariamn Purdum 1837-1913

*

* * Marguerite Antoinette Purdum 1838-1909

*

* * Elizabeth Washington Purdum 1840-1907

*

* * William Henry Harrison Purdum 1841-1923

*

* * Emily Jones Purdum 1843-1905

*

* * Eveline Webster Purdum 1845-1921

*

* * James Henning Purdum 1847-1923

*

* * Benjamin Franklin Purdum 1851-1882

CHAPTER 5

Jemima King
1805-1892

This daughter of John Duckett King (1778) was born either April or May 11, 1805, in Montgomery County, and died February 7, 1892 at Browningsville. She and her husband are buried there at the Bethesda Methodist Church cemetery. Married February 14, 1824, in Frederick, John Lewis Purdum, born December 27, 1798 in Montgomery County, died July 25, 1870, son of Joshua Purdum (1767) and Rachel Browning (1775). They had children, most of whom were married in Frederick County, Maryland. Each will be discussed in birth order following the general family listing:

1. Rufus King Purdum, born June 5, 1827
2. Sarah Rebecca Purdum, born January 29, 1829
3. John Dorsey Purdum, born October 25, 1830
4. Jemima King Purdum, born June 13, 1831
5. Joshua Hinkle Purdum, born November 21, 1833
6. Rachel Browning Purdum, born July 16, 1835
7. Mariamn Purdum, born March 21, 1837
8. Marguerite Antoinette Purdum, born July 2, 1838
9. Elizabeth Washington Purdum, born February 12, 1840
10. William Henry Harrison Purdum, born November 27, 1841
11. Emily Jones Purdum, born September 21, 1843
12. Eveline Webster Purdum, born February 17, 1845
13. James Henning Purdum, born February 27, 1847
14. Benjamin Franklin Purdum, born March 7, 1851

CHILD 1

Rufus King Purdum
1827-1909

This son of John Lewis Purdum (1798) and Jemima King (1805) was born June 5, 1827, and died November 23, 1905 at Appomattox, Virginia. Married January 12, 1850 to Emily Brandenburg, born April 5, 1827 in Frederick County, Maryland, died February 16, 1916 at Appomattox; a daughter of Lemuel M. Brandenburg and Charlotte Kindley (1805). Children, based largely on census records:

1. John Fillmore Purdum, born January 31, 1851 Frederick County, Maryland; died March 24, 1935 in Appomattox County, Virginia, where he is buried. Married January 21, 1873 to Laura Richard Hewitt, born May 1, 1855 in Bedford County, Virginia, and died July 10, 1917 at Appomattox, Virginia; daughter of George Hewitt (1815) and Rebecca Leftwich (1815). A daughter:

    a. Laura Purdum, born at Appomattox, Virginia, August 20, 1879, and died February 27, 1971 in East Orange, New Jersey. Married October 11, 1898 to Charles Cawthorn.

2. Samuel (or Lemuel) W. Purdum, born c.1853, married c.1874 to Margaret.
3. Jemima Purdum, born c.1855
4. Anna O. Purdum, born c.1858
5. Edward E. Purdum, born c.1860
6. Virginia L. Purdum, born c.1862
7. Cornelia G. Purdum, born c.1864; died October 8, 1865 at New Market, Virginia.
8. William Reich Purdum, born May 24, 1866 near New Market, Virginia.
9. Emma L. Purdum, born c.1869 at Appomattox, Virginia.

CHILD 2

Sarah Rebecca Purdum
1829-1911

This daughter of John Lewis Purdum (1798) and Jemima King (1805) was born January 29, 1829, and died November 10, 1911 at Kemptown. Married December 30, 1847 to Jesse B. Brandenburg, born June 16, 1824 and died April 6, 1896, son of Lemuel M.

Brandenburg (1801) and Charlotte Kindley (1805). They had children, all born in Montgomery County, Maryland:
1. Charlotte Lavinia Brandenburg, born 1851, died 1887. Married Basil F. Buxton, born 1843 and died 1927 at Kemptown, son of Brook Buxton and Kitty Mullinix. At least a daughter:
   a. Emma Rose Buxton, born August 21, 1874, died June, 1957. Married November 7, 1894 to William Eldridge Watkins, born 1867 and died April 1, 1943. Children:
      (1) Myra Lavinia Watkins, born February 16, 1896, died 1987. Married Emory Cross Woodfield, born June 17, 1889, died December 9, 1934, son of Thomas Griffith Woodfield (1856) and Emma Cassandra Boyer (1868), and had children:
         (a) Eldridge Woodfield.
         (b) Rose Woodfield.
         (c) George Woodfield.
      (2) Nellie Mae Watkins, born July 4, 1897 and married Mullinix.
      (3) Albert Dewey Watkins, born January 28, 1899, died 1969.
      (4) Cora Elaine Watkins, born March 1, 1901 and married Solomon.
      (5) Anna Louise Watkins, born February 16, 1903 and married Shoemaker.
2. Wilhemina Anna Brandenburg, born October 30, 1859, and died December 16, 1905. Married October 6, 1881 in Frederick County to Jesse William Moxley, born October 6, 1855 and died August 23, 1934, son of Risdon Moxley. Buried at Kemptown. They had eight children:
   a. Ernest Walter Moxley, born April 30, 1882, died September 12, 1973; married Mary Margaret Clay
   b. Lester Moxley, born July 26, 1886, died December 8, 1969. Married June 6, 1909 to Lottie May Burdette.
   c. Allison Moxley, born May 26, 1888, died March 19, 1952. Married October 30, 1912 to Margaret Gertrude Shoemaker.
   d. Lillie May Moxley, born June 30, 1890, died May 9, 1957. Married Milton Nash.

123

e. Stillbirth Moxley, son.
f. Jesse Herman Moxley, born June 5, 1893, died July 15, 1943; buried Prospect cemetery, Mt Airy, Maryland. Married December 2, 1914 to Mary Catherine Condon.
g. Elvira Moxley, born March 9, 1896, died October 1, 1986; buried St. Peter's Catholic cemetery at Libertytown. Married Edward Joseph Noonan.
h. Vivy Moxley, born November 17, 1900, and died October 15, 1903; buried at Kemptown.
3. Bradley Jefferson Brandenburg, born about 1863 and died November 10, 1945. Married first December 26, 1888 to Valerie Eveline Hyatt, born November 22, 1867 and died 1921 at Kemptown, daughter of Eli Hyatt, III, and Georgianna Lewis. Married second Nicie V. Lee. Seven children born to his first marriage:
a. Jessie Fay Brandenburg, born January 6, 1892 and died September 27, 1963. Married to Asa Hull Watkins.
b. George Floyd Brandenburg, born August 21, 1893 and died August 8, 1920. Married December 26, 1914 to Katherine Elizabeth Williams.
c. Bradley Claytus Brandenburg, born January 26, 1895, died February 24, 1972. Married March 5, 1919 to Leah Marie Williams.
d. Maysie Nadine Brandenburg, born November 18, 1897, died August 13, 1989. Married Lester Steele Watkins.
e. Fairy Brandenburg, born March 2, 1903; married to Lester William Burdette, son of Luther Melvin Burdette (1875). Children:
    (1) Carolyn Burdette, married Donald Bell. A son:
        (a) Michael Donald Bell.
    (2) Rosalie Nadine Burdette, married May 19, 1965 to William Harvey Rittase.
f. Evelyn Crothers Brandenburg, born November 5, 1907. Married Lester Baker Riggs.
g. Merhl Hyatt Brandenburg, born August 26, 1910, died January 9, 1980. Married Ethel L. Justice.

4. Mary Bert Brandenburg, born about 1866, and married to Calvin Watkins, born 1865 and died 1954 at Kemptown. Five children:
   a. Infant Watkins, born May 10, 1897; died June 1, 1897.
   b. Infant Watkins, born August 24, 1900, and died October 4, 1900.
   c. Okie Watkins.
   d. Grover Watkins.
   e. Virgie Watkins.
5. Ezra Brandenburg, born June 24, 1868, died January 28, 1936 at Fort Crockett, Texas; buried at Kemptown. He was a Marine Band musician, and was married April 11, 1889 in Frederick County, Maryland, to Tillie Renn, born c.1871 in the county, and died February 1, 1950 in Carroll County; buried at Mt. Airy, daughter of M. Luther Renn. Children, born in Frederick County:
   a. Osca Pearl Brandenburg, born January 31, 1892; married September 18, 1913 to Raymond Watkins.
   b. Earl D. Brandenburg, born c.1893, died August 22, 1965. Married Elizabeth, and had children:
      (1) Frances Brandenburg, married Sutherland.
      (2) Shirley Brandenburg, married Murray.
   c. Hanson Ezra Brandenburg, born March 4, 1895, died September 6, 1954 at Perry Point Veterans Hospital; buried at Kemptown; single.
   d. Sellman J. Brandenburg, born c.1898, died May 4, 1963 at Peculiar, Missouri; buried at Mt. Airy. Married Marian Kuhn. His obituary states that he had five grandchildren, and names one son:
      (1) Leroy Brandenburg.
   e. Windsor Brandenburg, died 1950 to 1954, probably in Baltimore.
6. Lucy Beatrice Brandenburg, born about 1871, died 1932. Married July 3, 1895 in Frederick County, to John Thomas Mullinix, son of Robert Mullinix and Evelyn Baker. They had children:
   a. Clyta Beatrice Mullinix; married December 24, 1914 to Joseph Leslie Woodfield, born March 4, 1891, and died

July 3, 1949, son of Thomas Griffith Woodfield (1856) and Emma Cassandra Boyer (1868). Children:
  (1) Willard Woodfield.
  (2) Beatrice Woodfield.
  (3) Dorothy Woodfield.
  (4) Vincent Woodfield.
  b. Leslie Mullinix.
  c. Aubrey Mullinix.
  d. Genevieve Mullinix.
  e. Dorothy Mullinix, married Leslie King.
7. Sybell R. Brandenburg, born January 7, 1873, and died March 15, 1873; buried at Kemptown.

CHILD 3

John Dorsey Purdum
1830-1896

This son of John Lewis Purdum (1798) and Jemima King (1805) was born October 25, 1830, and died April 6, 1896. Married December 29, 1852 to Sarah A. Baker, by whom he had six children. Married second January 3, 1878 to Lucinda Moxley, born July 18, 1840 and died January 13, 1911, daughter of Reuben M. Moxley and Kitty Ann Wolfe. The 1880 census of the Clarksburg District of Montgomery County lists John Dorsey as head of household, with Lucinda, born c.1841, and four children. The children were:
1. Alfred W. Purdum, born March 11, 1855, and died September 15, 1876 at Kemptown.
2. Josephine Purdum, born January 10, 1859, and died July 24, 1913; buried Mountain View Cemetery. Married November 2, 1876 to Homer F. King, born December 24, 1852 and died July 24, 1896, son of Luther Green King (1825). He is buried at the Mountain View Cemetery next to his wife. They appear in the 1880 census for Clarksburg District, where he is listed as working in a distillery (his father's, no doubt), and they have two children:
  a. Clarence E. King, born c.1878

b. Myrtle King, born December, 1879. Married first to Washington White and second Brockway. Three children from her first marriage:
    (1) Washington White, married to Louisa Griffith and had children:
        (a) Louisa White, married Darrington Riggs.
        (b) Dorothy White.
        (c) Washington White.
        (d) Charles White.
    (2) Myrtle White.
    (3) Frances White.
3. Louisa A. Purdum, born c.1864
4. Sarah E. A. Purdum, born c.1866
5. Reverdy Mason Purdum, born December 19, 1868, and died January 27, 1937; buried Kemptown. Married there June 7, 1898 Carrie Frances King, born May 30, 1876, died August 29, 1943; daughter of John Edward Howard King (1845) and Martha Elizabeth Linthicum (1844). One daughter:
    a. Mary Purdum; married to Albert Castir or Easter.
6. Eunice M. Purdum, born July 10, 1876 and died June 15, 1949. Married the Reverend Ferdinand Desoto Browning, born January 1, 1865, and died December 21, 1952 at Kemptown, son of Jeremiah and Georgette Browning. Three children:
    a. Mary Elizabeth Browning, born March 17, 1910.
    b. Glenn Ferdinand Browning, born February 26, 1912.
    c. Maxine Fern Browning, born September 2, 1914.
7. Emory Purdum, born c.1879 and died December 29, 1953. Married December 23, 1903 Alma V. Molesworth, born 1880, died 1930, daughter of John Molesworth. Buried Providence Methodist Church at Kemptown. They had children. He was married second to Mamie Baker, born July 29, 1888, daughter of Thomas Milton Baker and Anna Mary Lewis. His children from first marriage:
    a. Albert D. Purdum.
    b. Edna Leon Purdum, born July 29, 1906. Married November 20, 1919 Guy E. Leatherwood at Kemptown Church.

c. L. Eugene Purdum, born c.1919 at Kemptown, and died March 22, 1972 at Westminster, Maryland. He was married to Elsie Miller and had children:
   (1) Lewis E. Purdum, of Houghton, Michigan.
   (2) John E. Purdum, of Westminster.
d. E. Ralph Purdum.
8. Lillie Purdum; married William Scheel.
9. Lewis E. Purdum, a minister.

CHILD 4

Jemima King Purdum
1831-1886

This daughter of John Lewis Purdum (1798) and Jemima King (1805) was born June 13, 1831, and died October 29, 1886. Married December 13, 1850 to William H. Baker, born December 13, 1826 and died February 1, 1894 at Kemptown, son of Thomas Baker (1800) and Mary Day (1801). They had children:
1. John T. Baker, born November 4, 1851, died December 19, 1921. Married to Caroline Virginia Mullinix, born August, 1854 at Long Corner, died 1924, and buried at Damascus. They had children:
   a. William Andrew Baker, born August 28, 1880 at Poplar Springs, died May 28, 1942. A teacher, he married December 26, 1906 Isla May Young, born August 9, 1881 at Damascus; one child. Married second July 7, 1913 Norma Oleanda Brandenburg, born March 5, 1884 at Mt. Airy, died January 25, 1918. They had the second child listed. He married third July 6, 1921 Laura Belle Foard, born June 12, 1887 Forest Hill, Howard County, Maryland, died May 20, 1971. They had the last two children:
      (1) Isla Lorraine Baker, born April 4, 1909. Married August 5, 1933 to Roger Franklin Burdette, an economist, born May 20, 1909, son of Emory Whitehead Burdette (1890). Two children:

(a) Natalie Ann Burdette, born September 9, 1938 at Takoma Park, Maryland. A school teacher, she died August 20, 1966, single.

(b) Carol Baker Burdette, born January 5, 1942 at Takoma Park. Married February 19, 1960 to George Edgar Calahan, born December 21, 1937 at Miami, Arizona, a mining superintendent. Children, born at Tucson, Arizona:

    1. Kenneth Roger Calahan, born December 9, 1960

    2. Rebecca Lynn Calahan, born September 9, 1962

(2) Rudelle Brandenburg Baker, born January 4, 1914 near Damascus. Married June 28, 1943 Sarah L. Chain, born July 7, 1918 at Mt. Olive, Mississippi. A daughter:

    (a) Susan L. Baker, born November 5, 1954 at Miami, Florida.

(3) David William Baker, born August 3, 1922 at Baltimore. A mechanical engineer, he married June 30, 1950 June 30, 1950 Mabel Louise Collier, born December 3, 1927 Greene County, Virginia. Children:

    (a) Robert Gilmer Baker, born June 28, 1952

    (b) Carol Ann Baker, born February 23, 1954

    (c) William David Baker: November 16, 1956

    (d) John Morris Baker, born October 31, 1960

(4) Jean Gibson Baker, born December 24, 1923 Baltimore. A teacher, she married August 10, 1968 Wilbur Wallace Wilson, born March 27, 1922 at Roanoke, Virginia.

b. Della Day Baker, a twin, born February 29, 1884, and died October 18, 1911, single.

c. Stella Faring Baker, a twin, born February 29, 1884 and died August 10, 1885

d. James Vernon Baker, born January 5, 1886, died October 25, 1952. A teacher, he married December 22, 1909 to Rose Ethel Duvall, born June 14, 1898. Children:

(1) Ethel Duvall Baker, born October 26, 1910 Washington, D. C. Married July 11, 1928 Carl Edward Scherrer, born there August 17, 1905. He was a jewelry craftsman, and partner in Collins and Scherrer. Children:

    (a) Shirley Mae Scherrer, born September 9, 1931 at Washington, D. C. Married February 5, 1955 to Fletcher Reid Brande, born there May 18, 1931, a State Department employee. Children:

        1. Christie Lee Brande September 23, 1956
        2. Jesse Reid Brande: July 5, 1958
        3. Danny Shawn Brande: May 21, 1961

    (b) Patricia Ann Scherrer born May 29, 1941, married June 22, 1963 Hassell Frederick Bowman, born June 26, 1936, US Air Force. One son:

        1. Kenneth Edward Bowman.

(2) Elva Muriel Baker, born August 3, 1913. Married Fraley and divorced in 1942; no children.

(3) Russell Austin Baker, born November 16, 1916

(4) Betty Jean Baker, born January 17, 1926 in Washington. Married October 17, 1948 John Scott Small, born May 1, 1925 in East Riverdale. Two children:

    (a) Debra Jean Small, born July 17, 1952. A nurse, last reported in Anchorage, Alaska.

    (b) John Alan Small, born February 22, 1958 at Rockville, Maryland

(5) Allen Dale Baker, born October 10, 1931 at Washington. Married Ruth Lee Hoffman; children:

    (a) James Allen Baker.
    (b) Patrick Lee Baker.
    (c) Susan Farg Baker.

e. Lillian May Baker, born February 27, 1888. Married June 5, 1912 Bradley Clifford Leatherwood, born July 11, 1886 at Woodbine, died March 6, 1941. Three children, born at Mt. Airy, Maryland:

(1) Genevieve Leatherwood, born January 26, 1914.
Married February 5, 1938 John Mason Wilbur,
born August 15, 1911 at Devon, Pennsylvania,
died October 2, 1947. Two children:
(a) Elizabeth Fitch Wilbur, born August 25,
1940 at Dallas, Texas
(b) Susan Bradley Wilbur, born November 3,
1942 at Dallas, Texas. Married September
28, 1963 to Michael Denis Gauthier, born at
Cincinnati, Ohio, and divorced. She married
second March 5, 1971 Gary Lee Wamsley,
born Fall City, Nebraska. He was a professor
of political science at University of Kansas.
One child to each marriage:
1. David Bradley Gauthier: May 13, 1965
2. Jonathan Asbury Wamsley: October 20,
1973
(2) Helen Baker Leatherwood, born March 3, 1917.
Married June 15, 1941 to Vernon Ray Simpson,
born October 29, 1915 at Baltimore. He is a retired Vice Principal of the Damascus High School,
and has three children:
(a) Helen Dianne Simpson, born August 22, 1942
at Temple, Texas. Married September 20,
1969 Clisby Harrell Krell, Jr. and had a child:
1. Christine Ann Krell: November 29, 1973
(b) John Reynolds Simpson, born May 23, 1949
at Baltimore, Maryland. Married June 23,
1973 to Leslie Ann Jackson.
(c) David Vernon Simpson, born March 19, 1956
(3) John Francis Leatherwood, born June 17, 1920,
and died January 30, 1945. Buried Pine Grove
cemetery, Mt. Airy.
f. Franklin Lansdale Baker, born March 3, 1891 and died
March 15, 1891
g. Harold Levering Baker, born February 4, 1896, died
October 17, 1927 in Denver, Colorado, of tuberculosis
contracted in the first world war.

2. Mary W. Baker, born March 18, 1853; died July 13, 1942. Married to Eli Lawson and had two children:
   a.   Ola Lawson, married Nathan Burdette; no children
   b.   Annie Lawson, married Picket.
3. William H. D. Baker, born 1854; died 1936, single.
4. Eveline J. Baker, born September 7, 1856, died March 16, 1872.
5. Martha W. Baker, born September 25, 1860, and died October 13, 1881
6. Edna Elizabeth Baker, born January 31, 1863. Married October 4, 1883 John Edgar Hyatt, born August 11, 1859, died October 27, 1904. She married second to William Lewis. Four children from her first marriage:
   a.   William Eli Cleveland Hyatt, born October 8, 1884, died September 7, 1929. Married December 7, 1904 Mildred Survila Boyer, born July 2, 1883 at Damascus, daughter of John Wesley Boyer (1857). and had three children, born there:
      (1)   Edna Wilson Hyatt, born November 26, 1905. Married August 10, 1927 to Purdum Burdette Linthicum, born March 27, 1906, died November 28, 1973. Their children are discussed under their father's name, following, which see.
      (2)   John Cleveland Hyatt, born June 28, 1910. Married April 22, 1933 Madeline Kidd, born March 27, 1906 at Mt. Airy. No children reported.
      (3)   Clifford Boyer Hyatt, born April 20, 1915. Married October 24, 1942 Geraldine Von Sant, born November 10, 1923 at Frederick. Children:
         (a)   Barbara Lou Hyatt, born September 26, 1945 at Frederick. Married April 18, 1970 Donald Lynn Knotts, born February 1, 1943. They had a son:
            1.   Christopher Michael Knotts, born June 4, 1972
         (b)   James Cleveland Hyatt, born March 26, 1947 at Frederick, a mechanical engineer. Married August 4, 1973 to Jennifer Estelle Lucke,

born January 14, 1951 at Annapolis. No children reported.

    (c) Gregory Boyer Hyatt, born November 26, 1952 at Sunbury, Pennsylvania.

b. Charles Vester Hyatt, born 1886 at Kemptown. Married to Martha, who died 1974, and had children:

    (1) Gertrude Hyatt, born 1912

    (2) Edgar Hyatt, born 1915

    (3) Charles Hyatt, born 1922

c. Herbert Hyatt, born November 16, 1888, died December 17, 1955. Founder of Hyatt Building Supply Co. of Damascus. Married December 25, 1920 Beulah Souder, born September 21, 1889 at Damascus, died January 8, 1968. Buried at the Damascus Methodist Church cemetery. They had children:

    (1) Janice Pearl Hyatt, born November 12, 1912 Damascus. Married June 22, 1933 Roland Lee Green, born April 10, 1916, and had children:

        (a) Joy Hyatt Green, born July 13, 1940 at Gaithersburg. A teacher, married August 31, 1961 to Warren J. Schwab, born May 9, 1939 at Rockville.

        (b) Roland Lee Green, Jr., born October 4, 1941 at Gaithersburg. Married August, 1962 Joan Waters, born Clarksburg; divorced. Married November 17, 1967 Diane Ciccone, born November 13, 1946 at Worcester, Mass.

        (c) Roy Joseph Green, born August 22, 1947 at Gaithersburg. Bank manager, married March 3, 1966 Susan Riggs Meyer, born March 2, 1950 at Sandy Spring.

        (d) Philip Harvey Green, born October 28, 1949 at Gaithersburg. Married September 18, 1970 Linda Dianne Norwood, born April 3, 1951 Laytonsville.

    (2) Herbert Souder Hyatt, born April 10, 1916. President Bank of Damascus. Married December 16,

1936 to Ruby Mae Williams, born February 8, 1918 near Damascus, a teacher. One son:

- (a) Jerry Herbert Hyatt, born September 29, 1940 at Damascus. An attorney, member of the Maryland House of Delegates. Married August, 1964 to Virginia Home, divorced in 1968 after one son. He married second 1973 to Barbara Lutz Allen, and had three children, the four being:
  1. Stephen Williams Hyatt.
  2. Timothy H. Hyatt, adopted.
  3. John Lutz Hyatt, adopted.
  4. Jerry Williams Hyatt.

- (3) Hilda Mae Hyatt, born March 28, 1920 near Damascus. A teacher, married December 25, 1945 Guy Kenneth Howes, born September 1, 1917, and divorced. Married second February 14, 1948 Charles William Roelke, born March 7, 1919 at Frederick, and divorced. Married third October 8, 1966 to Arthur Leonard Watkins, Jr., born March 22, 1912 near Damascus, an auto dealer. She had three children, born to her second marriage:
  - (a) Robert Hyatt Roelke, born December 20, 1949 at Frederick. Married April 24, 1971 to Trudy Ann Redmond, born August 12, 1950 at Frederick.
  - (b) Charles William Roelke, Jr., born October 12, 1950, died December 13, 1950.
  - (c) Carol Mae Roelke, born July 31, 1953 at Frederick

d. John C. Hyatt, born 1891 at Kemptown, died 1934. Married 1917 to Ethel Moxley, born near Damascus. Children:
  - (1) Irving Hyatt, born 1920
  - (2) Bernard Hyatt, born 1923

7. Frances A. Baker, born January 29, 1864, died 1902. She married Jason Mullinix, and had children:

a. Myrtle Mullinix, married to William E. Miller and had children:
   (1) William W. Miller.
   (2) Richard Kenneth Miller.
   (3) Mary Frances Miller.
   b. Bertie Mullinix, married Harry Green.
8. Dorsey Lewis Baker, born February 23, 1867; died 1949. Married to Lillie Mabel Norwood, and buried Kemptown. Three children:
   a. Norwood Baker.
   b. Willard Baker.
   c. Bernard Baker.
9. Rufus E. Baker, born April 17, 1870, and died 1957 at Kemptown. Married Emma Edith Kemp. Children:
   a. Day Baker.
   b. Winfred Baker.
10. Alice Roberta Baker, born March 20, 1873, and died 1945. Married to Samuel Dorsey Warfield and had a son:
   a. Hamilton Deets Warfield, born December 21, 1897 near Browningsville, and died March 29, 1974. Owned and operated Damascus Chevrolet for 56 years, and married September 28, 1921 to Fairy Elizabeth Burdette, born February 14, 1902, daughter of William Hubert Burdette (1872) and Beda Cassandra King (1873). Their children are discussed under their mother's name in Chapter 8, devoted to the descendants of Singleton King (1810), which see.

CHILD 5

Joshua Hinkle Purdum
1833-1874

This son of John Lewis Purdum (1798) and Jemima King (1805) was born November 21, 1833, and died March 27, 1874 after being kicked by a horse. Buried at Bethesda United Methodist Church at Browningsville, Montgomery County, Maryland, along with many other members of the greater King family. Married No-

135

vember 5, 1864 to Martha Brown Burdette, born November 8, 1843 and died May 30, 1929, the daughter of James William Burdette (1813) and Cassandra Purdum (1804). They had children:

1. Mary L. Purdum, born January 18, 1866, and died September 6, 1956. Married April 25, 1887 in Montgomery County, Maryland, to Miel E. Linthicum, born February 28, 1865 and died September 8, 1928. They had children:

    a. Earle Linthicum, born November 22, 1893; died October 25, 1959 at Clagettsville. Married to Ada Oagle and had children:

        (1) Edwin Lee Linthicum; married to Leith Eileen Cline, born May 15, 1922, daughter of Carl Albert Cline and Esther Leith Moxley. Three children:

            (a) Edwina Larue Linthicum, born January 17, 1940. Married Francis Edward Harrison and had children:

                1. Francis Edward Harrison, Jr.: August 7, 1959.
                2. Christie Lee Harrison: January 29, 1961
                3. Gregory Allen Harrison: January 7, 1962
                4. John Franklin Harrison: March 13, 1963
                5. James Vinton Harrison: March 14, 1964

            (b) Eugenia Leith Linthicum, born September 2, 1944; married Harold Boyer Mullinix.

            (c) Anita Sue Linthicum, born March 26, 1956.

    b. Ethel Linthicum, died April 25, 1967. Married to Ivan Lawson, born November 21, 1886 and had children:

        (1) Arthur Lawson, married and divorced. Married second to Evelyn Cox.

        (2) Hanford Lawson; married Hazel Murisen.

    c. Miel Wright Linthicum; married Irma Watkins, born March 29, 1903, a daughter of Alonzo Claggett Watkins (1867) and Mary Louana Boyer (1870). Children:

        (1) Miel Wright Linthicum, Jr., born April 10, 1928, married Mary Emma Johnson, and had children:

            (a) James Miel Linthicum, born 1952
            (b) Robert Earl Linthicum, born 1954

       (c)   John Monroe Linthicum, born 1961
       (d)   Jill Suzanne Linthicum, born 1962
  (2)   George Morsell Linthicum, born April 4, 1926, married Jeanne Marie Brown, and had children:
       (a)   Mary Martha Linthicum.
       (b)   Beverly Jeanne Linthicum.
       (c)   Donna Joan Linthicum.
       (d)   George Morsell Linthicum, Jr.
       (e)   Ann Marie Linthicum, born 1962
  (3)   Joseph Linthicum, born April 21, 1930, married Gay Elizabeth Harding. No children.
  (4)   Bernard Lee Linthicum, born November 21, 1934. He married Martha Hooper and had children:
       (a)   Irma Jane Linthicum.
       (b)   Amanda Jean Linthicum.
d. Purdum Burdette Linthicum, born March 27, 1906, died November 28, 1973. Married August 10, 1927 to Edna Wilson Hyatt, born November 26, 1905, daughter of William Eli Cleveland Hyatt (1884) and Mildred Survila Boyer (1883). Children:
  (1)   Mary Mildred Linthicum, born May 9, 1930 at Damascus, and married May 19, 1948 to Jeremiah Elsworth Brandenburg, who was born January 22, 1925, the son of William Brandenburg and Bessie May Burdette. No children.
  (2)   Shirley Hyatt Linthicum, born July 10, 1931 at Browningsville. Married October 28, 1950 Paul Curtis Johnson, born February 15, 1929 at Glen Burnie, Maryland. Children:
       (a)   Paul Curtis Johnson, Jr., born May 21, 1953. Married April 5, 1975 Suzanne Marie Fritz, born October 5, 1955 at Mercersburg, Pa.
       (b)   Jerrie Wayne Johnson, born September 30, 1954 at Olney
       (c)   Maryanne Hyatt Johnson, born November 20, 1963 at Frederick
  (3)   Debora Kay Linthicum, born September 16, 1950 near Damascus; an elementary school teacher.

2. John W. Purdum, born c.1867. His wife's name is not now known, but he had at least seven children:
   a. Fred Purdum.
   b. Nellie Purdum; married Herndon.
   c. Emma Purdum.
   d. Georgianna Purdum.
   e. John Purdum.
   f. August Purdum.
   g. Virginia Purdum.
3. Rufus Elsworth Purdum, born 1869, and died c.1952. Married December 23, 1890 at Providence Methodist Church, in Kemptown, Maryland, Alice Sardinia Baker, born January 29, 1867, and died July 6, 1904, daughter of Thomas Milton Baker and Anna Mary Lewis. An infant death, and three surviving children:
   a. William Floyd Purdum, born December 10, 1894 and died August 14, 1898.
   b. Raymond Gaver Purdum, born 1896 and died February, 1971 in Havre DeGrace. Married to Mildred E. Rigler. Children:
      (1) Gail Purdum, married to Taylor.
      (2) Raymond Gaver Purdum, Jr.
      (3) Gary L. Purdum.
   c. Jessie Marie Purdum, born June 12, 1900; married to James Sellman Day, born c.1899 and died 1924 at Browningsville, Maryland. He was a son of James Start Day and Laura Helen Davis. Jessie Marie and James Sellman Day had two children, born at Pleasant Grove. Married second to R. Leslie Davis, born c.1891 and died 1948, son of R. Lee Davis and Cora Layton. They had one daughter. The children of Jessie Marie were:
      (1) Laura Helen Day, born October 3, 1920. Married February 15, 1939 to George Josiah Stup, born July 23, 1917 at Burtonsville, and had children:
         (a) George Larry Stup, born November 13, 1939. Married June 29, 1969 Judy Ann MacIntyre, born July 31, 1946 at Baltimore. Two children, born at Frederick:

      1. Lauren Davis Stup, born August 9, 1973
      2. Joel Lynn Stup, born March 18, 1975
  (b) Linda Jeanne Stup, born October 29, 1940. Married June 26, 1965 to Robert Easterday Broadrup, born October 17, 1940 Frederick. He is a dentist; three children, born Frederick:

      1. Elizabeth Easterday Broadrup, born March 20, 1968
      2. Robert Livingston Broadrup, born June 27, 1970
      3. Garrett Cade Broadrup: August 29, 1974

  (c) Darryl Leslie Stup, born July 22, 1943, and married May 2, 1970 to Judy Mae Roberts, born April 13, 1947 at Frederick. No children

  (d) Alison Elizabeth Stup, born March 15, 1949. A registered nurse, she married July 27, 1974 Gary Wayne Stitley, born May 30, 1944 at Catoctin Furnace, Maryland. No children.

  (e) Stephen Jay Stup, born July 31, 1951. Married February 3, 1973 to Sharon Ann Musial, born September 27, 1952 Bethesda. A child:

      1. Corey Stephen Stup, born May 24, 1973

(2) Alice Marie Day, born August 11, 1922. Married February 12, 1950 Clifford Hefner, born June 12, 1922 Lewisburg, West Virginia; no children.

(3) Betty Davis, born May, 1930; married January, 1951 to Mark Jeffers, born July 3, 1930, and had children:

  (a) Leslie Carolyn Jeffers, born April 7, 1956
  (b) Teresa Marie Jeffers, born April 5, 1958

CHILD 6

Rachel Browning Purdum
1835-1910

This daughter of John Lewis Purdum (1798) and Jemima King (1805), was born July 19, 1835, and died July 4, 1910. Married

June 16, 1858 to George Washington Wesley Walker, son of George Bryan Walker (1799) and Margaret Boyer (1805). He was born October 10, 1837 in a log cabin on the home farm near Browningsville, Montgomery County, Maryland, and died May 7, 1915. By deed dated December 20, 1875, George obtained clear title to the property from his brothers and sisters. George studied music under local teachers, and in the summer of 1870, at the Normal Institute in Florida, New York. In about 1880, he commissioned John Mount, a local builder, to build a Gothic Revival style manor house, which he named *Mendelsohn Terrace*. The house is a three bay by five bay, two and a half story, L-shaped frame house sitting on a hill, facing south, overlooking the valley of Bennett Creek. The front porch has a flat roof, with a turned balustraded railing and four wooden columns for support. There are three cross gables on the south elevation, each with eight-light Gothic windows. The home has been placed on the Historic Register, and is currently occupied by Stewart Eugene Walker, a descendant. For more than fifty years, *Mendelsohn Terrace* was the musical and literary center of the area. Local choirs and schools gathered there and George played the organ in the Bethesda United Methodist Church near his home for more than fifty-six years.

He appears as head of household in the 1880 census for the Damascus District, with his wife, and eight of their children. In 1904 (see Liber 180, folio 132, Montgomery County Land Records), he bought from his son, Muller M. Walker and Helen A. Day, a four acre parcel at Browningsville, being parts of the tracts known as *Flag Patch* and *Solomon's Roguery*, which apparently adjoined, or were very near, the home farm. In 1911, by deed recorded in Liber 224 at folio 318, George (then a widower) conveyed the home farm to his children. His will, dated May 16, 1914, and probated June 1, 1915, is filed in Liber HCA 14 at folio 479 among the Will Records of Montgomery County, Maryland. There, he names his seven living children, and five grandchildren, being the children of his deceased daughter. The will of his wife, dated July 10, 1910, and probated October 4, 1910, is found in Liber HCA 8 at folio 346. Their children, probably all born on the home farm near Browningsville, included:

1. Mary Alice Eudoria Walker, born September 14, 1859; married April 2, 1894 to Reverend Doctor Charles Scanlon, born October 5, 1869, died March 25, 1927. In 1902, they lived in Minneapolis, Minnesota. The place of birth of some of their children is questionable:
   a. Michael Scanlon, born November 22, 1894 at Valpariso, Indiana (or Orland, Pennsylvania ?), died May 13, 1970. Married Miriam Winifred Wallace.
   b. Mary Browning Scanlon, born October 5, 1896 at Wheaton, Minnesota. Single, a school teacher.
   c. Pauline Rosabelle Scanlon, born January 8, 1898 at Wheaton, Minnesota (or Brookline, Massachusetts). Married to Janel Gardescua from Romania.
   d. Helen Ruth Scanlon, born December 20, 1900, in Minneapolis, Minnesota (or Markham, Virginia). Married to Leon Block.
   e. Alice Walker Scanlon, born November 22, 1902; married August 8, 1933 to Edward Henry Wells, born in Chefoo, China, son of Mason Wells and Margaret Grier Wells. They had children, born in Orange, New Jersey:
      (1) Mary Alice Wells, born July 2, 1935
      (2) Ralph Scanlon Wells, born October 27, 1940
      (3) Edward Graham Wells, born September 1, 1944
   f. Ella (now Ellen) Hill Scanlon, born March 25, 1905 at Frederick, Maryland. Married Theodore Seipmann.
2. John Lewis Everett Walker, born March 4, 1861; died April 26, 1924. Married September 17, 1884 Harriet Ann Eugenia Hobbs, born 1854 and died 1924. Four children:
   a. John Raymond Gwinn Walker, born July 29, 1885; died January 6, 1962
   b. Fletcher Asbury Walker, born 1887; died 1924
   c. Eugene Samuel Wesley Walker, born December 10, 1892 near Browningsville, Montgomery County, Maryland, and died July 18, 1951. He was married November 4, 1916 to Ethel Virginia Day, born August 2, 1897; died January 8, 1939, daughter of James Start Day (1865) and Laura Helen Davis (1874). Buried at Bethesda United Methodist Church, Browningsville, Montgomery County,

141

as are numerous members of this branch of the family. (Eugene may have been married second to Mary R.). By deed dated 1925, recorded in Liber 372 at folio 42 in Montgomery County, Langdon S. and Sadie E. Day conveyed a four-acre tract to Eugene and his brother, J. R. Gwinn (above), being the same land that Day had obtained from their uncle and aunt, George Mendelsohn Muller Walker and Helen Augusta Day. Eugene had children:

(1)　Stewart Eugene Day Walker, born April 25, 1918 in the living room of the family home, *Mendelsohn Terrace,* and died before 1995. Married August 20m 1941 at the Clarksburg parsonage, to Eunice Evelyn "Bootsie" Burdette, born September 22, 1924 in Philadelphia, daughter of John Adolph Burdette and Margretha Johanna Janssen. Stuart was the owner of the home farm. They had two sons, born there:

(a)　Stewart Eugene Walker, born November 5, 1944; married June 1, 1968 to Patricia Ann Burdette, the daughter of Maxwell Elsworth Burdette and Elmira Parrish. Children:

1.　Stewart Eugene Walker, III: February 3, 1971
2.　Darryl David Walker, born December 22, 1973

(b)　Darryl Wayne Walker, born May 19, 1948

(2)　Evelyn Virginia Walker, born July 13, 1919, and married September 25, 1940 to Merhle Purdum Pickett, born June 1, 1916 at Poplar Springs. They had three children, born at Frederick, Maryland:

(a)　Merhlyn Virginia Pickett, born April 21, 1944 and married to William Barnes, son of Edgar and Dorothy Barnes, and had children:

1.　Melony Barnes.
2.　Sharon Barnes.

142

    (b)   Evelyn Eugenia Pickett, born November 5, 1948 and married John Cushwa, Martinsburg, West Virginia.

    (c)   Ann Selena Pickett, born January 10, 1951

   (3)   Edsel Davis Walker, born July 9, 1921; married first to Sarah Kemp, and second September 11, 1964 to Phyllis Ethel Stanley, born November 10, 1928 in Damascus, Maryland, daughter of Grover Mount Stanley and Rosa Lena Boyer. No children.

d.   A daughter Walker, died in infancy.

3.   Miriam Augusta Webster Walker, born February 14, 1864; and died in infancy.

4.   Margaret Jemima Roberta Walker, born January 7, 1866; died May 1, 1913. Married December 23, 1889 to Joseph Rinkly Linthicum, son of Lee Linthicum. The name of her husband has also been reported as Joseph Hamilton Linthicum. He was born September 28, 1866 and died January 7, 1942. In her mother's will, Margaret Jemima received a gold watch and chain. Five children:

a.   Walker S. Linthicum, born September 5, 1891, died September 26, 1930, single. One of the most popular young men in that part of Montgomery County; his funeral cortege from his home near Ridgeville to Bethesda United Methodist Church was one of the longest that the county had seen.

b.   Paul Linthicum, born 1893, died 1894.

c.   Infant Linthicum, stillbirth 1895.

d.   Rosia Rachel Linthicum, born November 11, 1899. Married Sherman Claude Kline; no children.

e.   Eleanor E. Linthicum, born July 30, 1902. Married David Everhart; no children.

f.   Parepa F. Linthicum, born June 4, 1904; single

g.   Roberta F. Linthicum, born September 22, 1907. Married Donald E. Pyle; children:

   (1)   Lynn Reece Pyle.

   (2)   Lorna Jean Pyle.

5.   William Alfred Baker Walker, born November 1, 1867; died August 8, 1947. Married December 24, 1890 to Laura Arvilla

Day, the daughter of Rufus King Day and Ann Priscilla Brandenburg. She was born at Browningsville. July 11, 1867, and died January 23, 1943. In 1907, William and Laura, then said to be of Frederick County, Maryland, executed a mortgage, recorded in Liber 195 at folio 356 in the Land Records of Montgomery County, Maryland. She died January 27, 1943, and in her will is said to be of Frederick County, although the will was probated in Montgomery. She names her husband, and their two sons, who were Executors. An inventory of the real property is included in the probate, and included one third interest in a farm of 154 acres, 2 roods and 20 perhces in Frederick County; and two parcels located partly in Frederick, Montgomery and Howard Counties, one containing 25 acres and the other, 10 acres. They had twelve children, all born at Ridgeville, Maryland:

a. Blanche Willard Walker, born January 19, 1892; died August 4, 1926. Married November 21, 1924 Ernest M. Ehrenberg, born August 15, 1891 at Ludington, Michigan; died September 13, 1966. No children.

b. Esther May Walker, born March 28, 1893; married May 28, 1921 to William Anderson Taylor, born at Inwood, Long Island, New York. He was an insurance agent in Mt. Airy, Maryland. Children, born at Mt. Airy:

    (1) Theodore Paul Ernest Taylor, born September 3, 1930; married to Marian Davis Faunce.

    (2) Jessie Laura Taylor, born November 24, 1932; married on September 5, 1953 to William Maxwell Tees Hanklin, a clergyman, born September 30, 1929 at Upland, Pennsylvania, and had children:

        (a) Judith Ann Hanklin, born August 22, 1954; married January 27, 1973 Mark A. Light, born at Lebanon, Pennsylvania. One son:

           1. Andrew Mark, born December 11, 1973.

        (b) William Maxwell Tees Hanklin, II, born July 15, 1956

c. Daughter Walker, born January 8, 1895; died July 3, 1895

d. Bessie Pauline Walker, born August 4, 1897; died March 7, 1916
e. William Paul Walker, born August 7, 1898 at Ridgeville, Maryland, died January 27, 1972. He was an educator and a scientist; and a professor at the University of Maryland. Married May 6, 1938 to Frances Myers, born at New Windsor July 17, 1907, and died July 14, 1973. They had at least one child:
    (1) William F. Walker, born December 23, 1942 at Takoma Park, Maryland.
f. Wesley Day Walker, born September 29, 1900, and died May 29, 1901.
g. Rufus Wesley Walker, born April 2, 1902; died February 5, 1903.
h. Dwight Talmadge Walker, born August 23, 1903 at Ridgeville, Maryland, and married August 23, 1925 to Ruth Davis, born February 22, 1904 at Linwood, Carroll County, Maryland; died January 22, 1972. They had five children, and he was married second February 14, 1973 to Marion Evangeline Barnes, born 1917. The children were all born near Mt. Airy, Maryland:
    (1) Dwight Talmadge Walker, Jr., born April 8, 1929
    (2) June Juanita Walker, born March 23, 1932; married June 10, 1955 to Charles Franklin Beck, II, born March 14, 1929 at Mt. Airy, Maryland, and had children:
        (a) Charles Franklin Beck, III: October 1, 1964
        (b) Beth Luella Beck, born March 26, 1969
    (3) Wava Jane Walker, born September 13, 1934; married December 23, 1952 to George Everet Emswiler, born December 13, 1931 at Timberville, Virginia, and had children:
        (a) David Leroy Emswiler, born August 9, 1953
        (b) Rodney Gordon Emswiler: December 2, 1954
        (c) Wanda Sue Emswiler: November 17, 1956
        (d) Kirk Walker Emswiler, born August 7, 1959
    (4) Mary Ann Walker, born February 6, 1936 at Mt. Airy, Maryland. Married June 28, 1956 to James

Oscar Brandenburg, born January 17, 1933. They had four children:

(a) Barbara Lynn Brandenburg: April 23, 1958
(b) Nancy Lee Brandenburg: December 24, 1962
(c) James Michael Brandenburg: July 9, 1966
(d) Randy Lee Brandenburg: November 25, 1969

(5) William Richard Walker: June 28, 1940. Married August 1, 1969 to Christa Sikken, born September 29, 1946 at Norden, West Germany.

i. Ernest Artman Walker, born August 29, 1904 at Ridgeville, Maryland; married August 28, 1929 to Irene Elizabeth Baker, born December 17, 1905 at Niagara Falls, New York, and had one child:

(1) Elizabeth Ann Walker, born April 21, 1944 Washington, D. C . Married June 14, 1989 John Arthur Gill, born May 4, 1925 Dubuque, Iowa. One son:

(a) David Ernest Gill, born December 17, 1970 at Madison, Wisconsin.

j. Wilfred Taft Walker, a twin, born May 21, 1908; died August 2, 1908.

k. Wilbur Bryan Walker, a twin, born May 21, 1908; died August 6, 1908.

l. Willing Wendell Walker, born July 9, 1910; married August 6, 1964 to Mary Vandevort Nicklas, born November 20, 1910 at Pittsburg, Pennsylvania; died April 13, 1977. Buried at the Bethesda United Methodist Church cemetery near the village of Browningsville, with numerous other family members. No children.

6. Rosabelle Walker, born January 31, 1870; died July 28, 1891. Could this be the same girl who married May 14, 1885 to Charles Bacon?

7. Fidelia Seward Walker, known as Della, born August 11, 1871; died August 28, 1960. In 1908, she and Parepa W. Walker, her sister, by deed recorded in Montgomery County, in Liber 196 at folio 475, obtained from James H. and Sallie Lawson of Frederick County, a tract containing 30 acres, 1 rood and 8 perches of land at Browningsville, being part of the tract called *Trouble Enough Indeed*. She was married at her

home November 4, 1908 to Preston L. Snyder, born May 7, 1885; died April 16, 1967; son of John L. Snyder and Corie Young. They had a daughter:

a. Carol Walker Snyder, born July 29, 1909 near Travilah, Montgomery County, Maryland. Married Joseph Sileck, and divorced, retaining her maiden name. They had one child:

(1) Joseph Snyder Sileck.

8. Parepa Wesley Wood Walker, born September 11, 1872; died 1937. Married June 16, 1913 to Thomas Harrison Day, son of Charles T. Day (1858) and Margaret E. Dronenburg (1863). As of 1902, they lived at St. Paul, Minnesota. Under her mother's will, she received a buggy, harness and lap robe. At least one son:

a. Wesley Harrison Day.

9. Rachel Vivia Cochel Walker, born September 16, 1874; died February 18, 1957. Married December 4, 1900 to Reverend Doctor Roby Franklin Day, born June 18, 1872, died July 28, 1964 in Allenwood, New Jersey; son of Jackson Day and Survila Ann Beall Day (1831). In 1902, they were living at Bloomington, Illinois. Ordained as a minister September 16, 1900 at Ferris, Illinois. He later assumed the pastorate at Tehuacana, Texas, where he served as Dean of Westminister College. He served other charges, including Kansas City, Missouri; and Long Island, New York. In the will of her mother, she is referred to as Rachel Viera Day, "*my youngest daughter and namesake.*" She received from her mother a gold necklace. The will is specific as to the ultimate ownership of the necklace, apparently considered a family heirloom, and is to be owned by any subsequent female of the family who carries the name Rachel. They had children:

a. Stockton Elderdice Day, born July 16, 1902 at Holder, Illinois and married August 10, 1929 in Chicago to Lois Esther Trunk, born May 17, 1902. No children.

b. Chapin Walker Day, born December 16, 1905 at Tehuacana, Texas; married November 23, 1932 at East Orange, New Jersey, to Dorothy Louise Morgan, born July

147

22, 1908. He was a high school biology teacher in Caldwell, New Jersey. Children, born in Patterson:

(1) Chapin Walker Day, Jr., born April 6, 1936, and married June 24, 1958 Mary Lynne Adams, born August, 1938. They had a son. He married second October 3, 1964 Sandra Marie Elder, born August 20, 1936 at Springfield, Massachusetts, and had three children, the four being:

    (a) David Jeffrey Day, born May 7, 1959 at Ludington, Michigan

    (b) Rosemarie Wells Day, born July 9, 1966 at Long Beach, California

    (c) Chapin Walker Day, III, born April 30, 1968 at Kingston, New York

    (d) Roby Haskell Day, born October 14, 1971 at Kingston, New York

(2) Jon Roby Day, born April 14, 1938 at Patterson, New Jersey. An opthalmologist, he married June, 1964 to Brenda Jenkins. Two children:

    (a) Mark Walker Day, born February 24, 1965

    (b) Lisa Elayne Day, born April 10, 1969

c. James Roby Day, born January 18, 1908 in Tehuacana, Texas. He was a high school music teacher in Oceanside, New York, and married June 29, 1941 to Joyce Elva De-Grishe, born May 6, 1922. They had children: first born at Oceanside, New York; last two at Rockville Centre, New York:

(1) James Roby Day, Jr., born April 26, 1942. Pilot in the Navy; married December 28, 1975 to Sharon Parrish.

(2) Richard Garrison Day, born November 30, 1945. A German teacher, he married April 13, 1960 to Dorte Elsa Alma Tiedemann, born August, 1950. They had a daughter, born Renssellaer, New York:

    (a) Christina Fredericka Day: February 8, 1970

(3) Jeanne Ann Day, born November 29, 1947. Married December 5, 1970 to George James Simmons,

a piano teacher and tuner. Children, both born at Rockville Centre, New York:
- (a) George James Simmons, III: June 30, 1971
- (b) Heather Joy Simmons: August 26, 1972
   (4) Bonnie Jean Day, born December 20, 1958
d. Jackson Wesley Day, born August 24, 1910 at Browningsville, Maryland. Married June 7, 1941 to Ruth Lydia Slayton, born December 2, 1903 at Auburn, New York, died May 8, 1975. He was a missionary of the Methodist Church and served in China, Malaysia and Indonesia. They had children:
   (1) Jackson Harvey Day, born March 18, 1942 at Oakland, California. Married May 30, 1964 to Martha Ann Taylor, born November 14, 1942. He is the author of *James Day of Browningsville and his descendants, A Maryland Family*, which lists numerous generations of that individual. He had one child from his first marriage, and was married second in 1971 to Emily Ann Roberts, born July 16, 1946 in Washington, D. C.. They adopted one child. His two children were:
- (a) James Wesley Day, born March 29, 1966 at Cumberland, Maryland
- (b) Catherine Lynn Day, born September 6, 1966 in Bethesda, Maryland

   (2) Vivia Ruth Day, born March 7, 1945 Ithaca, New York. Married June 26, 1968 James Earl Tatum, born June 26, 1947. Children, born at Pt. Pleasant, New Jersey:
- (a) Brenda Jane Tatum, born October 19, 1970
- (b) Carolyn Ann Tatum, born October 19, 1972

10. George Mendelsohn Muller Walker, known in most land record entries simply as Muller M. Walker, born June 27, 1880 and died September 24, 1953. Married August 19, 1904 to Helen Augusta Day, born April 8, 1878 near Kemptown, Maryland, and died July 18, 1957. She was a teacher, daughter of Luther Day (1832-1897) and Ann Elizabeth Lewis. They had children:

149

a. George Wesley Day Walker, born June 21, 1804 Browningsville, Maryland. He was a patent attorney in the District, listed in the 9th Edition, *Who's Who in the East.* Married December 25, 1930 to Ruth Elizabeth Worsham, born December 31, 1904 at Denver, Colorado, daughter of John Mettauer Worsham and Lillian McGill. They lived in Wilmington, Delaware, and had three children:

(1) George Muller Walker, born January 2, 1932 Washington, D. C. He was a minister; married in York, South Carolina, January 25, 1957 to Lillian Wanda Wiggins, born May 24, 1930 at Cowpens, South Carolina, and divorced after three children. He married second October 28, 1972 to Ruth Fowler Hilsberg, born February 9, 1936, who had four children from a prior marriage. His children included:

(a) Julie Ann Elizabeth Walker, born July 16, 1960 at San Antonio, Texas.

(b) Katherine Amelia Walker, born December 13, 1962 at Abilene, Texas

(c) George William Walker, born October 12, 1965 at Albany, Texas

(2) John Richard Walker, born March 14, 1942 at Wilmington, Delaware. He was a stockbroker there and married June 1, 1968 Marie Elizabeth Proud, born March 24, 1948. A daughter, born at Wilmington:

(a) Barbara Lee Walker, born March 23, 1969

(3) William Randolph Mettauer Walker, born September 9, 1944. An accountant in Wilmington, he married February 14, 1970 to Linda Low Steeley, born February 24, 1950 at West Chester, Pennsylvania, the daughter of Charles Steely and Flora Ganine. They had a daughter, born at Wilmington:

(a) Deborah Ann Walker, born April 6, 1974

b. Robert Muller Walker, born July 18, 1909. He was an examiner at the Patent Office; married October 22, 1945 to Louise Elizabeth Berchtold, born November 3, 1914

Washington, D. C., daughter of Joseph Frank Berchtold and Clara Pittman. Four children, born in Washington:

    (1)   Robert Louis Walker, born 1947; died 1948

    (2)   Frank Lawrence Walker, born July 7, 1949

    (3)   Helen Elizabeth Walker, born June 3, 1951

    (4)   Jean Louise Walker, born April 2, 1954. Married June 9, 1973 Charles Donald Boyer, born April 22, 1944 in Baltimore, Maryland.

  c. Helen Ruth Walker, born in Washington, September 2, 1917, and married August 14, 1948 Robert Otho Zeller, born November 21, 1917 at Hagerstown, Maryland. He was an oceanographer; she was a teacher; they had children born in Washington, D. C.:

    (1)   Evelyn May Zeller, born February 17, 1951

    (2)   Robert Otho Zeller, Jr., born July 19, 1952

CHILD 7

Mariamn Purdum
1837-1913

This daughter of Jemima King (1805) and John Lewis Purdum (1798), was born March 21, 1837 at Browningsville, Maryland, and died January 14, 1913 in Trinidad, Colorado. Married December 23, 1859 in Frederick County to Joseph Asbury Beall, born March 19, 1838 at Damascus, Maryland, and died October 15, 1898 in Trinidad, Colorado. The two are buried there in the Odd Fellows-Masonic Cemetery. Very soon after their marriage, they moved from Maryland to Lawrence, Kansas, travelling in an old horse-drawn jersey wagon. In 1872, they moved on west by train to Granada, Colorado, and from there by covered wagon to Trinidad, where they first lived in an adobe house. An account of their family appears in *Colorado Families, A Territorial Heritage*, from which much of this information has been taken.

In Maryland, Joseph had been a teacher for a time, and toward the end of the Civil War, was a volunteer in the Kansas State Militia. In Colorado, he was a builder, helped organize the Public Library, served as City Superintendent of Buildings, and was active

151

in other civic capacities. After moving to Colorado, Joseph changed the spelling of the family name from Beall to Bell, and it will be reported here in that fashion. They had children, born in Lawrence, Osage County, Kansas:

1. John Lewis Bell, born and died August 23, 1860.
2. Roberta Eugenia Bell, born August 22, 1861 and died August 21, 1927 of a heart attack in Denver, Colorado. Married September, 1892 to Dr. Robert Kettner of Michigan, in Trinidad, Colorado. He died March 8, 1947 in Albuquerque, New Mexico, and both are buried in Trinidad, Colorado. He was a dentist, practicing in Denver, and they had two children:
    a. Eugene Charles Kettner, born October 18, 1895 in Trinidad, Colorado, and died 1975 in Northport, New York. Married August, 1923 in Denver, Colorado, to Adaline Havens, born there March, 1900. A dentist, he served in Veteran's Hospitals, and had three children:
        (1) Jeanette Kettner, born c.1924 in Livermore, California. Married twice: first to Norris in New York, and second to Dzmas. Two children born to the first marriage at Northport, New York:
            (a) Brett Norris, born 1960
            (b) Mitchell Norris, born 1961
        (2) Robert Eugene Kettner, born June 19, 1925 in Alexandria, Louisiana. Married 1947 at Stockton, California, Beryl Fayette, born January 14, 1926 at Tillamook, Oregon, the daughter of John Fayette and Carolyne Chinn. Robert was a West Point graduate, served in the Army for seven years and later worked with power companies in Michigan, Georgia and California. Children:
            (a) Ronald Kettner, born May, 1950 in Albuquerque, New Mexico.
            (b) Michael Kettner, born July, 1952 in Alexandria, Louisiana; died November 15, 1973.
            (c) Mark Kettner, born July, 1956 in Pittsburg, Pennsylvania.
            (d) Eric Kettner, born January, 1958 at Pittsburg.

(e) Jill Kettner, born April, 1967 at Jackson, Michigan

    (3) Susan Kettner, born August 1, 1928 in Denver, and died there 1958. Married October, 1945 to Godfrey DeGilse Etter, and had a son:

        (a) Grady D. Etter, born July, 1947

b. Mariamne Jeanette Kettner, born November 28, 1900 in Trinidad, Colorado. Married July, 1929 in Estancia, New Mexico to Fred Jay Geyer, born September 18, 1889 in Niles, Michigan; died November 1, 1975 at Albuquerque, New Mexico, a son of Joseph Geyer and Anna Bliss.

3. Maretta Aletha Bell, born April 9, 1863 and died August 20, 1864

4. Exorenia Jemima Bell, born November 26, 1864 and died September 8, 1865

5. Joseph Charles Bell, born March 7, 1872 and died March 20, 1932. Married September 5, 1901 to Bessie Welton Sherman, born March 17, 1884 in Chillicothe, Missouri, and died January 4, 1953, daughter of William Owen Sherman and Nellie Mae Palmer. Joseph was a graduate of George Washington University in Washington, D. C., and practiced law in Colorado, also serving in a number of civic and public capacities. They had eight children:

a. Catherine Roberta Bell, born July 25, 1902, died June 11, 1975 in Denver. Married in Trinidad September 5, 1923 to Edgar Ernest Evans, born April 22, 1896 in Baltimore, Maryland, and died March 11, 1977 in Denver. He was a son of John Wesley Evans and Margaret Leland. They had children:

    (1) Catherine Roberta Evans, born July 8, 1924 in Boulder, Colorado. Married May 17, 1947 at Carney's Point, New Jersey, to John Allen Stroud. He was born September 17, 1921 in Berkeley, California, son of John Allen Stroud, Jr. and Anna Elizabeth Dodge. Three children:

        (a) Sally Palmer Stroud, born October 5, 1949 in Palo Alto, California

- (b) Thomas Whitney Stroud, born November 29, 1951 in San Francisco, California.
- (c) Elizabeth Randall Stroud, born December 18, 1955 in Sacramento
- (2) Robert Edgar Evans, born January 23, 1927 in Baltimore, Maryland. Married August 23, 1947 at Penn-Grove, New Jersey, to Faith Yvonne Marts. She was born September 7, 1928 at Bridgeton, New Jersey, daughter of William Raleigh Marts and Reba Ann Donaldson. Four children:
  - (a) Douglas Robert Evans, born March 23, 1948
  - (b) Eric Barclay Evans, born June 5, 1952 at Salem, New Jersey
  - (c) Todd Wesley Evans, born December 20, 1956 at Salem. Married June 11, 1977 at Denver, Colorado, Mary Lou Hitchcock, born March 31, 1959 at Kermit, Texas.
  - (d) Tamra Rachell Evans, born April 13, 1965 at Englewood, New Jersey.
- b. Joseph Asbury Bell, born March 27, 1904 in Trinidad, Colorado; died October 29, 1968 in Bethesda, Maryland. Married September 25, 1928 at Castle Rock, Colorado, to Margaret Mae Nichols. She was born November 1, 1906 at Louisville, Kentucky, the daughter of Benjamin Franklin Nichols and Wilmuth Augusta Nichols. Joseph was a doctor, serving in the Army from 1943 to 1945, and received the Legion of Merit, and the Distinguished Service Medal. They had two children:
  - (1) Margaret Joan Bell, born April 12, 1929 at Denver and married first March 17, 1951 Robert Powell by whom she had four children and divorced. She married second November 22, 1973 to Eugene Randall Cline at Naperville, Illinois; no children. Her children, born at Boulder, Colorado:
    - (a) Peggy Lee Powell, born October 11, 1951
    - (b) Joseph Dale Powell, born June 3, 1954
    - (c) Rebecca Lynn Powell: twin; October 9, 1960
    - (d) Bradford Scott Powell: twin; October 9, 1960

154

(2)   Shirley Mae Bell, born March 5, 1931 at San Francisco. Married first James William Kelly in 1964 and divorced. Married second at St. Louis, Missouri, to Burris D. LaMar, born December 20, 1923 at St. Louis, Missouri, who is a retired Navy Captain. Three children born to the first marriage and two to the second:

    (a) James Richard Kelly: September 16, 1948
    (b) William Michael Kelly, born May 30, 1953 at Bethesda, Maryland
    (c) Joseph Craig Kelly, born March 23, 1954 at Bethesda
    (d) Andrew Gilbert LaMar, born January 12, 1965 at Long Beach, California
    (e) Michelle Marie LaMar, born November 24, 1966 at Bethesda, Maryland

c. William Sherman Bell, born July 6, 1906 at Trinidad, Colorado and died February 4, 1962 in Houston, Texas. He was married there October 6, 1934 to Edythe Giraud Westerfield, born February 16, 1909, daughter of George Sumner Westerfield and Mary Edythe Giraud. He was an attorney with Shell Oil in Houston. Two children:

    (1) Earle Giraud Bell, born August 24, 1935, and died July 14, 1967. She was a concert pianist and the four-year Bell Scholarship for Excellence in Music was established in her memory.
    (2) William Sherman Bell, Jr., born February 6, 1939 at Houston, Texas. Married there January 18, 1969 Elizabeth Chesnut, born December 9, 1942 Miami, Oklahoma, daughter of Charles Caldwell Chesnut and Mary Elizabeth Bush. Children, born at Houston:
      (a) Elizabeth Anne Bell, born October 27, 1969
      (b) William Stuart Bell, born April 7, 1971
      (c) Edythe Elaine Bell: twin; November 3, 1972
      (d) Mary Katherine Bell: twin November 3, 1972

d. Charles Edward Bell, born July 16, 1909 in Trinidad, Colorado. Married June 10, 1934 to Billie Elizabeth Gra-

155

ham, born April 11, 1912 at Brainard, Minnesota, daughter of Frank Samuel Graham and Bessie Early. Charles was an electrical engineer, and was president of various banks in New Mexico, Colorado and Wyoming. After retirement, lived in Wytheville, Virginia. Children:

    (1)   Graham Edward Bell, born November 8, 1935

    (2)   Donald Early Bell, born August 31, 1937

    (3)   Charlene Elizabeth Bell, born August 28, 1939

    (4)   Bruce Charles Bell, born FEbruary 2, 1948

e.   Robert Franklin Bell, born October 21, 1912 in Trinidad, Colorado. Married December 3, 1937 in Baltimore, Maryland, Nellie May Trenkle. She was born in Alliance, Nebraska, April 3, 1910, daughter of Samuel Trenkle and Nellie Heath. Robert was a medical doctor and they had three children:

    (1)   Joseph Charles Bell, born November 11, 1940

    (2)   Robert Allan Bell, born January 12, 1942

    (3)   Catherine Marie Bell, born March 4, 1945

f.   Ely Eugene Bell, born December 26, 1915 in Trinidad, Colorado, and died July 20, 1973 at home in Columbus, Ohio. Married first June 18, 1942 in Colorado Springs to Jacqueline Barr, born there May 15, 1919 and died there February 14, 1946, daughter of Al M. and Edwina Barr. He married second March 20, 1948 to Alice Anderson, born October 9, 1917 at Sidney, Ohio. Ely held a PhD from Ohio State University, Phi Beta Kappa. He was a leading international authority on infrared radiation, and worked on the Sidewinder missile. He also taught physics at Ohio State for for thirty-one years. Two children were born to his first marriage, and one to the second:

    (1)   Robert Stuart Bell, born March 23, 1943

    (2)   Thomas Ely Bell, born February 11, 1946

    (3)   Barbara Alice Bell, born August 7, 1950

g.   Mariamne Elizabeth Bell, born July 17, 1918 in Denver. Married October 13, 1945 in Trinidad to Morris Fenton Taylor, born October 21, 1915 at Mt. Morris, New York, and died January 29, 1979 at Trinidad of cancer, son of Joseph Fenton Taylor and Mary Morris. Morris was a noted historian, and author of a number of publications and books on the history of Trinidad and the Southwest. They had children:

    (1)   Mary Elizabeth Taylor, born March 11, 1947

    (2)   Rebecca Bell Taylor, born November 28, 1950

h.   Sarah Jane Bell, born December 21, 1920 in Denver and married December 15, 1940 at Mosquero, New Mexico to Dean Caldwell Mabry. He was born August 26, 1920, son of John Nance Mabry and Letha Bryan Caldwell. He was an officer in the Army, and received the Purple Heart and the Bronze Star; later practiced law in Trinidad, and served as District Attorney and District Judge. They had three children:

    (1)   Sarah Jane Mabry, born October 27, 1941

    (2)   Letha Bell Mabry, born October 8, 1947

    (3)   Patricia Dean Mabry, born February 16, 1951

CHILD 8

Marguerite Antoinette Purdum
1838-1909

This daughter of John Lewis Purdum (1798) and Jemima King (1782) was born July 2, 1838 and died September 23, 1909. Married December 1, 1857 at her home to James Francis Penn, born February 12, 1829 in Carroll County, Maryland, and died December 11, 1909 at Browningsville; son of James Penn and Sarah Snyder. Buried there at Bethesda United Methodist Church. They had children, the first five born at Browningsville; the remainder in Howard County, Maryland:

1.   Sarah Jemima Penn, born January 17, 1859; died c.1941 at Long Corner, in Howard County; buried Bethesda United Methodist. Married December 23, 1879 in Howard to Charles Edward Mullineaux, born c.1848 in Howard County. At least two children:

a.   Roy Mullineaux.

b.   Paul Mullineaux.

2. Marianne Lewis Penn, born August 3, 1861; died July 30, 1890; buried Bethesda United at Browningsville
3. John Wilson Penn, born January 26, 1863; died January 13, 1930; buried at Howard Chapel at Long Corner. Married there March 31, 1897 to Ida May Burdette, born May 26, 1868 and died February 28, 1935, daughter of Caleb Burdette (1825) and Ann Elizabeth Brown (1832). At least two children:
    a. Marguerite Elizabeth Penn, born June 30, 1898 at Long Corner; married Leslie Kelley, born c.1895
    b. Louise Ardell Penn, born December 8, 1906; married John Gaver.
4. Edna Rachel Elizabeth Penn, born March 31, 1864; died July 1, 1866 at Browningsville
5. Lucy Gabriella Penn, born April 4, 1866; died January 22, 1952 at Mt. Airy, Maryland. Married August 16, 1893 at Long Corner to Willie Edgar Mullinix, born December 5, 1866 in Carroll County; died June 27, 1946, son of John Thomas Mullinix and Laura Virginia Dillon. Children:
    a. Julia May Mullinix, born May 21, 1899 at Long Corner in Howard County; died January 16, 1919. Married October 18, 1917 in Frederick, to John Mercer, born there c.1895
    b. Ruth Augusta Mullinix, born August 6, 1901 Ridgeville in Carroll County; died May 8, 1975 at Baltimore.
    c. Eva Virginia Mullinix, born April 18, 1903 at Mt. Airy, and died January 21, 1984 at Poplar Springs, Howard County, Maryland. Married December 22, 1923 in Frederick, to Edgar Eugene Wilson, born October 8, 1900 at Mt. Airy Junction, Frederick County.
6. James Albert Clinton Penn, born September 4, 1867, and died December 14, 1908 in Baltimore, Maryland. Married there December 13, 1893 to Mary Elizabeth Wood. He married second July 30, 1898 Ella Farrell at Baltimore.
7. Emma Roberta Belle Penn, born March 14, 1869; married at Long Corner to Ernest Benson. At least one son:
    a. Glen Benson.
8. George Washington Wesley Penn, born January 13, 1871, and died June 30, 1871

9. Wellington May Penn, born May 1, 1873; died c.1942; married to Edna J. Feaser about 1900
10. Jennie Fidelia Stern Penn, born December 7, 1873
11. Effie Augusta Penn, born April 23, 1876, and married October 4, 1916 at Hebbville, Maryland, George C. Keigler.

CHILD 9

Elizabeth Washington Purdum
1840-1907

This daughter of Jemima King (1805) and John Lewis Purdum (1798), was born February 12, 1840, and died September 26, 1907. Buried in the Damascus Methodist Church cemetery. Married November 20, 1856 to Milton Boyer, born July 13, 1834 at Browningsville; died October 24, 1912; son of John Boyer and Elizabeth Day, who were married in February 24, 1816 in Montgomery County, Maryland. In county tax lists between 1793 and 1813, the Boyer family is shown as owners of various tracts of land in the county, including parts of *Henry and Elizabeth Enlarged, Flag Patch,* and *Solomon's Roguery,* names which appear in records of other related families over the years. Milton Boyer and Elizabeth Washington Purdum had children, born in Montgomery County:

1. John Wesley Boyer, born November 15, 1857, and died February 9, 1937. Married to Amanda Wilson Day, born June 17, 1857 at Silent Valley, and died December 5, 1925, daughter of Jackson Day and Survila Ann Beall (1831). Both buried at Montgomery Chapel, Claggettsville, north of the town of Damascus. Children:
    a. Mildred Survila Boyer, born July 2, 1883 at Damascus; married December 7, 1904 William Eli Cleveland Hyatt of Mt. Airy, Maryland, born October 8, 1884, died September 7, 1929, son of John Edgar Hyatt (1859) and Edna Elizabeth Baker (1863). The family of William Eli and Mildred Survila is discussed under the father's name, in an earlier section of this Chapter 5, subtitled Child 4, dealing with the descendants of Jemima King Purdum (1831), which see.

159

b. Cora Elizabeth Boyer, born December 31, 1884, and
    married Willard Lansdale Souder, born 1885, died April
    21, 1968. They had children:
    (1) Willard Lansdale Souder, Jr., born May 15, 1908,
         died September 6, 1974. Married February 14,
         1955 Mabel Delores Pomeroy. No children.
    (2) Evelyn Elizabeth Souder, born November 19,
         1911, and married September 5, 1936 to Lewis
         Philip Allnutt, Jr., born September 25, 1910. They
         had children:
         (a) Barbara Lynn Allnutt, born December 6,
              1942. Married September 28, 1963 Thomas
              Cushman, born October 27, 1942. Children,
              perhaps born in Saco, Maine:
              1. Robin Marie Cushman: April 6, 1965
              2. Tracey Lynn Cushman: July 31, 1967
         (b) Lewis Philip Allnutt, III, born July 26, 1944,
              and married September 4, 1965 to Karen
              Christie, born June 24, 1943. Both were
              schoolteachers.
    (3) Mary Wilson Souder, born November 20, 1918.
         Married October 13, 1937 Adrian Stout Norris;
         children:
         (a) Mary Ellen Norris, born December 20, 1939
              and married January 24, 1959 to Joseph
              Aaron Green, born December 5, 1939. Lived
              at Mt. Airy, and had children:
              1. Joseph Aaron Green, III: September 23,
                  1959
              2. Melanie Suzanne Green, born January
                  26, 1961
              3. Christopher Scott Green, born February
                  20, 1964
              4. Mary Beth Green: November 7, 1965
         (b) Patricia Ann Norris, born December 29, 1940
              and married April 30, 1960 to Charles David
              McVey, born October 27, 1941. Lived at Mt.
              Airy and had children:

160

1. Roxanne Anita McVey, born October 29, 1963
2. Paula Ann McVey: July 31, 1965
(c) Charles Lansdale Norris, born March 1, 1942
(4) Philip Boyer Souder, born January 7, 1920. Married June 10, 1950 Margaret Elizabeth Hood, born April 27, 1913, died January, 1968. He was married second Virginia Hungerford. No children.
(5) Eleanor Day Souder, born June 9, 1921. Married July 24, 1941 to Fred Roscoe Gosnell, born July 5, 1919, and had children:
(a) Fred Roscoe Gosnell, Jr., born December 21, 1942, married October 21, 1967 to Dorothy Annis Townsend, born August 19, 1955 St. Petersburg, Florida. A daughter born at Aza Kuwae, Okinawa:
1. Melissa Lynn Gosnell: March 10, 1969
(b) Donna Lee Gosnell, born December 28, 1948
(6) Hazel Eileen Souder, born January 10, 1927.
c.. Willard Day Boyer, born July 11, 1888, a pharmacist. Married December 11, 1920 to Eleanor Gleason Miles, born August 4, 1895 at Cedar Grove, died 1957. Two children, born at Washington, D. C.:
(1) Donald Day Boyer, born May 5, 1925. Married June 9, 1956 to Cynthia Alice McEvoy, born September 4, 1929 at Cambridge, Massachusetts. They had children, born in New York:
(a) Richard Day Boyer, born June 20, 1958
(b) Penelope Alice Boyer: December 24, 1960
(c) Katherine Eleanor Boyer: January 17, 1963
(2) Eleanor Gleason Boyer, born January 17, 1929, and married November 16, 1958 to Larry Clemons Messick, born Washington, June 23, 1930. Two children, born in Oklahoma:
(a) Kent Clemons Messick: January 23, 1962
(b) Eric Miles Messick: June 15, 1964
d. Rosa Lena Boyer, born August 7, 1891 near Damascus, Maryland, and married October 23, 1912 at Laytonsville

161

Grover Mount Stanley, born July 28, 1892 at Damascus, and died December 17, 1949, son of Richard Harry Stanley and Fanny Gertrude Mount Stanley. Four children, born at Damascus:

(1)   Gertrude Wilson Stanley, born June 14, 1914. A teacher.

(2)   Doris Eleanor Stanley, born November 13, 1916; married Perry George Burdette, born January 16, 1915, son of John James Burdette (1875) and Cora Idella King (1878). Their children are discussed under their father's name in Chapter 8, devoted to descendants of Singleton King (1810), which see.

(3)   Hazel Margaret Stanley, born June 23, 1922; married to Joseph Haddaway Warfield, born July 8, 1921, and had children:
    (a) Margaret JoAnn Warfield: October 15, 1942
    (b) Terrence Wayne Warfield, born June 6, 1946 and married October 14, 1972 Tana Kaye Denn, born June 19, 1944.

(4)   Phyllis Ethel Stanley, born November 10, 1928. Married September 11, 1964 Edsel Davis Walker, born July 9, 1921 at Browningsville, son of Eugene Samuel W4esley Walker (1892) and Ethel Virginia Day (1897). No issue.

e.   Doris Addell Boyer, born May 8, 1899 at Monrovia, Maryland

f.   John Milton Boyer, born February 23, 1902, and married November 28, 1925 to Helen Virginia Gue, born December 24, 1905. Children:

(1)   John Alton Boyer, born December 12, 1926. Married September 22, 1956 to Cynthia Frances Rau, born May 12, 1933 in New York. He was an attorney; children, born in Washington, D. C.:
    (a) John Henry Boyer, born June 18, 1959
    (b) Bruce Alton Boyer, born September 15, 1960

(2)   Audry Virginia Boyer, born May 30, 1934. Married May 5, 1956 to Francis Keefe, born July 26,

1932. Four children, probably born in Silver Spring, Maryland:
   (a) Sharon Patricia Keefe: February 17, 1957
   (b) JoAnne Frances Keefe: November 25, 1959
   (c) Glenn Matthew Keefe: November 23, 1963
   (d) Kenneth Richard Keefe: December 24, 1966
  (3) Edna Maxine Boyer, born September 13, 1936. Married December 30, 1958 to Edmund Henry Lloyd, Jr., born August 29, 1934 in Washington. Children, born there:
   (a) Donna Jean Lloyd, born January 9, 1962
   (b) Teresa Diane Lloyd, born December 12, 1964

2. James Wellington Boyer, born December 23, 1859, and died January 15, 1934. Married Alice Hicks Lewis, born October 10, 1861 and died February 18, 1952; buried at Salem United Methodist Church at Cedar Grove, Maryland. Children:
  a. Mary Bird Boyer, born June 25, 1885, and married to W. Lafayette Bowman.
  b. Lyndall Lewis Boyer, born December 18, 1895; married to Fred Blaine Kitterman and had children:
   (1) Richard Kitterman.
   (2) John Kitterman.

3. Jemima Elizabeth Boyer, born October 9, 1864 at Browningsville, and died January 23, 1952; buried at Damascus. Married October 23, 1901 at Laytonsville to Adam McKendree Bowman, born October 23, 1852 and died March 15, 1932. They had children, born at Damascus:
  a. Mary Elizabeth Bowman, born April 20, 1903; married September 8, 1932 to Harry Lee Browning.
  b. McKendree Boyer Bowman, born July 17, 1911; single.

4. Jesse Darby Boyer, born October 7, 1866; married to Caroline Watkins. An infant death, and:
  a. Ruth Landella Watkins Boyer, died of measles at age 20.

5. Emma Cassandra Boyer, born August 11, 1868, and died February 11, 1950. Married Thomas Griffith Woodfield, born October 1, 1856 and died March 30, 1920. He established the Woodfield Ford dealership, and had children:

a.   John Dorsey Woodfield, born November 3, 1887; died
     July 25, 1953. Married December 20, 1910 to Mazie
     Marie Watkins and had children:
     (1)   John Woodfield.
     (2)   Thomas Dorsey Woodfield, born January 22, 1915
           at Woodfield, died September 16, 1990 at Olney,
           Maryland. He owned and operated the Thomas D.
           Woodfield and Sons electrical contracting business
           in Damascus. Married January 22, 1934 at Rock-
           ville, to Sarah Jane King, born May 24, 1916 at
           Kemptown, in Frederick County, and died De-
           cember 16, 1988 in North Fort Myers, Florida;
           buried at Upper Seneca Baptist Church cemetery,
           in Cedar Grove, Maryland. She was the daughter
           of Reginald Windsor King (1878). The children
           are discussed under her name in Chapter 3, de-
           voted to descendants of Middleton King (1801),
           which see.
     (3)   Paul Woodfield.
     (4)   Jane Woodfield.
     (5)   Elizabeth Woodfield.
     (6)   Grace Woodfield.
b.   Emory Cross Woodfield, born June 17, 1889, and died
     December 9, 1934. Married Myra Lavinia Watkins, born
     February 16, 1896, died 1987, daughter of William Eld-
     ridge Watkins (1867) and Emma Rose Buxton (1874),
     and had children:
     (1)   Eldridge Woodfield.
     (2)   Rose Woodfield.
     (3)   George Woodfield.
c.   Joseph Leslie Woodfield, born March 4, 1891, and died
     July 3, 1949. Married December 24, 1914 Clyta Beatrice
     Mullineaux and had children:
     (1)   Willard Woodfield.
     (2)   Beatrice Woodfield.
     (3)   Dorothy Woodfield.
     (4)   Vincent Woodfield.

d. Bradley Milton Woodfield, born July 12, 1893. Married September 4, 1919 to Marian Norman Howard. Children:
   (1) Henry Howard Woodfield.
   (2) Carolyn Woodfield, married Richard Bennett.
   (3) Bradley Milton Woodfield, Jr., born September 12, 1920; died May 9, 1923.
e. Thomas Franklin Woodfield, born January 7, 1897, and died February 23, 1897.
f. William Dewey Woodfield, born May 2, 1897, and died March 3, 1955. Married Sue Madesta Lansing. Children:
   (1) William Woodfield.
   (2) Susan Woodfield.
g. George Washington Woodfield, born January 25, 1908. Married Elizabeth Shaw Virts. Children:
   (1) Nancy Woodfield.
   (2) David Woodfield.
   (3) Mary Ann Woodfield.
6. Mary Louana Boyer, born March 9, 1870, and died June 28, 1945. Married Alonzo Clagett Watkins, born July 28, 1867, died January 25, 1946, son of Edward King Watkins (1837) and Sophronia R. Phelps. Their descendants are treated under the father's name, which see.
7. George Milton Boyer, born May 22, 1872 and died September 21, 1956; buried at Boyer Memorial Chapel. This is the Reverend Doctor George Milton Boyer, married December 24, 1902 to Annie Marie Bowman, born January 27, 1877 and died January 20, 1974, only daughter of Aden McKendree Bowman. They had children:
a. Susan Elizabeth Boyer, born May 14, 1905 in Damascus, and died February 26, 1993, single. She held a master's degree from George Washington University, and taught school in Montgomery County.
b. Milton McKendree Boyer, a doctor, born March 25, 1907. Married March 20, 1954 Helen Warfield Souder, daughter of Archie W. Souder (1884), and had children:
   (1) Sally Ann Boyer.
   (2) George Boyer.
   (3) McKendree Warfield Boyer.

c. George Wesley Boyer, born December 25, 1911. Married April 24, 1934 to Willie Beatrice Drye, daughter of John Drye of North Carolina. At least one child:
   (1) Mary Jo Boyer, married William Lambert.
d. Annie Mary Boyer, born November 20, 1916. Married April 30, 1943 to Charles Benjamin Cramer, III. They had children:
   (1) Charles Benjamin Cramer, IV. Married to Nancy Browning.
   (2) McKendree Cramer.
   (3) George Cramer; married Norma.
8. Sarah Rebecca Boyer, born October 6, 1874, and died August 11, 1926. Married to Claude H. Burdette, born May 17, 1872; died May 29, 1938, son of John Edward Burdette (1845) and Elizabeth J. King (1845). They had children, discussed under their father's name in Chapter 13, devoted to descendants of Edward J. King (1821), which see.
9. William Everest Boyer, born May 4, 1878, died July 8, 1951. Married to Amelia C. Baker, who died July 8, 1951 at Damascus, and had children:
a. Wilfred Everest Boyer, born November 12, 1905; died March 19, 1975. Married August 4, 1929 to Evelyn Deardoff.
b. Milton Baker Boyer, born December 15, 1906; died May 2, 1975, single.
c. Ethel Boyer, born July 17, 1908, and died November 18, 1908
d. Ralph Lewis Boyer, born 1910, and died February, 1965. Married to Barbara Shorter.
e. Helen Amelia Boyer, born May 16, 1912, died July 18, 1970. Married first June 6, 1934 to Herndon Maloney, and second to Francis Carter. One child, first marriage:
   (1) Robert Maloney.
10. Alice Orlean Boyer, born c.1881 at Damascus, died December 8, 1946. Married December 24, 1902 to Granville Eggleston Kinsey, born January 1, 1880 and died August 17, 1942. They had children:

a. Edwin Reese Kinsey, born October 14, 1903, died June 12, 1963. Married September 1, 1925 to Jane Ayton. At least one son:
   (1) Edwin Reese Kinsey, Jr.
b. Mary Columbia Kinsey, born October 27, 1906, married November 3, 1923 to Arnold Raymond Stull. Children:
   (1) Mary Orlean Stull.
   (2) Arnold Raymond Stull, Jr.
   (3) Carolyn Stull.
   (4) Jane Stull.
c. Howard Granville Kinsey, born September 22, 1908 and married March 9, 1929 to Edna Elizabeth Gosnell, and had children:
   (1) Dorothy Kinsey.
   (2) Robert Kinsey.
d. George Milton Kinsey, born January 9, 1910, and died September 17, 1910.
e. Alice Elizabeth Kinsey, born April 1, 1919, and married December 25, 1941 to Albert Thomas Phillips. Children:
   (1) Thomas Phillips.
   (2) Albert Phillips.
11. Washington Roby Boyer, born September 17, 1883, died December 5, 1931. Married Myrna Miles; no children.

CHILD 10

William Henry Harrison Purdum
1841-1923

This son of John Lewis Purdum (1798) and Jemima King (1805) was born November 27, 1841, and died September 18, 1923; buried at Browningsville. Married November 5, 1864 Mary E. Lewis, born January 6, 1843 and died February 22, 1917, the daughter of Arnold T. Lewis and Sarah Watkins. William Henry and Mary had children:
1. Roberta Grant Purdum, born September 17, 1865; died January 12, 1903 at Browningsville, Maryland. Married June 16, 1887 in Frederick to Preston Clairsville Day, born c.1860, a

167

distant relative. He was born October 21, 1859 and died October 21, 1931, son of Rufus King Day (1827) and Ann Priscilla Brandenburg (1831). Roberta and Preston had children:

    a. Harold Lewis Day, born November 7, 1888

    b. Wilfred Preston Day, born July 13, 1890

    c. Ralph King Day, born September 6, 1897

2. John W. Purdum, born c.1867

3. Florida J. Purdum, born August 9, 1868; died June 13, 1953. Married December 27, 1898 George M. Linthicum, born July 28, 1869; died January 20, 1948. No children.

4. Rosa Belle Purdum, born April 8, 1870; died January 13, 1952. Married December 24, 1896 to Samuel H. W. Browning, born August 15, 1866; died August 25, 1937. They had children:

    a. P. Maurice Browning; married Nell E. Thompson.

    b. Harry L. Browning, married Elizabeth Bowman.

    c. Mary Ellen Browning, married William Leroy Williams, born 1902 and died 1940. Children:

        (1) Browning Williams.

        (2) Robert Williams.

        (3) P. Maurice Williams.

        (4) Franklin Williams, married Shirley Newman.

5. William L. Purdum, died 1950. Married December 28, 1892 to Ethel Jean Hobbs, and had children:

    a. Ethel Joice Purdum, a twin, born December, 1902. Married Rex Ruggles and had children:

        (1) Purdum Ruggles.

        (2) Bryan Ruggles.

    b. Erica Purdum, a twin, born December, 1902 and married Harold Brown Hobbs.

    c. William Carl Purdum, born March 8, 1916; and married Virgie Eleanor Day, born April 17, 1897. Children:

        (1) Rosemary Ethel Virginia Purdum, born January 10, 1917.

        (2) Erica Joyce Purdum, born November 27, 1919

        (3) William Wilfred Purdum, born August 23, 1925

        (4) Eleanor Jean Purdum, born March 7, 1922.

6. Frank C. Purdum, born 1872; died 1946. Married to Gertrude Berger. Children:
   a. Arthur Purdum, married to Eleanor Spielman.
   b. Frank C. Purdum, Jr., married to Betty. At least one son:
      (1) Frank C. Purdum, III
7. Bradley Kindley Purdum, born September 24, 1874 at Monrovia, Frederick County, Maryland. A biography of his life appears in the *Tercentenary History of Maryland*, in which it is explained that his family surname was originally Prudhomme, changed to Purdham when the family went from France to England with William the Conqueror, and finally to Purdum in Wales, where the family was found prior to emigration to America. In 1917, he organized the Hamilton Bank and was prominent in real estate as president of the Hamilton Real Estate Company, the Parkwood Cemetery Company, and the Berwick Land Company; as well as having been licensed as a pharmacist in 1900. He was married September 17, 1912 in Baltimore to Evelyn Darling, daughter of Doctor Edwin G. Darling and Anna Brendel. No children.
8. Harry D. Purdum, a doctor; married Beatrice.

CHILD 11

Emily Jones Purdum
1843-1906

This daughter of Jemima King (1805) and John Lewis Purdum (1798), was born September 21, 1843 at Browningsville, and died October 20, 1906 at Daisy, Howard County. Married November 15, 1860 to John Joseph Mullinix, born January 15, 1839 in Montgomery County; died April 13, 1912 at Daisy, the son of Asbury Mullinix and Elizabeth Fleming. The 1870 census of Montgomery County reports the family, with John owning property. The 1879 Atlas of the county records his ownership of a grist mill, a saw mill, and other property. The 1878 Atlas of Howard County indicates that he was a large land owner there as well. It should be noted that the name appears in public and private records spelled both Mullinix and Mullineaux, both of which appear to stem from

French origins, there being a town of Molineus near Paris. We will report here using the spelling Mullinix, which appears to be the most prevalent, with apologies to any member of the family accustomed to the other spelling. They had fourteen children:

1. James Asbury Mullinix, born October 29, 1861; died May 30, 1923. Married November 14, 1888 at Howard Chapel Church to Fannie Ernestine Mullinix, born August 20, 1868 and died September 20, 1950 (or 1959); buried at Howard Chapel in Howard County, Maryland. She was a daughter of Andrew Day Mullinix and Susan Jane Becraft. James and Fannie had eight children:

   a. Millard F. Mullinix, born November 24, 1889, and died May 3, 1959; buried at Howard Chapel. Married Ethel D. Buxton born January 22, 1893, died August 11, 1950.

   b. Roscoe Mullinix, born December 21, 1891, and died February 2, 1892; buried at Howard Chapel.

   c. George D. Mullinix, born September 1, 1893, and died March 25, 1915, after being kicked in the stomach by a horse. Single; buried at Howard Chapel.

   d. James Herbert Mullinix, born November 13, 1894, died December 7, 1980; buried at Howard Chapel. Married December 3, 1919 at the Kemptown parsonage to Lottie F. Watkins, born at Damascus December 10, 1898, and died June 5, 1979, daughter of Frank Watkins and Fidelia Reed. James and Lottie had children, including:

      (1) James Albert Mullinix, born January 20, 1921 and died November 22, 1994 at Sun City Center, Florida. Married to Vina Patton.

      (2) H. Winford B. Mullinix, born June 5, 1928

      (3) Margaret E. Mullinix, born December 16, 1929

      (4) Edward L. Mullinix.

      (5) David R. Mullinix.

      (6) Robert B. Mullinix.

   e. Sherman M. Mullinix, born March 21, 1898, died August 19, 1957, and buried at Poplar Springs. Married to Alta Elizabeth Molesworth, born March 15, 1904 at Poplar Springs, died November 29, 1994, daughter of William Molesworth and Margaret Cook. Two children:

     (1)   Maynard S. Mullinix.

     (2)   Margaret E. Mullinix, married to Shipley.

f.   J. Fletcher Mullinix, born 1899, died September 2, 1931. Married to Lillian White; no children.

g.   Ellsworth Mullinix, buried at Kemptown; married Louise and had one infant daughter, died June 29, 1934.

2.   John Webster Mullinix, born March 12, 1863. Buried at Damascus. Married October 2, 1897 Louise C. Etchison, born April 24, 1867 and died August 9, 1923; also buried at Damascus. She was the daughter of Lonza and Hepsibah Etchison, and the mother of three children, two of whom died quite young and are buried at Damascus:

    a.   Sheldon Mullinix, born March 9, 1900; died August 30, 1900.

    b.   Webster E. Mullinix, born March 16, 1903; died August 4, 1904

    c.   Dyson F. Mullinix, died November 6, 1993. Married at Ridgeville, Maryland, April 13, 1933 to Thelma Ruth Farrier, born July 24, 1907 at Carter, Illinois and died June 15, 1994 at the Avalon Manor Nursing Home, in Hagerstown, Maryland, while living at Middletown. She was a daughter of Charles Ephraim Farrier and Patience Derkey; attended the University of Virginia, and graduated from Towson State Normal School. Buried at the Grossnickle Church of the Brethren cemetery, Myersville, Maryland. There were three sons surviving, and her obituary names five grandchildren: Eric Mullinix, Sonji Jernigan, Charles Mullinix, Robert Mullinix, and Barbara Mullinix. The children, and their residence in 1994, were:

      (1)   Vernon Mullinix, of El Paso, Texas.

      (2)   Harry Mullinix, of Hagerstown, Maryland.

      (3)   Guy Mullinix, of Clear Spring, Maryland.

3.   American Addison Ellsworth Mullinix, born August 29, 1864, and died March 14, 1948 at Daisy, in Howard County. Married December 16, 1886 to Laura Belle Mullinix, born March 25, 1864; died April 2, 1933 at Daisy; the daughter of Andrew Day Mullinix and Susan Jane Becraft. They had children, born in Howard County, Maryland:

a. Hattie Willard Mullinix, born November 14, 1887; died June 14, 1888 at Daisy; buried at Howard Chapel.

b. Harrison Ellsworth Mullinix, born January 20, 1888; died about December 25, 1956. Married December 14, 1914 to Edna Hobbs.

c. Norman Ernest Mullinix, born August 19, 1890 Howard County, Maryland; died December 24, 1971 at Woodbine, while living at Ellicott City, Maryland. Buried in McKendree cemetery, Howard County. Married November 25, 1914 Pauline Kathryn Hartsock, born January 25, 1894, daughter of Archie Clifton Hartsock (1869) and Cora Virginia Slagle (1866). Children:

(1) Walter Clifton Mullinix, born November 16, 1915 and died October 2, 1979; buried at Montgomery Methodist Church. Married at Kemptown, August 3, 1940 Elizabeth Mae Hurley, born May 20, 1910, the daughter of Harry Gilmore Hurley and Bessie Varina Warthen. It should be noted here that this branch of the Hurley families is descended from Michael Hurley, born September 29, 1811 at Kinaugh, County Cork, Ireland. Other Hurleys discussed in this study as living in or near Clarksburg, Montgomery County, are descendants of Daniel Hurley, born c.1658, who immigrated to Talbot County, Maryland, in 1676 aboard the *Maryland Merchant*. The two branches do not appear to be related, unless centuries ago in Ireland. Children:

(a) Elaine Mullinix, born October 31, 1942, and married September 14, 1963 to Edward Blake White, born March 5, 1940. Two children:

1. Richard Edward White, born January 13, 1964.

2. Susan Elaine White, born October 21, 1965.

(b) Wayne Edwin Mullinix, born November 14, 1943; married July 8, 1967 to Judith Gude and had at least one child:

1. Sarah Frances Mullinix: September 22, 1973.
(2) Esther Mullinix, married to Walter.
(3) Paul E. Mullinix.
(4) N. Ernest Mullinix.
(5) Virginia Mullinix, born 1931, died 1972; buried at McKendree cemetery, Howard County. Married Dietrich.

d. John Day Mullinix, born October 4, 1892, died June, 1971; buried Mountain View cemetery, Alpha, Maryland. Married November 26, 1919 to Mary Musgrove, born c.1896, and died June 1, 1959, a daughter of William Musgrove and Catherine Lyons Crooks. His obituary states there were fourteen grandchildren and a number of nieces and nephews. His children included:
(1) John David Mullinix.
(2) Katherine Mullinix, married to Dorcus.
(3) Ruth Mullinix, married to King.
(4) Lois Mullinix, married to McEveny.
(5) Mary Grace Mullinix, married to Shriver.

e. Asbury Mullinix, born May 31, 1895; died 1964 at Woodbine. Married August 3, 1918 Lillian T. Thomas, born c.1897 on the Eastern Shore of Maryland, and died 1993. She was a teacher at Cooksville, Maryland, living at Lisbon. Children:
(1) T. Straugn Mullinix, born July 6, 1920, and died May 14, 1926.
(2) Asbury Mullinix, Jr., born November 14, 1921 and died May 14, 1980 at North Fork, Pennsylvania. Married Margie June Skinner and had four grandchildren, and at least a son and a daughter:
    (a) Asbury S. Mullinix of Raleigh, N. C.
    (b) Lois Mullinix; married Busky
(3) Leonard Owens Mullinix, born June 5, 1923
(4) Robert Allen Mullinix, born October 2, 1926
(5) Sterling Mullinix, lived in Ellicott City, Maryland
(6) Eileen Mullinix, married H. Calvin Day.
(7) Dorothy Mullinix, married Lloyd Boore.

f. Ada May Mullinix, born May 1, 1897; died February 8, 1981 at Daisy. Married November 21, 1917 Leonard Leo Lewis, born January 5, 1894

g. Addison Robey Mullinix, born August 15, 1899; died December 4, 1980 at Woodbine. Married Mildred Irene Martin, the daughter of George Dorsey Martin and Una Estelle Stier. At least two sons, born at Daisy, Howard County:
(1) Kenneth Robey Mullinix, born December 28, 1925
(2) Donald Martin Mullinix, born August 9, 1928

h. Spencer Jones Mullinix, born April 7, 1902; died September 24, 1970 at Daisy; buried near Mt. Airy. Married Elizabeth Poole. Children, according to his obituary:
(1) Daughter, married Murat Seibert.
(2) Daughter, married Paul Hanigan.
(3) Daughter, married Alvin J. Irvin, Jr.
(4) Daughter, married Paul Embrey.
(5) Richard S. Mullinix.

i. Edwin Warfield Mullinix, born August 19, 1904; died June 17, 1941. Married October 27, 1929 to Lula May Cook, born May, 1907 and died May, 1969. Children:
(1) Hazel Mullinix.
(2) Laura Louise Mullinix.

j. Marie Mullinix, born October 8, 1908 at Daisy, died November 29, 1991 in Frederick, Maryland. Married to John Milton Glennon.

4. Alice Flavilla Mullinix, born Februry 28, 1867, died March 22, 1955; buried at Mt. Lebanon. Married December 29, 1886 to Basil T. Warfield, born August 24, 1859, died May 19, 1931. They had children:

a. Raymond L. Warfield, married first Bessie Allnutt, and second Dorothy Elizabeth Watkins, born April 28, 1900, died September 28, 1970, daughter of Alonzo Claggett Watkins (1867) and Mary Luana Boyer (1870). Two children from his first marriage; three from his second:
(1) Tommy Warfield, died at age 19.
(2) Clyde G. Warfield.
(3) Raymond Lafayette Warfield, Jr.

    (4)   Dorothy Warfield.
    (5)   Ellis Warfield, died at six months.
    b.   Mamie E. Warfield, married Charles Murphy; children:
    (1)   Cortney Murphy.
    (2)   Mary Alice Murphy.
    (3)   Merhle Murphy.
    (4)   Casper C. Murphy.
    (5)   Rockney E. Murphy, married Arnold.
    (6)   Harry A. Murphy.
    (7)   Wilford Murphy.
    c.   Bessie C. Warfield, born October 29, 1895 near Damascus, and died February 23, 1982 at Mt. Airy; buried at Howard Chapel United Methodist cemetery at Long Corner. Married Raymond L. Murray, who died January 1, 1946. One son:
    (1)   Calvin M. Murray.
    d.   Merhle Warfield, married Mary Leishear.
5.   Rachel J. E. Mullinix, born August 11, 1869; died February 15, 1893 in childbirth; buried at Howard Chapel. Married Arpil 11, 1892 in Montgomery County, Maryland, to Charles Edward Hilton. No children.
6.   Robert Monroe Mullinix, born October 4, 1871; died c.1945. Married October 10, 1893 to Cecilia Becraft, born 1871 and died January 9, 1964; buried at Mt. Lebanon near Damascus; daughter of Milton Becraft and Rebecca Watkins. Children:
    a.   Maud R. Mullinix; married George Gillis.
    b.   Ethel Mullinix, married Purdum Poole.
7.   Emory Elijah Mullinix, born June 4, 1874, and died October 26, 1926. Married Clara May Benson, born November 6, 1871, died February 29, 1964, daughter of Thomas Edwin Benson and Annie Green. Buried at the Damascus cemetery; Children:
    a.   E. Edwina Mullinix, born c.1900, died August 25, 1985, single. Member of the Maryland State Retired Teachers Association, the DAR, and other organizations.
    b.   Harold W. Mullinix, born 1902, died February 25, 1975. Married Leone Williams. They made their home at Maple Hieghts Farm near Damascus, and had children:

(1)   Harold W. Mullinix, Jr. At least these children:
  (a)   Deanna Lee Mullinix, married November 26, 1988 at Damascus, Gary Wayne Clever, son of Carl Clever of Middletown.
  (b)   Rodney Mullinix.
(2)   Betty Mae Mullinix, married to Barry Morris of Richmond, Virginia. They had children:
  (a)   John B. Morris, a minister; married and had children:
    1.   Jennie Morris.
    2.   John Morris.
(3)   Joyce Mullinix, married Glenn Little of Salisbury
(4)   Barbara Mullinix, married Grigg of Damascus.
  c.   Constance C. Mullinix, unmarried, a charter member of the Pleasant Plains of Damascus Chapter NSDAR.
8.   Joseph Hinkle Mullinix, born January 3, 1876; died c.1951. Married about 1902 Molley (or Mary) Evelyn Mullinix, born April 20, 1881, died 1959; the daughter of James Leonard Mullinix and Mary E. Young. Children:
  a.   James Newman Mullinix, born May 30, 1903, died July 13, 1990 at his home in Mt. Airy. Married to Gertrude Marie Poole. Children:
    (1)   Candice Mullinix.
    (2)   Newman Truman Mullinix.
    (3)   Ronnie Leakins, a stepson.
  b.   Stella Virginia Mullinix, born March 5, 1905, married August 24, 1921 to George Earl Hilton, born December 24, 1901 in Howard County, and died April 20, 1984 in Carroll County, Maryland. Children:
    (1)   Mary Amelia Hilton.
    (2)   Earl Leroy Hilton.
    (3)   Kathryn Virginia Hilton.
    (4)   Robert Philip Hilton.
  c.   Mary Adaline Mullinix, born February 12, 1907, and died November 15, 1975; buried Damascus cemetery. Married Roscoe F. Purdum. They had children:
    (1)   Allan R. Purdum of Dania, Florida (1975).
    (2)   Ernest F. Purdum.

d. Sanford Winstead Mullinix, born August 3, 1908
e. Helen Marie Mullinix, born 1911, an infant death
f. Vergie Emmeline Mullinix, born September 1, 1917. Married Clayton Grube Crouch.
g. Edith Caville Mullinix, born April 19, 1919, and married Carroll Aubrey Burdette.
h. Mazie Mullinix, born December 29, 1921, and married Frank Leslie.

9. Andrew Thomas Mullinix, born December 15, 1877, died February 20, 1929. Married Nancy Pickett.
10. Rufus Henning Mullinix, born August 20, 1880, died May 5, 1881 or February 15, 1893.
11. Mary Exeline Mullinix, born June 9, 1882; died January 16, 1941. Married November 12, 1901 to Clinton Duvall, born 1875 and died 1927, son of Celius Duvall. Children:
   a. Ralph Clinton Duvall, born July 28, 1911, and died December 7, 1915; Damascus.
   b. Purdum Duvall, died February 5, 1920 at 16 days of age.
12. Bessie Belle Mullinix, born September 26, 1884; died January 17, 1934. Married February 18, 1902 Matthew Pickett, born October 8, 1882. Children:
   a. Leland Pickett, married Elizabeth Rippeon.
   b. Emily Pickett, married Dewey Brown.
   c. Selena Pickett, married McMahon.
   d. Merhle Pickett, married Evelyn Walker.
   e. Clarence Pickett, died at about age fourteen.
13. Dorsey LaSalle Mullinix, born April 12, 1887; died May 29, 1967 at home in Lisbon, Howard County. Married September 29, 1909 to Cora Elizabeth Grimes of Baltimore, born June 12, 1891, died February 18, 1967. They are buried at Howard Chapel Methodist Church at Long Corner, and, at the time of death, he was survived by seventeen grandchildren and seventeen greatgrandchildren. His children, born at Mullinix, Montgomery County, Maryland, included:
   a. Jerome John Mullinix, born June 29, 1910; married Mary Flynn, born August 16, 1915.
   b. Helen Elizabeth Mullinix, born June 15, 1917; married Carpenter; and second to Selby.

c. Norman Dorsey Mullinix, born September 25, 1921, died December 26, 1995 at Montgomery General Hospital; buried at Sunshine. Married to Hazel M. Gordon. He was a veteran of the second world war, and a retired construction superintendent, he was a member of the American Legion and the Lisbon Bible Church, at Lisbon. At the time of his death, there were nine grandchildren and his three children:

(1) Greg L. Mullinix, of Woodbine
(2) Glenn N. Mullinix, of Mount Airy. Married August, 1979 to Barbara Jean Loy, daughter of Ernest M. and Alice J. Loy.
(3) Diana J. Mullinix, married Price of Arnold, Md.

d. Meade Claude Mullinix, born February 24, 1923, and died January 6, 1987 at Washington Hospital Center; buried at Mt. Carmel, Sunshine, Maryland. Married to Evelyn B. Gordon. At the time of his death, there were seven grandchildren, and three children:

(1) John M. Mullinix.
(2) Larry W. Mullinix.
(3) Patti L. Mullinix, married Dennison.

14. King Jones Mullinix, born August 19, 1890. Married to Anna P. Gillis, and had children:

a. Vincent Mullinix.
b. Emily Frances Mullinix, born November 1, 1909, and died January 3, 1910. Buried Howard Chapel.

CHILD 12

Eveline Webster Purdum
1845-1921

This daughter of Jemima King (1805) and John Lewis Purdum (1798), was born February 17, 1845, and died March 27, 1921; buried Bethesda United Methodist Church. Married February 16, 1864 Robert Emory Burdette, born January 18, 1841, the son of James William Burdette (1813) and Cassandra Purdum (1804), and had children:

1. Abraham Lincoln Burdette, born November 17, 1864 and died March 24, 1931. Married February 23, 1886 in Montgomery County to Georgia Ellen Waters King, born c.1867, daughter of John Middleton King (1830) and his first wife, Amy C. Brewer (1836). The descendants of Abraham and Georgia are discussed under their mother's family in Chapter 3, dealing with the families of Middleton King (1801), which see.

2. Cassandra Elizabeth Burdette, born December 29, 1866 and died May 3, 1952. Married July 29, 1895 William M. Beall.

3. John Purdum Burdette, born 1868; married December 29, 1898 to Emma Jones.

4. James Franklin Burdette, born 1870 and died October 19, 1936. Married February 20, 1897 to Iona M. Snyder, born 1878, died 1965. Burial at Wesley Grove Methodist Church in Woodfield, Maryland. and had children:

    a. James L. "Dick" Burdette, born 1907, died September 12, 1984 at Shady Grove Hospital. Married to Edna Benson, born c.1911, and died July 16, 1951 at their home in Rockville. She was resident manager of the Blandford Apartments, employed by the Town Council office for some time, and the former Miss Rockville in 1941. She was a daughter of Orion R. Benson. After her death, James L. was apparently married second to Martha R. He was a retired police officer in Montgomery County, Maryland, and had a daughter, born to his first marriage:

        (1) Barbara Burdette, born c.1940. Married Klix, and had children at Burke, Virginia:

            (a) Kathleen Klix.
            (b) Steven Klix.
            (c) Sharyn Klix.

    b. Edith Burdette, married George P. Woodfield.

    c. William Edwin Burdette, born June 22, 1917 and died July 16, 1964. Buried at Hyattstown Methodist Church cemetery. Married to Elizabeth Miles, born October 11, 1921. Children:

        (1) Judith Ann Burdette.
        (2) James William Burdette.
        (3) William M. Burdette, born June 23, 1942.

CHILD 13

James Henning Purdum
1847-1923

This son of Jemima King (1805) and John Lewis Purdum (1798), was born February 27, 1847, and died c.1923. Married first November 9, 1871 to Martha Rebecca Burdette, born January 22, 1848 and died August 26, 1883 at her home near Clarksburg, daughter of Hamilton Burdette (1794). James was married second, April 5, 1884, to Sarah Edith Lewis, born c.1856 and died February 12, 1933 at Browningsville. Children, four born to his first marriage and four to the second:

1. Jemima Elizabeth Purdum, born April 7, 1874; died June 30, 1935. Married April 12, 1892 to Elias Vinson King, born August 28, 1869 and died June 17, 1937, son of Charles Miles King (1814) and Harriet Brewer (1830). Elias and Jemima Elizabeth are buried at the Clarksburg United Methodist Church. Two of their children are buried nearby; there were at least three:
   a. Charles Maury King, born February 3, 1896, and died August 10, 1978
   b. Myrtle Purdum King, died July 7, 1898; lived eight days
   c. Ora Henning King, born July 18, 1910; died September 26, 1968. Married to Iris Watkins, born November 16, 1914; died May 24, 1984. Both are buried at Clarksburg United Methodist cemetery. A son:
      (1) Oliver Henry King, born August 12, 1941
2. Exie Purdum, married December 19, 1899 to Eugene Angelo Jamison and had children:
   a. Estelle Jamison, married Bryan Barr.
   b. Edith Jamison, single.
   c. Claude Jamison, married Morningstar.
   d. Purdum Jamison, single.
   e. Leo Jamison, single.
3. William H. Purdum, died March 27, 1873 at two months
4. James F. Purdum, born August 11, 1876 and died June 23, 1944; buried at Clarksburg United Methodist Church ceme-

tery. Married October 25, 1905 Nettie E. Burdette, daughter of William A. Burdette (1849). Two children:

    a.   James William Purdum, born April 4, 1908, died July 14, 1990 and married to Julia E. Davis, born January 24, 1910 and died February 22, 1937. He was married second to Velma Ray, who survived him. Children, perhaps one born to each marriage:

        (1)   James J. Purdum; married Lorraine Cole, and had a daughter:

            (a)   Kimberly Purdum, born 1966

        (2)   William R. Purdum.

    b.   Mary Evelyn Purdum, born May 3, 1912; married to Claude Rufus Purdum, the son of Urner S. Purdum (1878) and Ollie Burdette (1882); and had children:

        (1)   Catherine Purdum, born 1936; married to Darryl Armstrong and had a son.

        (2)   Jefferson L. Purdum, born 1940 and had children.

5.   Manie Purdum, born January 29, 1886; married April 19, 1905 to William Milton Dutrow and had children:

    a.   Grace Dutrow.

    b.   Robert Dutrow.

6.   Louis Windom Purdum, born December 7, 1892 and died November 27, 1893.

7.   Edith Lillian Purdum, born February 19, 1895; married 1913 Elwood Elliott Barr of Gaithersburg. Two children were born, and she married second to William Pearre. Her children were:

    a.   Velma Barr.

    b.   Margarette Barr.

8.   An infant death, September 16, 1897.

CHILD 14

Benjamin Franklin Purdum
1851-1882

This son of Jemima King (1805) and John Lewis Purdum (1798), was born March 7, 1851, and died June 29, 1882. Married

November 20, 1875 Sybelle M. Browning of Frederick, born c.1856. They had children, and after his death, she was married secondly December 22, 1885 in Frederick County to Richard H. Bennett, born c.1857. The children of Benjamin Franklin were:

1. Imogene Purdum, born December 5, 1878 and died 1944. Married December, 1901 to Edward Louis Baker, born 1876 and died 1939 at Kemptown. A daughter:
    a. Estelle Baker, married Bernard Gloyd; two children.
2. William Franklin Purdum, born January 8, 1880, and died November 4, 1933 at Kemptown. Married February 1, 1910 to Elsie M. Warfield; no children.
3. Edith E. Purdum, born December 9, 1876 and died September 26, 1966 at Browningsville. Married April 25, 1899 to Maurice M. Snyder, born February 20, 1876 and died August 31, 1967 at Browningsville. Four children:
    a. Purdum Snyder.
    b. Forest Snyder.
    c. Parepa Snyder, born July 1, 1913 at Browningsville, and died September 1, 1990 at Tucker, Georgia. Married Albert E. Andelman; no children.
    d. Elsie Snyder, married Bun Kinsey.
4. Ethel M. Purdum, born February 6, 1883, a little more than seven months after her father's death; died August 14, 1885.

Edward King
1740-1784
*

*

John Duckett King
1778-1858
*

*

Harriet Ann King
1807-

*   *   *   *   *

*

* * Elizabeth M. Day 1826

*

* * Rufus King Day 1827

*

* * Harriet Ann W. Browning 1838

*

* * Luther Henry Harrison Browning 1840

CHAPTER 6

Harriet Ann King
1807-

This daughter of John Duckett King (1778) was born c.1807 (1811, according to the census), and married December 16, 1824 in Frederick, Maryland, to Luther Day, born August 26, 1803, son of James Day (1762), and his second wife, Sarah "Sallie" Warfield. She and Luther Day had two children. She married secondly c.1835 Luther Martin Browning, born c.1810, son of Archibald Browning. Luther Martin was a blacksmith and a farmer, and they had at least two children, listed last following. They appear in the 1850 census for Montgomery County, where he is listed as born c.1813, and Harriet born c.1808. There are just the two youngest children in the household. In the 1860 census, Luther and Harriet appear, with only their youngest son still living at home. After her death, Luther Martin Browning was married second to Corilla Soper, who was apparently born c.1829, the daughter of Ignatius Soper (1785) and Ann Browning (1796). They had two children.

The descendants of Luther Day and Harriet Ann King are discussed through several generations in *James Day of Browningsville and his descendants: A Maryland Family,* published by Jackson H. Day at Columbia, Maryland, February, 1976. We will not attempt to cover all the detail found there, and highly recommend that publication to the serious researcher into this particular branch of the greater King family. The book can be found at the library of the Montgomery County Historical Society, Rockville, Maryland.

The four known children of Harriet Ann King from her two marriages are listed following. Each of them will be discussed in further detail following the general family listing:

1.   Elizabeth M. Day, born c.1826
2.   Rufus King Day, born May 13, 1827
3.   Harriet Ann W. Browning, born c.1838
4.   Luther Henry Harrison Browning, born March 11, 1840

CHILD 1

Elizabeth M. Day
1826-1915

This daughter of Luther Day (1803) and Harriet Ann King (1807) was born c.1826, died c.1915. Married Elmon G. Burdette, born March 6, 1823 and died April 29, 1901. Buried at Kingstead Farm cemetery near Damascus, Maryland. Marriage license issued December 27, 1848 in Frederick County, Maryland, for marriage to Elizabeth J. Day. The family appears in the 1850 census for the Clarksburg District of Montgomery County, with their first child, in the 1860 census with three, and in the 1870 census with three. Children:

1. Harriet Ann H. Burdette, born 1850 and died September 21, 1931; married Richard Jefferson Watkins. Her obituary states that she died in Baltimore at the home of her granddaughter, Mrs. James Dayhoff, and was buried at the Pine Grove Cemetery, in Mt. Airy, Maryland. Children:
   a. Lizzie Watkins, married Horn; lived in Baltimore.
   b. Mary Laura Watkins, married to James Davis Windsor and had a daughter:
      (1) Elaine Virginia Windsor, born May 11, 1924 at Mt. Airy, and married November 25, 1950 to Guy Kenneth Howes, born July 5, 1916 at Etchison. They have a daughter:
         (a) Connie Dianne Howes, born October 2, 1955 at Frederick. Married December 28, 1974 to Richard Sheldon English.
2. Eveline H. Burdette, born c.1850, and died October October 7, 1927. Married to William S. Poole, born October 4, 1836, died February 7, 1910. Children:
   a. Lula Blanche Poole, born near Damascus, July 7, 1881; died May 17, 1951. Married June 30, 1914 to Richard Jefferson Brown, born March 8, 1867 at Purdum, and died November 17, 1942; buried at Mountain View Church. A daughter, born at Purdum:

(1) Lillian Blanche Brown, born April 10, 1918 and married December 24, 1942 to Richard Marvin Day, born May 24, 1913 near Browningsville, son of James Start Day (1865). No children.

b. Rufus Greenberry Poole, born June 1, 1882, died June 4, 1932. Married Ella Murray Miles, and had children, born at Clarksburg, Maryland:

(1) William Lemuel Poole, born May 3, 1918, and married September 25, 1947 Christina S. Smith. Married second on April 10, 1967 to Alice Rae Williamson, born February 24, 1920 at Meridian, Mississippi.

(2) Evelyn Martha Poole, born December 14, 1921. Married November 28, 1946 to William W. McKimmy, born March 4, 1917 at Dickerson, Maryland. Children:
(a) William H. McKimmy, born May 21, 1948
(b) Carol Ann McKimmy, born April 24, 1950. A nurse, she married October 19, 1974 to Richard Paul Hefner.

c. Clarence Robert Poole, born July 14, 1888; and married to Lillie Mae Beall and had three children. Married second February 26, 1933 to Dora Irene Beall, born 1893 in Purdum; no children. The three children were:

(1) Thelma Mae Poole, born June 16, 1912, buried at Fort Rosecrans, California. Married to Laurence Unglesbee. One daughter. She married second Milton Hubbard. Her daughter was:
(a) Doris Unglesbee, born September 21, 1928 at Germantown. Married Emahiser and had two children. Married second Noyes and had one child. Married third James Gervice Fouts of Winston-Salem, North Carolina, and had two children:
1. Frank Wayne Emahiser: April 12, 1947
2. Dorene May Emahiser: July 16, 1948
3. Cheryl Lynn Noyes: October 29, 1950
4. Geri Sue Fouts: La Mesa, California

          5.   James Gervice Fouts, Jr., born August 11, 1959

    (2)   Mary Evelyn Poole, buried at Methodist cemetery in Laytonsville. Married to William G. Linthicum, and had three children:

        (a)   William G. Linthicum, Jr.

        (b)   Clarence Robert Linthicum.

        (c)   Betty Linthicum, married to Emory J. Nester, and lived at Dublin, Virginia

    (3)   Etta Poole, died single.

d.   Ethel L. Poole, married Cleveland Beall, born March 8, 1883, died March 8, 1942; no children. She married second Charles Orme; no children.

3.   Frances America Cornelia Burdette, born January 21, 1857 and died October 29, 1919. Married John Wesley Brown, born April 9, 1850, died October 29, 1919, son of Ephraim Brown and Rhoda J. Watkins. Buried at Montgomery Chapel cemetery, Claggettsville, Maryland. Eleven children, born at Purdum, Maryland:

a.   Charles Monroe Brown, born October 11, 1878, died March 6, 1900 of measles, single.

b.   Dorothy Bell Brown, born August 8, 1881 near Purdum, Maryland, and died November 15, 1952. Married Arthur Burdette, born March 5, 1881, died November 19, 1951, son of Perry G. Burdette (1849). Buried at Montgomery Chapel, Claggettsville. Children:

    (1)   Arthur Russell Burdette, born December 1, 1905 at Poplar Springs. Married November 6, 1929 Goldie Marie Harrison, born January 18, 1906 at Woodbine. No children; divorced. He married second Margaret Marie Shepard, born March 25, 1915. No children.

    (2)   Beatrice Ardean Burdette, born February 11, 1910 at Poplar Springs, died November 2, 1966; buried at Montgomery Chapel, Claggettsville. Married August 22, 1929 to Elbert Welsh, born April 27, 1904 at Mt. Airy, son of William Thomas Welsh and Elsie Pearl Lowman. One son:

(a) Elbert Welsh, Jr., born March 29, 1930 at Frederick. Married June 23, 1951 Martha Eloise Reed, born November 26, 1932 at Blacksburg, Virginia, the daughter of Chymer Reed and Effie East. Two children:
1. Terry Lee Welsh: November 28, 1953
2. Michael Stevens Welsh, born September 1, 1957

(3) Albert Austin Burdette, born September 14, 1912 at Poplar Springs. Married September 17, 1936 to Julia Mae Buck, born August 26, 1912 at Murdo, South Dakota, daughter of Francis Marion Buck and Ada Iola Billips. Children:
(a) Joan Marie Burdette, born May 1, 1939. Married July 18, 1964 Alvin Ambrose Lehr, born October 19, 1933 at Baltimore, son of Lenard Harry Lehr and Mamie Mary Dare. A daughter, born there:
1. Ann Marie Lehr: September 2, 1965
(b) Joyce Mae Burdette, born July 5, 1941. Married February 14, 1958 John Stanley Goodwin; four children and divorced. Married second December 14, 1968 to John Frederick Spaulding, born July 9, 1941 at Ogdensburg, New York. One child. He adopted her children from the first marriage in May, 1969, and they had one child. Her children were:
1. Michael Allen Goodwin: August 4, 1958
2. Kathy Lynn Goodwin, born May 8, 1960
3. John Stephen Goodwin: March 19, 1964
4. Linda Kay Goodwin: August 13, 1965
5. Debora Jean Spaulding: July 7, 1970

c. Roby Harriman Brown, born August 6, 1884 near Purdum, Maryland. Married August 17, 1911 to Virgie Estelle Price, born July 15, 1893 at Dickerson, died February 25, 1966. Children:

189

(1) Nora May Brown, born March 7, 1912. Married February 15, 1930 to Maurice Alton Shipley, born July 13, 1905 at Browningsville. Children:

(a) Fred Alton Shipley, born March 2, 1931. Married June 15, 1952 to Doris Lorraine Remsburg, born December 10, 1932 and had children, born at Frederick:
  1. Dianne Marie Shipley: June 27, 1959
  2. Joan Michelle Shipley: May 11, 1963

(b) Carroll Wilson Shipley, born July 28, 1932, and married July 11, 1961 Kathleen Virginia Kane, born January 8, 1932 in Washington, D. C.; no children.

(c) Donald Lee Shipley, born September 5, 1934, and married October 21, 1961 Louise Frances St. Clair, born August 28, 1939. No children.

(d) Robey Lewis Shipley, born August 31, 1937, and married September 2, 1962 Patricia Ellen Loun, born August 26, 1943 at Frederick. Children, born there:
  1. Robey Lewis Shipley, Jr., born February 29, 1964
  2. Roxanne Rene Shipley: March 24, 1968

(e) Maurice Linwood Shipley, born October 10, 1942. Married December 29, 1967 Beverly Jean Allnutt, born August 13, 1945 at Frederick. A daughter:
  1. Lynda Jeanne Shipley, born December 11, 1968 at Frederick

(f) Norita Mae Shipley, born December 15, 1944

(g) Mary Ellen Shipley, born October 26, 1948

(2) Woodrow Wilson Brown, born November 27, 1914. Married Nellie Wright and had a daughter:

(a) Violet Brown, born March 26, 1954

(3) Price Leo Brown, born June 22, 1922. He was a police officer in Montgomery County, married January 17, 1944 to Eva Mae Wright; no children, divorced. Married second March 21, 1953 Sarah

190

Beatrice Nix, born August 28, 1922 in Satolah, Georgia. No children, and divorced.

d. Hattie Ardean Brown, born February 8, 1886. Married November 5, 1910 to Delaney Floyd Brown, born November 23, 1889 at Burnt Hill, died November 7, 1966; buried at Mountain View cemetery, Purdum. Child:

  (1) Delaney Pearl Brown, born August 27, 1919, died April 24, 1974. A produce merchant, he married January 6, 1953 to Margarette Ruth Wolfe, born May 17, 1929 in Edenburg, Virginia. Children, the first two born at Gaithersburg; last at Damascus:

    (a) Terry Lee Brown, born July 21, 1955, and married Gwendolyn Mae Hilton, born September 1, 1955, daughter of Robert Maurice Hilton (1932). Children:

      1. Scott Delaney Brown: March 14, 1980

      2. Kevin Robert Brown: October 19, 1984

    (b) Delaney Anthony Brown: February 10, 1959

    (c) Pamela Ruth Brown: July 17, 1960

e. Willard Harrison Brown, born August 29, 1888, died March 28, 1969. Married June 4, 1917 Sarah Elizabeth King, born August 16, 1888 at Purdum, died January 25, 1952. Their descendants are discussed under her name in Chapter 3, devoted to the descendants of Middleton King (1801), which see.

f. Viva J. Brown, born 1889, died June 12, 1890

g. Addie Mae Brown, born September 21, 1891. Married March 31, 1920 to William Edward King, born April 9, 1860, died June 27, 1936. She was his second wife, and the family is discussed under his name in Chapter 10, dealing with the descendants of Charles Miles King (1814), which see.

h. Filmore Cleveland Brown, born October 12, 1893 near Purdum, Maryland. Married July 20, 1914 to Frances Marian Watkins, born July 15, 1895 at Cedar Grove, daughter of Noah Watkins (1846) and Julia Ann Linthicum (1850). Children:

(1)   Francis Earl Brown, born February 9, 1915. Married August 18, 1937 to Glenrose Mary Flair, born May 12, 1916 in Frederick. Children:

    (a) Allen Wayne Brown, born October 27, 1938, and married Mach 18, 1959 to Margaret Klug, born July 12, 1941 in Germany.

    (b) Francis Earl Brown, Jr., born October 5, 1941, and married November 6, 1959 Evelyn Jeanette Lawson, born August 4, 1942. They had a son, born in Frederick:

        1. Ricky Allen Brown: September 20, 1960

    (c) David Anthony Brown, born March 27, 1950, and married May 29, 1969 to Nancy Jo Nash, born September 10, 1950. One son:

        1. David Anthony Brown, Jr.

(2)   Julian Wilson Brown, born April 14, 1918, and married September 2, 1937 to Mary Virginia Purdum, born August 28, 1919, and had one child. Married second October 14, 1946 to Violet Marie Jessee, born July 18, 1927, and had three children. His four children were:

    (a) James Richard Brown, born October 19, 1940 at Shady Grove. Married April 11, 1966 to Carolyn Delores Davidson, born April 30, 1948 at Saltville, Virginia. One son, born at Olney, Maryland:

        1. Steven Gary Brown: October 18, 1971

    (b) Julia Wilhelmina Brown, born November 2, 1947 at Frederick.

    (c) Benita Lee Brown, born September 30, 1949 at Olney.

    (d) Kay Arlene Brown, born January 18, 1959 at Olney.

(3)   Doris Virginia Brown, born April 9, 1925, and married November 18, 1945 to Forrest Chipman Beane, born March 16, 1927 in Washington, D. C. They had no children.

(4) Ruth Evelyn Brown, born March 25, 1931, and married to Leon Hladchuk. One son:

    (a) Craig Sheldon Hladchuk: February 18, 1958.

i.   Norman P. Brown, born June 12, 1895, died July 23, 1895

j.   Dorsey Brian Brown, born July 22, 1896, died March 8, 1955. Married January 24, 1920 to Daisy M. Gregg, and had a son:

    (1) Irvin F. Brown, born July 8, 1921, died 1968. He married May 2, 1942 to Doris Rene Smith, born at King's Mountain, Kentucky. Married second to Florence, and is buried in the Mountain View cemetery at Purdum. Children from first marriage:

      (a) David Brown.

      (b) Lynda Brown.

k.   Lynda Pearl Brown, born November 18, 1899. Married May 5, 1929 Mertlen Long Dutrow, born July 19, 1899 at Frederick, and had a son:

    (1) Merhle Eugene Dutrow, born July 13, 1937, and married in 1957 to Mary Jane Baker. A son:

      (a) Rickey Eugene Dutrow: February 9, 1958.

CHILD 2

Rufus King Day
1827-1902

This son of Luther Day and Harriet Ann King (1807), was born May 13, 1827 at Kings Valley, in Montgomery County, Maryland, and died December 1, 1902 in Frederick, Maryland; buried at Bethesda United Methodist Church at Browningsville. Married October 23, 1849 in Frederick to Ann Priscilla Brandenburg, born February 11, 1831; died October 10, 1915 in Frederick, buried with her husband. They had children, born either in Frederick or Montgomery County, Maryland:

1.   Titus Granville Day, born September 16, 1850, died November 23, 1931. A schoolteacher, he was married October 16,

1885 to Laura Dorcas Watkins, born February 22, 1858, died September 20, 1940. No children.

2. Lattimer W. Day, born c.1852, died 1935. A farmer near Kemptown, he married after November 12, 1878 to Venia W. Browning, born 1857, died 1933; buried Providence cemetery at Kemptown. Three children:

  a. Venia Wynonia Day.

  b. Ira Eugene Day, born c.1880 near Kemptown, Maryland, and died April 10, 1955. He was a farmer in the Richmond, Virginia, area. Married December 19, 1903 to Sallie Caskie Lester, born there December 9, 1882, died 1963; buried Doswell, Virginia. Eight children, first three born at Kemptown, the rest at Doswell, Virginia:

    (1) Janice June Louise Day, born June 5, 1904, and married October 14, 1921 to Carl Paul Pflugradt, born March 11, 1900. Children:

      (a) Evelyn Damaris Pflugradt, born September 19, 1922 at Richmond, Virginia. Married April 5, 1941 Joseph Bernard Collier, born September 16, 1921, died December 29, 1970 and had children:

        1. Beverly Diane Collier, born October 20, 1944 at Richmond, Virginia. Married June 10, 1961 to Howard Sterling Mann, born March 25, 1942. Two children and divorced. Married second August 21, 1971 Eddie Steven Rusak, born August 7, 1924. Her two children were:

          a. Deborah Leigh Mann, born July 28, 1962

          b. Howard Sterling Mann: January 11, 1965

        2. Janice Gayle Collier, born April 19, 1946. Married July 25, 1964 Wesley Earl Smith, born October 9, 1942. Two children and divorced February 16, 1968. Married second August 14, 1971

Kenneth Howell Boyle, born February 9, 1934. Children from the first marriage:
  a. Wesley Earl Smith, Jr., born July 30, 1965
  b. Lisa Gayle Smith, born December 6, 1966
  3. Jayne Blair Collier, born September 21, 1953, and married June 22, 1974 Terry Crew, born March 4, 1957.
(b) William John Roger Pflugradt, born August 7, 1924. Married August 21, 1948 Margaret Earle Johnston, born April 26, 1926. Live in Virginia, and have children:
  1. Bruce Alan Pflugradt: October 3, 1954
  2. Susan Elaine Pflugradt: July 18, 1965
(c) Gretchen Anne Pflugradt, born August 6, 1926. Married April 10, 1944 Warren George Harding, born September 10, 1923. Live in Virginia and have children:
  1. Paul Jeffrey Harding: March 30, 1946
  2. David Michael Harding: June 2, 1950
(2) Claude Randolph Day, born October 21, 1906 and died October 23, 1973; buried Forest Lawn cemetery at Richmond, Virginia. Married June 20, 1933 to Alberta Mae Mehl, born November 20, 1907. No children.
(3) Thelma Lester Day, born August 27, 1910, and married December 2, 1932 Raymond Charles Traylor, born November 9, 1902. They lived at Mechanicsville, Virginia; children:
  (a) Pauline Fay Traylor, born January 18, 1944. Married July 3, 1969 Richard Daniel Paine, born July 30, 1941. One son:
    1. Richard Daniel Paine, Jr.
  (b) Forrest Raymond Paul Traylor, born February 18, 1947. Married January 2, 1969 Marilyn Paige Wilkinson, born May 30, 1948. One son:

1.   Shawn Paul Traylor September 10, 1969

(4)   Clara Lavinia Day, born March 1, 1913. She was a registered nurse, and married March 27, 1936 to Julian Leigh Richardson; divorced 1938. Married second November 30, 1940 to Gene Richard Davies; one child and divorced. Clara was married third in 1954 to Herbert Loving; divorced 1956. Married fourth December 5, 1960 Walter Lewicki, who died August 12, 1958. Married fifth November 5, 1960 to Claude Swenson Chandler and divorced April, 1964. Her child was:

(a)   Shirley Jean Davies, born July 21, 1943. Married June 29, 1962 Lloyd Michael Mounce, born October 13, 1942. Live in Oneonta, New York, with children:

1.   James Robert Mounce: June 30, 1964

2.   Tammara Lynn Mounce: August 7, 1967

(5)   Robert Adrian Day, born November 4, 1915. Married February 5, 1938 Althah Ernestine Latham, born January 8, 1918. Children:

(a)   Barbara Loretta Day, born July 4, 1939. Married August 17, 1959 Patrick L. Wright, born March 13, 1940, and had children:

1.   Robert Ashby Wright: August 7, 1961

2.   David Patrick Wright, born November 25, 1967

3.   Thomas Wright: September 25, 1968

(b)   Roberta Angela Day, born February 19, 1944. Married August 4, 1962 Shelton Lamar Brunson, born November 27, 1938. Children:

1.   Eugene Lamar Brunson: June 27, 1965

2.   Angela Elizabeth Brunson December 26, 1969

(6)   Margaret Antonia Day, born June 21, 1918. Married November 22, 1938 Thomas Otway Snead, born December 18, 1917, died November, 1962; one child. She married second July 18, 1946 to John Wallace Pecawicz, born August 23, 1915;

Major, USA retired. They had two children. The
three children of Margaret were:

(a) Judith Loraine Snead, born September 2,
1939 Richmond and married October 4, 1958
Alan G. Blewett, born February 2, 1931 at
Minneapolis, Minnesota. Live in Florida, and
have children:
1. Carla Elaine Blewett: January 3, 1960
2. Ronald Rush Blewett: October 21, 1961
(b) Brenda Inez Pecawicz, born March 14, 1949,
Richmond.
(c) Alan Eugene Pecawicz, born July 27, 1950 at
Frankfurt, Germany.

(7) Emil Rodney Day, born August 12, 1921. Married
first to Lillian Penny and divorced. Married second
September 16, 1946 to Opal, and divorced after
two children. Remarried Lillian. His children were:
(a) Susan Day, adopted.
(b) Karen Day, born January 14, 1957
(c) Scott Ronald Day, born August 14, 1958

(8) Leroy Edward Day, born January 1, 1927. Married May 18, 1947 to Mary Elizabeth Hornbuckle,
born September 3, 1925. Children:
(a) David Franklin Day, born January 13, 1949,
married to Ingrid Korth and lived in Hawaii
(b) Jean Shirley Day, born August 3, 1951. Married July 27, 1974 to Allen Cary.
(c) Michael Philip Day, born May 15, 1957

c. Melissa B. Day, born c.1883. Married John Watkins,
born 1881, died 1960. Two children:
(1) J. Latimer Watkins, married Mary. No children.
(2) Roland Watkins, married Ruth; no information.

3. Addison Singleton Day, born January 8, 1856, and died December 19, 1929. A farmer in Frederick County, Maryland, he
married Laura Washington Beall, born in Montgomery
County, January 9, 1859, died March 2, 1936. Buried at
Bethesda Methodist Church at Browningsville. Four children:

a. Harrison Edward Day, born January 6, 1888 in Frederick County, died 1920. Single.

b. Daisy May Day, born November 18, 1891, died April 26, 1968. Married to her cousin, Murray Otis Day, born September 29, 1888 in Montgomery County, died April 26, 1968. Two children:

    (1) Laura Ann Day, born May 19, 1915. Married June 21, 1938 to Jesse Downey Day, Jr., born June 30, 1914 near Mt. Airy, Frederick County. He was a farmer, raising beef cattle; she was an elementary teacher. Two sons:

        (a) David Ellis Day, born January 4, 1943

        (b) Douglas Edsel Day, born July 11, 1945

    (2) Ruth Edna Day, born November 20, 1918; married April 17, 1940 to Henry Cornelius Krantz, Jr., born September 15, 1917 in Frederick County. They had children:

        (a) Kenneth Edward Krantz: October 10, 1941

        (b) Beverly Kaye Krantz, born January 8, 1947

c. Annie Griffith Day, born August 18, 1896, died February 8, 1905.

d. Rufus Addison Day, born February 21, 1901 in Frederick County, died June 19, 1932; buried at Providence Church in Kemptown. Married to Myrtle Day, born September 7, 1901, and had children:

    (1) Rufus Addison Day, Jr. Married Mary Jane Pryor; no children.

    (2) William Emory Day, married Helen Willier; a son:

        (a) Howard Michael Day, born June 24, 1948 at Baltimore. Married April 4, 1966 to Cheryl Jeanne Harrison, born August 30, 1948. They live in Baltimore; two children, first born at Olney; second at Baltimore:

            1. Gregory Robert Day, born November 27, 1966

            2. Joelle Denise Day: April 27, 1971

4. Altona Bovincia Clintinchia Day, born October 22, 1857 and died November 19, 1934. She died single, remaining at home

to care for her invalid mother. Buried Bethesda Methodist Church cemetery at Kemptown.

5. Preston Clairsville Day, born October 21, 1859, died October 21, 1931. A pharmacist in Washington, D. C., he was married after June 14, 1887 to Roberta Grant Purdum, born September 17, 1865, died January 12, 1903. Buried at Bethesda Methodist Church at Kemptown. Three children:

   a. Harold Lewis Day, born November 7, 1888, died September 13, 1968. A pharmacist who operated his father's store after his death, he was married November 28, 1914 to Julia Wrightman Denham, born September 3, 1885, died January 17, 1969. A daughter:

      (1) Virginia Lee Day, born July 14, 1918. Married June 10, 1939 to Theodore W. Chase, Jr., born December 13, 1914. Divorced after children, and later married Will Browning Kern. Her children:

         (a) Theodore W. Chase, III, born May 8, 1940 at Schenectady, New York, and married Marilyn R. Moore, born at Baltimore.

         (b) Julia Ann Chase, born October 31, 1941 at Columbus, Georgia. Married to Richard M. King, born in Baltimore. Children:

           1. Douglas M. King: September 10, 1963

           2. Holly Ann King: December 28, 1965

         (c) Philip Scott Chase, born August 20, 1953

   b. Wilfred Preston Day, born July 13, 1890, a pharmacist. He married Lucille Hill, born January 1, 1904 Marietta, Ohio. No children.

   c. Ralph King Day, born September 6, 1897, died August 23, 1858. Buried at Rose Hill cemetery, Oklahoma City, Oklahoma. Married to Dell Pemberton Slaughter, born October 20, 1892 at Woods Hole, Massachusetts. They had no children.

6. Harriet Emma Day, born c.1863 at Kemptown, and died October 29, 1949. Married February 16, 1887 to James Oliver Barnes, born April 2, 1860, died January 11, 1939. A farmer, buried at the Bethesda Methodist Church cemetery near Browningsville, Maryland. Two children:

a. Herbert Day Barnes, born March 6, 1891, died April 7, 1958. Married July 29, 1916 to Rosa May Lewis, born January 9, 1896; died September 21, 1968. Like many of the family members, she is buried at Bethesda Methodist Church cemetery, Browningsville, Maryland. Children:

(1) Dorothy Pauline Barnes, born December 4, 1917. Married June 19, 1935 to George Franklin Burdette, born September 2, 1912, died May 31, 1970, and buried at Damacus Methodist cemetery. Children:

(a) James Larry Burdette, born April 2, 1936, died February 13, 1974

(b) Dinah Elaine Burdette, born March 21, 1947 at Frederick. Married October 14, 1967 Larry Wayne Mullinix, born July 14, 1948. Live at Damascus and have a child:

1. Tammy Dawn Mullinix: July 28, 1974

(2) Anna Louise Barnes, born March 23, 1920, and married October 11, 1940 to Brandon Woodrow Duvall, born March 4, 1913 near Damascus. He was a Maryland State Policeman. Children, born at Frederick:

(a) Jerry Brandon Duvall, born March 19, 1943, and married January 9, 1971 Karen Ann Rosapepe, born November 9, 1945 at Youngstown, Ohio. He is professor of economics at Montgomery College.

(b) Jeannette Louise Duvall, born July 27, 1944, and married July 15, 1966 Meredith Hall MacKusick, III, born August 8, 1940 in Chicago. A daughter:

1. Elizabeth Ann MacKusick: December 24, 1974 at Washington, D. C.

(c) Herbert Sherwood Duvall, born December 12, 1945. Married September 22, 1967 Sandra Lynn Eagle, born November 1, 1944 at Galesville, Illinois. Two children:

1. Christopher Brandon Duvall: January 9, 1969
2. Alice Louise Duvall: October 14, 1971

(3) Vivian Bernice Barnes, born July 23, 1923, and married December 10, 1941 to Charles Hanford Browning, born December 7, 1921. Children:

   (a) Charles Hanford Browning, Jr., born July 13, 1943 and married June 20, 1964 to Patricia Lee Barnes, born October 14, 1945 at Frederick. President of Browning Construction Company; three children:

      1. Charles Hanford Browning, III: July 8, 1967
      2. Duane Edward Browning: November 23, 1968
      3. Aaron Robert Browning: May 27, 1974

   (b) Nancy Rosalie Browning, born October 21, 1945. Married July 5, 1970 Ormus Durrett Bennett, born June 19, 1946 at Cumberland, Maryland. Children:

      1. Belinda Berniece Bennett: February 26, 1971
      2. Clifton Wayne Bennett: July 31, 1972

(4) Mazie Emma Barnes, born November 8, 1926, and married July 12, 1947 to Albert Francis Rebert, born October 11, 1916 at Pottstown, Pennsylvania. Children:

   (a) Nelson Wayne Rebert, born July 2, 1952.
   (b) Debra Louise Rebert, born March 22, 1954. Married July 14, 1974 to Robert Francis Davis, born August 17, 1954 at Olney, Maryland. Child:

      1. Kathryn Debra Davis: January 29, 1975

   (c) Dennis Alan Rebert: September 19, 1958

b. Raymond Oliver Barnes, born June 11, 1893. Married to Lula Norene Day, born April 12, 1899, died October 1, 1966. They had children:

(1)   Marion Evangeline Barnes, born May 5, 1917. Married June 15, 1938 to John William Lawson, born September 21, 1912, died November 3, 1969. They had three children, and she married second February 14, 1973 to Dwight Talmadge Walker, born 1903. Her children were:

    (a) Sylvia Elaine Lawson, born August 5, 1939 and died June 10, 1943

    (b) Dianne Cecil Lawson, born February 4, 1941

    (c) John William Randolph Lawson, born May 19, 1950.

(2)   James Raymond Hamilton Barnes, born May 31, 1927. Married Mary McClairy, and had a child. He married second Pat Brashears. The child was:

    (a) Jamie Luanne Barnes, married April 29, 1973 to Gordon Alan Chertoff.

(3)   Eleanor Irene Virginia Barnes, born October 9, 1934. Married June 3, 1960 David J. Sessa, born March 3, 1938 at Hackensack, New Jersey, and had children:

    (a) Brian David Sessa, born April 5, 1963

    (b) Valerie Irene Sessa, born August 20, 1964

    (c) Kenneth Gregory Sessa, born August 4, 1969

    (d) Jennifer Danielle Sessa, born April 11, 1972

7. James Start Day, born c.1865 near Kemptown, Maryland, and died November 9, 1949. He was a farmer, and was married December 26, 1894 to Laura Helen Davis, born November 5, 1874, died February 14, 1942 and buried at Bethesda Methodist Church, at Browningsville. Twelve children, born near Browningsville:

a. Rufus Wilson Day, born November 2, 1895, died December 30, 1918, single.

b. Ethel Virginia Day, born August 2, 1897, died January 8, 1939. Married November, 1916 Samuel Wesley Walker, born December 10, 1892, died July 18, 1951. Buried at the Bethesda Methodist Church, Browningsville. Their descendants are discussed in her husband's section.

c. James Sellman Day, born July 6, 1899, died June 21, 1924. Married November 19, 1919 to Jessie Marie Purdum, born July 12, 1900, daughter of Rufus Elsworth Purdum (1869) and Alice Sardinia Baker (1867). Their children are discussed under their mother's name in Chapter 5, dealing with descendants of Jemima King (1805), which see.

d. Clarence Emory Day, born January 25, 1901, and died September 23, 1901

e. Anna Lucille Day, born July 16, 1902. Married December 27, 1924 to Rudy Leroy Brandenburg, born December 4, 1905 near Kemptown, died April 10, 1960. They had children:

(1) Betty Elaine Brandenburg, born July 25, 1925 and married June 1, 1943 to Earl Edward Dixon, born May 11, 1920 Frederick. Children, born Frederick County:

(a) Bernard Leroy Dixon: February 11, 1945

(b) Janice Elaine Dixon: October 3, 1946. Married March 2, 1963 to Dewey Douglas Tibbs, born August 22, 1943 in Virginia. Children, born in Frederick:

1. Jacqueline Elaine Tibbs, born August 12, 1963

2. Dewey Douglas Tibbs, Jr.: April 9, 1965

3. Joanne Marie Tibbs: July 22, 1966

(c) Linda Louise Dixon, born December 15, 1947 and married December 23, 1966 to Donald Wayne Linton born August 22, 1948 at Frederick. One child; divorced. She married second October 19, 1974 to Clarence John Shull, III, born January 31, 1947 at Frederick. Her child was:

1. Don Wayne Linton: December 29, 1966

(2) Mary Helen Brandenburg, born August 5, 1926. Married August 30, 1947 to Earle Lynwood Browning, born February 28, 1924. Children:

(a) Marlene Carol Browning, born June 18, 1950 and died June 11, 1972

(b) Lynette Adele Browning, born June 18, 1950, married December 20, 1972 Edward Leroy Sellers, born April 30, 1948 in Virginia. A daughter:

    1. Cresent Carol Sellers: July 14, 1973

(c) Gary Martin Browning, born April 26, 1952.

(3) Robert Leroy Brandenburg, born November 11, 1927; died November 17, 1927

(4) Charlotte Virginia Brandenburg, born March 15, 1929. Married December 3, 1954 to Paul Burlin Rosencrantz, born at Stockdale, Pennsylvania, November 27, 1922. No children.

(5) James Oscar Brandenburg, born January 17, 1933. Married June 28, 1956 to Mary Ann Walker, born February 6, 1936 at Mt. Airy. Children:

(a) Barbara Lynn Brandenburg: April 23, 1958

(b) Nancy Lee Brandenburg: December 24, 1962

(c) James Michael Brandenburg: July 9, 1966

(d) Randy Lee Brandenburg: November 25, 1969

(6) Shirley Ann Brandenburg, born June 28, 1934, and married December 4, 1951 to Charles William Emswiler, born December 24, 1925 at Timberville, Virginia. Live at Kemptown and have children:

(a) Larry Wayne Emswiler: January 30, 1953

(b) Donald Lee Emswiler: January 30, 1954

(7) Rosalie Brandenburg, born June 15, 1936. Married October 19, 1951 to Marvin W. Hubble, born June 1, 1932 at Nebo, Virginia. They live at Monrovia: children:

(a) Robert Lee Hubble, born April 27, 1952

(b) Kevin Richard Hubble: September 15, 1957

(c) Keith Allen Hubble, born July 12, 1959

(d) Brenda Lee Hubble, born December 23, 1961

(8) Franklin Rudell Brandenburg, born November 28, 1940. Married November 25, 1959 to Carolyn

Maye White, born February 15, 1942 at Sandy Spring, Maryland. Live at Kemptown; children:

    (a) Ricky Franklin Brandenburg, born November 12, 1960

    (b) Sherri Ann Brandenburg: September 21, 1963

    (c) Jeffrey Keith Brandenburg: October 11, 1966

f.   Murray Davis Day, born May 20, 1904. Married December 26, 1925 to Lois Elaine Burdette, born August 18, 1906. Children:

(1)   James Murray Day, born November 3, 1926, and married July 23, 1947 Betty Marie Beall, born December 8, 1926 at Browningsville. Children:

    (a) Brenda Jean Day, born August 20, 1948. Married September 13, 1969 Robert Osborne Drisch, born June 13, 1946 at Dickerson. Daughter:

        1.   Christy Lynn Drisch: January 23, 1973

    (b) Gary Wayne Day, born October 22, 1952. Married July 6, 1974 Wanda Kaye Shiers, born November 10, 1956 at Olney.

    (c) Joan Marie Day, born January 5, 1954. Married September 5, 1973 to Roy Stanley, born June 29, 1953 at Olney.

(2)   Kenneth Lee Day, born May 26, 1930. Married March 31, 1950 to Rowena Jane Lee. Children:

    (a) Kenneth Berkely Day, born December 6, 1964 at Bethesda, Maryland

    (b) Sherri Lee Day, born March 5, 1968

(3)   Carroll Davis Day, born July 31, 1944. Married January 9, 1965 to Jessie Darlene Kaufman, born October 22, 1946 Gaithersburg. Children, born Bethesda, Maryland:

    (a) Carol Ann Day, born January 10, 1968

    (b) Patricia Ann Day, born September 13, 1971

g.   Raymond Fout Day, born April 26, 1906. Married December 25, 1928 to Annie Sophronia McElfresh, born February 11, 1906 near Browningsville. Children:

(1) Dorothy Jean Day, born October 16, 1929, and married July 30, 1948 to Willis Webster Beall, born September 7, 1927, son of Barry Beall and Edith Burdette. Live near Clarksburg and have children:

    (a) Mark Willis Beall, born December 19, 1950, and married January 11, 1973 to Pamela Ann Mandy, born at Birmingham, Alabama.

    (b) Melanie Ann Beall, born June 10, 1953. Married June 9, 1973 Jeffrey Thomas Valcourt, born October 5, 1953 at Coronado, California.

    (c) Wendy Jeanine Beall, born March 17, 1959 at Olney, Maryland

(2) Raymond Harold Day, born December 12, 1930. Married January 27, 1951 Shirley Ann Woodfield, born January 9, 1931 at Galesville, Maryland, and had children, born at Annapolis:

    (a) Judith Elaine Day, born March 13, 1953. Married June 10, 1972 David Lee Loftice, born April 8, 1952 in Virginia. Daughter:

       1. Amanda Leigh Loftice: June 20, 1974

    (b) Cheryl Ann Day, born December 14, 1954

    (c) Cindy Lou Day, born May 18, 1957

(3) Barbara Ann Day, born July 30, 1938. Married December 20, 1958 Ralph Eugene Kemp, born October 17, 1938 in Frederick County. Children, born there:

    (a) Michael Allen Kemp, born July 20, 1959

    (b) Julie Renee Kemp, born December 11, 1960

    (c) Janiele Anita Kemp, born December 24, 1962

h. Kelsel Williams Day, born October 2, 1907. His birth has also been reported as May 20, 1904. Married December 21, 1929 to Mildred Jane Burdette, born June 12, 1910 near Damascus, daughter of Claude H. Brudette (1872) and Sarah Rebecca Boyer (1874). Six children:

(1)   Kelsel Williams Day, Jr., born March 15, 1931. Married August 24, 1951 Elizabeth Ann Lockard, born December 22, 1931 at Eldersburg. Children:
    (a) Gayle Marie Day, born August 27, 1953 at Anchorage, Alaska. Married June 25, 1971 Larry Hood.
    (b) Kevin Scott Day, born August 22, 1955

(2)   Evelyn Jane Day, born March 26, 1933 and died March 11, 1934

(3)   Maxwell Latimer Day, born March 4, 1935, and married to Shirley Ann Crum, born June 23, 1935 at Frederick. Children, born at Olney, Maryland:
    (a) Alan Christopher Day, born August 14, 1962
    (b) Brian Keith Day, born December 13, 1968

(4)   Basil Boyer Day, born July 15, 1936. Married June 9, 1957 to Sally Jo Eisenbeis, born October 10, 1937 at Williamsport, Pennsylvania. Her name has also been reported as Eisenberg. Children:
    (a) Basil Boyer Day, Jr., born January 14, 1958 at Olney, Maryland
    (b) Polly Jo Day, born November 16, 1964 at Frederick, Maryland

(5)   Janet Louise Day, born November 23, 1937, and married December 14, 1957 to Austin Delmar Rippeon, born December 11, 1932 at Frederick. Children, born at Frederick, Maryland:
    (a) Austin Delmar Rippeon, Jr.: August 11, 1958
    (b) Wesley Pierre DeVoe Rippeon: June 25, 1960
    (c) Hope Dayon Rippeon: November 23, 1974

(6)   John Marvin Day, born May 5, 1951. Married October 6, 1973 to Amanda Lou Helwig, born October 10, 1951 at Hanover, Pennsylvania.

i.   Helen Mildred Day, born June 8, 1909. Married October 20, 1927 to Carl Oscar Mullican, born June 22, 1906 near Lewisdale, Maryland, died 1978; son of Oscar Thomas Mullican (1886). The children of Helen Mildred are discussed under their father's name in Chapter 3, dealing with the descendants of Middleton King (1801).

j. Effie Madeline Day, born January 14, 1912. Married December 25, 1929 Raymond Merson Moxley, born March 6, 1909 near Kemptown. They had children:
  (1) Gloria Alvin Moxley, born December 20, 1930; married September 2, 1948 Merhle Basil Warfield, born February 26, 1927 at Etchison. Children:
    (a) Merhle Wayne Warfield, born December 15, 1950. Married June 19, 1971 to Sharon Lee Smith, born May 8, 1951 at Damascus.
    (b) Raymond Curtis Warfield: January 20, 1952
  (2) Leonard Wayne Moxley, born December 28, 1941. Married September 10, 1960 Alfrieda Mae Duvall, born June 23, 1940. Children:
    (a) Kevin Harold Moxley: November 5, 1961
    (b) Kristen Leon Moxley: July 28, 1964
    (c) Kelly Wayne Moxley: July 8, 1969
  (3) Donna Jeanne Moxley, born April 13, 1948, and married December 20, 1969 Arthur Howard Isaacs born April 6, 1948 at Thurmont. Children:
    (a) Aaron Jeffrey Isaacs, born June 6, 1972 Hialeah, Florida
    (b) Chad Jeremy Isaacs, born December 31, 1974 near Damascus, Maryland
k. Richard Marvin Day, born May 24, 1913. Married December 24, 1942 to Lillian Blanche Brown, born April 10, 1918 at Purdum, the daughter of Richard Jefferson Brown (1867). No children.
l. Hanford Perry Day, born January 28, 1916. Married December 24, 1938 to Marie Allen Chick, born September 18, 1921 near Clarksburg. Children:
  (1) Robert Perry Day, born July 26, 1940. Married July 12, 1959 Rosia Mary Green, born October 11, 1942 near Mt. Airy. Children:
    (a) Terry Ann Day, born March 7, 1960
    (b) Douglas Robert Day, born October 23, 1961
    (c) Michael Allen Day, born July 10, 1964

(2)   Evelyn Louise Day, born April 7, 1943. Married May 9, 1962 Wayne Sellman Watkins, born May 15, 1938 near Lewisdale. Children:
(a)   Catherine Marie Watkins, born June 15, 1963
(b)   Patricia Lynn Watkins, born August 12, 1967
(3)   Doris Jane Day, born March 16, 1946. Married January 19, 1967 to Alexander Paul Watkins, born January 26, 1938 at Mineola, New York. They had no children.

8.   Laura Arvilla Day, born July 11, 1867; married on December 24, 1890 to William Alfred Baker Walker, born November 1, 1867. He was the son of George Washington Wesley Walker and Rachel Browning Purdum Walker. At least eleven children, who are discussed under her husband's family, which see

9.   Langdon Storrs Day, born c.1871, died July 2, 1954. He was a pharmacist in the city of Washington, and was married November, 1896 to Maude Ozella Day, born February 16, 1871 at Browningsville, died February 4, 1924. They had three infant deaths, and one surviving child. He was married second September 2, 1924 to Sadie Elizabeth Gue, born February 18, 1901 at Laytonsville, and had a son. His two children were:

a.   Ivah May Day, born September 3, 1901. Married June 14, 1923 Trago Winter Lloyd, born December 30, 1893 at Inwood, West Virginia. He was a Methodist minister, and they had children:
(1)   Carroll Langdon Lloyd, born January 19, 1925 at Martinsburg, West Virginia. Married October 31, 1952 Phyllis Barnes, born September 5, 1928 at Lisbon, Maryland. No children.
(2)   Jeanne Winifred Lloyd, born July 1, 1930 at Frederick, Maryland. Married August 22, 1953 to Harry Nevin Keller, born May 13, 1925 at Millheim, Pennsylvania. Children, born in New Jersey:
(a)   Anne Margaret Keller: February 24, 1957
(b)   Paul Nevin Keller, born March 5, 1959
(c)   Joyce Helen Keller, born July 11, 1961
b.   Quentin Langdon Day, born October 17, 1926. Married July 30, 1961 to Ruth Virginia Woodfield, born July 26,

1942 near Claggettsville. Children, the first and third born at Frederick; the second at Sandy Spring, Maryland:
  (1)   Larry Langdon Day, born December 5, 1962
  (2)   Joseph Loren Day, born February 3, 1965
  (3)   Lisa Carol Day, born July 20, 1967
10. Nora May Day, born August 14, 1875; died March 26, 1879.

CHILD 3

Harriet Ann W. Browning
1838-

This daughter of Harriet Ann King (1807) and her second husband, Luther Martin Browning (1810), was born c.1838 in Montgomery County, Maryland. We have not yet discovered any information relative to her life, or if she reached adulthood.

CHILD 4

Luther Henry Harrison Browning
1840-1908

This son of Luther Martin Browning (1810) and Harriet Ann King (1807), was born March 11, 1840, and died January 26, 1908 at his home in the New Market District, Frederick County, Maryland. Married April 25, 1861 Sarah Louisa Brandenburg, born February 4, 1843 in Frederick County, died April 8, 1917; the daughter of Lemuel M. Brandenburg (1801) and Charlotte Kindley (1805). Like his father, he was a blacksmith and a farmer, occasionally mended clocks, and was known to practice a bit of medicine. They had children:
1. Harrison McGill Browning, born February 9, 1862; a machinist, who lived in Baltimore. Married to Mary Virginia Young, the daughter of Mrs. Sarah F. Young, and had two children:
    a.   Earl Harrison Browning.
    b.   Marie Elmer Browning.
2. Melville Newton Browning, born January 12, 1864

3. Lina M. Browning, born February 2, 1866; married Jackson Clay, and had five children:
   a. Linda Clay.
   b. Carol Clay.
   c. Sterling Clay.
   d. Mabel Clay.
   e. Thelma Clay.
4. Harriett Charlotte Browning, born c.1868, died 1934. Married to Franklin E. Spurrier and had four children:
   a. Clarence Spurrier.
   b. Stella Spurrier.
   c. Everett Spurrier.
   d. Margaret Spurrier.
5. Luther L. Browning, born March 14, 1869; married to Ida Barton. Lived in Baltimore and had three children:
   a. Holly Browning.
   b. Lawrence Browning.
   c. Agnes Browning.
6. Elizabeth Browning, born December 2, 1871
7. James Monroe Browning, born August 1, 1873, and died December 1, 1948. Married to Nannie L. Thompson and had two children, one of whom was:
   a. Algie Browning.
8. Eldridge M. Browning, born September 20, 1875, died September 3, 1947. Lived in Mt. Airy; married Annie R. Trout. One child:
   a. Layman Browning.
9. Rosella May Browning, born December 29, 1877. Lived near Frederick; married to Lewis White and had three children:
   a. Lillian White.
   b. Paul White.
   c. Murr White.
10. Agnes Matilda Browning, born May 3, 1880, died September 11, 1949. Married to Titus E. Brown in Montgomery County
11. Hepzi Edith Browning, born February 26, 1882. Married Nathan Clagett.
12. Raymond Atlas Browning, born December 10, 1884. Married Della Fleming.

Edward King
1740-1784
*

*

John Duckett King
1778-1858
*

*

**John A. King
1808-1888**
*

*

*   *   *   *   *
*

* *   Sarah N. King 1831-1901
*

* *   Jemima A. King 1934-1909
*

* *   John Duckett King 1835-1905
*

* *   Thomas Peter King 1840-
*

* *   Edward T. King 1842-
*

* *   Charles C. King 1846-1920

CHAPTER 7

John A. King
1808-1888

This son of John Duckett King (1778) was born October 1, 1808 and died February 7, 1888; and buried in the Kingstead Farm Cemetery. Family group records of the Mormon Church indicate that he was married August 29, 1829 to Susan Day, but I have found no other record to support that statement, unless she was a first marriage, and died quite early. This is perhaps the same individual listed as head of household in the 1850 census for Clarksburg District of Montgomery County, aged 41, listed as a blacksmith. Some records list his wife's name as Mary A., but the census lists Elizabeth, born c.1807. She was Elizabeth Norwood, born April 5, 1805, died September 5, 1873, and they were married January 22, 1831. She and her husband are buried on the Leslie King farm in Kings Valley, Montgomery County, Maryland. There are five children listed. The family also appears in the 1860 census, again listing the wife as Elizabeth, and this time with only three of the children, but also including one of their daughters, with her husband, and their infant child, living with her parents. They appear again in the 1870 census, this time with their son, John D. King, living with them, with his wife, and three small children. Also in the household is one Hannah Norwood, aged 60 (born c.1810), not identified, but perhaps the sister of Elizabeth Norwood, wife of John A. King. The 1880 census lists only John A. and Hannah, there listed as a King, perhaps a third marriage. The children of John will be discussed in detail following the general family listing, and included:

1. Sarah N. King, born April 22, 1831, died March 4, 1901.
2. Jemima A. King, born December 1, 1834, and died March 7, 1909.
3. John Duckett King, born c.1836, died August 22, 1905.
4. Thomas Peter King, born c.1840; married December 6, 1867 to Elvira London. Nothing more is known.

213

5. Edward T. King, born c.1842, of whom nothing is known
6. Charles C. King, born September 18, 1846, and died February 12, 1920.

CHILD 1

Sarah N. King
1831-1901

This daughter of John A. King (1808), was born April 22, 1831, and died March 4, 1901. By Montgomery County marriage license dated March 25, 1852, she was married to Obediah Stillwell Layton, born March 11, 1832, died October 18, 1895; both are buried at Clarksburg cemetery. He and his wife are found in the 1860 census of Clarksburg District, in the household of his parents, John Layton (1796) and Catharine Layton (1797). In the Renunciation books for Montgomery County, in Liber GCD 9 at folio 304, dated April 27, 1901, Charles C. King, John D. King and Jemima Browning, described as "heirs at law" in the estate of Sarah N. Layton, deceased, renounce their rights of administration in the estate. These three are two of her brothers, and a sister, which leads me to the conclusion that we are here dealing with the right person. A daughter:
1. Ettie Layton, born 1858, died 1958; married John T. Burdette, and had one daughter:
    a. Ethel Burdette.

CHILD 2

Jemima A. King
1834-1909

This daughter of John A. King (1808), was born December 1, 1834, and died March 7, 1909. Married January 5, 1859 to William T. Browning, born c.1832, died November 26, 1900. Parents of, at least:
1. Emma King Browning, born January, 1860

CHILD 3

John Duckett King
1836-1905

This son of John A. King (1808), was born c.1836, died August 22, 1905 and is buried at Salem United Methodist Church in Cedar Grove. His wife, Lucinda A. Watkins, born c.1842; died December 25, 1923, and is buried there also. They were married February 21, 1862 in Montgomery County. As mentioned above, he was living with his parents during the 1870 census, with a wife and three small children. The 1880 census carries the family, this time with five children listed. This appears to be John Duckett King, whose death on August 22, 1905 was reported in the Montgomery County *Sentinel* "in his 69th year." His wife is not reported there by name, but his five sons were:

1. Hiram G. King, born January 10, 1863; died September 11, 1936
2. Thomas O. King, born c.1864, perhaps died 1927 and buried in Damascus Methodist cemetery. May be the same individual married November 15, 1888 to Ida E. Burns, born 1867, died 1945, and also buried there. Two sons are buried with them; there were more:
   a. Barry J. King, born 1889. The obituary of this individual appeared in the *Frederick Post* of November 7, 1970. It stated that he died November 5, 1970 at the age of eighty-one, a retired B. & O. Railroad employee. He had a brother, Howard T. King, of Halethorpe, and two sons:
      (1) Richard B. King, of Park Forest, Illinois
      (2) Thomas M. King, of Baltimore
   b. Howard T. King.
   c. Clinton C. King, born 1898; died 1936
3. Henry J. King, born c.1867, died 1949; buried at Salem Methodist Church in Cedar Grove. Married Manona E., born 1873, died 1958; also buried there.
4. Edward Carlton King, born c.1872, and died 1934. Married February 5, 1895 to Harriet M. Dutrow, born March 7, 1876,

died May 11, 1899. Married second March 11, 1901 at Clarksburg, Maryland, to Nonie M. Lydard, born 1881, died about September 23, 1968, daughter of John C. Liddard and Mary Ella Hobbs. Marriage license records list him as a widower, 28 years of age. Buried Salem United Methodist Church, Cedar Grove. They had children:

a. Carlton King, born 1902, died 1955; buried Salem United Methodist Church, Cedar Grove
b. Mildred King, married John Thompson. A son:
    (1) Fulton Perry Thompson.
c. Mary Norene King, born July 21, 1909. Married to William Windsor. At least one daughter:
    (1) Ann Windsor, married Frank Thompson, and had at least two children:
        (a) Sally Thompson: January 12, 1945
        (b) William Thompson.

4. R. Delaney King, born June 30, 1874; died February 15, 1946, buried at the Damascus Methodist Church cemetery, with his wife, Mary Sybil (or Sybell) Ward, born April 3, 1880; died January 28, 1961. They were married September 3, 1896, at Rockville, and had at least these children:

a. Archie C. King, born May 20, 1897; died young
b. Ida Landella King, born November 22, 1902, died July 4, 1903
c. Maude Alverta King, married September 21, 1921 at Grace Methodist Church in Gaithersburg, to Walter M. Magruder.
d. Glenwood Dawson King, born c.1918 in Cedar Grove, died May 6, 1996 in Damascus. He was, for many years, chief of employee services for the Montgomery County government, prior to his retirement. He was also a Nationwide Insurance agent for 44 years, and chairman of the board of the Bethesda United Methodist Church, where he and his wife are buried. Married September 2, 1939 Olive Virginia Burdette, born January 3, 1919, died April 16, 1995 at home in Damascus, the daughter of Ira Lansdale Burdette (1900) and Fannie C. Cutsail. The children of Glenwood were:

(1)   Bonnie Elaine King, born June 16, 1940 at Browningsville, and married Delmas Foster of Damascus. Two daughters:
       (a) Penny Sue Foster, born 1961
       (b) Tammy Lynn Foster, born May 21, 1964
(2)   Judy N. King, and married to Thomas Knoll, of Mt. Airy.

CHILD 6

Charles C. King
1846-1920

This son of John A. King (1808), was born September 18, 1846, and died February 12, 1920. Married December 18, 1865 in Montgomery County, Maryland, to Mary E. Watkins, born August 13, 1846, and died June 8, 1911. Both are buried at Clarksburg United Methodist Church. They appear in the 1870 census of Damascus, Montgomery County, with two children. Also in the household is George G. King, born c.1854, not otherwise identified. The 1880 census includes the family, with five of their children. The children were:

1.   Bradley T. King, born c.1867 and died 1959; married June 14, 1892 to Sarah Wilson Dowden, born May 31, 1867 and died 1948, daughter of Zachariah Dowden (1829) and Rebecca Miller (1831). They are buried at Salem United Methodist Church at Cedar Grove. They had children:
     a.   Wallace C. King, born 1903 at Cedar Grove, and died March 13, 1977. Buried with his parents.
     b.   Bertie Madeline King, born 1897; died 1983. Married May 26, 1937 William E. Crutchley, born 1868 and died 1942; no children were reported. He was apparently first married to Lydia M., born 1870 and died 1933, the mother of his children. The family is buried at the Clarksburg Methodist Church cemetery.
2.   Hannah M. King, or Annie M. King, born c.1869, and married December 12, 1894 to John E. Harding.

3. Norris M. King, born c.1871. Married March 13, 1907 to Elizabeth Penner, both of them being of Montgomery County.
4. Florence G. King, born c.1875
5. Maggie M. King, born c.1877
6. George King.
7. Bud King.

Edward King
1740-1784
*
*
John Duckett King
1778-1858
*
*
**Singleton King
1810-1897**
*
*
* * * * *
*
* * William H. King 1835
*
* * Mary Jane King 1838
*
* * James Harrison King 1841
*
* * Singleton Lewis King 1843
*
* * Manzella L. King 1845
*
* * Edmund Dorsey King 1847
*
* * Caroline Columbia King 1851
*
* * Roberta Isabell King 1853
*
* * John Bell King 1860

CHAPTER 8

Singleton King
1810-1897

This son of John Duckett King (1778) was born October 21, 1810 and died January 30, 1897. Married January 9, 1834 Jane Rebecca Lewis, daughter of Jeremiah Lewis and Mary Windsor. He was married a second time; beside him at the Urbana Methodist cemetery is the grave of Mary A., as his wife. She was Mary Ann Lewis, born September 9, 1820 and died November 16, 1880, and they were married March 23, 1844 in Frederick County. He was married third in Frederick County, May 14, 1885 to Caroline Lewis, born c.1835; perhaps his three wives being sisters. His family is listed in the 1850 census of Frederick County, with Mary A., his wife, and seven of the children. The family appears also in the 1860 census of the Urbana District of Frederick County, with Singleton, his wife, and nine children (the entire family). His children, apparently four born to his first marriage, five to the second, and none to the third, were as follows. Each child reaching maturity will be discussed in birth order, following the complete family listing:

1. William H. King, born c.1835
2. Mary Jane King, born May 20, 1838
3. James Harrison King, born December 15, 1841
4. Singleton Lewis King, born November 23, 1843
5. Manzella L. King, born May 18, 1845; died November 25, 1874.
6. Edmund Dorsey King, born August 23, 1847; died October 16, 1910.
7. Caroline Columbia King, born February 5, 1851; died February 11, 1900.
8. Roberta Isabell King, born October 1, 1853, and died April 6, 1865. Buried Wesley Chapel, Urbana, Maryland.
9. John Bell King, born June 3, 1860; died May 7, 1909.

CHILD 1

William H. King
1835-

This son of Singleton King (1810) was born c.1835; buried Mt. Olivet, Frederick. He was married in Frederick County, Maryland, December 30, 1856, to Susan E. Mercer, born c.1835. The family appears in the 1870 census of Urbana District, Frederick County, with two of their children. Also in the household is one Ida Madary, ten years of age (born c.1860), not otherwise identified. Their children included:

1. William W. King, born c.1865
2. Perry M. King, born c.1867

CHILD 2

Mary Jane King
1838-

This daughter of Singleton King (1810) was born May 20, 1838, and died January 4, 1905. She was married March 1, 1859 to her cousin, Charles T. Browning, born July 9, 1827; died February 14, 1885 at the age of 57 years, 7 months and 2 days. He was the son of Perry Browning (1799), and Elizabeth Miles King (1802). Mary Jane was reportedly married second to Nathan Burdette; no further information. The children of Mary Jane and Charles T. Browning were:

1. Cornelius H. Browning, born June 28, 1861, died January 28, 1935; married November 25, 1890 in Montgomery County, his cousin, Eveline Rebecca Walker, born May 6, 1864 and died October 30, 1943. She was a daughter of Nathan James Walker (1824) and Eveline King (1828). Children:
   a. Carrie Evelyn Browning, born September 2, 1894; married Robert Crawford Green, born April 5, 1902 and died March 26, 1972.

b. Raymond Carleton Browning, born November 30, 1898; married Ethel Patrick, and had at least three children:
  (1) Robert Carleton Browning, born 1924; married to Catherine Buckler, born 1924, and had children:
    (a) Robert Carlton Browning, Jr., born 1956
    (b) Janet Browning, born 1956
  (2) Mary Patricia Browning, born 1926; married Joseph N. Willis, born 1923, and had children:
    (a) Susan Marie Willis, born 1951
    (b) Robin Browning Willis, born 1954
  (3) Harriet Rebecca Browning, born 1927; married Charles T. Ashecroft, born 1919, and had children:
    (a) Cynthia Lynn Ashecroft, born 1957
c. Russell W. Browning, born December 17, 1896, and died April 14, 1897.
2. Florence E. Browning, born c.1871; died October 26, 1886 at age 14 years, 11 months and 5 days.
3. Mary Helen Browning, born c.1873, and died November 6, 1888 at 15 years and 5 days.
4. Charles Everett Browning, married Lavinia Estelle Windsor, born December 25, 1866 and died July 29, 1905. They had children:
  a. Florence M. Browning, born February 29, 1888, and died August 7, 1888
  b. Everett Monroe Browning, born 1889, married Christena Thorn Mailler.

CHILD 3

James Harrison King
1841-1907

This son of Singleton King (1810) and his first wife, Jane Rebecca Lewis, was born December 15, 1841, and died August 8, 1907. Married Mary Emma Essex, born April 5, 1845; died July 4, 1920. Both buried in the Mount Olivet Cemetery, Frederick; two sons and a daughter are buried with them. They appear in the 1870 census of New Market District, Frederick County, Maryland, with their first child, then less than a year old. The census indicates that Mary Emma Essex, and her first child, were born in the District of Columbia. Also in the household are an older couple, probably her parents. They are Josiah Essex, a carpenter, born c.1817 and Ruth Essex, born c.1815. There is also a domestic servant, Susan Roberts, just thirteen years old (born c.1857). They had several children:

1. Charles Edward King, born September 16, 1869 (or June 27, 1869), and died November 24, 1951; buried at Mt. Olivet Cemetery in Frederick, Maryland. Married Mary C. Remsburg born c.1877, died November 6, 1930, and buried with her husband. Children, apparently born in Frederick County:
   a. Irma King, perhaps, born c.1898; died December 20, 1916
   b. John Russell King, born December 19, 1900, and died July 19, 1976; buried at Damascus Methodist Church. Married to Dorothy Mulllineaux, he was a past master of the Pentalpha Lodge 194, KF&A Masons of Gaithersburg, member of the Farm Bureau and the Agricultural Center. Two daughters and a son:
      (1) Anita K. King, married Lawrence Heller; lived in Darnestown and had children:
         (a) Caroline Heller.
         (b) Jacqueline Heller.
         (c) Barbara Heller.
      (2) Florence E. King, married Warfield, of Clarksburg
      (3) John Russell King, Jr.
   c. Nannie A. King, born c.1905. Married June 21, 1924 at Clarksburg, Montgomery County, Maryland, George F. Ray, Jr.; lived at St. Leonard, Maryland. Children:
      (1) Frances Ray.
      (2) George Ray, Jr.
      (3) Robert Ray.
   d. Mabel King, married to Clark Poole; lived in St. Leonard.
   e. Charles Edward King, Jr., married to Ursula Edwards and had children:
      (1) Elizabeth King, married Donald Sailors.
      (2) Linda King.

2. Mary A. King, perhaps. She may have been a stillbirth twin to Charles Edward, but not proven.
3. James Otis King, born July 2, 1872, died May 2, 1956; buried at Mt. Olivet in Frederick with his wife and two of his children. Married to Nettie Beatrice Yingling, born January 4, 1880, died February 21, 1944, a daughter of William Thomas Jefferson Yingling and Eveline Louise King; and had children:
   a. Mary Evelyn King, or Mary Emma King, born December 11, 1898, died December 19, 1916, single. Buried at Mt. Olivet, Frederick.
   b. Carleton Theodore King, born February 20, 1902, died May 6, 1960, single. Buried Mt. Olivet, Frederick.
   c. Helen Irene King, born October 14, 1904 near Urbana, died January 9, 1989. She was single, a teacher with a masters degree from the University of Maryland, and assisted in operating the Ideal Farms Dairy, after the death of her father.
   d. Dorsey Edward King, born 1909, died 1949; buried at Mt. Olivet in Frederick. Married Ruth Rebecca Keeney. His middle name is also reported as Edwin, although the obituary of his sister Helen clearly reads Edward. He had seven children:
      (1) June Esther King.
      (2) James Dorsey King, married Rebecca Fauver and had a son:
         (a) Michael King.
      (3) Larry Edwin King, married Julia Keim. A son:
         (a) Bradley King.
      (4) Thomas Hill King, married to Zandra Zimmerman and had a daughter:
         (a) Christina Dawn King.
      (5) Carlton Lamar King, was married to Susan Jean Hammond, and had a son:
         (a) Carlton Theodore King, II.
      (6) Marlin Lee King.
      (7) Lois Ruth King.
   e. Virginia Lorenz King, born May 26, 1911, died February 17, 1959; buried at Mt. Olivet, Frederick.

225

4. Albert Essex King, born 1876; died 1948. Married December 26, 1905 Lola Edna King at her home; daughter of Elias Dorsey King (1863). Their marriage license at Rockville states that they are not related, but they were, in fact, second cousins, once removed (pretty distant). They had common ancestry in John Duckett King (1778). Reportedly had three children:
   a. Gertrude King.
   b. Francis King.
   c. Margaret King.
5. Cordelia E. King, born January 5, 1881, died July 14, 1907
6. Everett J. King, born April 1, 1883, and died August 6, 1902
7. May King, married Henry Flook.
8. Bessie King, married Lusby.
9. Frank Singleton King.

CHILD 4

Singleton Lewis King
1843-1909

This son of Singleton King (1810) was born November 23, 1843, and died November 1, 1909 at his home near Woodfield, Montgomery County, Maryland. As a young man, he moved from Frederick County to Montgomery, acquiring a large farm in the Woodfield area, known as *Ray's Adventure*. It was there that he built his home in the late 1870s; a two-story frame dwelling, with a columned porch across most of the front. The house contained sixteen rooms, with a large open hallway, and two stairways leading to the second floor. The house was removed in early 1974, and a new home has been built where it stood on what is now Garfield Drive. Part of the land was donated by the family to the Wesley Grove Methodist Church, which contains stained-glass windows honoring various family members. The family Bible is still in existence, with entries made by the wife of Singleton Lewis, from which many of the dates reported here were taken. Singleton Lewis King was married February 17, 1870 in Frederick, to Mary Rachel Elizabeth Burdette, born June 9, 1852 and died April 17, 1923. They were married at the home of her parents, James William Burdette (1813)

226

and Cassandra Purdum (1804). Her obituary in the *Sentinel* states that she was survived by four daughters and seven sons, none of them named. However, in a set of books titled "Final Releases, Renunciations and Indentures" found in the office of the Register of Wills for Montgomery County, there is significant information relative to the family. In Liber HCA 11 at page 222 (and subsequent pages), there are renunciations filed by various family members relative to the administration of the estate, with the request that the Court issue letters of Administration to James R. King. All of the children appear to be listed there. In Liber HCA 7 at folio 198, can be found the first and final account in the estate, which concludes by listing the heirs and the manner of distribution. The widow received one-third, and the remaining two-thirds is divided into eleven equal shares for the children, all named. One daughter, an infant death, is buried with the parents at Wesley Grove Methodist cemetery in Montgomery County. The 1880 census for Clarksburg District lists the family, with five of the twelve children. Children were:

1.   James Rufus King, born May 13, 1871, according to the 1880 census, and the family Bible; and included in the distribution of his father's estate, as well as being the Administrator. He died July 23, 1946, buried at Wesley Grove Methodist Church in Woodfield, Maryland. Married there December 30, 1895 to Della Waters Woodfield, born March 1, 1879, died April 26, 1945. They had children:

   a.   Lyndall Victoria King, born August 10, 1901, Woodfield, died June 4, 1994, Frederick Memorial Hospital. Married first July 24, 1920 at the Cedar Grove Baptist Church to Walter Wilson Nicholson, born June 24, 1896, and married second to George Leonard Fuller, born July 30, 1903, died July 27, 1974. She had one son from her first marriage:

      (1)   James Kenneth Nicholson, born 1931, and married Amelia Ann Jarboe. They had a son:

         (a)   John Wilson Nicholson, born 1957

   b.   Maynard Wilson King, born March 11, 1903, and died March 27, 1969. Married Ruth Ethel Kinna, born April 4, 1906, and had a daughter:

(1)   Patricia Ann King, born 1934, married to Joseph Patrick Mallon, born 1934, and had two children:
(a)   Linda Marie Mallon, born September, 1960. Married Thomas Clark Marshall, born 1963.
(b)   Joseph Patrick Mallon, Jr., born October, 1962. Married Elizabeth Helen Murray, and had children:
1.   Jennifer Clarissa Mallon, born 1982
2.   Ashton Brynn Mallon, born 1986
c.   John Lewis King, born March 7, 1905 in Woodfield, in Montgomery County, Maryland. He died January 5, 1989 and is buried at Mt. Olivet Cemetery in Frederick. He was a charter member of the Damascus Lions Club, served on the Montgomery County Soil and Conservation Committee, and a number of other organizations dealing with agricultural issues. Married August 30, 1927 at Etchison to Mary Lee Stanley, daughter of Robert L. Stanley (1874) and Alma C. Purdum (1881). Children:
(1)   Sandra Lee King, born September 18, 1940, and married Willard Coulson Speace, born 1937, and had children:
(a)   Stanley Coulson Speace, born July 1, 1968
(b)   Brandon King Speace, born 1972
(2)   John Lewis King, Jr., born March 23, 1942, and married Roberta Ann Messer, born 1941, and had children:
(a)   Kimberly Ann King, born June 1, 1963 and married Matthew James Kempel. Children:
1.   Megan Ann Kempel, born 1987
2.   Matthew James Kempel, Jr., born 1989
(b)   Kenneth Stanley King, born March 4, 1965, and married Jill Marie Kempel. Children:
1.   Pamela Beth King, born 1988
2.   Donald John King, born 1989
(c)   Karl Lewis King, born March 19, 1969
d.   Marjorie Lee King, born March 21, 1907; lived 2 months

e. Mabel Waters King, born January 30, 1908. Married July 8, 1933 at Rockville to Raymond Benson Turner, born February 7, 1895, died 1976. They had children:

(1) James Robert Turner, born July 10, 1935. Married Mary Joyce Arnot, born 1934, and had children:

(a) Laura Lynn Turner, born February 17, 1960. Married November 13, 1993 to Henry Clay Raynes.

(b) Gary Dwayne Turner, born May 11, 1963. Married December 30, 1989 to Katherine Ann Yeszerski, born December 13, 1965. They had a daughter:

1. Danielle Marie Turner, born February 26, 1994 at Arlington, Virginia.

(c) Lisa Jean Turner, born May 1, 1964

(2) Mary Alice Turner, born April 23, 1940. Married Karl Raymond Deidrich, born 1938. Children:

(a) Beth Adele Deidrich, born May 10, 1958

(b) Mark Lee Deidrich, born April 2, 1960, and married 1979 Deborah Lynn Greenway, born December 10, 1960. They had a daughter:

1. Bridgette Lea Diedrich: May 19, 1980

(3) Margaret Louise Turner, born June 24, 1945, and married to Robert Sherman Ross, born 1942, and had children:

(a) Robert Sherman Ross, Jr.: March 23, 1967

(b) Katherine Amelia Ross, born 1973

f. Nettie Elizabeth King, born May 21, 1910, and married to William Henry Radcliffe, born 1907. They had a son:

(1) William Henry Radcliffe, Jr., born 1936, and married to Verna Elaine Hiponia, born 1940. They had children, the first and last born at Olney; the second at Washington, D. C.:

(a) Teresa Lee Radcliffe, born July 1, 1959, and married December 31, 1988 at Woodfield, Maryland, to Charles Albert Appleby, born October 11, 1948 at Frederick, Maryland.

(b) William Henry Radcliffe, III, born 1963

(c) Dawn Radcliffe, born July, 1965, and married November 7, 1987 at Libertytown, Maryland, to Michael Gregory.

g. James William King, a native of Woodville in Frederick County, Maryland, born July 8, 1913, and died August 25, 1970 after falling at a sister's home in Rockville, Montgomery County. He lived and worked on the dairy farm of William Lawson King until 1967, when he moved to Charlestown, West Virginia. He was married in 1938 to Nellie Mae Wilson, born 1911, and was survived by a number of sisters and brothers, as well as his children. Children were:

(1) Irvin Elmer King, born 1939 at Charlestown, West Virginia. Married Mary Jane Shroyer, born 1940, and had children:
   (a) Patricia Lou King, born 1970
   (b) Ronald Irvin King, born 1972
   (c) Janet Elizabeth King, born 1974
   (d) Kevin Wayne King, born 1979

(2) Anita Mae King, born 1941 at Emmitsburg, and married to James Ray Hill, born 1938. They had children:
   (a) Diane Anita Hill, born 1960, died June 21, 1961.
   (b) David Stewart Hill, born 1962. Married Sally M., and had children:
      1. Dennis J. Hill, born 1986
      2. Rachel N. Hill, born 1987
      3. James Ray Hill, Jr., born 1989
   (c) John Michael Hill, born 1963
   (d) Susan Elaine Hill, born 1965

(3) Jean Elizabeth King, born 1943 at Long Island, New York. Married John Bancroft Dietz, Jr. They had a son and a daughter:
   (a) Stephen Bancroft Dietz, born October, 1964. Married to Wendy Herbert.
   (b) Sharon Elizabeth Dietz, born 1968. Married to Andrew Hogg.

(4) Samuel Rufus King, born 1949. Married Mildred Virginia Creamer; no reported children. Married second Joann Hummer, and had children:
   (a) Brandi Lynn King, born 1973
   (b) Samantha Lynn King, born 1979
h. Edith Pauline King, born c.1915, and married to Wilfred Morgan Watkins, born in 1914. They had children:
   (1) John Edward Watkins, born October, 1940, and married to Sandra Mae Keilholtz, born July, 1941. Children:
      (a) Stephen Edward Watkins: December 8, 1964. Married Jeanne Weller.
      (b) Douglas Allen Watkins: September 11, 1966
      (c) Wayne Stuart Watkins, born 1968
      (d) Crystal Elaine Watkins: born 1970
   (2) Richard Morgan Watkins, born 1944; died in 1947 of leukemia.
   (3) Rachel Paulette Watkins, born November, 1949. Married February 3, 1968 William Donald Wivell, born 1946, and had children:
      (a) Todd Anthony Wivell, born 1970
      (b) Timothy Albert Wivell, born 1973
   (4) Deborah Susan Watkins, born November, 1954. Married William Charles Clarke, born 1954, and had children:
      (a) Amanda Marie Clarke, born 1979
      (b) Michael Richard Clarke, born 1986
i. Mary Jane King, born c.1923, married to Thomas Joseph Mullen, born June, 1926, and had children:
   (1) Judith Ann Mullen, born November, 1947; married Robert S. Ertter, born 1950 and had a son:
      (a) Matthew S. Ertter, born 1981
   (2) Joan Marie Mullen, born April, 1949. Married to Larry Yeatman, born 1948.
   (3) Jacqueline Elaine Mullen, born July, 1954; married Harry S. Lancaster, born 1951, and had children:
      (a) Harry S. Lancaster, III, born 1974
      (b) Aaron M. Lancaster, born 1977

231

(4) Janette Frances Mullen, born August, 1956, and married to Joseph M. Scrivener, born 1952. A son:
    (a) Joseph M. Scrivener, Jr., born 1980
(5) Jennifer Lee Mullen, born March, 1960. Married to Keith A. Nathe.
(6) Juliet Maureen Mullen, born November, 1961

2. Beda Cassandra King, born April 7, 1873; married August 11, 1897 at Wesley Grove to William Hubert Burdette, born c.1872. They had children:
a. Hubert Perry Burdette, born 1898. Married to Louise Harned and had a son:
    (1) Kenneth Burdette, born 1923; married to Evelyn Clark, born 1925, and had children:
        (a) Peter Thomas Burdette, born 1948. Married Joan Pearl Fort, born 1953, and had children:
            1. Jeffrey Burdette, born 1985
            2. Caitlin Burdette, born 1987
        (b) Linda Ann Burdette, born 1949
        (c) Michael Harned Burdette, born 1953; married Elizabeth Dale Buzard, born 1954. Children:
            1. Daniel Adam Burdette, born 1982
            2. Erin Kathleen Burdette, born 1985
            3. Katrina Elizabeth Burdette, born 1990
        (d) Susan Clark Burdette, born 1956
        (e) Steven Andrew Burdette, born 1958. Married Karen McCue, born 1959.
        (f) David William Burdette, born 1960. Married Susan Annette Otts, born 1964. A child:
            1. Curtis Lee Burdette, born 1990.
b. Fairy Elizabeth Burdette, born February 14, 1902. She married September 28, 1921 to Hamilton Deets Warfield, born December 21, 1897 near Browningsville, and died March 29, 1974, son of Samuel Dorsey Warfield and Alice Roberta Baker (1873). He owned and operated Damascus Chevrolet for 56 years. Children:
    (1) Hamilton Deets Warfield, Jr., born September 19, 1931. Married October 24, 1953 Juanita Louise Seboda, born April 6, 1932, and had children:

(a) Teresa Ann Warfield, born August 29, 1954. Married to Gordon Miles Cooley, and had children:
1. Adam Warfield Cooley: March 4, 1981.
2. Allison Leigh Cooley: May 2, 1984
(b) Hamilton David Warfield, born October 29, 1957.
(2) Joyce Elaine Warfield, born April 18, 1937. Married February 13, 1959 to Edmond Hamilton Rhodes, Jr., and had children:
(a) Mark Hamilton Rhodes, born November 19, 1960. Married to Sharon Lynn Hilton, born April 21, 1961, and had a son:
1. Matthew Hamilton Rhodes: February 5, 1987.
(b) Kenneth David Rhodes, born November 23, 1963. Married Kimberly Joyce Gartner, born May 11, 1964.
(c) Wayne Patrick Rhodes, born February 10, 1968. Married Kimberly Ann Hairfield, born April 15, 1966, and had children:
1. Ashley Elizabeth Rhodes, born February 25, 1985.
2. Timothy Wayne Rhodes, born August 31, 1990.
c. Roger William Burdette, born c.1909. Married Dorothy Laurene Souder, born 1912, daughter of Archie W. Souder and Sallie L. Purdum. Children:
(1) Roger William Burdette, Jr.
(2) Richard Souder Burdette.
3. Martha Rebecca King, born December 4, 1874, died January 4, 1950. Buried at Bethesda United Methodist Church cemetery near Browningsville, Maryland with her husband. Married to Maurice Watkins, born December 15, 1867, died March 31, 1940, son of William Thomas Watkins (1837), and Sarah E. Williams (1844). The family Bible states that Martha and Maurice were married on January 9, 1894 at Wesley Grove Methodist Church. Nine children:

a. Otis Lewis Watkins, born June 22, 1895, died September 15, 1958. Married Byrd Butler Kidd, born March 4, 1889, died November 6, 1977, daughter of Jesse and Martha Jane Butler. She had a daughter born to her first marriage: Madlyn Kidd, married Hyatt of Damascus. Buried together at the Bethesda United Methodist Church, Browningsville. No children

b. Infant Watkins daughter, August, 1897

c. Iva May Watkins, born December 13, 1897, died May 15, 1960. Married Ray Hilton, who died 1966. They had children:

(1) Catherine Hilton, born August 23, 1928; married Jesse Lee Riggs, born January 25, 1925. Children:

    (a) Charles Larry Riggs, born December 1, 1948. Married Patricia Kirchgassner. Children:

        1. Andrew Hilton Riggs, born December 13, 1973

        2. Carolyn Patricia Riggs: March 19, 1975.

    (b) James Bryan Riggs, born September 10, 1950 and married Linda Ann Driskill, born April 12, 1953, and had children:

        1. James Bryan Riggs, Jr.: May 6, 1972

        2. Jessica Christine Riggs, born November 6, 1975.

    (c) Julie Marie Riggs, born August 8, 1957, and married C. Wayne Frum. A child:

        1. Kelly Marie Frum, born April 20, 1979

(2) Robert Maurice Hilton, born November 29, 1932. Married Evelyn May Day, born March 30, 1930, daughter of James Day and Edna Beall. Children:

    (a) Gwendolyn Mae Hilton, born September 1, 1955. Married to Terry Lee Brown, born July 21, 1955, son of Delaney Pearl Brown (1919) Children:

        1. Scott Delaney Brown: March 14, 1980

        2. Kevin Robert Brown: October 19, 1984

(b) Gail Dianne Hilton, born December 21, 1957. Married Joel Thomas Hudlow, born September 23, 1955. A son:
1. Jesse Thomas Hudlow: April 20, 1984
(c) Suzanne Marie Hilton, born August 13, 1959. Married Jefferson Donald Federmeyer, and had a child:
1. Lindsay Marie Federmeyer: September 12, 1984.
(d) Sharon Lynn Hilton, born April 21, 1961
(e) Robert Ray Hilton, born August 31, 1963
d. Flora Elizabeth Watkins, born May 1, 1900; married Joseph Russell Sibley, born August 9, 1901. A child:
(1) Flora Elizabeth Sibley, born February 2, 1935, and married first to Vickroy, by whom she had a child. Married second to Martin Alexander Case, born October 18, 1932, and had a son. Children:
(a) Donna Lynn Vickroy, born August 1, 1958
(b) David Martin Case, born May 4, 1964
e. William Maurice Watkins, born April 17, 1902, died November 14, 1971; buried at Bethesda United Methodist Church cemetery, Browningsville. Married November 11, 1922 to Fannie Wagner McElfresh, born August 4, 1903. Children, born Browningsville:
(1) Dorothy Janice Watkins, born May 6, 1924, and married to Edward Warfield Mullinix, born December 11, 1921, and had children:
(a) Everett Wayne Mullinix, born October 29, 1946. Married Sharon Williams, born March 21, 1952, and had children:
1. Angelique Mullinix: December 2, 1969
2. Jessica Amy Mullinix: July 3, 1976
(b) Thomas William Mullinix, married Brenda Jane Gadow. Married second Margaret Palozi and had children:
1. Megan Ruth Mullinix, born September 18, 1980

2. Noah Warfield Mullinix, born October 3, 1983.
(c) Stephen Earl Mullinix, born November 6, 1952. Married Carol Williams, born April 5, 1953, and had children:
   1. Jason Robert Mullinix: March 7, 1977
   2. David Ryan Mullinix: April 11, 1980
   3. Lindsay Michelle Mullinix, born August 29, 1984.
(d) Kevin Patrick Mullinix, born April 9, 1958. Married Deanna Dawn Watson, born October 16, 1962, and had a child:
   1. Brooks Grayson Mullinix: July 4, 1985
(2) Ruth Evelyn Watkins, born October 25, 1926. Married John Cronin Beall, son of Barry Beall and Edith Burdette, and had five children. Married second Rudell C. Beall; no children. The children were:
(a) Carolyn Ann Beall, married to Glenn Kenneth Shriver, Jr., and had children:
   1. Sarah Kathryn Shriver.
   2. Carolyn Ann Shriver.
   3. Glenn Kenneth Shriver, III.
   4. Susan Lynn Shriver.
(b) Sandra Ruth Beall, and married Randall Allen Grear. Children:
   1. Jennifer Ann Grear.
   2. John Robert Grear.
   3. Matthew David Grear.
   4. Aaron Ray Grear.
(c) John Cronin Beall, Jr., born December 14, 1949, died in Vietnam, October 31, 1971 and buried at Browningsville, Maryland.
(d) Patsy Lee Beall, married to Robert Wayne Pickett, and had children:
   1. Lisa Ann Pickett.
   2. Rachel Marie Pickett.
   3. Nathan Robert Pickett.

(e) Barry William Beall, born April 14, 1959 and married Melissa Martin, born December 27, 1963. They had children:
   1. Teresa Elizabeth Beall, born September 14, 1983
   2. Heather Marie Beall: June 21, 1986

(3) Robert Lee Watkins, born October 29, 1932; and married Ardis Mae Hanson, born July 17, 1932. Two children:
  (a) Sharon Lynn Watkins, born June 13, 1958, and married to Larry E. Hunt, born December 27, 1956. They had children, and she married second James Fraley. Her children were:
    1. Robin Marie Hunt: August 20, 1974
    2. Katherine Hunt: November 21, 1978
    3. Erin Michelle Hunt: October 27, 1980
    4. Daniel Robert Hunt: October 28, 1982
  (b) Robin Leigh Watkins, born July 2, 1960, and married Charles E. Cole, Jr., born September 22, 1961.

f. Mary Rebecca Watkins, born April 12, 1905, married November 27, 1924 at the Bethesda United Methodist Church parsonage at Browningsville, Maryland, Milton W. Burdette, born 1900, the son of Willie H. Burdette and Mamie Pugh. At least one daughter:
 (1) Ann Burdette, born 1932, married to Alfred Freysz and had children:
  (a) Alfred Freysz, Jr., born October 7, 1953, and married Brenda McDonald. Children:
    1. Michelle Freysz, born July 11, 1977
    2. Richard Allen Freysz, born 1989
  (b) Sandra Kay Freysz, born January 26, 1957, and married Wayne Johnson, born September 30, 1954. Children:
    1. Courtney Elizabeth Johnson, born December 22, 1984.
    2. Merridith Ann Johnson, born 1988
    3. Jeremiah Paul Johnson, born 1990

g. Grace Alice Watkins, also found as Grace Olive Watkins and Olive Grace Watkins, born May 6, 1907. Married to David Irvin Ward, born February 4, 1907, and had children:
- (1) Lloyd Irvin Ward, born July 2, 1931. Married to Mary Helen Talbot, born June 23, 1932. One son:
  - (a) David Lloyd Ward, born November 5, 1957 and married Robyn Barklay. One son:
    1. Robert Christopher Ward, born March 22, 1983
- (2) Carleton Wendell Ward, born October 7, 1935. Married Sandra Norson, born October 30, 1936. Children:
  - (a) Thomas Carleton Ward, born August 6, 1958 and married Jo Ann Wilkes. A daughter:
    1. Jennifer Ward: October 13, 1986
  - (b) Steven Craig Ward, born May 12, 1967
  - (c) Boy Ward, stillbirth July 25, 1960
  - (d) Boy Ward, stillbirth March 16, 1961
h. Carlton T. Watkins, born May 8, 1914, died January 15, 1915; buried with his parents
i. Harold Willard Watkins, born October 31, 1919, married to Catherine Beall, born 1925, daughter of Barry Beall and Edith Burdette. Children:
- (1) Martha Joanne Watkins, born 1947, and married to Ted Hawk, born 1944. They had children:
  - (a) Donald Harold Hawk: December 28, 1969
  - (b) Jody Theodore Hawk, born 1971
  - (c) Travis Lavern Hawk, born 1973.
  - (d) Catherine Jean Hawk, born 1974
  - (e) Angela Marie Hawk, born 1982
- (2) Beverly Elizabeth Watkins, born 1956. Married to Paul Duerksen, born 1953, and had children:
  - (a) Benjamin Harold Duerksen, born 1984
  - (b) Joseph Michael Duerksen, born 1987
  - (c) Emilee Grace Duerksen, born 1988
- (3) Dwayne Maurice Watkins, born 1960, and married to Dorothy Station, born 1961. Children:

238

        (a)   Wesley Willard Watkins, born 1984

        (b)   Christopher Dwayne Watkins, born 1987

4.   Franklin Monroe King, born January 5, 1876 and died June 8, 1935. Married June 8, 1898 at Cedar Grove Methodist Church to Mary Avondale Watkins, born February 25, 1878 and died February 15, 1958, the daughter of Noah Watkins and Julia Ann Linthicum. Franklin and Mary are both buried at Wesley Grove Methodist Church cemetery. Children:

   a. William Oliver King: April 29, 1899, and died April 5, 1974 at Damascus. Married to Dorothy Craft, born 1912, and at the time of his death, there were twenty-seven grandchildren. Their children were:

     (1)   Roberta Olivia King, born 1931

     (2)   Herbert Charles King, born April 5, 1932 and died May 31, 1951

     (3)   Pearle Avondale King, born 1933, married John Malcomb Clarke, and had children:

        (a) Patricia Jean Clarke, born 1956. Married to Grover and had a son:

          1. Benjamin John Grover, born 1974

        (b) Wade Malcolm Clarke, born 1958

        (c) Barry Kevin Clarke, born 1962, and died September 29, 1962

        (d) Kimberly Ann Clarke: February 29, 1964

        (e) Gary Barton Clarke, born August 2, 1966

     (4)   Earl Raymond King, born 1934, married Esther Lucille Hargett, and had children:

        (a) Katherine Ann King, born September 9, 1959. Married to William Gregory Miller; children:

          1. Kathleen Michelle Miller, born 1981

          2. Stephen Andrew Miller, born 1985

        (b) Susan Elizabeth King, born May 9, 1961 and married John Wandishin.

        (c) Sandra Jean King, born January 28, 1964

     (5)   Henry Franklin King, born 1936, married Eleanor Marie Weber, born 1939, and had children:

(a) Lorena Marie King, born July 29, 1961, and married 1984 at Woodfield, Maryland, to Harold Kenzel. One child:
1. Dustin Robert Kenzel: April 30, 1987
(b) Wayne Allen King, born 1963. Married 1985 to Dawn Fountain and had children:
1. Sarah King, born May 12, 1990
2. Hannah King, born November 1, 1991
(c) Neil Herbert King, born 1965. Married May 12, 1990 to Teri Kline, and had a child:
1. Tayler Lynn King, born March 23, 1992
(d) Dale Edward King, born February 12, 1969
(e) Kari Lynn King, born 1971. Married July, 1992 to Andrew Mitchell.

(6) Margaret Ann King, born 1937, married 1958 at Woodfield, Maryland, James Boyette, born 1934 at Pensacola, Florida, son of Green Lester Boyette and Eva Boutwell. Children, the first child born at Riverdale, Maryland; the rest Frederick, Maryland:
(a) Teresa Ann Boyette, born 1958. Married 1981 at Tallahassee, Florida, Timothy Mullen born 1956 at Baltimore, Maryland.
(b) Deborah Faye Boyette, born June 17, 1961 and married 1984 at Tallahassee, Florida, to Eugene Borovsky, born 1954.
(c) Gretchen Noel Boyette: December 17, 1964 and married 1989 at Lake Wales, Florida, to Jesse Pennington.
(d) Renee Lynn Boyette, born January 24, 1968. Married 1991 at Orlando, Florida, Edward Grubb.

(7) Dorothy Olivia King, born 1939 at Woodfield, Maryland. Married April, 1961 to Carrol Don Hunter, born 1936 at Abilene, Texas, son of John Hunter and Velma Huchingson, and had children, born at Lubbock, Texas:
(a) Donna Yvonne Hunter, born November, 1961

(b) Jennifer Jean Hunter, born January 16, 1963. Married November, 1987 at Monterey, California, to Christopher Harrison. Children:
1. Daniel Harrison, born 1989 in Germany
2. Amanda Harrison, born 1992, Germany
(c) Gwynn Ellen Hunter, born April 2, 1965 and married June, 1988 at Midland, Texas, Kevin Albright.
(8) Opal Elena King, born 1940 Woodfield, Maryland. Married 1961 to Eugene Wilson Brown, Jr., born 1935 at Rich Square, North Carolina, the son of Eugene Wilson Brown and Hollie Parker, and had children, born at Ahoskie, North Carolina:
(a) Elena Rene' Brown, born November 24, 1963
(b) Eugene Wilson Brown, III, born July 20, 1966. Married 1993 Kathryn Ann Jones.
(9) William Oliver King, Jr., born 1942, married Joan Marie Watkins, born 1943 and had children:
(a) William Oliver King, III, born 1964
(b) Karen Marie King, born 1972
(c) Brian Charles King, born 1974
(10) James Thomas King, born 1943, married Martha Maelou Miller, born 1946, and had children:
(a) Shannon Sherelle King, born March 25, 1968
(b) Herbert Thomas King, born 1971
(c) James Thomas King, Jr., born 1973
b. Mary Frances King, born December 9, 1900. Married August 27, 1919 to James Raymond Kemp, born August 14, 1898 at Clarksburg, died August 7, 1970, son of James Monroe Kemp and Sarah Elizabeth Duvall. Mary Frances and James Raymond had children:
(1) Julia Louise Kemp, born July 18, 1920 at Woodfield, Maryland, and died October 18, 1990. Married October 10, 1946 to Donald Elisha Warfield, born August 19, 1918 at Damascus, died September 3, 1985; son of Elisha S. and Ethel P. V. Warfield. Julia was the mother of two children:

(a) James Harvey Warfield, born August 25, 1947 Frederick. Married November 29, 1974 Jennifer Lynn Hamm, born May 13, 1954 at Fairfield, Alabama, daughter of James Hamm and Florence Y. Anthony. Children:
1. Sarah Elizabeth Warfield: November 5, 1981.
2. Jennifer Lynn Warfield: November 11, 1987.

(b) Diane Louise Warfield, born October 2, 1948 Frederick.

(2) Mary Elizabeth Kemp, born October 20, 1921, died December 27, 1921.

(3) Edith Roberta Kemp, born March 25, 1925. She was married September 19, 1946 at Wesley Grove Presbyterian Church in Woodfield, Maryland, to Charles Oscar Baker, born June 25, 1922 at Mt. Airy, Maryland, son of Oscar Lee Baker and Bessie Clay Beshears (or Brashears). He was Fire Chief at National Bureau of Standards. Children, born at Frederick Hospital, Maryland:

(a) Glenn Charles Baker, born February 20, 1948. He was married September 26, 1976 at Damascus Methodist Church to Beryl Alta Andrews, born May 23, 1947 at Bethlehem, Pennsylvania, daughter of Richard and Aileen Andrews. Divorced after having children, two of whom died young. He married second to Kimberly Cuthbert, born May 1, 1958. His children were:
1. Matthew Aaron Baker, born January 25, 1973 and died February 18, 1973
2. Aimee Elizabeth Baker, died December 27, 1974
3. Seth Ashley Baker, born June 7, 1977

(b) Jerry Wayne Baker: January 27, 1951, and married August 7, 1984 Carson City, Nevada, to Ada Katherine Poole, born February 27,

1952 Frederick, Maryland, daughter of Harry and Doris Poole. A son, born Frederick:
1. Carson Remington Baker, born October 12, 1985.
(c) Dennis Raymond Baker, born March 17, 1955 and married October 26, 1985 in the Catholic Church at Sykesville, Maryland, to Sherry Harrison, born 1959.

c. Julian Pearre King, born December 5, 1903, and died January 18, 1973. Married June 17, 1925 in Methodist Church at Damascus to Sarah Elizabeth Burdette, born March 15, 1904 in Damascus, Maryland, died August 15, 1982, the daughter of Claude H. Burdette (1872) and Sarah Rebecca Boyer (1874). Julian and his wife are buried at Salem United Methodist Church in Cedar Grove. For a time, Julian operated the garage and service station at Cedar Grove, and was a member of the Damascus Lions Club. Elected to the Maryland House of Delegates 1946, he served two four-year terms. Children:
(1) Elizabeth Jean King, born September 10, 1927 at Woodfield, Maryland. Married February 7, 1948 to Oliver Lee Baker of Mt. Airy, born June 5, 1927. Children, born at Frederick:
(a) Terry Lee Baker, born February 6, 1949. Married January 24, 1970 to Lucinda Louise Lare, born there August 20, 1950, and had at least two children:
1. Valerie Jill Baker: February 2, 1973
2. Jeffrey Lee Baker, born 1975
(b) Marilyn Jean Baker, born March 28, 1951. Lived at Berryville, Arkansas. Married to Patrick Ronald Salisbury, Jr., born 1950.
(c) Darlene Dee Baker, born October 29, 1952. Married May 19, 1973 Michael David Wilt, born July 1, 1950 at Leesburg, Virginia, and had at least one daughter:
1. Veronica Rae Wilt, born 1981

243

(2) Julian Pearre King, Jr., born February 26, 1932 at Cedar Grove, Maryland. Married June 26, 1954 to Gloria Thomisina Reichard, born August 15, 1933 at York, Pennsylvania; divorced. Three children born in Los Angeles, California:

    (a) Susan Burdette King, born April 27, 1956

    (b) John Brian King, born January 19, 1962

    (c) Jay Michael King, born June 28, 1963

(3) Patricia Ann King, born December 1, 1933 at Cedar Grove. Married April 24, 1954 to Elmer Dale Allgood, born May 26, 1931 at Sasakwa, Seminole County, Oklahoma, son of Charles H. Allgood and Carrie Hardesty. He was a Montgom-ery County police officer; they had four children, born Montgomery County, Maryland:

    (a) Brooks Dale Allgood, born October 20, 1954. Married August 3, 1974 at Salem United Methodist Church, Cedar Grove, to Bina Sue Miller, born October 23, 1954 at Baltimore, daughter of Richard Miller and Dorothy Heil. They had children, born at Carroll Hospital, Westminster, Carroll County, Maryland:

        1. Blake Dale Allgood: March 12, 1985

        2. Brent Denning Allgood: May 26, 1987

    (b) Gilbert Blake Allgood, born April 15, 1956 and died October 13, 1956

    (c) Nita Ann Allgood, born September 8, 1957. Married October 1, 1988 at Salem Methodist Church, Cedar Grove, to Mark Lawson, born November 27, 1957, son of Richard Lawson and Kay Gladhill.

    (d) Stacy Ann Allgood, born September 12, 1968 and married February 14, 1993 at Salem United Methodist Church, Cedar Grove, to John Patrick Calloway.

d. Marjorie Roberta King, born September 3, 1908. Married Marvin Louis Spooner, and divorced. One daughter:

(1) Margaret Louise Spooner, born May 30, 1936 and married November 12, 1955 in Washington, D. C., to Kenneth Allen Hughes, born July 17, 1935 in Washington, son of Arnold Victor Hughes (1894) and Helen Cecilia Dove (1904). Children, born Washington:

(a) Donna Lee Hughes, born August 15, 1956. Married December 29, 1977 in Bloomsburg, Pennsylvania, to Raymond Eugene Goodwin, born March 28, 1952, and had children, born in Bloomsburg (Note: the source of this information lists the children with the surname of Phillips; we assume that to be an error):

1. Christopher Eugene Goodwin, born July 10, 1979.
2. Adam Lee Goodwin, born June 16, 1980

(b) Kenneth Allen Hughes, Jr., born October 29, 1957. Married September 4, 1982 at East Riverdale, Maryland, to Joan Carol Evans, born February 18, 1961. They had children, all born in Houston, Texas:

1. Alexander Evans Hughes, born April 21, 1986
2. Kelsey Victoria Hughes, a twin, born February 10, 1989
3. William Kenneth Hughes, a twin, born February 10, 1989.

(c) Robin Marie Hughes, born April 6, 1960 and married June 15, 1981 to Christopher Honeycutt, and divorced. They had a son:

1. Jason Tanner Honeycutt: July 1, 1983

(d) David Arnold Hughes, born October 24, 1964

e. Noah Franklin King, born December 16, 1912. Married first December 23, 1933 to Cecil Lawson; second Martha Hillery, born April 4, 1916 at Kemptown, Maryland, daughter of John Hillery and Gertrude Estelle Purdum. No children.

f. Jeremiah Lewis King, born November, 1915 Woodfield, Maryland. Also reported as Jeremiah Louis King; neither spelling as yet positively confirmed. Married at Delmar, Maryland, to Lillian Estelle Jones, born October 3, 1914 at Kemptown, Maryland; the daughter of Louis L. Jones and Bessie Bellison; and had twin girls, born Washington:

   (1) Janet Louise King, born November 24, 1937. Married 1961 to David Wesley McCloughan, born 1934 at Clarksummit, Pennsylvania; son of Donald C. McCloughan and Elizabeth Gose. Children:

      (a) Dwight David McCloughan: May 17, 1963; married August, 1991 in St. Louis, Missouri, to Laura Turpin.

      (b) Stephen Wayne McCloughan, born August 21, 1965 at Annapolis, Maryland.

   (2) Nancy Roberta King, born November 24, 1937. Married December 16, 1967 in Washington, D. C. to James Henry Coonrod, born September 1, 1923 at Waterloo, Iowa.

g. Calvin Lee King, born April, 1925. Married first Delora Simonds, and second to Millie Ikner. Three children, born to his second marriage:

   (1) Charles Lee King, born 1946, and married Marilyn Kornegay, born 1947; one child. Married second to Tamara Rasner, and had a second child:

      (a) Calvin Edward King, born 1969

      (b) Tegan King, born 1979

   (2) David Franklin King, born 1947; married Karen Hook and had a son. Married second Suzanne Marie Hack, and had a second son:

      (a) Christian King, born 1971

      (b) Brian David King, born 1982

   (3) Linda Marie King, born 1949, and married Jerry Burriss. Two children. She married second Bruce Butler, and had a child:

      (a) Nikki Burriss, born 1972

      (b) Barbara Burriss, born 1973

      (c) Kimberly Butler, born 1979

5. Cora Idella King, born March 11, 1878; married first to John
    James Burdette, born c.1875; and second to William Jefferson
    Mathers, born c.1876; according to the family Bible. She had
    six children born to her first marriage, and none to the second:
    a. John Norman Burdette, born 1899, died June 2, 1967 at
        Woodfield, Maryland. Married Dorcas Virginia Ifert,
        born 1901, died April 8, 1979, daughter of Daniel Ifert
        and Anna Ridenour. Children, probably born Woodfield:
        (1) Virginia Mae Burdette, born 1923, and married
             October 9, 1940 to Lindsey Leo McElfresh, born
             October 8, 1918, son of Colvin Hasey McElfresh
             and Sophronia Burdette. The family of Lindsey
             Leo and Virginia Mae is discussed under the name
             of the father in Chapter 14, devoted to descendants
             of Luther Green King (1825), which see.
        (2) Jean Evelyn Burdette, born January 12, 1927 at
             Woodfield, Maryland. Married June 15, 1946 to
             Harold Clayton Morris, born October 19, 1923 in
             Kirksey, Kentucky, son of Dallas Estie Morris and
             Ruby Smith. Harold served as a City Councilman
             of the City of Gaithersburg from his election in
             1962 until June 26, 1967. At that time, he was ap-
             pointed Mayor of the City, serving the unexpired
             term of Mayor John W. Griffith, who died in of-
             fice. Harold was reelected Mayor in 1970 for a
             four-year term. He was also a well-known builder
             in Montgomery County, Maryland, being one of
             the original partners in Heritage Builders; and
             served in a number of other appointive and elective
             capacities in the civic and political life of his state
             and county. They had children:
             (a) Michael Burdette Morris, born December 19,
                  1948; married Cheryl Lee Young. Children:
                  1. Christopher Gene Morris, born 1976
                  2. Melanie Jo Morris, born 1980
             (b) John Patrick Morris, born September 29,
                  1954, and married to Patricia Fisher, born
                  June 27, 1955, daughter of Thomas Warren

Fisher (1921) and Lois Jean Foster (1926); children:

1. Joseph Guy Morris, born 1989
2. Andrew Madison Morris, born 1991

(c) Michelle Jean Morris, born May 20, 1962.

(3) John Norman Burdette, Jr., married Patricia Poole and had children:

(a) Glen Curtis Burdette, born 1955.
(b) Gary Wayne Burdette, born 1958
(c) Eric Eugene Burdette, born 1967

b. Lucinda Mae Burdette, born c.1904, and married to Paul Lawrence Braun, born 1900.

c. Russell Lewis Burdette, born 1906, married twice: first to Helen Margaret Allport, by whom he had two children. Second to Elizabeth Viola Allport; no children:

(1) Lewis Allport Burdette, married Betty Kinna, and had children:

(a) Randy Burdette, born 1957
(b) Lu Ann Burdette, born 1960; married to Allen Knott, and had children:

1. Ashley Elizabeth Knott, born 1984

(c) Pamela Sue Burdette, born 1965

(2) Joyce Eileen Burdette, married to George Albert Burroughs, and had children:

(a) Mark Joseph Burroughs, born 1966, married Deborah Jane Swift, and had a child:

1. Marlee Jane Burroughs, born February 15, 1992.

(b) John Albert Burroughs, born 1970
(c) Rebecca Eileen Burroughs, born 1971

d. Albert Maurice Burdette, born 1909. Married, and had at least three children:

(1) Mary Louise Burdette, born 1931, and married to Howard Leslie Shores, born 1926. Children:

(a) Robert Leslie Shores, born 1952, married to Nancy Estes Houston, and had a daughter:

1. Amanda Houston Shores, born 1985

(b) Bruce Albert Shores, born 1954; married Lisa and had children:
   1. Sarah Dawn Shores, born 1980
   2. Christina Alexie Shores, born 1982
   3. Jesse Aaron Shores, born 1986
(2) James Albert Burdette, born 1935; married first to Ina Marie Lee, and had three children. Married second to Mary Jane Lane, born 1940; no children. His children were:
   (a) Alice May Burdette.
   (b) James Garland Burdette, born 1960
   (c) Kathy Louise Burdette, born 1965
(3) Margaret Estelle Burdette, born September 7, 1940. Married Leonard Thurston King, born April 21, 1942 at Clarksburg, son of Kenneth Thurston King (1921) and Olivia Jewell (1923). Children:
   (a) Lisa Ann King, born September 10, 1962
   (b) Kelly Lynn King, born July 28, 1965
   (c) Leonard Thurston King, Jr., born February 19, 1969
e. Mary Elizabeth Burdette, born 1911, married Woodrow Wilson Ward, born 1912. They had children:
   (1) Woodrow Wilson Ward, Jr., born 1944, married to Linda Sue Reece, born 1943. Children:
      (a) Mark Ward, born 1972
      (b) Tracey Ward, born 1974
   (2) Pauline Estelle Ward, born 1947. Married Robert Thomas Rosensteel, born 1947, and had one child. She married second Graig Daniel Mallgrave. Her daughter was:
      (a) Hillary Ward Rosensteel, born 1971.
f. Perry George Burdette, born January 16, 1915. Married Doris Eleanor Stanley, born November 13, 1916, daughter of Grover Mount Stanley (1892) and Rosa Lena Boyer (1891). Four children. He was married second to Betty Jo Sawyer. Perry was a good friend of the author, and was engaged in several business ventures. Among other things, he was a builder, and a building inspector

for the Veteran's Administration. They lived in a large home in the village of Woodfield. His children were:

(1) Barbara Ann Burdette, born October 3, 1933; married John Edward Burdette, born September 12, 1932 at Cedar Grove, a builder. Children, first two at born Selma, Alabama, last three Olney, Maryland:

    (a) Brenda Ann Burdette, born April 12, 1952 and married February 1, 1975 to Bertrand Merson Magin, born April 16, 1948 at Frederick. Children:

        1. Corey Lee Magin, born 1977
        2. April Renee Magin, born 1979

    (b) Vivian Dianne Burdette: September 25, 1953. Married Robert Eyler.

    (c) Jacqueline Kay Burdette: September 1, 1957. Married Steven Wayne Strunk. Children:

        1. Steven Wayne Strunk, Jr., born 1981
        2. Carrie Strunk.
        3. Infant Strunk.

    (d) Dale Curtis Burdette: September 24, 1959

    (e) Timothy Edward Burdette: November 6, 1963

(2) Ruth Ellen Burdette, born June 15, 1937; married July 13, 1957 to Donald Ray Hobbs, Jr., born October 9, 1934 in Washington, D. C. He is a landscaping contractor. Children, born at Olney:

    (a) Lori Lynn Hobbs: February 23, 1961

    (b) Lana Rae Hobbs: April 12, 1963

    (c) Donald Ray Hobbs, III: January 23, 1965

(3) John Grover Burdette, born April 26, 1945

(4) Doris Rosemary Burdette, born June 15, 1950 and married October 28, 1972 David George Friend, born February 18, 1950 Norristown, Pennsylvania. They had children:

    (a) Marcus Samuel Friend, born 1976

    (b) Matthew Friend, born 1980

6. Emma Estelle King, born September 27, 1880, and died November 6, 1880

7. Mary Garfield King, born September 29, 1881; (called Mollie in her father's will), died November 30, 1968. Married March 30, 1904 to Eli Granberry Ward, born January 30, 1877, died July 15, 1937, son of Enoch George Ward and Mary Rebecca Ward. Lived on part of the tract called *Ray's Adventure*, locally known as Pleasant View Farm. They had a son:

a. James Roland Ward, born May 6, 1909, died March 1, 1984 at Woodfield, Maryland. Married June 28, 1932 at Old Epworth Church, Gaithersburg, Maryland, to Mary Elizabeth Johnson, born June 22, 1913 at Sellman, Maryland, daughter of James Edgar Johnson (1885) and Georgia Mae Cecil (1886). Children:

(1) Mary Ann Ward, born August 13, 1933 Salisbury, Maryland. Married December 29, 1955 at Wesley Grove Church in Woodfield, Clifford James Davis, Jr., born October 27, 1932 at Berlin, Maryland, son of Clifford James Davis (1908) and Anna Frances Brittingham (1911). Children, all born at Montgomery General Hospital, Olney, Maryland:

(a) Debora Sue Davis, born September 17, 1956. Married August 29, 1981 at Epworth United Methodist Church, Gaithersburg, Maryland, David Torrance Speier, born April 18, 1956 in Philadelphia, son of William Farren Speier (1930) and Nancy Mae Torrance (1929). One daughter:

1. Georgia Mae Speier, born February 3, 1989 at Bryn Mawr, Pennsylvania.

(b) Molly Lynn Davis, born December 12, 1960, a twin.

(c) Michael James Davis, born December 12, 1960, a twin; married August 2, 1985 in Huntsville, Alabama, Mary Lou Drake, born March 15, 1960 at Decatur, Alabama. She was a daughter of Billy Gene Drake (1930) and Eva Garnett Hobbs (1933). They had two children, born at Huntsville:

1. Stephanie Michelle Davis: June 29, 1987

2. James Drake Davis: March 22, 1992

(2) Thomas Roland Ward, born January 3, 1938 on the home farm at Woodfield. Married August 10, 1955 at Damascus, to June Harloe Snapp, born October 6, 1938 at Frederick, daughter of Carl Henry Snapp (1911) and Pauline May Lewis (1917). They lived at Woodfield, and had children:

(a) Cherrie Lynn Ward, born Janury 20, 1957. Married at home October 25, 1980 to William Harry Gartner, born October 27, 1946, son of Robert Ernest Gartner (1918) and Harriet Catherine Wachter Perry (1917). William Harry had been first married to Katherine Lorraine Soper, by whom he had one child, and was divorced. Cherrie Lynn had one son:

1. Jason Thomas Gartner: March 6, 1987

(b) Terrie Lee Ward, born June 9, 1959

(c) Thomas Jeffry Ward, born June 30, 1963 and died July 1, 1963

(d) Vickie Sue Ward, born December 30, 1964, and married May 21, 1994 to Todd Douglas Edwards, born August 19, 1969. A daughter:

1. Ashley Mae Edwards: January 29, 1995

(3) James Edgar Harold Ward, born July 16, 1944 at Frederick, Maryland. Married January 29, 1969 at Berkley Heights, New Jersey, to Pamela Frances Rundlet, born January 20, 1945, Summit, New Jersey, daughter of George Taylor Rundlet and Mildred Goekemeyer. They had children, the first two born at Baltimore, Maryland; the last at York, Pennsylvania:

(a) Jennifer Lee Ward: September 8, 1970

(b) Susanna Rebecca Ward: January 20, 1973

(c) Carolyn Elizabeth Ward: September 20, 1975

8. Roberta Columbia King, born June 8, 1885, died February 2, 1966. Married December 24, 1906 to Norman Bliss Jacobs, born November 17, 1883, and had children:

a. Mary Hazel Jacobs, born October 31, 1912, died May 2, 1981. Married to Everett Rufus Jones, born January 25, 1914, son of Ira Leroy Jones (1877) and Amy Matrona King (1881). He has been active throughout his life in civic and political activities in Montgomery County, having served on the Maryland-National Capital Park and Planning Commission, as well as chairing a number of important committees and commissions concerned with planning and growth policies of the county. He has been active as well in the affairs of his church, serving on foreign missions. They have children:
   (1) Everett Rufus Jones, Jr., born July 22, 1944; married to Barbara Dowell.
   (2) Mary Beth Jones, born March 25, 1950, married to Richard C. MacLeay, born February 12, 1950, and had children:
       (a) Andrew Cameron MacLeay, died young
       (b) Daniel Gregory MacLeay: February 9, 1979
       (c) Mark Robert MacLeay: May 13, 1981
       (d) Benjamin Samuel MacLeay: June 13, 1983
       (e) Steven Joseph MacLeay: February 4, 1987
       (f) Anna Marion MacLeay: January 18, 1990
   (3) David Stanley Jones, born November 11, 1952. He married first Mary Hamilton, and had children. Married second to Kathleen Yates. Children:
       (a) Amanda Catherine Jones: April 11, 1984
       (b) Michael David Jones: July 31, 1986
b. Norman Bliss Jacobs, Jr., born 1917; married Virginia Woolman and had children:
   (1) Catherine Ann Jacobs, born 1944
   (2) Patricia Elizabeth Jacobs, born 1950, and married to John Theodore Hanson. On son:
       (a) William Bliss Stephen Hanson, born August 16, 1985.
c. James Wriley Jacobs, born July 25, 1923, and married September 13, 1947 to Elizabeth Jeanne King, born December 6, 1927, daughter of William Lawson King

(1897). Their children are discussed in Chapter 3 dealing with descendants of Middleton King (1801), which see.

9. Stauzy Lewis King, (called Stanzy G. in his father's will, but the name used here in his obituary and the family Bible). Born May 20, 1887; died March 21, 1959 in Rockville, Maryland. His wife was Irene Ernest Dodson, of Rockville and St. Petersburg, Florida, and died December 13, 1968. Both buried at Fort Lincoln Cemetery. She may have been married first to Dodson, since the obituary of both of them mentions children, apparently bearing that surname. They had children:

a. S. Allen King, born November 18, 1912 and died April 13, 1987. Married April 18, 1934 at Washington Grove to M. Eloise Fraley, born November 3, 1914. He was a retired horseman, having moved first to Aiken, South Carolina, and then to Easton, Maryland, where he died. Survived by two sons:

(1) S. Allen King, Jr., of Easton, Maryland, born September 4, 1935 and married to Sue Archibald, born June 16, 1944. They had children:
(a) Wendy Ann King, born April 23, 1964
(b) Stuart Allen King, born November 26, 1969

(2) Robert A. King, of Lahaska, Pennsylvania, born March 19, 1940 and married Esther Vliet, born April 2, 1943. They had children:
(a) Shane Scott King, born March 10, 1964
(b) Timothy Wade King, born April 10, 1969

b. Raymond Singleton King (1987 living at Lusby, Calvert County), born April 8, 1914. Married October 17, 1936 Miriam Ruth Fink, born January 20, 1918, died January 11, 1992 at Montgomery General Hospital, daughter of Casper and Rhoda Fink. Children:

(1) Sharon Lee King, born October 4, 1941. Married December 31, 1959 at Riverdale, Maryland, to George Thomas Crown, born June 23, 1942 at Sandy Spring, Maryland; son of George Wallace Crown and Ellen Crown. They had children:
(a) George Thomas Crown, Jr., born November 15, 1960

(b) Kimberly Ruth Crown: October 20, 1963

(c) Todd Raymond Crown: September 27, 1966

(2) Gary Raymond King, born October 13, 1944 and married to Francee Understein.

(3) Melvin Eugene King, born December 14, 1946 and married Deborah Marie Best. Children:

(a) Gary Alan King: October 28, 1969

(b) Tracey King: June 30, 1971

10. Roby Harrison King, born September 1, 1889; died December 15, 1962. Buried at Wesley Grove Methodist Church, single.

11. Hattie Mae King, born January 22, 1893, according to the Family Bible, but contains no date of death. She is reportedly buried at Hyattstown Christian Church cemetery. Married to James Bradley Hawkins, born 1886, and had children:

a. Mary Belle Hawkins, born May 6, 1915, married to Charles Edward Watkins, born 1914, and had children:

(1) Joanne Marie Watkins, born 1939. Married James Edward Musson, born 1936, and had a son:

(a) Larry Edward Musson, born June 22, 1966

(2) Charles Edward Watkins, Jr., born 1940, known as Bucky. Married Barbara Joan Beall, born 1943. One daughter:

(a) Cynthia Elaine Watkins: November 5, 1962. Married to Dexter Gordon Mathis; children:

1. Sarah Diane Mathis, born 1984

2. Jason Kyle Mathis, born 1987

(3) Carol Lee Watkins, born 1953. Married Richard Harold Collins, born 1945.

b. James Wilson Hawkins, born 1916, and married Janie Elizabeth Grimes, born 1920. Children:

(1) Sharon Louise Hawkins, born 1946. Married on December 6, 1969 John Daniel Jones, born 1937 and had children:

(a) Jennifer Lynn Jones, born 1971

(b) Jeffrey Daniel Jones, born 1974

(2) James Floyd Hawkins, (or James Wilson Hawkins, Jr.), born 1950 . Married Sharon Ann Watkins.

c.   George Wesley Hawkins, born 1919, married to Doris Peacock, born January 27, 1920, died June, 1964. They had children, and he married second Georgia Lee Scott, no children. His children were:

    (1)   George Wesley Hawkins, Jr., born April 16, 1942, and married Sarah Patricia Gray. Children:
        (a)   Patricia Ann Hawkins, twin: January 2, 1964
        (b)   Teresa Ann Hawkins, twin: January 2, 1964
        (c)   John Wesley Hawkins: August 4, 1967
        (d)   Joseph Hawkins: March 23, 1969

    (2)   Alice Mae Hawkins, born 1944, married Charles Eugene Fritz, born 1938. Children:
        (a)   Ronald Wayne Fritz: June 8, 1965
        (b)   Charles Eugene Fritz, Jr.: July 10, 1972

    (3)   Leroy Bradley Hawkins, born January 4, 1946, married to Charlotte Mullinix, born 1947, and divorced, after one son. He was married second to Linda Webb, and had two children. His children:
        (1)   Richard William Hawkins: March 12, 1969
        (2)   Thomas Hawkins.
        (3)   Travis Hawkins.

d.   Sterling Lewis Hawkins, born 1921, and married to Ella Eugenia Elder, born 1921. Children:

    (1)   Sterling Lewis Hawkins, Jr., born 1945. Married Susan Burton (or Cathie Burton). Children:
        (a)   Annie Laurie Hawkins, born December, 1964 (also reported as Laurie Marie Hawkins).
        (b)   Amy Sue Hawkins.

    (2)   Wayne Elder Hawkins, born 1948.

    (3)   Donald Lee Hawkins, born 1952. Married Colleen Faye Hamann, born 1956, and had children:
        (a)   Jessica Lynn Hawkins, born 1984
        (b)   Michael Lee Hawkins, born 1985

    (4)   Gloria Jean Hawkins, born 1958. Married Rod Gunthrum, born 1959.

e.   Eleanor Mae Hawkins, born 1926. Married Richard Franklin Stup, born 1921. Children:

  (1) Brenda Dianne Stup, born February 1, 1950.
     Married Tulloss and had a daughter:
     (a) Katherine A. Tulloss, born 1981.
  (2) Shirley Mae Stup, born March 31, 1959. Married
     Brice Greenville.
 f. Charles Benjamin Hawkins, born 1932. Married Joyce
  Elaine Riggs, born 1933, and had children:
  (1) Karl Benjamin Hawkins, born May 12, 1968
  (2) Franklin Riggs Hawkins, born 1971

12. Cramwell McKinley King, born September 24, 1895 and died
 May 18, 1971, intestate. His estate was filed and settled by his
 only son and heir, his daughter having predeceased her father.
 Cramwell is buried at Wesley Grove Methodist Church. His
 wife is there; she was Ivy Blanche Broadhurst, born February
 23, 1891 and died April 5, 1971; they were married March 19,
 1913 at Clarksburg. One daughter is buried there; and there
 was one son who survived his father:
 a. Ellsworth McKinley King, born c.1914; died November
  29, 1989 at the Kensington Gardens Nursing Home in
  Montgomery County. Married June 29, 1935 at Woodfield to Mary Lewis Ward, born 1917, daughter of Mrs.
  Norine Lewis Ward. Survived by a son and a daughter:
  (1) Eugene McKinley King, born 1936; lived in
    Kensington, Maryland. Married three times: first
    to Joanne Irene Beglin, two children and divorced.
    Married second Anita Joyce Strait, and had one
    daughter. Married third Betsy. Children were:
    (a) Jeffrey McKinley King, born November 22,
     1964. Married Barbara Easto, born 1963, and
     had a child:
     1. Alyson Anita King: August 24, 1991
    (b) Bryan Eugene King: November 27, 1966
    (c) Deborah Anita Clair King, born 1975
  (2) Esther Mae King, born 1948. Married June 8,
    1968 Charles Gregory Senseney, born 1948. She
    married second Charles Falstick, and had children:
    (a) Jennifer Falstick, born 1982
    (b) Charles Falstick, Jr., born 1983

b. Lillian Carolyn King, born January 4, 1915; died August 4, 1920
c. Roby King.

CHILD 5

Manzella L. King
1845-1874

This daughter of Singleton King (1810), was born May 18, 1845, and died November 25, 1874. Buried at Wesley Chapel, Urbana. Married August 17, 1873 in Frederick to James F. Beall, born c.1833, a widower and a merchant. At least one daughter:
1. Bertie J. Beall, married Bradley Dutrow.

CHILD 6

Edmund Dorsey King
1847-1910

This son of Singleton King (1810), was born August 23, 1847; died October 16, 1910. Married June 17, 1879 to Mary Fannie Lewis, born c.1848, and died November 25, 1916 at age of 67 years, 5 months, 15 days. Both buried at the Mount Olivet Cemetery in Frederick, Maryland. No children. She was a daughter of John R. Lewis.

CHILD 7

Caroline Columbia King
1851-1900

This daughter of Singleton King (1810), was born February 5, 1851; died February 11, 1900. Buried Hyattstown Methodist cemetery. Married March 1, 1881 to John P. Harris, born c.1846.

CHILD 9

John Bell King
1860-1909

This son of Singleton King (1810), was born June 3, 1860; died May 7, 1909; buried Mt. Olivet, Frederick. Married to Ruth E. Duvall, born April 24, 1862; and died October 10, 1940. Both buried at Mt. Olivet in Frederick. At least these children:

1. Infant death, July 27, 1891, buried at Wesley Chapel, Urbana.
2. Mabel Sharretts King, born February 3, 1895. Married to Charles L. Butterfield.

Edward King
1740-1784
*

*

John Duckett King
1778-1858
*

*

Mary Ann T. King
1813-1894
*

*

*   *   *   *   *
*
* *   John A. Lewis 1832
*
* *   Mahlon T. Lewis 1834
*
* *   Elizabeth A. Lewis 1837
*
* *   Mary Catherine Lewis 1839
*
* *   Iraneus Lewis 1849
*
* *   Jerome C. Lewis 1851
*
* *   Bettie Lewis 1857

CHAPTER 9

Mary Ann T. King
1813-1894

This daughter of John Duckett King (1778) and Jemima Miles (1782) was born March 20, 1813, and died May 25, 1894. Married Edward King Lewis, born November 19, 1808, died August 30, 1884 at Boyds, Maryland; son of Jeremiah Lewis and Mary Windsor. The family appears in the 1850 census of the Clarksburg District of Montgomery County, with children, and one George Stewart, born c.1834, a laborer. The 1860 census provides more information as to the family. Edward King Lewis is mentioned in the biography of his second son in *Portrait and Biographical Record,* in which it is stated that there were only four children who attained years of maturity. Edward was a school commissioner in the Clarksburg District of Montgomery County, and a member of the Whig party, later becoming a Democrat. The first four children will be discussed in detail, individually, following the family listing. The last three children apparently died young:

1. John A. Lewis, born February 13, 1832
2. Mahlon T. Lewis, born August 24, 1834
3. Elizabeth A. Lewis, born January 10, 1837
4. Mary Catherine Lewis, born April 25, 1839
5. Iraneus Lewis, born c.1849
6. Jerome C. Lewis, born c.1851
7. Bettie Lewis, born c.1857

CHILD 1

John A. Lewis
1832-1886

This son of Edward King Lewis (1808) and Mary Ann T. King (1813), was born February 13, 1832, died April 27, 1886. He married Julia King Shaw, born December 23, 1833, died June 24, 1900, daughter of William Shaw. They had children:

1. William E. Lewis, born May 12, 1859, died March 27, 1949, buried at Clarksburg United Methodist Church cemetery. He was married April 6, 1889 to Vernona Gibson, born January 4, 1863, died October 6, 1948. Also buried at Clarksburg. They had a son:

    b. Edward Lewis, married to Mary A. Hughes, daughter of George Edward Hughes and Mary Louise Dutrow. Two children:

        (1) Mary Louisa Lewis, born February 13, 1920, and married October, 1942 Walter Hazwell Magruder. Two children:

            (a) Walter Hazwell Magruder, Jr., born August 18, 1945. Married Diane Halfronda.

            (b) Mary Magruder, born October 18, 1948 at Lancaster, Pennsylvania, and married Joseph Glenn.

        (2) Margaret Vernona Lewis, born January 16, 1926; married March 11, 1949 George Herbert Phelps. No children.

2. Percival T. Lewis, born October 17, 1871, died June 3, 1945; buried at Boyds Presbyterian Church. Married Hattie Leaman, born October 4, 1872, died January 9, 1937; buried at Upper Seneca Baptist Church, Cedar Grove, Maryland. Children, the first two born at Clarksburg, the rest at Boyds, Maryland:

    a. John Lewis.

    b. Myrtle Lewis, died in California. She married Bradley Clark Riggs.

    c. Augusta Lewis, married to an eye specialist, and lived in Youngstown, Ohio.

    d. Bessie Lewis, died in Sarasota, Florida.

    e. John Robert Lewis, died at Augusta, Georgia.

    f. Harriett Lewis, lived in New York.

    g. Rosalie Lewis, died in Hawaii.

    h. Lawrence Lewis, died at Martinsburg, West Virginia.

    i. Linwood Lewis, a twin, lived in Mobile, Alabama.

    j. Oscar Lewis, a twin, killed in a hunting accident at 15.

k. Randolph Lewis, died at Augusta, Georgia.
3. Annie Elizabeth Lewis, born September 8, 1857, died March 6, 1944; buried at Hyattstown Methodist Church. Married to James Latimer Warfield, born September 25, 1850, and died October 20, 1899; buried at Hyattstown. Two children:
    a. Charles Edwin Warfield, born December 14, 1884, died April 18, 1958, single. Buried at Hyattstown Methodist.
    b. Edith Warfield, married Oscar Tabler and had children:
        (1) Bernice Tabler, married Bernard Hillard.
        (2) Harold Tabler, born at Waldorf, Maryland. He was married and had two sons.

CHILD 2

Mahlon T. Lewis
1834-

This son of Edward King Lewis (1808) and Mary Ann T. King (1813), was born August 24, 1834, died 1920, buried at the Boyds Presbyterian Church cemetery, in Montgomery County, Maryland. A biography of Mahlon T. Lewis appeared in *Portrait and Biographical Record*. Married December 12, 1876 at the Methodist Church in Laurel, Maryland, to Georgianna Milstead, born 1850 in Prince George's County, died April 20, 1920, daughter of William Milstead and Mary Hamill. She had been previously married to Moriarity, by whom she had one son. For a time, Mahlon taught school in the western part of Montgomery County. He worked in the store of Claggett, Newton, May & Co. in Washington, but returned to the farm. In 1860, he began work in a store at Clarksburg, which he later acquired with a partner, forming the firm of Lewis and Neil. Later, he was a partner in the firm of Williams & Lewis, with stores in Clarksburg and Boyds, later buying the interest of his partner. Two children were born to the Mahlon T. Lewis marriage:
1. J. Frank Lewis, died June 26, 1944, single. Buried at Boyds.
2. Georgianna Lewis, married Walter Norris. One daughter.

CHILD 3

Elizabeth A. Lewis
1837-1911

This daughter of Edward King Lewis (1808) and Mary Ann T. King (1813), was born January 10, 1837, died April 20, 1911, and buried at Boyds Presbyterian Church cemetery, in Montgomery County, Maryland. Single.

CHILD 4

Mary Catherine Lewis
1839-1896

This daughter of Edward King Lewis (1808) and Mary Ann T. King (1813), was born April 25, 1839, and died January 8, 1896, single. Buried at Boyds.

Edward King
1740-1784
*

*

John Duckett King
1778-1858
*

*

**Charles Miles King
1814-1886**
*

*

* * * * *
*

* * Luther N. King 1850-1940
*

* * John Brewer King 1852-1919
*

* * Frances L. King 1856-
*

* * Crittenden King 1857-1918
*

* * William Edward King 1860-1936
*

* * Charles Miles King, Jr. 1861-1879
*

* * Harriett W. King 1864-
*

* * Thomas D. King 1868-1947
*

* * Elias Vinson King 1869-1937

CHAPTER 10

Charles Miles King
1814-1886

This son of John Duckett King (1778) was born April 5, 1814, probably in the Clarksburg District of Montgomery County, Maryland, and died February 2, 1886. Married December 8, 1848 in Frederick, Maryland, to Harriet Brewer, born December 28, 1830 and died September 7, 1877, the daughter of Vincent Brewer (1803) and Catherine Lewis (1806). Charles Miles King and his wife are buried in Kingstead Farm cemetery. A Bond for the administration of the estate of Charles M. King was filed March 3, 1886 in Liber RWC 16 at folio 23, office of the Register of Wills for Montgomery County, signed by Luther N. King as Administrator, with four other King family members joining in the Bond. Three of them are readily identified as his brothers; the fourth is Rufus B. King, whom we have not yet identified, but could be yet another brother.

In RWC 17 at folio 185, in the Inventory, Sales, Debts and Accounts records of Montgomery County, dated March 16, 1886, there appears an evaluation of the real estate of Charles Miles King, deceased. It is rather interesting, giving us some idea of the way the family lived in that period. The list includes: one 2-story dwelling house; one barn, newly repaired; two corn houses; three tobacco houses; one meat house; one dairy; one old log dwelling house, with stable (both in bad condition); one orchard; and a garden. The property is said to contain about 240 acres, of which one-fifth is woodland; one-fifth is swamp; and three-fifths is tillable. First and final accounts of the estate were filed November 21, 1888, in Liber RWC 18 at folio 341, in which the heirs were named, one daughter being deceased as of that date.

The family appears in the 1860 census for Damascus, Montgomery County, and again in the 1870 census, with several children. In the 1880 census, Charles Miles King appears without a wife, but with five of his children. His family included the following children, each of whom will be discussed in detail after the general family listing:

1. Luther N. King, born c.1850
2. John Brewer King, born November 11, 1852
3. Frances L. King, born c.1856
4. Crittenden King, born August 31, 1857
5. William Edward King, born April, 1860
6. Charles Miles King, Jr., born October 28, 1861
7. Harriett W. King, born c.1864
8. Thomas D. King, born August 15, 1868
9. Elias Vinson King, born August 28, 1869

CHILD 1

Luther N. King
1850-1940

This son of Charles Miles King (1814) was born c.1850, and died 1940. Apparently married twice; first to Ida F. Burdette, born c.1861 and died January 3, 1895 at the age of 34 years, 9 months and 28 days, daughter of John E. Burdette (1835). She is buried at the Hyattstown Christian Church. He married second to Clara Mullineaux, born 1872; died 1953. Both are buried at Upper Seneca Baptist Church cemetery at Cedar Grove. At least two daughters:

1. Lucille Clara King, born July 3, 1908, married November 27, 1926 at Kings Valley to Ira King of Boyds, born May 6, 1902, son of Pearl Clark King (1879) and Alice E. Price (1866), as reported in the *Sentinel* newspaper and county marriage records, which state that they were not related. Married second to Jacobs and third to Gavin L. Brown.
2. Hazel Ethel King, born January 7, 1912, and died May 15, 1977. Buried at Upper Seneca Baptist Church with her sister and brother-in-law.

CHILD 2

John Brewer King
1852-1919

This son of Charles Miles King (1814) was born November 11, 1852, and died May 13, 1919, he is buried at Salem United Methodist Church at Cedar Grove. There are three ladies buried with him, each recorded as his wife: Laura, born December 3, 1856 and died December 29, 1879; Lillie M., born August 30, 1864 and died April 27, 1892; and Emily L., born November 1, 1866 and died January 31, 1902. In the 1880 census, he appears without a wife, which would follow after the death of his first wife a few months earlier. With him in the census is a daughter. There was apparently also a son, probably born to his first marriage:

1. John Brewer King, Jr., married to Lavinia Burns and had at least four children, born near Kemptown:
   a. Burtie May King, born June 26, 1893
   b. Walden V. King, born July 7, 1894 near King's Valley, in Montgomery County; died February 20, 1978; buried in the Clarksburg United Methodist Church cemetery. His wife, Violena Shipley, was born October 27, 1899; died September 4, 1979; buried with her husband. He was survived by two daughters and six grandchildren, one of whom was Mrs. Mickey Greene of Monrovia:
      (1) Mary Esther King, born July 3, 1919; married to Forrest N. Haney of Clarksburg, born October 27, 1918, died September 4, 1981, and had children:
      (a) Richy Haney.
      (b) Mary Eloise Haney, born June 28, 1940 at Clarksburg, married August 9, 1957 to Thomas Leslie Woodfield, born June 20, 1939 in Damascus. They had children:
         1. Alethia Kae Woodfield, born March 9, 1961; married in Clarksburg to Michael Craig Watkins, born June 17, 1964, a son of Donald Watkins and Barbara Wright, and had a child:

        a.   Kelsey Lynn Watkins, born May 17, 1992
2.   Tara Lee Woodfield, born July 19, 1966, and married November 6, 1993 at Gaithersburg, Kevin Michael Pumphrey, son of Frank Pumphrey of Damascus and Anne Smiley of Clarksburg. Tarra was named Maryland Dairy Princess for 1984-1985.

(2)   Lillian May King, born January 3, 1921; married to Clarence Ellis Hood, of Libertytown, Frederick County. Children, all born there:

(a) Dixie Hood, married to Flynn

(b) Glenn Hood

(c) Denis Rex Hood, born September 26, 1952. Married May 20, 1978 to Nancy Lee Moxley, born February 7, 1957, daughter of Floyd Keen Maloy Moxley (1926) and had children:

    1.   Andrea Lee Hood: September 1, 1982
    2.   Daryl Ellis Hood: January 7, 1986

c. Lenia King, born October 7, 1895

d. Lavinia Nene King, born August 19, 1899

2. Estella B. King, born c.1875

CHILD 3

Frances L. King
1856-

This daughter of Charles Miles King (1814) was born 1856; married to Etchison. Deceased prior to 1888, but reportedly had children.

CHILD 4

Crittenden King
1857-1918

This son of Charles Miles King (1814) was born August 31, 1857 near Damascus, and died January 13, 1918, at his home near Cedar Grove. Crittenden is buried at the Upper Seneca Baptist Church, at Cedar Grove, Maryland. His wife is buried there, also: she was Margaret Florence Watkins, born December 7, 1862 and died January 11, 1924, daughter of Lorenzo Dallas Watkins (1835) and Jane Dorsey Purdum (1840). They were married April 24, 1882. The will of Crittenden King is found in Liber HCA 19 at folio 421 in the will records of Montgomery County, Maryland. Dated March 12, 1917, it was entered for record February 12, 1918. He leaves his farm and personal property to his wife for her lifetime, so long as she remains single, and names four of his children. Final accounts in his estate are filed in Liber HCA 17 at folio 482, dated January 14, 1919, in which division is made equally between the four children:

1. Leslie Crittenden King, born May 24, 1896 at Kings Valley; died December 2, 1974 at his home called Kingstead Farms, near Damascus. Buried Upper Seneca Baptist Church at Cedar Grove, Maryland. Married October 28, 1920 at Cedar Grove his second cousin, Bertha Marie Beall, born September 12, 1901, died September 23, 1968, daughter of Edward Maurice Beall (born September 30, 1870; died November 24, 1938) and Mary Jane Purdum (1882). Leslie Crittenden and his wife are buried at Upper Seneca Baptist Church at Cedar Grove. Four sons are buried there with them, and there were other children:

    a. Maurice Crittenden King, born February 21, 1922, and married February 21, 1952 to Anne Riggs White, born August 13, 1931. They had children:

        (1) Maurice Crittenden King, Jr., born November 27, 1957

        (2) Ann Lyn King, born August 8, 1959. Married to Steven Palmer, and had children:

271

(a)   Amy Nichole Palmer: January 4, 1986

(b)   Stephen Joseph Palmer: October 29, 1987

(3)   Jane Marie King, born June 14, 1963. Married to Bertali Rojas, born April 24, 1954. Child:

(a)   Mauricio Rojas, born January 29, 1996

b.   Leslie Irving King, born June 26, 1924; died October 27, 1995.

c.   Harold Rufus King, born September 10, 1927, and died August 30, 1994. Served in the 101st Airborne, Army.

d.   Douglas Edward King, born March 16, 1929

e.   Robert Lee King, born April 4, 1931; died 1934

f.   Charles Carroll King, born March 27, 1933; died 1935

g.   Bertha Jane King, born January 18, 1935

h.   James Franklin King, born January 2, 1937; died January 1, 1996 at Frederick, Maryland. Married October 20, 1966 Dorothea Moran, born October 5, 1931. A son:

(1)   James Franklin King, Jr., born May 12, 1968

i.   Paul Richard King, born May 22, 1938 at Cedar Grove. Married October 9, 1960 to Kathleen Ann Beall, born March 8, 1942, and had children:

(1)   Peter Brandon King, born May 17, 1963. Married May 22, 1983 to Tracey Marie Copp, born July 3, 1963. Children:

(a)   Krista Lyn King, born January 6, 1984

(b)   Josiah Brandon King, born July 29, 1996

(2)   David Andrew King, born March 13, 1966, and married November 26, 1994 to Susan Marie Hockenberry, born December 6, 1974. Children:

(a)   Amber Nichole King: September 12, 1996

(3)   Leslie Lyn King, born October 28, 1968. Married August 20, 1988 Richard Wager Bailey, born July 24, 1964, and had children:

(a)   Richard Wager Bailey, Jr.: July 24, 1989

(b)   Christian Paul Bailey: September 10, 1991

(c)   Luke Henry Bailey: October 4, 1993

j.   Gloria Elaine King, born December 22, 1942. Married to John Joseph Daly, born August 31, 1944. Children:

       (1)   John Joseph Daly, Jr., born November 3, 1966 and married to Mary Bodden, born July 9, 1967. They have a daughter:

           (a)   Brittany Christian Daly: June 25, 1990

       (2)   Christopher Edward Daly: August 13, 1972

   k. Mary Florence King, born October 10, 1945

2. Orida Jane King, born c.1883, married April 25, 1907 at Kings Valley to J. Garnet Ward.

3. Beulah Hattie King, born c.1887; married April 25, 1907 at Kings Valley to Harry L. Nicholson.

4. Charles Dow King, born January 13, 1890 in King's Valley, near Damascus, Maryland, and died August 26, 1962. Married December 29, 1911 at Rockville to Augusta Ward, born November 10, 1888; died April 2, 1922, daughter of Harrison Gilmore Ward (1853) and Ara Matilda Thrift (1857) of Travilah. Charles Dow King was married second June 20, 1923 at Darnestown, to Albertis Ward, born December 20, 1883 and died March 24, 1970, sister of his deceased wife. Buried at Upper Seneca Baptist Church at Cedar Grove. At least one son, born to his first marriage:

  a. Harrison Crittenden King, born October 1, 1912 at Kings Valley, near Damascus, Montgomery County, Maryland; died February 17, 1995. Married March 25, 1933 at the Methodist Parsonage in Laytonsville, to Gladys Louise Allnutt, born January 28, 1915 at Etchison, Maryland, and died March 11, 1988; daughter of Walter and Ida Allnutt. She was a member of Montgomery County Fair Board, and numerous other agricultural and home-maker related organizations. He was a farmer, charter, and founding member of the Laytonsville Fire Department and the Laytonsville Lions Club; member of the Agricultural Center, the Farm Bureau, and Montgomery County School Board. They were survived by three children, eight grandchildren, and six great grandchildren. Children:

       (1)   Augusta Mae King, born March 30, 1936; married to Donald Wayne and had children:

273

(a) Cynthia Louise Wayne, born October 9, 1957, married to David Bowman. Children:
 1. Stephanie Ann Bowman: November 15, 1988.
 2. Andrew Bowman, February 15, 1992
 3. Amy Bowman, December 23, 1993
(b) Donna Marie Wayne, born November 27, 1960; married August 1982 to Michael Hill and adopted two children from Korea:
 1. Scott O. Sung Hill, June 23, 1989
 2. Kathryn Won Hill, December 21, 1991
(c) Mary Beth Wayne, born June 9, 1968, married May, 1994 Brian Grant. No children.

(2) John Dow King, married and had children:
(a) Michael Harrison King, born April 20, 1968 and married to Teresa Start. No children.
(b) Susan Lynn King, born February 28, 1970
(c) David Henry King, born June 1, 1975

(3) Thomas Gilmore King, married and had children:
(a) Patrice Marie King, born March 6, 1967, and married to Scott Brickman. One daughter:
 1. Anna Brickman.
(b) Joel Thomas King, born April 30, 1969, and married to Tierney. One daughter:
 1. Adelain King.

CHILD 5

William Edward King
1860-1936

This son of Charles Miles King (1814) was born April, 1860, and died 1936; buried at Upper Seneca Baptist Church at Cedar Grove. With him is a wife, Annie T., born 1864, died September 13, 1931, and a son, who died quite young. He was granted a divorce from Annie during October of 1919, apparently after first having two children. Married second March 31, 1920 at Rockville to Addie Mae Brown, born September 21, 1891 at King's Valley, and died November 29, 1975, daughter of John Wesley Brown (1850, and Frances America Cornelia Burdette (1857). The marriage record clearly indicates that the groom was then 59 years of age, and divorced. His will, dated August 8, 1933, was entered July 20, 1936 in Liber HGC 11 at folio 459 in the will records of the county. He mentions a son and two daughters, listed below, as well as Hattie Lorraine King, whom he calls "daughter of my wife" without further explanation. There is a will of Annie T. King, dated June 21, 1920 and entered September 29, 1931 in Liber PEW 20 at folio 198, which lists the same daughter, Vivian Burdette. It also mentions two brothers: Webster V. and Willie H. Burdette. There is also an obituary from the *Frederick Post* of September 14, 1931, reporting the passing of Anna Temple King (or Temple Anna King, as there reported). She was the daughter of John E. and Mary Watkins Burdette, and it is reported that she was survived by the daughter, Mrs. Charles Burdette, and her two brothers, mentioned above. We are therefore dealing with the same individual in each case. It would appear probable that Annie Temple Burdette King may have been married prior to her marriage to William E. King, and had one daughter. They had children:

1. Willie Harold King, born c.1893; died April 8, 1905
2. Vivian M. King, born September 15, 1888; died January 15, 1982; married Charles Burdette, born June 21, 1885; died March 11, 1970. Buried in the Clarksburg United Methodist Church cemetery.
3. William Edward King, Jr., born January 31, 1921; buried at Upper Seneca Baptist Church in Cedar Grove, Montgomery County, Maryland. He was a Vice President of Riggs Bank; married November 27, 1944 to Catherine Marie Leda, born March 2, 1924 at Baltimore. Six children, born Bethesda:
    a. Ronald Edward King, born September 18, 1945. Banker with Riggs; married August 31, 1968 to Patricia Marie Sterling, born July 6, 1948 at Princeton, West Virginia
    b. Robert Charles King, born January 21, 1948
    c. Richard William King, born November 26, 1948, married November 8, 1969 Benie Lou Lasher, born July 13, 1951 at Denver, Colorado
    d. William Edward King, III, born December 5, 1953

e. David Wesley King, born February 13, 1959
f. John Charles King, born August 2, 1963
4. Frances Addie King, born April 13, 1923, married Josephson
5. Hattie Lorraine King, born May 19, 1926

CHILD 6

Charles Miles King, Jr.
1861-1879

This son of Charles Miles King (1814) was born October 28, 1861; died June 8, 1879; buried at Kingstead Farm near Damascus, in Montgomery County, Maryland.

CHILD 7

Harriett W. King
1864-

This daughter of Charles Miles King (1814) was born c.1864, and married to Williams.

CHILD 8

Thomas D. King
1868-1947

This son of Charles Miles King (1814) was born August 15, 1868; died April 8, 1947; buried at Mountain View Cemetery. Probably same who was married August 2, 1900 to Della Hilton at Purdum.

CHILD 9

Elias Vinson King
1869-1937

This son of Charles Miles King (1814) was born August 28, 1869 and died June 17, 1937. He is buried at the Clarksburg United Methodist Church. His wife is also buried there; he was married April 12, 1892 to Jemima Elizabeth Purdum, born April 7, 1874; died June 30, 1935, daughter of James Henning Purdum (1847) and Martha Rebecca Burdette (1848); see Chapter 5. Elias Vinson had children:

1. Charles Maury King, born February 3, 1896, and died August 10, 1978
2. Myrtle Purdum King, died July 7, 1898; lived eight days
3. Ora Henning King, born July 18, 1910; died September 26, 1968. Married to Iris Rebecca Watkins, born November 16, 1914; died May 24, 1984. Both are buried at Clarksburg United Methodist cemetery. A son:
   a. Oliver Henry King, born August 12, 1941

Edward King
1740-1784
*

*

John Duckett King
1778-1858
*

*

**Rufus King
1816-1899**
*

*

*   *   *   *   *
*
* *   Sommerville King 1841
*
* *   Eugeniah E. King 1842
*
* *   Mary Louisa King 1845-
*
* *   Frances E. King 1846-1929
*
* *   Sarah Jemima King 1852-1853
*
* *   Anna Gertrude King 1856-
*
* *   Rufus King

CHAPTER 11

Rufus King
1816-1899

This son of John Duckett King (1778) was born January 25, 1816, and died May 10, 1899, and buried in the Kingstead Farm Cemetery. Married October 28, 1839 in Frederick, Maryland, to Amanda Elizabeth Mobley, born May 20, 1822, daughter of Basil Mobley and Elizabeth Miles. She died March 1, 1861 at the age of 41 years, 9 months and 26 days, and is buried in the Kingstead Farm cemetery. They appear in the 1850 census of the Clarksburg District of Montgomery County, Maryland, with two children. Also in the household is a young boy, Joseph F. Lowe, born c.1842. In the 1860 census for Clarksburg, Rufus appears with three of his children, and an apparent boarder, Joseph J. Benson, born c.1839, a school teacher. He also appears in the 1870 census, but this time without his wife, Amanda E., who died in 1861. There are two identified daughters; Frances E. and Annie G; and, for the first time, one Susan C. King, born c.1846, as well as a one-year old, Rufus King. In the 1880 census, he appears again, without a wife, and the one child, Rufus, born c.1869. Also in the household is one Helen A. Hurley, thirteen years old (born c.1867), not otherwise identified. His will, dated May 18, 1892, was entered May 23, 1899 in Liber GCD 12 at folio 158 in the will records of Montgomery County. He states that he is a citizen of Clarksburg, then living in the District of Columbia, and mentions real estate on the road from Clarksburg to Damascus, which is to be sold and divided between his four named children. In the office of the Register of Wills for Montgomery County, Maryland, in Liber GCA 9 at folio 242, there are receipts dated March 20, 1900 for payments to the heirs of Rufus King, deceased. They are signed by Anna G. Brown; Frances E. Ayton; and Rufus King. His children included the following. Those reaching adulthood will be discussed in detail following the family listing:

1.   Sommerville King, born April 11, 1841; died August 11, 1841

2. Eugeniah E. King, born July 26, 1842; died September 25, 1844
3. Mary Louisa King, born c.1845, of whom more
4. Frances E. King, born September 7, 1846, of whom more
5. Sarah Jemima King, born November 11, 1852; died April 4, 1853.
6. Anna Gertrude King, born April 19, 1856, of whom more
7. Rufus King, married 1867, of whom more

CHILD 3

Mary Louisa King
1845-1926

This daughter of Rufus King (1816) was born c.1845, and died March 25, 1926. Married March 20, 1860 to Samuel Benson Talbert, who died December 6, 1900. Children, the last four of whom were named in her father's will, included:
1. William Olonzo Talbert, born January 2, 1862 or 1863
2. Rufus Franklin Talbert, born February 3, 1869, and died June 16, 1894.
3. Charles Talbert.
4. Clifton Talbert.
5. Maud Talbert.

CHILD 4

Frances E. King
1846-1929

This daughter of Rufus King (1816) was born September 7, 1846, and died December 5, 1929. Married November 10, 1870 to James Edward Ayton, born January 16, 1847; died August 20, 1910. Lived at Laytonsville, Maryland, where both are buried, and had at least three children, all buried there:
1. Elizabeth "Neen" Ayton, born 1871, and died 1912. Married Thurman.

2. Susie A. Ayton, born January 29, 1876; died March 3, 1877
3. George Edward Ayton, born 1881; died 1937

CHILD 6

Anna Gertrude King
1856-1934

This daughter of Rufus King (1816) was born April 19, 1856, died March 25, 1934. Married December 10, 1872 to Reuben Middleton Brown of the District of Columbia, where he operated a paint store on Seventh Street. Son of Reuben Brown and Jemima P. King (1826), Reuben Middleton was born June 9, 1851 and died March 6, 1927. He and Anna are buried at Glenwood cemetery. They had children, born in Washington:

1. George Mobley Brown, born November 3, 1873, died October 24, 1875
2. Frederick Reuben Brown, born July 21, 1875, and married October 20, 1897 to Louise Tilleau, and divorced. Married second Mary Katherine Hurley, born July 27, 1915, daughter of Harry Mankin Hurley (1853) and Rosa E. Brown (1860). Frederick Reuben and Mary Katherine were both crippled. They had one son:
   a. Leo Reuben Brown, born November 23, 1917. He was struck by a train, and lost both legs.
3. Rufus Carey Brown, born June 20, 1877, died March 4, 1943, single.
4. Bessie Mae Brown, born May 21, 1880, died August 7, 1881
5. Frank Stearns Brown, born September 1, 1883, and died September 8, 1935, single. He was the father of one child by an English girl:
   a. Francis Brown, born March 23, 1921 in England.
6. Annie Gertrude Brown, born September 8, 1884, died July 10, 1966. Married November 2, 1904 to Ivan J. Riley, born June 21, 1886 at Tenleytown, D. C. and died October 4, 1950. Two children:
   a. Royce Middleton Riley, born September 11, 1905, died July 24, 1970. Married June 2, 1935 to Mary Specht,

born April 4, 1908 at Savage, Howard County, Maryland daughter of Isaac Jacob Specht and Viola Wasky. They had children:

    (1)   William Middleton Riley, born July 12, 1938

    (2)   Dorothy Lucinda Riley, born March 26, 1944

  b.   Andrew Jackson Riley, born December 11, 1910, and married Gertrude Locke, no children. He married second Marie Marshall, born in England near Scottish border.

7.   Mabel Amanda Brown, born September 30, 1887, and died October 30, 1890.

8.   Reuben Middleton Brown, Jr., born May 27, 1889, and died November 21, 1893.

CHILD 7

Rufus King
m/1867

This son of Rufus King (1816), was married March 7, 1867 to Susie E. Brown, born 1844 in Washington, D. C., died December 2, 1873. He was known as "Little Rufe" to distinguish him from his father. They had a son, who lived near Clarksburg:

1.   Rufus King, Jr., born May 26, 1869

Edward King
1740-1784
*

*

John Duckett King
1778-1858
*

*

Sarah Rebecca King
1818-1902
*

*

*   *   *   *   *
*

*   *   Martha Warfield 1845-
*

*   *   John E. Warfield 1847-
*

*   *   Amanda Warfield 1849-
*

*   *   Pradby Warfield 1855-
*

*   *   William Warfield
*

*   *   Exaline Warfield

CHAPTER 12

Sarah Rebecca King
1818-1902

This daughter of John Duckett King (1778) and Jemima Miles (1782) was born March 6, 1818, and died July 10, 1902 at Kemptown, Maryland. Married December 1, 1843 at Rockville, Maryland, to Horace Warfield, born April 2, 1814, died April 11, 1873 at Kemptown. They had children, according to the 1850 census for Clarksburg, Montgomery County. In the household is also one Hamilton G. Warfield, born c.1820 and what is perhaps his wife, Elizabeth Warfield, born c.1810. The will of Sarah Rebecca is filed in liber GCD 12, at folio 502, in the records of Montgomery County, Maryland. She lists five of her children.The children will be discussed in detail, by birth order, following the family listing:

1. Martha Warfield, born February 22, 1845.
2. John E. Warfield, born c.1846.
3. Amanda Warfield, born c.1849
4. Pradby Warfield, born c.1855
5. William Warfield, deceased before 1902. Nothing more known
6. Exaline Warfield.

CHILD 1

Martha Warfield
1845-1906

This daughter of Sarah Rebecca King (1818) and Horace Warfield (1816), was born February 22, 1845, and died April 15, 1906. Married to Franklin B. Day, born November 10, 1836 at the Parson Day Farm near Browningsville, son of the Reverend James Day and Sarah Mark. No children.

CHILD 2

John E. Warfield
1846-1925

This son of Sarah Rebecca King (1818) and Horace Warfield (1816), was born c.1846 in Montgomery County, Maryland, and died about July 10, 1925, according to his obituary in the *Frederick Post*. He was buried at Providence Methodist Episcopal Church in Kemptown, Maryland. He was married in Montgomery County, April 28, 1887 to Mary E. Molesworth, who apparently predeceased her husband, and had no children.

CHILD 3

Amanda Warfield
1849-1941

This daughter of Sarah Rebecca King (1818) and Horace Warfield (1816), was born c.1849 and died 1941. Married to Columbus Purdum, born 1838, died 1917; buried at Kemptown. He was a son of Joshua Purdum and Rachael Browning. Was assigned the post office position under Grover Cleveland, which was held in Al Smith's store and called Purdum Post Office, from which the name of the village derived. He and Amanda had children:
1. Eunice Elizabeth Purdum, born September 18, 1869, died June 25, 1870; buried at Kemptown.
2. Leah W. Purdum, born c.1870, died May 19, 1877 at the age of 7 years, 9 months, 11 days. Buried at Kemptown.
3. Hepsi Gertrude Purdum, born June 2, 1875, died May 15, 1951; buried at Kemptown. Married Newton "Knute" Poole, and had children:
   a. Gertrude Poole, married William Johnson. Children:
      (1) Guy Johnson.
      (2) James V. Johnson, married Mary Stanley, and had children:
         (a) Larry E. Johnson.

       (b)   Vernon "Pete" Johnson. Married to Melody Brown.

    (3)   Ruth Johnson, married to Lindy N. Beall, son of Barry Beall.

    (4)   Dorothy Lillian Johnson, born June 3, 1928. Married June 29, 1946 at Mountain View Church to Franklin Webster King, born March 31, 1927, the son of Harvey Webster King (1890) and Martha Pauline Burdette (1893). The children are discussed under their father's name in Chapter 3 devoted to the descendants of Middleton King (1801), which see.

    (5)   Walter Johnson.

  b.   Lucy Poole, married William Haller King, born May 18, 1893, died November 11, 1972; buried at Mountain View Cemetery in Montgomery County. He was a son of Holady Hix King (1857) and Amy Jane Musgrove (1860) and the family is discussed in Chapter 13, dealing with the descendants of Edward J. King (1821), which see.

  c.   Purdum Poole, married Ethel Mullinix.

  d.   Roger Poole, born May 14, 1905. Married Susie Gue.

  e.   Robert Poole, married Pearl Gartrall.

  f.   Wallace Poole.

4.   Umer S. Purdum, born 1878, died 1963. Married to Ollie Burdette, born 1882, died 1956; buried at Kemptown. They had two children:

  a.   Roscoe Franklin Purdum, born September 3, 1904 on the Johnson farm. Married in Frederick County, Maryland on September 20, 1924 to Mary Adaline Mullinix, born February 12, 1907 on Mullinix Mill Road in Montgomery County, daughter of Joseph H. and Evea Mullinix. Two children:

    (1)   Allen Purdum, born October 12, 1934 in Gaithersburg, Maryland. Married August 20, 1966 to Linda Monee.

    (2)   Umer Purdum, born February 15, 1951.

b. Claude Rufus Purdum, born 1913, and lived at Clarksburg. Married Evelyn Purdum, born 1912, daughter of James Purdum and Nettie Burdette. Children:
   (1) Catherine Purdum, born 1936; married to Darryl Armstrong and had a son.
   (2) Jefferson L. Purdum, born 1940 and had children.
5. Alma C. Purdum, born 1881, died 1928. Married Robert L. Stanley, born 1874, died 1925. Children:
   a. Mary Lee Stanley, married August 30, 1927 John Lewis King, born March 7, 1905 at Woodfield, Maryland, son of James Rufus King (1871) and Della Waters Woodfield (1879). John Lewis and Mary Lee had children, discussed under their father's name in Chapter 8, devoted to the descendants of Singleton King (1810), which see.
   b. Esther Stanley, married Edwin Warfield.
   c. Louise Stanley.
   d. Roland Stanley, never married.
   e. Estelle Stanley, married Steve Thomson.
   f. Jeanne Stanley, married Bryan Falcone.
6. Lynee Purdum, married Reverend Clough, and had children:
   a. Elizabeth Clough.
   b. Hobart Clough.
   c. Eunice Clough.
7. Sallie L. Purdum, born April 29, 1886, died March 13, 1966. Married to Archie W. Souder, born January 15, 1884, died July 1, 1933 at Damascus. They had children:
   a. Ruth Souder; married Irving Gue, a prominent builder and businessman, and had a son:
      (1) John Gue, married Nancy Davay.
   b. Jane Souder; married Hubert Snapp, who was also a locally well-known builder of quality homes and small communities. They had children:
      (1) Carol Snapp.
      (2) James Snapp.
      (3) John Snapp.
   c. Helen Warfield Souder. In 1989, she was invited to become the first woman member of the Damascus Lions Club. Married March 20, 1954 to Doctor Milton

McKendree Boyer, born March 25, 1907, son of George Milton Boyer (1872). Children:
(1) Sally Ann Boyer.
(2) George Milton Boyer, II.
(3) McKendree Warfield Boyer.
d. Dorothy Laurene Souder, born 1912. Married Roger William Burdette, born 1909, son of William Hubert Burdette (1872) and Beda Cassandra King (1873). They had children:
(1) Roger William Burdette, Jr.
(2) Richard Souder Burdette.
e. Grace Wilson Souder, born July 23, 1913; married Clark Fout King, born August 16, 1910, son of Filmore Clark King (1890) and Emma Jane Lydard (1890). He is a retired Corporate Counsel, living in Damascus. Children are listed under his name in Chapter 14, dealing with the descendants of Luther Green King (1825), which see.

CHILD 4

Pradby Warfield
1855-1915

This son of Sarah Rebecca King (1818) and Horace Warfield (1816), was born c.1855 and died 1915. In the obituary of his mother, he is listed as Bradley Warfield. Married Mary Browning.

CHILD 6

Exaline Warfield

This daughter of Sarah Rebecca King (1818) and Horace Warfield (1816), was married February 22, 1881 in Montgomery County, Maryland, to Jacob M. Allnutt. Her name is found in some records spelled Exerline, although Exalene appears to be correct.

Edward King
1740-1784
*
*
John Duckett King
1778-1858
*
*
**Edward J. King
1821-1899**
*
*

* * * * *
*
* * Elizabeth J. King 1845-
*
* * Somerville King 1848-1922
*
* * Rufus Kent King 1850-
*
* * Franklin Scott King 1852-1894
*
* * James Edward King 1854-
*
* * Holady Hix King 1857-
*
* * Lewis Bell King 1861-
*
* * Eva Lee King 1864-1928
*
* * Amanda Cornelius King 1870-1946

CHAPTER 13

Edward J. King
1821-1899

This son of John Duckett King (1778) was born January 10, 1821 and died July 21, 1899. Married January 15, 1845 to Mary Jane Burdette, born October 20, 1825; died March 3, 1885, daughter of Hazel Burdette and Elizabeth Miles. He is buried in the Kingstead Farm Cemetery in upper Montgomery County. They appear in the 1850 census of Clarksburg District of Montgomery County, Maryland, with four of their children, and several other persons in the household. There is Elizabeth Burdette, born c.1795, who is probably Elizabeth Miles Burdette, the mother of Mary Jane, as well as Emeline Burdette, born c.1833; Julia Ann Burdette, born c.1837; and John E. Burdette, born c.1835; the three perhaps being siblings of Mary Jane, with their widowed mother. There is also one William Hammond, born c.1832, a laborer. The census of 1870 for the same district contains the names of eight of their children, as well as Elizabeth Burdette, still living in the household. The 1880 census contains the family, with four of their children, and the wife of Holaday Hix, listed as a daughter-in-law. There are a number of entries in various books relative to administrations, in the office of the Register of Wills for Montgomery County, having to do with the estate of Edward J. King. In Liber GCA 9 at folio 195, dated August 1, 1899, four of his children renounce their rights of administration, and request that Rufus Kent King be named as Administrator. In liber HCA 2 at folio 370, dated April 16, 1901, there is the first and final account of the estate by Rufus K. as Administrator. After the usual listing of accounts, the distribution is set forth in one-ninth shares to each of the children. In liber GCA 9 at folio 299 and following, dated April 25, 1901, there are receipts from eight of the children, indicating that they were paid their share of the estate, with Rufus Kent King as the Administrator. There is also a Petition filed with the Orphan's Court in Liber GCD 7 at folio 138, dated June 28, 1899, wherein the Court is requested to order a deed for the lands of Edward J. King, whereon he resided, which he had sold by contract prior to his death. Rufus Kent King, as Administrator, acknowledged that he was aware of the transaction, and the deed was ordered. The children will each be discussed in detail after the family listing:

1. Elizabeth J. King, born c.1845
2. Somerville King, born May 28, 1848
3. Rufus Kent King, born January 28, 1850
4. Franklin Scott King, born c.1852
5. James Edward King, born October 22, 1854
6. Holady Hix King, born December 12, 1857
7. Lewis Bell King, born c.1861
8. Eva Lee King, born August 31, 1864.
9. Amanda Cornelius King, born February 17, 1870

CHILD 1

Elizabeth J. King
1845-1924

This daughter of Edward J. King (1821) and Mary Jane Burdette (1825) was born c.1845, and died 1924. Married to John Edward Burdette, born May 20, 1845 and died May 31, 1908 at Clarksburg; son of Greenbury Burdette and Martha Ward (1821). Greenbury was born March 14, 1818 and died February 13, 1891. He was perhaps also married to Sarah E., born April 6, 1836 and died December 1, 1898, since they are buried together at the Clarksburg United Methodist Church cemetery. Elizabeth J. King and John Edward Burdette had children:

1. Claude H. Burdette, born May 17, 1872; died May 29, 1938. Married to Sarah Rebecca Boyer, born October 6, 1874, and died August 11, 1926, the daughter of Milton Boyer (1834) and Elizabeth Washington Purdum (1840), and had children:
   a. Basil Boyer Burdette, born June 9, 1899, and married October 29, 1921 to Emily Lorraine Moxley, born May 1, 1903, died September 18, 1968, daughter of Harry B. Moxley and Eleanor Hyatt. No children.

b. Earl Hamilton Burdette, born February 4, 1902, and died April 21, 1937. Married December 22, 1926 to Marjorie Jane Nicholson, born February 8, 1908 at Gaithersburg, and had children, born at Gaithersburg:

    (1) Harry Hamilton Burdette, born October 17, 1927, died c.1995. Damascus business-man, operating bowling alley, car wash and convenience store. He married November 18, 1954 Miriam Janet Reber, born July 7, 1930 at Washington Grove, and had a daughter, born at Olney, Maryland:

        (a) Bonnie June Burdette, born June 26, 1963

    (2) Earl Leroy Burdette, born October 25, 1930

    (3) Robert E. Burdette, born 1932, died May 13, 1933

    (4) Marjorie May Burdette, born May 2, 1933, and married January 5, 1952 Charles Stanley Carter, born May 11, 1928 at Frederick. Children, the first three born at Olney, the fourth at Silver Spring:

        (a) Charles Stanley Carter, Jr.: January 22, 1954

        (b) Earl Dorsey Carter: February 15, 1955

        (c) Robert Arthur Carter: August 8, 1957

        (d) John Francis Carter: October 3, 1965

    (5) James Arthur Burdette, born April 16, 1936, and married Donna Whitzel, and had children:

        (a) James Arthur Burdette, Jr., born February 18, 1960. Married Cecelia Agnes Stout, born October 3, 1955 at Loretto, Pennsylvania.

        (b) Tina Marie Burdette, born November 2, 1965

c. Claude Edward Burdette, born October 9, 1905 at Damascus, Montgomery County, Maryland; died April 8, 1994. He was retired from the county school system, where he was a carpenter. Married November 20, 1920 to Marjorie Rebecca McElfresh. At the time of his death, there were fourteen granchildren and eight great-grandchildren. His children were born at Damascus:

    (1) Hazel Mae Burdette, born May 21, 1932. Married March 16, 1951 Gene Hoyle, born August 4, 1928 at Barnesville. They had children:

        (a)   Richard Eugene Hoyle: July 8, 1952. Married August 22, 1975 Joanne Offutt.

        (b)   Kenneth Edward Hoyle: December 24, 1957

        (c)   Mark Joseph Hoyle: February 2, 1959

        (d)   Scott Warren Hoyle: September 18, 1960

        (e)   Steven Michael Hoyle: July 25, 1966

(2)   Donald Edward Burdette, born May 1, 1935. Married June Watkins and had a child. He married second July 2, 1960 Mary Ann Kosta, born June 18, 1936 in New York, and had three children:

        (a)   Tina Marie Burdette.

        (b)   Bruce Edward Burdette: May 13, 1961

        (c)   David Allen Burdette: February 27, 1963

        (d)   Dawn Lora Burdette: January 6, 1964

(3)   Grace Rebecca Burdette, born June 30, 1937. Married November 7, 1958 to Robert Ray Snapp, born July 18, 1937 at Olney. Children, all born in Montgomery County, Maryland:

        (a)   Kimberly Rebecca Snapp: August 10, 1961

        (b)   Linda Mae Snapp: November 25, 1963

        (c)   Barbara Claudine Snapp: July 20, 1965

(4)   Clifford Warren Burdette, born June 9, 1941. Married August 3, 1968 Verla Phyllis Jones, born December 31, 1941 at Desloge, Missouri, and had children, born at Leonardtown, Maryland:

        (a)   Gregory Warren Burdette: May 19, 1969

        (b)   Keith Adam Burdette: November 5, 1971

(5)   Claude Michael Burdette, born June 1, 1943. Married October 4, 1963 to Eunice Elaine Staub, born July 30, 1945, and had a son:

        (a)   Kevin Michael Burdette, born May 16, 1964

d.   Sarah Elizabeth Burdette, born March 15, 1904; married June 17, 1925 to Julian Pearre King, born December 5, 1903 and died January 18, 1973, son of Franklin Monroe King (1876) and Mary Avondale Watkins (1878). Their children are discussed under their father's name in Chapter 8, dealing with descendants of Singleton King (1810), which see.

e. Mildred Jane Burdette, born June 12, 1910; married December 21, 1929 to Kelsel Williams Day at Frederick, Maryland, born May 20, 1904, son of James Start Day (1865) and Laura Helen Davis (1874). His birth has also been reported as October 2, 1907. Their children are discussed under their father's name in Chapter 6, dealing with descendants of Harriet Ann King (1807), which see.

f. John Milton Burdette, married Evelyn Virts. One son:
   (1) John Milton Burdette, Jr.

g. Martha Catherine Burdette, born July 17, 1915; married November 25, 1932 to George Chester Pearce, born September 19, 1914, son of Harry Lord Pearce, and Ruth Ann Sheckels. Children, born in Montgomery County:
   (1) Ruby Mae Pearce, born March 28, 1933, married June 6, 1953 to Robert Eugene Bellison, born September 10, 1931. Children, born at Olney:
       (a) Lisa Kay Bellison: April 21, 1958
       (b) Lori Sue Bellison: October 13, 1962
       (c) Lynn Michelle Bellison: May 28, 1965
   (2) Chester Ray Pearce, born March 18, 1934 married July 20, 1955 Violet Mae Gue, born April 27, 1934, daughter of Irving Gue of Boyds. Children, born at Olney, Maryland:
       (a) Daryl Ray Pearce, born May 23, 1956
       (b) Paul Douglas Pearce, born September 1, 1958
       (c) Dana Lou Pearce, born November 17, 1959
   (3) Roscoe Milton Pearce, born June 15, 1935, and married June 15, 1955 Jett Lorraine Flook, born at Myersville, and had children, the first two born at Frederick, the last three at Olney:
       (a) Milton Ashley Pearce: October 16, 1959
       (b) Valerie Ann Pearce: May 13, 1961
       (c) Jeffery Alan Pearce: November 16, 1963
       (d) Melinda Jean Pearce: April 14, 1966
       (e) Paul Benjamin Pearce: February 27, 1975
   (4) George Hamilton Pearce, born January 30, 1941 and married Ernestine Shoemaker. Divorced after one child:

(a) Cathy Pearce.

(5) Harry Alvin Pearce, born May 5, 1943, married May 3, 1964 June Ann Burdette, born September 7, 1944 in Frederick, daughter of Paul Burdette and Martha Ann Ifert. Two children:

    (a) Harry Todd Pearce, born December 24, 1969 at Bad Cannstatt, West Germany

    (b) Kimberly Martha Pearce, born April 15, 1971 at Olney, Maryland

h. Charles King Burdette, born December 10, 1917, and married to Lois Watkins, daughter of Ray Watkins and Bessie King. Married second August 6, 1946 to Ruby Clay, born April 22, 1925. Two children from his second marriage:

    (1) Charles King Burdette, Jr.: December 27, 1947

    (1) Rebecca Elaine Burdette: February 6, 1949

2. Mamie Burdette, born April 26, 1875; died March 16, 1877

3. Oscar W. Burdette, born 1878; died 1919. Married May 21, 1902 to Annie Jennie Pugh, born 1878; died 1919.

4. Martha J. Burdette, born c.1877; died May 25, 1936. Married first to Harry Thompson, and second to Ryland or Reilly.

5. Lola Burdette; married Howard Yingling.

6. Estelle Burdette, born March, 1880

7. Della Maude Burdette, born November 6, 1882 at Clarksburg and died January 15, 1952 in Washington, D. C. Married October 1, 1901 William Jose, born March 25, 1871 in Rhaunen-Trier, Germany; and died July 6, 1953 in Washington. They had children, born in Washington:

a. William Jose, Jr., born July 9, 1905; died January 16, 1955; Married c.1923 to Mary Young Davis, born January 6, 1906 in Washington; died May 29, 1975. At least one daughter:

    (1) Betty Jane Jose, born November 7, 1926; married in Washington, September 27, 1947, William Henry Scrivener, Jr., born there April 16, 1925; died there May 10, 1945.

8. Charles Burdette, born June 21, 1885; died March 11, 1970. Married to Vivian M. King, born September 15, 1888; died January 15, 1982. Clarksburg United Methodist.
9. Basil Vernon Burdette, born May 3, 1887; died January 3, 1892
10. Fred E. Burdette; married Lucille Penn; lived at Ohiopyle, Pa.

CHILD 2

Somerville King
1848-1922

This son of Edward J. King (1821) was born May 28, 1848, and died March 7, 1922. His name has also been reported as Sommerville W. King. Married to Joan Elmon Beall and buried at Damascus Methodist Church.

CHILD 3

Rufus Kent King
1850-

This son of Edward J. King (1821) and Mary Jane Burdette (1825) was born January 28, 1850, and died April 22, 1916. He was married June 19, 1879 to Emma F. Bowman, born February 5, 1862, died October 14, 1936. Buried at the Damascus Methodist Church cemetery. The 1880 census for Clarksburg District carries a household headed by William H. Bowman, born c.1821, with his wife, Sarah, born c.1819. Living in the household at the time is Rufus Kent King, listed as son in law, with his wife, Emma F., listed as daughter, and their first child, then only one month old. His obit in the Sentinel stated that he left his wife, "the former Miss Bowman," and children. In a set of books titled Inventories, Sales, Distributions and Administrations, found in the Register of Wills Office for Montgomery County, in Liber GCA 9 at folio 280, dated November 23, 1900, there is the receipt of Emma F. King for her share of the estate of her father, William H. Bowman. There is a similar receipt from her sister, Sarah Bowman. Administrator of the estate was Rufus Kent King. Other documents indicate that he was also a Justice of the Peace for the county. The children, most of whom are buried at the Damascus Methodist Church, included:

1. Laura Cornelia King, born May 8, 1880, died December 18, 1939. Married April 18, 1908 to Wilbur Stone Day, born January 31, 1882; died April 14, 1955, son of James Edward Day (1855) and Emma Jane Lawson (1859). Buried at Damascus, no children.

2. Ardella Mae King, born April 29, 1882, died November 10, 1959. Married December 31, 1908 at Damascus to Howard Montgomery Miles, born September 12, 1879; died December 17, 1952. His will is found in liber WCC34, folio 11, in the records of Montgomery County, Maryland. Her will is filed in liber VMB 118, folio 418. They had children:
   a. Howard Montgomery Miles, Jr., married Diamond
   b. Thomas Miles, married Janet Etchison
   c. Laura Virginia Miles, married Thomas Aston Garrett
   d. Mary Katherine Miles, a Major in the US Army; married to Whitaker
   e. Henry K. Miles, married Eleanor

3. Effie Lee King, born October 3, 1883, died May 20, 1972. Married June 10, 1903 to Arthur Monroe Burdette, born October 26, 1880; died April 9, 1964, son of William W. Burdette and Mary Wooten Lawson. Effie Lee was survived by three children, eight grandchildren and fourteen great grandchildren. Children were:
   a. Lois Burdette, born August 18, 1906; married December 26, 1925 to Murray Davis Day, born May 20, 1904 near Browningsville, son of James Start Day (1865) and Laura Helen Davis (1874). The descendants of Lois and Murray are found under his name in Chapter 6, dealing with descendants of Harriet Ann King (1807), which see.
   b. Mary Emma Burdette, born August 18, 1913; married April 18, 1931 to Amos O'Neal Twenty, born September 1, 1908, son of John Twenty and Della Irene Reeder. Children:

(1) Amos O'Neal Twenty, Jr., born June 7, 1932, and married July 1, 1954 to Charlotte Lee Welsh. They had children:
    (a) Larry Leroy Twenty, born 1958
    (b) Linda Lee Twenty.
    (c) Lisa Lee Twenty, born 1963
(2) Donald Lee Twenty, born July 3, 1933, died July 3, 1934.
(3) Mary Jane Twenty, born October 13, 1937, and married June 6, 1958 to John Edgar Fleming, Jr.
(4) Larry Monroe Twenty, born October 11, 1942 and drowned August 8, 1956
(5) Thomas Michael Twenty, born December 2, 1947. Married July 25, 1970 to Linda Kay Butler.
c. Arthur Monroe Burdette, Jr., born December 11, 1911, and married June 4, 1938 to Elaine Agnes MacKenzie, born January 23, 1920, daughter of Joseph Stanislaus MacKenzie and Amy Ruth Twenty. Children:
    (1) Carolyn Lee Burdette, born February 2, 1944 at Frederick. Married twice: first Davis, no children. Married second December 3, 1968 to Gene Autry King, born September 12, 1945 at Frederick, son of Woodrow King and Margaret Holt.
d. William Kent Burdette, died in an auto accident; married to Eleanor M. Burgess and had children:
    (1) Ronald Monroe Burdette, born 1943
    (2) Eleanor Marie Burdette.
4. Sally Jane King, born January 19, 1886; died February 15, 1953. Married December 25, 1907 at Damascus to William Jackson Day, born December 12, 1886 at Silent Valley, and died August 28, 1970, son of James Elisha Day (1862) and Mamie Mullinix (1868). The will of William Jackson Day is filed in Case No. 052-09-70J in Montgomery County records. He had children:
a. James Kent Day, born March 7, 1909 at Damascus, and married December 28, 1939 Helen Lolita Burdette. They had one son:

(1) James Kent McKendree Day, born March 18, 1942 at Washington, D. C. A lawyer, he married May 1, 1971 Yvonne Margareta Eriksson, born August 28, 1943 at Stockholm, Sweden. A son:
    (a) James Kent McKendree Day, Jr., born July 12, 1975 at Asheville, North Carolina.

b. William Jackson Day, Jr., born September 29, 1920, and married December 27, 1948 Nancy Ellen Watson, born February 27, 1923. One child, adopted:
    (1) Lee Ellen Day, born February 3, 1959, died 1978 in an auto accident.

5. William E. King of Damascus. This individual is perhaps the son of Rufus Kent King (1850). The obituary of Rufus in 1936 listed several daughters, and his one son, William E., then living in Damascus. According to his own obituary appearing in the Montgomery County *Journal* of May 15, 1987, this William E. was born c.1899 in Damascus, and died May 13, 1987 in Culpeper, Virginia; buried at Damascus Cemetery. He was married to Elsie Young, and at the time of his death, was survived by twenty grandchildren, sixteen great grandchildren, and seven children, whose place of residence was listed as of 1987:

a. William E. King, Jr. of Ednor, Maryland. He died prior to 1994, and was married to Mary C. Beall, born 1922 and died March 29, 1994, the daughter of Charles H. Beall and Carmilla Chisolm; and is buried at Union Cemetery, Burtonsville. They had three children, with their residence listed, and a grandchild, Lindsay King, whose father is not specified. The children were:
    (1) William E. King, III, of Takoma Park
    (2) Gerald Hayward King, of Gaithersburg
    (3) Mary C. King, married to Hull of Manassas, Virginia, who had at least one child:
        (a) Wendy Hull.

b. Rufus King, of Clearwater, Florida, and perhaps named for his grandfather

c. Audrey King, married to Shorter, of Annapolis, Maryland

d. Arnold King, of Hagerstown, Maryland

e. Shirley King, married to Alton M. Martin, a Montgomery
    County policeman. Lived in Laytonsville.
f. Betty King, married Gum, of Valley Head, West Virginia
g. Barbara J. King, married Brenner, of Silver Spring, Md

CHILD 4

Franklin Scott King
1852-1894

This son of Edward J. King (1821) and Mary Jane Burdette
(1825) was born born c.1852, and died September 29, 1894 at the
age of 42 years, 4 months and 14 days. Married October 18, 1876
to Elizabeth E. Williams, born c.1855; died June 2, 1907, daughter
of William Williams. The couple appear in the 1880 census with
their first child. All are buried at Salem Methodist Church in Cedar
Grove, Montgomery County. His known children were:
1. Wootie Lee King, daughter, born December 20, 1877
2. Agatha W. King, born c.1885; died January 2, 1901 at the age
    of 16 years, 8 months and 21 days.
3. Robey F. King, lived in Washington in 1907, married to Mae
    Keefer.
4. Mabel P. King, married Perry Anderson.

CHILD 5

James Edward King
1854-1934

This son of Edward J. King (1821) and Mary Jane Burdette
(1825) was born October 22, 1854 and died November 21, 1934.
Married November 1, 1876 Addie Cassandra Hurley, born March
7, 1859 and died 1942, daughter of Obed Hurley (1800) and Maria
Louise Waters Peters (1819). Both buried at the Clarksburg United
Methodist Church cemetery. In the 1880 census, the young couple
appear, with their first child at the age of two. Also in the household is Obed Hurley, listed at 79 years of age. The family Bible of

James Edward King is now in the possession of James R. King of Clarksburg, and contains a number of references to family members. The will of James Edward King, dated November 14, 1930, is recorded in liber HGC 5 at folio 439. He leaves his estate to his wife for her lifetime, and at her death or her remarriage, to their seven children:

1. James Obed King, born June 18, 1878, died December 13, 1962. Married June 12, 1901 at the bride's home to Alma Owings Johnson of Buck Lodge, then the teacher in the one-room school at Cedar Grove, in Montgomery County. She was born March 28, 1874 and died January 5, 1939, and both are buried at Salem Methodist Church in Cedar Grove. Her parents were Thomas Johnson and Katharine Stewart. James Obed operated the general store there, and was a life-long member of the church. His will, dated November 5, 1930, was probated December 17, 1962, and filed in liber VMB 155 at folio 868 in the office of the Register of Wills for Montgomery County, Maryland. In the will, he names his wife as a legatee, and specifically names "my legally adopted daughter" Catherine L. King, also known as Katherine L. King. An infant death, and one daughter:

   a. Infant King, April 16, 1904
   b. Katherine L. King, born March 21, 1910, died November 18, 1983 in an auto accident at Hagerstown. Married September 1, 1934 at Damascus, Richard George Hunt. Children:
      (1) Alma Jean Hunt.
      (2) Richard Hunt.

2. Ettie May King, born July 16, 1881, died January 9, 1976. Her will is recorded in liber TME 8 at folio 482 in Montgomery County, and provides numerous names of family members. Married December 27, 1905 at Clarksburg, to James Russell Boyer, born August 7, 1881, died August 8, 1948, son of John Wesley Boyer and Vera Day. No children

3. Dora Sophronia King, born January 29, 1884; christened December 10, 1885 at Clarksburg Methodist Church. Married there December 18, 1907 to Claude Gyspon Mullinix, born January 6, 1882 near Damascus, died September 3, 1964 at

Olney hospital, a farmer. He was a son of William A. Mullinix and Elizabeth Bowman. No children.

4. Raymond King, born December 7, 1886; died February 25, 1972. Married December 20, 1913 at Barnesville, Montgomery County, Anna Edmonia Gardiner, born January 5, 1891; died August 30, 1960. Both buried Clarksburg United Methodist Church. They had children:
   a. Dorothy King, married Allen W. Dallas and had a child:
      (1) Mary Ann Dallas, married Bandy.
   b. James Raymond King, born January 31, 1917 Clarksburg and died June 19, 1982 at Winterhaven, Florida. Known as Pete, he was married September 3, 1946 to Sarah L., born 1922. Both buried at Clarksburg United Methodist Church cemetery. He had children:
      (1) James E. King.
      (2) Margaret Ann King.
      (3) Michael Ray King.
5. Forrest Edward King, born August 4, 1889 at Clarksburg, and died December 14, 1955 in Baltimore. Married April 23, 1916 at Ellicott City, Maryland, to Ida Elizabeth Behn, born September 6, 1891 in Washington, D. C., died June 16, 1961 in Baltimore, the daughter of John E. Behn and Clara A. Englemeyer. Forrest and Ida had a son:
   a. James Forrest King, born November 30, 1916 Baltimore. Married there December 21, 1946 Carolyn Louise Prout, born October 7, 1916 in Calvert County, Maryland, the daughter of Carrow Tolson Prout and Mary A. Merrick. James Forrest is an Air Force Colonel and had children:
      (1) James Forrest King, Jr., born January 9, 1949 at Salina, Kansas. Married June, 1971 at Andrews Air Force Base, Maryland, Mary Louise Meehan.
      (2) Sallie Behn King, born March 22, 1952 at Walter Reed Hospital. Married December 17, 1977 at *Elmwood,* Calvert County, Maryland, Steve Keffer
      (3) Caroline Prout King, born August 3, 1953 at Ft. Meade Hospital, Maryland
      (4) Mollie Merrick King, born May 30, 1961 at Scott Air Force Base, Illinois.

6. Addie Maria King, born May 8, 1893, and died April 30, 1962. Married November 29, 1922 at Clarksburg, Clarence Gorman Griffith, born May 31, 1899, died February 28 1967, son of Clarence M. Griffith and Grace Etchison. Gorman Griffith was postmaster of Gaithersburg for a number of years. He and his wife are buried at Forest Oak in Gaithersburg. No children.

7. Pauline Almabelle King, born August 21, 1900, and died November 22, 1991 at the Wilson Health Care Center in Gaithersburg, Maryland; buried at Clarksburg. According to marriage records of Montgomery County, Pauline King, aged 19, was married October 25, 1919 at Clarksburg to Milton Thompson, born November 6, 1899, died February 22, 1945, son of William and Gertrude F. Thompson. They had two daughters. She married second Charles Jackson Rabbitt, born December 17, 1878, but had no children. Active in Red Cross volunteer work during World War II; the Epworth Methodist Church; Daughters of America; Order of the Eastern Star; and Pythian Sisters. Survived by two daughters:

   a. Ettie Grace Marie Thompson, born August 9, 1920. Married Marion Blain Dayhoff, who retired as a Captain of the Montgomery County police, born September 5, 1909, and died July 27, 1970, son of Willford Ellis Dayhoff and Margaret Thompson. One daughter:
      (1) Tanya Lee Dayhoff, born January 12, 1943, and married to Albany Grubb and had children:
         (a) Scotty Grubb, born December 5, 1967
         (b) Nichole Grubb, born September 17, 1971
         (c) Keith Grubb, born February 28, 1973
   b. Dora Catherine Thompson, married to Ivens Buchanan and had children:
      (1) Ivens Buchanan, Jr., born February 12, 1960
      (2) Cynthia Ann Buchanan, born April 8, 1962

CHILD 6

Holady Hix King
1857-1935

This son of Edward J. King (1821) and Mary Jane Burdette (1825) was born December 12, 1857, and died August 9, 1935. Buried at Clarksburg United Methodist Cemetery with his wife. His name is found spelled Holliday in his father's will. Married October 1, 1879 in Frederick County to Amy Jane Musgrove, born April 3, 1860, and died October 2, 1927. Two sons are buried there with them, as well as two infant deaths. The obituary of their son, Thurston B. King, provides the names of three more of the children:

1. Protes E. King, born c.1880, died January 31, 1882 at age 1 year, 6 months and 27 days.
2. Flora S. King, born December 26, 1886, died August 13, 1952 at Clarksburg. Married to Edward Smith and had children:
    a. King W. Smith.
    b. Edward H. Smith.
3. Thurston B. King, born December 28, 1889, and died September 14, 1972 at the Frederick Nursing Center. His will was dated October 18, 1963 and was probated in Rockville, Maryland. There, he leaves his entire estate to his wife, with the provision that should she predecease him, the estate is to be divided between their children. At the time, he lived in a brick home on Ridge Road in Damascus, and owned a farm of 123.16 acres on Lewisdale Road. He was married c.1912 to Pomona Burdette, born December 22, 1894 and died January 1, 1967, daughter of Abraham Lincoln Burdette and Georgia Ellen Waters King (1867). Thurston and his wife are both buried at Clarksburg United Methodist Church cemetery in Montgomery County. He was a farmer and a building contractor. They had at least three daughters and two sons who survived their father, and 12 grandchildren and 14 great grandchildren. Children were:
    a. Mildred Ardean King, born c.1913. Married July 11, 1931 at Clarksburg to E. Calvin Burdette, born c.1910 and died September 1, 1987. Born in Hyattstown, the son

of Edgar Luther Burdette and Lucy Benson. A farmer, living near Clarksburg, in Montgomery County. Children:

(1) E. Allen Burdette of Boyds; married Mary Ann Beall, and had children:
  (a) Ruth Ann Burdette.
  (b) Joseph Allan Burdette. Married; two children:
    1. Andrea C. Burdette.
    2. Mickey Allan Burdette.
  (c) Alana Linda Burdette.

(2) Shirley B. Burdette, born February 3, 1935, and married Jack Kling, born April 17, 1933, son of Thomas Maynard Kling (1908) and Edna Mae King (1908). Children:
  (a) Ronald Maynard Kling: December 29, 1958
  (b) Laurie Gayle Kling: June 10, 1964

b. Bernice Louise King, married Raymond Mills. Children:
  (1) Gordon Mills.
  (2) Harold Mills.
  (3) Kenneth Ray Mills, married Natha Ruth May.

c. Kenneth Thurston King, born February 20, 1921 at Clarksburg, and was a Montgomery County policeman. Married to Olivia Jewell, born November 24, 1923 at Comus. One son:
  (1) Leonard Thurston King, born April 21, 1942 at Clarksburg. Married to Margaret Estelle Burdette, born September 7, 1940, the daughter of Albert Maurice Burdette (1909), and had children:
    (a) Lisa Ann King, born September 10, 1962
    (b) Kelly Lynn King, born July 28, 1965
    (c) Leonard Thurston King, Jr., born February 19, 1969

d. Doris Jane King, Born August, 1926. Married to Calvin Kemp Burdette, born August 6, 1924 at Long Corner, and died October 25, 1969, son of Amos D. Burdette and Nellie Kemp. They had children:
  (1) Norma Jean Burdette.
  (2) Elizabeth Ellen Burdette, born September 5, 1961

e. Robert Hilton King, married Doris Thompson.

4. William Haller King, born May 18, 1893 and died November 11, 1972, buried in Mountain View Cemetery, Montgomery County. He was first married to Lucy Poole, daughter of Newton "Knute" Poole and Hepsi Gertrude Purdum (1875); and second to Daisy I. Price, born c.1891 and died February 8, 1974. She had first been married to Wesley R. Smith, by whom she had a daughter and a son. William Haller's will was dated April 5, 1972 and probated in Montgomery County, in which he names his wife, and both of her children from her first marriage. Only one daughter is named in the will, Lucille M., and a daughter-in-law, Eileen M. King. He also names a grandson, Robert M. King, and two granddaughters: Catherine Jones and Patricia Lucille King. His stepchildren and children appear to have included:

    a. Haller Howard King, born December 9, 1912; married to Eileen M., and father of the grandson and granddaughter bearing the King name:

        (1) Robert M. King.

        (2) Patricia Lucille King.

    b. Lucille M. King, married to Junkin.

    c. Frances Lucille King, born May 29, 1914, perhaps married to Jones, and the mother of the granddaughter bearing that name and mentioned in the will.

5. Claude H. King, probably the same who was born 1901 and died 1972; buried at Salem United Methodist at Cedar Grove. Married Oda May Cline, born 1902, and had at least the following children:

    a. Katherine King, married William V. Mullinix.

    b. Dorothy May King, born December 27, 1924 and died September 14, 1925. Buried at Clagettsville

    c. William E. King; married to Kathryn A.; children:

        (1) Janet Elaine King; married Runkles. A son:

            (a) Michael W. Runkles.

        (2) Deborah M. King; married Lowman. A son:

            (b) Jeffrey D. Lowman.

    d. Betty J. King; married to Nicholson

6. Bessie King, married Ray Watkins (or Roy), son of Garrett Webster Watkins (1872) and Vertie A. Mullinix (1873). Children:
   a. Lois Watkins, married to Charles King Burdette, born December 10, 1917, son of Claude H. Burdette (1872) and Sarah Rebecca Boyer (1874); no children.
   b. Grace Watkins.
   c. William Watkins, married a daughter of Joe Abrams.

CHILD 7

Lewis Bell King
1861-1932

This son of Edward J. King (1821) and Mary Jane Burdette (1825) was born c.1861, and died September 29, 1932. Married February 6, 1883 to Emma Jane Hurley, born 1863 and died 1942. She was a daughter of John W. Hurley (1831) and Frances M. Richardson (1838). They are buried in the Clarksburg United Methodist Church cemetery, with one named son, and twin infant deaths. They had other children:

1. Howard Monroe King, born 1883; died 1910, single.
2. Sherwood C. King, born c.1885, died February 12, 1958. Married to Grace Lawson, born c.1882, died March 13, 1954, daughter of George Lawson, and had children:
   a. Allen King, married and had children:
      (1) Betty King, died of cancer, single.
      (2) George King.
      (3) Alice King.
   b. Evelyn King, married Richard Duell and had a daughter:
      (1) Patsy Duell.
   c. Frances King, married to James G. Raley.
3. Marian T. King, married July 1, 1910 in Rockville, to Elmer E. Williams. One daughter:
   a. Dorothy Williams, married Ernest Boyden.
4. Helen King, married Hamilton Duvall; had a daughter:
   a. Grace Duvall, married Benjamin McMahon; children:
      (1) Douglas McMahon.

       (2)   Glen McMahon.

       (3)   Lynn McMahon.

5.   Grace King, single.
6.   Infant King, born August 6, 1889; died August 10, 1889
7.   Infant King, born August 6, 1889; died August 15, 1889
8.   Madeline Virginia King, born July 13, 1890, and died July 23, 1955. Married December 8, 1909 to Albert Russell Scott of Long Corner, Maryland. He was a son of Samuel Norris Scott and Margaret Ellen Burdette, and the father of two children:

a.   Ethel Madeline Scott, born November 23, 1910. Married June 13, 1931 to Bernard Diehl Gladhill. He was a son of Franklin S. Gladhill and Mollie W. Baker, and widely known in Montgomery County, Maryland, simply as Buck Gladhill. Children, born near Kemptown, Frederick County, Maryland:

    (1)   Samuel Upton Gladhill, born May 17, 1933, and married February 14, 1959 Rebecca Osie Savage, born October 30, 1934 at Liberty, Maryland, the daughter of Harry Randolph Savage and Bertha Osie Poole. Children, born in Frederick County:
        (a)   Evelyn Marie Gladhill: November 6, 1959
        (b)   Susan Rebecca Gladhill: October 30, 1960
        (c)   Walter Martin Gladhill: April 5, 1963

    (2)   Mary Virginia Gladhill, born August 20, 1935 and married October 1, 1953 Neill Barclay Davis, born February 26, 1930 in Washington, D. C., adopted son of Marshall Davis and Louise Gude. Children, the first three born in Washington, the last born in Frederick. Mary Virginia married second Ray Albert Grimes, born September 1, 1926 at Mt. Airy, Maryland, son of Albert Grimes and Edith A. Harrison; no children. Her children were:
        (a)   Virginia Louise Davis: September 5, 1954
        (b)   Wilhelmina Gude Davis: July 25, 1956
        (c)   Scott Edwin Davis: December 13, 1957
        (d)   John Barclay Davis: January 14, 1963

    (3)   Bernadine Gladhill, born July 9, 1937 and married April 27, 1956 Fred Parker Beall, born November

17, 1930 at Lewisdale, son of Barry R. Beall and
Edith Burdette. Children, born Frederick County:
- (a) Joy Julia Beall, born March 4, 1957
- (b) Bernard Barry Beall, born April 20, 1958
- (4) Maurice Albert Gladhill, born November 6, 1950
b. Helen Scott, born April 16, 1915. Married George
Washington Horman and had children:
- (1) Louis Randolph Horman, married with children:
  - (a) Adam Horman.
  - (b) Daniel Horman.
- (2) Dawn Ellen Horman.
- (3) Nancy Kay Horman.

CHILD 8

Eva Lee King
1864-1928

This daughter of Edward J. King (1821) and Mary Jane Burdette (1825) was born August 31, 1864 and died January 11, 1928.
She also appears in some records as Eveline Lee King. Married to
John Oliver Thomas Watkins, born November 3, 1860; died January 11, 1928, son of Oliver T. Watkins (1828) and Eleanor Jane
Brewer. They had twelve children:
1. Frederick B. Watkins
2. James Norman Watkins.
3. Eleanor Jane Watkins; married Thomas H. C. Flynn.
4. Mazie Marie Watkins. Married December 20, 1910 to John
   Dorsey Woodfield, born November 3, 1887; died July 25,
   1953. They had children:
   - (1) John Woodfield.
   - (2) Thomas Woodfield.
   - (3) Paul Woodfield.
   - (4) Jane Woodfield.
   - (5) Elizabeth Woodfield.
   - (6) Grace Woodfield.
5. Lodge Watkins, died in Washington, D. C., February 7, 1973.
   Married Rosie C. and had children:

a. John D. Watkins
b. Ollie L. Watkins
6. Eva Louise Watkins; married Joseph Waters Woodfield
7. Archibald Brett Watkins. Montgomery County marriage records report the marriage of Archie B. Watkins on March 18, 1921 at Monrovia, to Marie King, born c.1903, which is this individual. He is shown in other records as being just Archer Brett Watkins, born July 16, 1895 at Cedar Grove. His wife is Amanda Marie King, born July 1, 1902, daughter of Edward Walter King (1869) and Fannie Dutrow (1876). They had children, discussed under their mother's name in Chapter 3 dealing with descendants of Middleton King (1801) which see.
8. May Grace Watkins; married Richard T. Schaeffer.
9. Paul Watkins.
10. Earl Watkins.
11. Willis B. Watkins
12. Avie C. Watkins; married James Paul Warfield.

CHILD 9

Amanda Cornelius King
1870-1946

This daughter of Edward J. King (1821) and Mary Jane Burdette (1825) was born February 17, 1870; died November 4, 1946. Called Minnie in her father's will, and listed as Minnie A. in church records, and in the 1880 census, she was married February 20, 1889 to Charles Jefferson Lee Watkins, born 1864 and died 1937, son of Lorenzo Dallas Watkins (1836) and Jane Dorsey Purdum (1840). Buried at Upper Seneca Baptist Church in Cedar Grove. They had at least two sons and a daughter:
a. Charles Jefferson Lee Watkins, Jr., married Rose Mae Johnson. At least one daughter:
(1) Margaret E. Watkins, born April 18, 1917; died December 27, 1995. She is perhaps Margaret Ellen Watkins, who was married June 19, 1943 to Samuel Sylvester Gloyd, born October 12, 1914, son of

311

Henry Dorsey Gloyd (1879) and Margaret Lavina Arnold (1876).

b. Talmadge Lodge Watkins, born 1891, died 1975; married Myrtle Bryan Burns, born June 25, 1896, and died 1979; daughter of Nicholas Edward Burns (1865) and Laura Gertrude King (1873). Talmadge and his wife are buried in the cemetery of Upper Seneca Baptist Church at Cedar Grove, Montgomery County, Maryland. Nearby are the graves of two of their sons:

(1) Charles Edward Watkins, born May 24, 1914 and died March 2, 1975. Married to Mary Belle, born May 6, 1915.

(2) Royce T. Watkins, born 1918, died 1972. Married to Agnes S., born 1919.

c. Gladys D. Watkins, born 1894, died 1897.

Edward King
1740-1784
*

*

John Duckett King
1778-1858
*

*

**Luther Green King
1825-1909**
*

*

*   *   *   *   *

*

* *   Calvin H. King 1846-

*

* *   Eveline L. King 1849-

*

* *   Rufus Fillmore King 1850-1926

*

* *   Homer F. King 1853-

*

* *   Roberta King 1855-

*

* *   Laura Belle King 1862-

*

* *   Edna Estelle King 1905-

CHAPTER 14

Luther Green King
1825-1909

This son of John Duckett King (1778) was born March 10, 1825 in the Clarksburg area of Montgomery County, Maryland, and died March 7, 1909. Buried in the Kingstead Farm Cemetery. He must have been ill for a time, since, according to the Montgomery County *Sentinel* of January 24, 1908, he offered his grist mill at Boyds for sale. Married October 14, 1845 in Frederick, Maryland, to Tabitha Browning, born c.1823, died 1873. He appears as head of household in the 1850 census for the Clarksburg District of Montgomery County, with his wife, Tabitha, and at least two of their children. The household also contains one Edward Holland, born c.1833, a mulatto; and James Shedrick, born 1840, a negro. He appears as head of household in the 1880 census, at the age of 55, listed as a distiller. He was married September 11, 1873 in Frederick County, to Mary A Howe, a widow, then listed at 46 years of age. He was married again, for the third time, c.1899 to Mary Lurena King, his great niece, born October 13, 1880, daughter of John Edward Howard King (1845), and they had one child. She married twice again after his death: first December 1, 1909 to Charles A. Heagy, and then to Herbert Clayton Smith, both at Kemptown; and died May 1, 1964 in Cincinnati, Ohio. He appears as head of household in the 1860 and 1870 census for Montgomery County, with his wife, and several children. His will, dated February 24, 1905, was entered for record March 16, 1909 in the will records of Montgomery County, Maryland, liber HCA 8, at folio 98. He leaves to his son, Rufus F. (Filmore) King, the farm he obtained from John Snowden on June 7, 1868 (EBP5, folio 341); to his grandson, John R. Lewis, land he obtained from John D. King on September 4, 1857 (JGH 6, folio 213), "where my distillery is located". He states in his will that the "major portion of my personal estate will consist of whiskey in bond" and instructs his executor in the disposition of those assets. He also mentions a stepson, William E. Howe. On March 16, 1909, in liber HCA 9 at folio 212 in the office of the Register of Wills for Montgomery County, his widow, Mary L. King, filed a document wherein she reserved the right to take inheritance by dower, rather than under the will, should she so deside. In that document, she lists all the heirs, and mentions that there is the quantity of 49,000 gallons of whiskey in bond. She later decides to inherit under the will. An inventory and appraisal of the personal estate was filed with the Court March 22, 1909, in liber HCA 6 at folio 466, Register of Wills office of Montgomery County, indicating a rather substantial estate for the period. All the whiskey was listed, which ranged in barrel age from June of 1904 to March of 1909. The rest of the appraisal provides us with an idea of the possessions an affluent farmer and business-man of that time required. It included:

176 acres of land	2 acres around distillery
mill, tenant house & 2 acres	70 acres of land (Rufus farm)
1st National Bank stock	90 bushels of rye
50 bushels of malt	19 new whiskey barrels
2 1/2 barrels of flour	600 barrels of feed
95 bushels of wheat	75 cords of wood
furniture in dwelling	1 surveyor's compass
1 horse	1 cow
2 buggies	400 paper bags
9 pea fowls	cash in the house
cash in 1st National Bank	

According to the first account of the estate, dated November 9, 1909, liber HCA 7 at folio 439, the whiskey sold for $6,443.31. The children of Luther Green King will be discussed in individual detail following the general family listing:

1. Calvin H. King, born c.1847
2. Eveline Louise King, born c.1849
3. Rufus Filmore King, born October 7, 1850
4. Homer F. King, born December 24, 1852
5. Roberta King, born c.1855
6. Laura Belle King, born c.1862
7. Edna Estelle King, born July 13, 1905

CHILD 1

Calvin H. King
1847-

This son of Luther Green King (1825) and his first wife, Tabitha Browning, was born c.1847, and was a miller. Married October 9, 1869 to Mary E. Pryor at Browningsville. They appear to be living in his father's household during the census of 1870.

CHILD 2

Eveline Louise King
1849-1928

This daughter of Luther Green King (1825) and his first wife, Tabitha Browning, was born c.1849, died April 21, 1928. Married to William Thomas Jefferson Yingling, born c.1849, died April 11, 1928. They had children:

1. Nicie T. Yingling, born 1885, died 1938. Married Morgan L. Trail, born c.1890, died 1967; buried at St. Rose Catholic Church at Cloppers. At least two sons:
   a. Morgan L. Trail, Jr., married Mary.
   b. Leo V. Trail, married Margaret Rowe, and had a son:
      (1) Leo V. Trail, Jr.
2. Hattie Yingling, married William Luhn, and had a daughter:
   a. Beulah, or Bessie, married Leslie Lawson. Children:
      (1) Wayne Lawson.
      (2) Robert Lawson.
      (3) Darleen Lawson.
3. Lola Yingling, married Horace Washington Smith, who died October 28, 1944.
4. Billy Yingling, married Edith O'Hara, and had children:
   a. John William Yingling, married Anna Lilly.
   b. Joyce Yingling, married Joseph Hender. Six sons.
   c. Jean Yingling.

5. Vernon Yingling, married Exie E. Moxley, born February 24, 1878, died July 29, 1949; buried at Mt. Olivet in Frederick. Three children:
   a. Windsor Yingling, married Grace Harmon. A child:
      (1) Vernon Yingling.
   b. Virginia Yingling, married Joseph Cutsail. A child:
      (1) Melvin Cutsail.
   c. Exel Yingling, married Jean McCurdy.
6. Nettie Beatrice Yingling, born January 4, 1880, died February 21, 1944. Married James Otis King, born July 2, 1872, died May 2, 1956, son of James Harrison King (1841) and Mary Emma Essex (1845). Nettie Beatrice and James Otis had five children, who are discussed in Chapter 8, dealing with the descendants of Singleton King (1810), which see.
7. Belle Yingling, married Cleveland Lawson.

CHILD 3

Rufus Filmore King
1850-1926

This son of Luther Green King (1825) and his first wife, Tabitha Browning, was born October 7, 1850, and died April 26, 1926 at his home near Purdum, Montgomery County. Married March 25, 1874 to his cousin, Ursula Mahala King, born August 30, 1857 and died December 2, 1940, daughter of John Middleton King (1830). Both are buried at Damascus United Methodist Church. The family appears in the 1880 census for Clarksburg District, with Rufus and his wife; and their son, Genoa, then five years old. Also in the household is Ursula M. J. Orme, eleven (born this is Ursula M. Jemima Orme, born c.1868), listed as a cousin. His will, dated May 31, 1919, was entered for record June 3, 1926 in liber HGC 33 at folio 319, will records of Montgomery County. He directs that his farm of 72.75 acres be sold, and the proceeds distributed to his wife and children. The estate was not finally closed until December 1, 1940. Children were:
1. Genoa King, born May 16, 1875 and died November 3, 1943, He is buried at Damascus Methodist Church cemetery. Mar-

ried at Mountain View Methodist Church, October 20, 1898 to Vinnie Edna Lawson, born August 26, 1875; died July 25, 1954; buried with her husband. She was a daughter of James Uriah Lawson and Katherine Elizabeth Turner of Frederick County. An infant daughter is buried with them, the first listed. The Montgomery County *Sentinel* of July 5, 1901 announced that he was building a mill at Damascus. His will, dated March 18, 1943, is found in Liber OWR 6 at folio 486 in the will records of Montgomery County, entered March 6, 1945. It names his wife, and a daughter:

a. Catherine Elizabeth King, infant death April 3, 1906

b. Edna Mae King, born September 17, 1908, died February 26, 1969; buried Westhaven Memorial Gardens. Married Thomas Maynard Kling, born August 15, 1908, died May 4, 1928, the son of Thomas Kling and Fannie Montgomery. Children:

    (1) Jack Kling, born April 17, 1933. Married at Clarksburg, Maryland, July 31, 1953, Shirley B. Burdette, born February 3, 1935, the daughter of E. Calvin Burdette (1910) and Mildred Ardean King (1913). Children:

        (a) Ronald Maynard Kling: December 29, 1958

        (b) Laurie Gayle Kling: June 10, 1964

    (2) Frances Edna Kling, born March 17, 1941. Married May 9, 1964 to Leonard Grayson "Jack" Phelps, born January 6, 1938, son of Albert Grayson Phelps and Catherine Alberta Miller. Children, including at least:

        (a) Boy Phelps, stillbirth June 13, 1965

        (b) Gregory Scott Phelps: September 6, 1966

        (c) Thomas Leonard Phelps: June 11, 1968

2. Amy Matrona King, born September 7, 1881, died August 8, 1955. At least one compilation of marriage records gives her date of birth as c.1872, which would appear to be incorrect. Married July 24, 1900 to Ira Leroy Jones, born October 6, 1877, died December 13, 1970, and had children:

a. Ira King Jones, married Margaret Miller.

b. Everett Rufus Jones, born January 25, 1914. Married first to Mary Hazel Jacobs, born October 31, 1912, died May 2, 1981, daughter of Norman Bliss Jacobs (1883) and Roberta Columbia King (1885). Everett married second to Jacquelyn Schroder, who is currently minister at Kemptown Providence Church. Children born to the first marriage only, discussed under the name of Mary Hazel Jacobs in Chapter 3, devoted to descendants of Middleton King (1801), which see.

3. Ethyl Lansdale King, born May 26, 1886, died June 15, 1971; buried at Damascus. Married December 22, 1904 at the Methodist Episcopal Parsonage in Frederick, Maryland, to Millard Diehl Burdette, born October 24, 1885, died September 29, 1950; also buried at Damascus; son of John F. Burdette (1856-1935) and Ella Florence Turner (1864-1939). Children:

a. Paul Winfred Burdette, born October 22, 1905, died July 24, 1977 in Bethesda, Maryland. Married at Mt. Tabor Methodist Church in Etchison, Maryland, June 19, 1930, to Nettie Estelle Griffith, daughter of Walter and Mary Estelle Griffith. Children, born in Washington, D. C.:

(1) Jacolyn Burdette, born October 28, 1939. Married January, 1959 to Richard Conklin of Frederick. They had children:

(a) Jean Michele Conklin: December 29, 1967

(b) Richard Walter Conklin: March 12, 1961

(2) Paul Douglas Burdette, born July 11, 1944, and married August 23, 1969 to Jane Regina Long of Bowie, Maryland.

b. Gladys Marie Burdette, born March 13, 1907. Married to Urban Lynch. She married second to Charles Osgood of Catonsville.

c. Mildred D. Burdette, born August 4, 1909. Married in 1929 George Allan Lathrop of Stockton Springs, Maine. He was born June 8, 1904, died July 24, 1941. Children:

(1) George Allan Lathrop, Jr., born August 15, 1930 and died March 27, 1949

      (2)   Marden Burdette Lathrop, born March 26, 1932 and died August, 1933

      (3)   Douglas Allen Lathrop, born August 18, 1941.

d.   Mabel Leone Burdette; married to Paul E. Wagner of Katmandu, Nepal.

e.   Rodney Leoland Burdette, born April 30, 1914. Married Della Boyce of Charlestown, West Virginia. Children:

      (1)   Leoland Burdette, born 1940 at Lewisdale.

      (2)   Rodney Wesley Burdette, born May 10, 1942, and married twice. His second marriage was June 24, 1962 to Shelva Jean (Wright) Burdette, born March 16, 1940, who was first married to his cousin, Allen Eugene Burdette (see following). They had a son:

          (a)   Kevin Brian Burdette: September 9, 1963

      (3)   Danny Lee Burdette, born October 12, 1943 in Frederick; lived in South Dakota.

f.   Millard Diehl Burdette, Jr., born April 16, 1917, died August 6, 1990 at Montgomery General Hospital, Olney, Maryland. Married July 31, 1937 at the parsonage in Clarksburg, Madalyn Willard Bennett, born 1919. They had children, born at Browningsville, Maryland:

      (1)   Allen Eugene Burdette, born July 31, 1937, and married 1956 to Shelva Jean Wright. Children:

          (a)   Theresa Wright Burdette: December 19, 1956

          (b)   Dawn Michele Burdette: May 28, 1958

          (c)   Kimberly Dee Burdette: April 21, 1961

      (2)   Carol Arlene Burdette, born September 3, 1940. Married David Willis Flynn. Divorced, children:

          (a)   David Curtis Flynn: August 23, 1960

          (b)   Robin Carol Flynn: May 7, 1966

      (3)   Baby Burdette, stillbirth July 27, 1942

g.   Betty Lou Burdette; married William E. Garris.

h.   Elsie Janis Burdette, born June 23, 1919, died March 1, 1970; buried at Bethesda United Methodist Church near Browningsville, single.

i.   Elva Mae Burdette; married to Charles D. Dunlap of Langhorn, Pennsylvania. Three girls and a boy.

4. Filmore Clark King, born July 3, 1890, and died August 6, 1971. He is buried in the Damascus Methodist Cemetery with his second wife and her son, whom he adopted. Married first August 10, 1907 in Frederick to Emma Jane Lydard, born March 12, 1890 and died August 16, 1974, daughter of John C. Lydard (1850); buried at Upper Seneca Baptist Church at Cedar Grove. She was noted for wildlife conservation and for years raised pheasants, quail, wild ducks and other birds and animals for release into the wild. For her efforts, she was appointed Game Breeder and Deputy Game Warden in 1927 by Mr. E. Lee LeCompte, State Game Warden of Maryland. The farm, located on Game Preserve Road near Gaithersburg, is now a part of the Seneca State Park. She had four sons, one of whom predeceased his mother; eleven grandchildren and nineteen great grandchildren. Filmore was married second September 3, 1935 to Pearl Winstead (Hawkins) Green, born May 17, 1896 and died April 20, 1980, daughter of George W. and Ida Hawkins. Her obituary appeared in the *Frederick Post*, in which it was stated that she was survived by one son, last listed below, and two grandchildren. That son was from her first marriage to Green, and was adopted by her second husband. The five sons of Filmore C. King from his two marriages, were:

a. Clark Fout King, born August 16, 1910 at Clarksburg; a retired District of Columbia Corporation Counsel. Lives at Damascus and married Grace Wilson Souder, born July 23, 1913, daughter of Archie W. Souder (1884) and Sallie L. Purdum (1886) and had children, born in the city of Washington, D. C.:

   (1) Daniel Clark King, born August 30, 1939; married to Daria Nadja Hentish, born in the Ukraine, and had children, born in Washington, D. C.:
      (a) Michael Andrew King: July 4, 1966
      (b) Christine Anne King: January 19, 1968
   (2) John MacDonald King, born June 2, 1942. Married February 18, 1962 in Reingold, Georgia, to Alice Keith Myers, born June 2, 1942 at Knoxville, Tennessee, daughter of Richard Myers and

322

Sara Nell Hasson. Children, born in Washington, D. C.:
- (a) Mark Sheridan King: October 19, 1962
- (b) Bryan MacDonald King: October 19, 1965

b. Orin Woodrow King, born January 13, 1912 at Kings Valley; died August 25, 1973, and is buried at Neelsville Presbyterian Church, in Montgomery County. He had retired from the National Institutes of Health, and lived in Gaithersburg, Maryland. His stone carries the name of his wife, who was Ida R. Howard, born January 15, 1914, and predeceased her husband. He had children:
- (1) Jane King, married Musser
- (2) Diane King, married Neal
- (3) Dorothy King, married O'Quinn
- (4) Peggy King.
- (5) Orin Woodrow King, Jr.
- (6) William King.
- (7) Paul King.

c. Malcolm Elwood King, born August 13, 1913 at Kings Valley, and died May 24, 1994. He was a public information officer for the Department of Natural Resources, and founder of the state's *Save-Our-Streams* program. Having served in the CBs during the second world war, he was active in the Izaac Walton League, and was responsible for the donation of land for its national headquarters site from Otis Beall Kent. He received numerous honors and recognitions for his efforts on behalf of conservation of natural resources. He was survived by a very special friend of many years, Jean Serf, of Gaithersburg; his brothers and several nieces and nephews.

d. Donald Genoa King, born April 10, 1917 at Lewisdale; an active member of Grace United Methodist Church in Gaithersburg for many years. Married to Betty Freize, who operated a beauty salon in the town. In 1995, Don was honored for his fifty years of service to Gaithersburg Lions Club. At least one daughter:
- (1) Sandra King.

e. Thomas R. King, son of Pearl Green, adopted by Filmore C. King after their marriage. Married to Jane.
5. William C. King, born July 3, 1894

CHILD 4

Homer F. King
1852-1906

This son of Luther Green King (1825) and his first wife, Tabitha Browning, was born December 24, 1852, and died July 24, 1896, leaving two children, according to his father's will. He is buried at the Mountain View Cemetery, next to his wife. He was married November 2, 1876 to Josephine Purdum, born January 10, 1859, died July 24, 1913, daughter of John Dorsey Purdum (1830) and Sarah A. Baker. Homer and his wife appear in the 1880 census for Clarksburg District, where he is listed as working in a distillery (his father's, no doubt), and they have two children:
1. Clarence E. King, born c.1878
2. Myrtle King, born December, 1879; married to Washington White and second to Brockway. Three children from her first marriage:
    a. Washington White, married Louisa Griffith. Children:
        (1) Louisa White, married Darrington Riggs.
        (2) Dorothy White.
        (3) Washington White.
        (4) Charles White.
    b. Myrtle White.
    c. Frances White.

CHILD 5

Roberta King
1855-1894

This daughter of Luther Green King (1825) and his first wife, Tabitha Browning, was born c.1855, died July 13, 1894 at the age of 38 years, 8 months and 14 days; buried at Bethesda United Methodist Church, Browningsville. Married December 12, 1872 in Frederick County to the Reverend Caleb Joshua Burdette, born January 6, 1849, died January 10, 1920, son of James William Burdette (1813) and Cassandra Purdum (1804). Nine children, many of them buried at Bethesda United Methodist Church, Browningsville. After the death of Robert, Caleb Joshua Burdette was married second October 22, 1895 in Baltimore to Mrs. Arlene G. Robinson, born 1856, died 1934. They had a son. The nine children of Roberta King and Caleb Joshua Burdette were:

1. Emory McNemar Burdette, born October 9, 1873; died July 5, 1874

2. Rebecca Zerah Burdette, born October 14, 1877, died June 24, 1945. Married October 9, 1896 in Montgomery County, to Bradley Watkins, born February 14, 1870, died March 11, 1941, son of William Thomas Watkins and Sarah E. Williams and had children:

   a. Lena Elizabeth Watkins, born February 22, 1898, died March 23, 1982. Married June 2, 1917 to Floyd Moxley, born July 19, 1895, died July 23, 1974, son of Cornelius Edward Moxley and Florence E. Poole. At least one son:

      (1) Floyd Keen Maloy Moxley, born August 16, 1926. Married June 28, 1951 to Ruby Jo Garland, born June 6, 1930 in Tennessee, daughter of Dave W. Garland and Nora Ledford. Two children:

         (a) Glenn Floyd Moxley, born April 4, 1953, and married April 19, 1985 Barbara Ann Peterson born December 19, 1964, daughter of Roger J. Peterson, Sr.

         (b) Nancy Lee Moxley, born February 7, 1957. Married May 20, 1978 Denis Rex Hood, born September 26, 1952, son of Clarence Ellis Hood and Lillian Mae King (1921). Children:
            1. Andrea Lee Hood: September 1, 1982
            2. Daryl Ellis Hood: January 7, 1986

   b. Roberta E. Watkins, born 1901, died 1961. Married to George Lincoln Burdette, born July 9, 1897, died January 25, 1918, son of Abraham Lincoln Burdette (1864) and

Georgia Ellen Waters King (1867). No children. She married second to Charles F. Burdette, born 1898, died 1947, son of Willie H. Burdette and Mamie Pugh, and had two children. Married third to Tightus E. Brown, born 1880, died June 11, 1966, son of Thomas Ephraim Brown and Sarah E. Hilton. No issue. Her two children, born to the second marriage, were:

(1)   Wallace Franklin Burdette, married Dolly Keeney and had children:

    (a)   Robert Franklin Burdette, born 1947, married February 19, 1966 to Barbara Ann Schaffer.

    (b)   Steven Burdette.

    (c)   Teresa Ann Burdette, born 1960

(2)   Ella Irene Burdette, married Gordon Hall, and had children:

    (a)   Lawrence Hall.

    (b)   Beverly Hall.

    (c)   Judy Hall.

    (d)   Patti Hall.

    (e)   Donald Hall.

c.   Howard R. Watkins, born December 19, 1903, died October 30, 1954; buried at Bethesda United Methodist Church, Browningsville, Maryland. Married Lois Lillian Davis, born May 23, 1911, and had children:

(1)   Marjorie Ann Watkins, married Charles J. Green, Jr., born September 5, 1925, died August 10, 1984, son of Charles J. and Helen E. Green. At least two children:

    (a)   Charles Raymond Green.

    (b)   Rita Lynn Green.

(2)   Bradley Parker Watkins, married to Patricia Rae Smith and had children:

    (a)   Jay Bradley Watkins.

    (b)   Patti Gail Watkins, born 1956

    (c)   Jan Parker Watkins, born 1960

3.   Herbert Karsner Burdette, born November 29, 1879, died March 7, 1950. Married Lillie Mae Piquette, born August 26,

1881, died October 21, 1952; buried at Browningsville, Maryland. They had children:

a. Luther Melvin Burdette, born June, 1925/26, and lived two months.

b. Mabel Burdette, married Francis F. Dahler, born November 29, 1887, died April 10, 1951. Buried at Bethesda United Methodist Church, Browningsville. They had children:

    (1) Lillie Amelia Dahler, born 1919, died August 10, 1965. Married Walter B. Alexander. Children:

        (a) Michael James Alexander.

        (b) Joan Anne Alexander.

    (2) Ernest Herbert Dahler, married Wilma Ford, and had a child:

        (a) Francis Frederick Dahler.

c. Sarah Ella Burdette, married first to Wallace Littleford, born 1899, died 1963, and was divorced. Married second Bob Davis, and third William T. Oden. Three children from her first marriage:

    (1) Mabel Alice Littleford, married George Anderson and had children:

        (a) George Anderson.

        (b) William Anderson.

        (c) Mary Alice Anderson.

        (d) David Anderson.

    (2) Helen Edna Littleford, married Norman Sanbower and had children. She married second 1969 Harry L. Hubble. First marriage children:

        (a) John Charles Sanbower.

        (b) Kristine Sarah Sanbower.

        (c) Andrew Francis Sanbower.

    (3) Wallace Charles Littleford, died June 24, 1994 at Hyattsville, Maryland. Married Alice G. and had children:

        (a) Nora Littleford, married Cincotta.

        (b) Christina Littleford, married Huddleston.

        (c) C. H. Michael Littleford.

        (d) William W. Littleford.

(c)   Thomas John Littleford.
d.   Edward Fisher Burdette, born May 16, 1910, died April 18, 1978, sergeant, US Army, retired. Married Birdie V. Sturgis, and had children:
(1)   George Herbert Burdette, married Clara.
(2)   Edward Lewis Burdette.
(3)   Ella Lorraine Burdette, married Carl Williams.
(4)   Robert Francis Burdette.
(5)   Margaret Ann Burdette, married Armas.
(6)   Walter D. Burdette.
(7)   Barbara Ellen Burdette.
e.   Woodrow W. Burdette, married to Evelyn Mann, born c.1908, died November, 1985. Children:
(1)   Francis Bernard Burdette.
(2)   Lois Evelyn Burdette, married Rodney Titus.
(3)   Jo Ann Burdette, married John D. Ewan, Jr.
f.   Herbert Malcolm Burdette, born c.1915 in Washington, D. C., died March 13, 1985, and buried at Bethesda United Methodist Church cemetery, Browningsville, Maryland. He was a retired mechanic, and had been a member of the Browningsville Cornet Band. Married Ellen Elizabeth Miller, born October 2, 1921 in Virginia, died February 12, 1984 at Pleasant View Nursing Home in Mt. Airy, Maryland. She was a daughter of Rogers F. Miller and Margaret Elizabeth Jacobs, and had been first married to Richards, by whom she had a son, Lawrence L. Richards. Children born to Herbert Malcolm Burdette and Ellen Elizabeth were:
(1)   Jerri Lynn Burdette, graduate of Shepherd College, and a Montgomery County teacher. Married Albert C. Oglesby, Jr., and had a child:
(a)   Matthew Jacob Oglesby.
(2)   Sue Ellen Burdette.
(3)   Herbert Malcolm Burdette, Jr., born 1952 and died 1953.
g.   James Daniel Burdette, born December 15, 1921 at Clarksburg, Montgomery County, Maryland; died September 29, 1972 at Suburban Hospital in Bethesda. He

was a builder, and a veteran of the second world war; buried at Gettysburg National Cemetery. Married Eileen Hamilton Paxton, born c.1922, and had children. They were divorced, and Eileen married second to Cordell. The children were:

> (1) James Lawson Burdette, born January 12, 1947 at Columbia Hospital in Washington, D. C.; married May 2, 1970 at the Damascus United Methodist Church, to Margaret Elizabeth Sellers, daughter of Jasper Lee Sellers of Damascus.
>
> (2) Pamela E. Burdette.

h. Guy Putman Burdette, married Julia Mary Margaret Dronenburg, born September 11, 1921 Frederick County, the daughter of William Lee Dronenburg and Ellender Virginia Catherine Kemp. Two children:

> (1) Guy Martin Burdette.
>
> (2) Lee Burdette.

i. John Wesley Burdette, married Ellen Snedecker, who died in 1955. Children:

> (1) Bonnie Jean Burdette.
>
> (2) Lou Ellen Burdette.

4. Luther Melvin Burdette, born 1875, died 1947. Married Effie D. Davis, born 1875, and died 1946; buried at Browningsville, the daughter of Richard Plummer Davis (1844) and Virginia Ruth Williams. Children:

a. Virginia Marie Burdette, died April 5, 1908 at 4 months and 23 days of age.

b. Melvin Burdette, married first Esther Jones and divorced. Married second to Katherine.

c. Lester William Burdette, married Fairy Brandenburg, born March 2, 1903, the daughter of Bradley Jefferson Brandenburg (1863), and Valerie Eveline Hyatt (1867). (See Chapter 4, dealing with the descendants of Elizabeth Miles King [1802] for further information about the Brandenburg family.) Children:

> (1) Carolyn Burdette, married Donald Bell. A son:
>
> > (a) Michael Donald Bell.

(2) Rosalie Nadine Burdette, married May 19, 1965 to William Harvey Rittase.
d. Helen Burdette, married Ray Carter, and had children:
(1) Robert Carter.
(2) Bruce Carter.
5. Simpson Burdette, born July 24, 1884; died August 24, 1885
6. Sadie Burdette, died 1959; married first to Russell Lewis and second Warren Keats. No children either marriage.
7. Sophronia Burdette. Married November 10, 1901 to Calvin Hughes McElfresh. His name is also reported in some records as Colvin Hasey McElfresh. They had children:
a. Fannie Wagner McElfresh, married William Maurice Watkins, born 1902. Their family is reported under the father's name in Chapter 8, devoted to the descendants of Singleton King (1810), which see.
b. Annie Sophronia McElfresh, born February 11, 1906 near Browningsville. Married Raymond Fout Day, born April 26, 1906, son of James Start Day (1865) and Laura Helen Davis (1874). Descendants are discussed under the father's name in Chapter 6, devoted to the family of Harriet Ann King (1807), which see.
c. Marjorie Rebecca McElfresh, married to Claude Edward Burdette, born October 9, 1905 at Damascus, Maryland, and died April 8, 1994, son of Claude H. Burdette (1872) and Sarah Rebecca Boyer (1874). The children are discussed under Claude Edward's name in Chapter 13, devoted to the descendants of Edward J. King (1821), which see.
d. John Hughsie McElfresh, married Evelyn Rippeon and had children:
(1) John Calvin McElfresh, born 1934/36, died 1954 in a car accident.
(2) Evelyn Irene McElfresh, married Urban Wendric Moore and had children:
(a) Debra Mae Moore, born 1954
(b) Urban Wendric Moore, III, born 1955
(c) Patricia Irene Moore, born 1956
(d) Teresa Ann Moore, born 1958

        (e)   John Michael Moore, born 1960

        (f)   James Kevin Moore, born February 4, 1962

        (g)   Cynthia Mary Moore, born October 20, 1964

        (h)   Joseph Allen Moore, born May 11, 1966

  (3)   Ann Louise McElfresh, married to Emmett Ray Pearre and had children:

        (a)   Douglas Ray Pearre, born 1957

        (b)   Pamela Ann Pearre.

  (4)   Kenneth Ray McElfresh, married Carol Welty, and had children:

        (a)   Kenneth Ray McElfresh, Jr.: March 12, 1965

        (b)   Dawn Michelle McElfresh: June 8, 1968

  (5)   Margaret Virginia McElfresh, born 1938, and died 1941 of spinal meningitis.

e. Lindsey Leo McElfresh, married Virginia Mae Burdette, born 1923, daughter of John Norman Burdette (1899) and Dorcas Virginia Ifert (1901), and had children:

  (1)   Linda Mae McElfresh, born May 6, 1943. Married Meredith H. Alexander, Jr., born February 16, 1939, son of Meredith H. Alexander and Mary Martha Booker, and had two daughters:

        (a)   Jennifer Lynn Alexander, born May 5, 1969, married October 14, 1990 Joseph Hedinger.

        (b)   Shiela Kay Alexander, born March 16, 1974

  (2)   Terrence Lee McElfresh, born July 17, 1949 and married June 15, 1974 Linda Hilton, born November 13, 1954, daughter of James Hilton and Esther Harrison. At least one son:

        (a)   John Terrence McElfresh, born 1978

  (3)   Cora Bonita McElfresh, born April 8, 1957, died January 7, 1958

  (4)   Joyce Ann McElfresh, born April 11, 1960, and married William Kavanaugh.

8. Eveline Burdette, twin: May 25, 1894; died August 3, 1894

9. Martha Burdette, twin: May 25, 1894; died August 17, 1894

CHILD 6

Laura Belle King
1862-

This daughter of Luther Green King (1825) and his first wife, Tabitha Browning, was born about April 1, 1861, died August 25, 1882; buried Hyattstown Methodist Church cemetery. Married November 5, 1878 at the home of the bride, to William Filmore Lewis, born May 11, 1901, died February 4, 1961. They had a child, and after Laura's death, William Filmore was married second to Olive Watkins. The child was:

1. John Robert Lewis, born c.1880, and died 1957; married Bessie Lansdale, born 1882, died 1963. Both buried at Pine Grove Chapel cemetery, Mt. Airy, Maryland. They had a son:
   a. Robert Lewis, married Margaret Scott.

CHILD 7

Edna Estelle King
1905-

Edna Estelle King was born July 13, 1905, the only child born to the second marriage of Luther Green King, when he was eighty years of age. Married October 31, 1925 at Ann Arbor, Michigan, to Bennie Emanuel Brierton, born July 16, 1901 in Arkansas, died August 1, 1988 in Miami, Florida, son of Frank and Maude Brierton; divorced. Children:

1. Marabee Jeanne Brierton, born March 1, 1927 at Stuttgart, Arkansas. Married first to Leslie W. Grunenwald and had a daughter, who used the surname of her mother's second marriage to John Seifert, although she was not adopted. Two children born to that marriage, all of them being:
   a. Mary Susan (Grunenwald) Seifert married Merle Fellows
   b. John, Jr. Seifert, lived to marry, but died young

c. Patricia Seifert, married and divorced twice, having a daughter by each marriage. Married first Robert Coma and second to Reza Khairghadam. Her daughters were:

   (1)   Angela Coma.

   (2)   Audrey Khairghadam.

2. Benned King Brierton, born September 16, 1929 in Stuttgart, Arkansas. Married first Mary and had four children; he married second Roberta; no children.

   a.   Benned King Brierton, Jr.

   b.   Bryan Alan Brierton.

   c.   Barry Wayne Brierton.

   d.   Bradley Brierton, an infant death

Edward King
1740-1784
*

*

John Duckett King
1778-1858
*

*

Eveline King
1828-1899
*

*

*   *   *   *   *
*
* *   John Wesley Walker 1849-
*
* *   George Edward Walker 1851-
*
* *   James King Walker 1852-
*
* *   Amanda E. Walker 1854-
*
* *   Charles William Waters Walker 1855-1921
*
* *   Crittenden Henning Walker 1857-
*
* *   Margaret Jemima Walker 1860-1862
*
* *   Eveline Rebecca Walker 1864-
*
* *   Nathan Asbury Walker 1865-
*
* *   Miriam W. Walker 1867-
*
* *   McKendree Bond Walker 1870-1954

CHAPTER 15

Eveline King
1828-1899

This daughter of John Duckett King (1778) and Jemima Miles (1782), was born July 4, 1828 and died July 5, 1899. She was married July 27, 1848 to Nathan James Walker. Son of George Bryan Walker (1799) and Margaret Boyer (1805), he was born October 27, 1824 on the family farm near Browningsville, Montgomery County, Maryland, and died May 4, 1913. At the time of his death, he had 32 grandchildren and 21 great grandchildren. He is the subject of a biographical sketch appearing on page 833 of *Portrait and Biographical Record of the Sixth Congressional District, Maryland*, 1898. It is reported there that Nathan:

> *"advocates the temperance cause, not only in precept, but in example also, for he has never tasted a drop of liquor or smoked a cigar in his life. He is a man of sterling character, respected by all who know him for his ability, industry, perseverance and uprightness."*

Eveline's tombstone in Forest Oak Cemetery, Gaithersburg, Maryland, reports her name as given here, but in other records as Amanda. The 1850 census for the First District of Montgomery County, Maryland, reports the household of the young couple, including Nathan James at age 25, his wife Eveline at age 21, and their first son, John Wesley, at seven months. However, the *Sentinel* newspaper of July 7, 1899 reports her death and there lists her name as Amanda Walker, which may have been a little-used first or second given name. It is of some interest to note that the first daughter of this couple was named Amanda E. Walker, perhaps in reality Amanda Eveline, the full name of her mother.

On November 18, 1849, Nathan James Walker purchased, for nine hundred dollars, part of the tracts of land called *Lost Knife* and *Crabb's Fortress*, containing 190 acres, from Charles H. C. Orme

335

and his wife, and named his new home *Rolling Knoll Farm*. In that deed, Nathan was said to be from Frederick County, Maryland. On March 13, 1867, by deed recorded in Liber EBP 4 at folio 2, he acquired lands from Joseph Mills and his wife, Martha E. Mills. Additional purchases increased the holdings to more than 450 acres of land, on both sides of Goshen Road, and extending into the town of Gaithersburg. Many years later, in the early 1960s, part of his farm, still in the Walker family, became the nucleus of the new town of Montgomery Village. Lost Knife Road, named for the early land grant name, will always preserve some of the history of the area, although newcomers may well not understand its meaning.

In 1877, Nathan Walker built a grist mill on part of the farm, with a wicker dam located on the opposite side of Goshen Road, feeding the mill through a head race running under the road. Many years later, the mill site was acquired by Dolly Becraft Irvine and her husband, Winfree Irvine. At the time of this writing, they still live on the property, and have restored the mill.

Nathan served as Superintendant of the Sunday School of the Methodist Episcopal Church, South, from 1861 to 1891. It is now known as Grace United Methodist Church, the oldest in continuous service in Gaithersburg, and one of the beautiful stained-glass windows commemorates his service there. His will, dated October 5, 1904 and probated May 20, 1913, is found in Liber HCA 14 at folio 188 in the will records of Montgomery County, Maryland. He mentions that his son, Nathan A. Walker, has purchased the grist mill property, and names his surviving children, as well as two grandchildren. He had eleven children, all born on the home farm:

1. John Wesley Walker, born October 29, 1849
2. George Edward Walker, born July 27, 1851
3. James King Walker, born November 24, 1852
4. Amanda E. Walker, born March 19, 1854
5. Charles William Waters Walker, born December 1, 1855
6. Crittenden Henning Walker, born November 19, 1857
7. Margaret Jemima Walker, born May 6, 1860
8. Eveline Rebecca Walker, born May 6, 1864
9. Nathan Asbury Walker, born January 12, 1865
10. Miriam W. Walker, born October 16, 1867
11. McKendree Bond Walker, born October 17, 1870

CHILD 1

John Wesley Walker
1849-1929

This son of Nathan James Walker (1824) was born October 29, 1849 in Frederick County, Maryland, and died June 4, 1929. His parents moved to Montgomery County when he was about one year old, and he lived the remainder of his life there. Married twice: first February 21, 1870 in Montgomery County, Maryland, to Amanda C. Thompson, born November 29, 1843, and died August 17, 1909; daughter of Captain Elijah Thompson and Elizabeth Ricketts. The seven children listed following were theirs, as well as an infant death, most of whom were buried at Forest Oak Cemetery in Gaithersburg.

John Wesley married October 6, 1910 in Washington, D. C. to Frances Eleanor Sibley, born 1872 and died 1949, a daughter of Joshua Sibley and Alcinda Dowden. The report of their marriage in the *Montgomery County Sentinel* lists her name as Nora Sibley, although his death notice some years later in the same newspaper lists the full name first reported above. No children.

In 1876, John Wesley purchased the farm of Eveline Gaither Hughes, and made his home there. The farm is the site of the present Asbury Methodist Village, in the City of Gaithersburg, and Walker Avenue was the farm lane leading from the Frederick Road to his home. By deed dated May 15, 1877, recorded in Liber EBP 16 at folio 335, Montgomery County, John Wesley and his wife conveyed 24 square perches of the tract known as *Deer Park* on the Frederick Road to Eveline Hughes. He served as Montgomery County Commissioner from 1897 to 1898, and six terms on the Board of Commissioners for the town of Gaithersburg. He was the Mayor of the town from 1906 to 1908, and again from 1918 to 1924. In 1892, he was supervisor of roads, and in 1914 and 1917, town assessor. His biography appears at page 659 (with an impressive photograph), in *Portrait and Biographical Record of the Sixth Congressional District, Maryland*, 1898, Chapman Publishing Company of New York and Chicago. His will, dated March 2, 1926 and probated June 11, 1929, is found in Liber PEW 14, at folio 226 in Montgomery County records. He mentions his second wife and his children, as well as his grandson, John Wesley Walker. To the grandson, he left two Bibles, one of which he had received from his own father. His children included:

1. Lula B. Walker, born November 23, 1870; died December 24, 1942. She inherited the family pictures of her father that he acquired prior to his second marriage. She was married June 9, 1896 to Willis B. Burdette, a teacher, born October 26, 1871, and died February 21, 1930. They had one child:

   a. Aubrey Wilson Burdette, born March 2, 1897 and died May 26, 1943. Buried at Forest Oak cemetery in Gaithersburg, Maryland. Married March 1, 1915 to Ruby Adelaide Gloyd, born July 16, 1898, daughter of Edmund Alexander Gloyd (1863). They had children, including:

      (1) Audrey Marie Burdette, born November 24, 1915; married August 25, 1934 James Robert Millan and had children:

         (a) Robert Lawrence Millan, born November 21, 1937

         (b) William Bradford Millan, born October 4, 1939, and died October 30, 1940

         (c) David Lewis Millan; September 25, 1942

         (d) . Dale Alexander Millan; July 12, 1948

      (2) Vera Regina Burdette, born April 8, 1919; married May 17, 1941 Robert Ford Sheffield.

2. Elijah Wilson Walker, born May 9, 1872; died November 9, 1924 at Gaithersburg, Maryland. He was married March 1, 1899 at the bride's home in Mifflinburg, Pennsylvania, to Emma Gertrude Thomas, born 1865 and died May 18, 1921. Deed dated 1904, recorded in Liber 176 at folio 161 in Montgomery County, Maryland, conveys to the couple Lot 14, Block 1, *Russell and Brooks Addition to Gaithersburg*. Their children included:

   a. Calphurnia Walker, who married first Hughes Monday and had two children, following. Married second James Moulden. Her two children were:

      (1) May Lee Monday, married John Woodrow Croft, of Kraft.

       (2)   Joyce Monday.
b.   John Wesley Walker, married July 22, 1931 to Mildred Burton.
c.   Jessamine Walker, married to Joseph Dawson; children:
       (1)   Janet Dawson.
       (2)   JoAnn Dawson.
3. Gertrude Elizabeth Walker, born January 3, 1874, and died August 16, 1957. She was married April 30, 1895 to Edgar Fulks, born April 29, 1873; died March 7, 1938, son of Ignatius Thomas Fulks (1832). His will is found in Book HGC 23, folio 15, dated September 8, 1937 and probated March 15, 1938 in Montgomery County. Edgar was very active in real estate in the county, as were most members of the family, with a number of entries appearing in the index books of the land records. Children included:
a.   Iva Catherine Fulks, born February 20, 1896; died October 30, 1958. Married William T. Lewis, born April 1, 1883 and died July 26, 1961
b.   Thomas Walker Fulks, born January 25, 1898; died November 8, 1913
c.   Leona Gertrude Fulks, born May 27, 1900
d.   Alma Lucille Fulks, born October 13, 1903, and died April 25, 1911.
e.   Evelyn Fulks, born April 16, 1906; died April 20, 1973. She was married to Samuel Thomas and had children:
       (1)   Lawrence Thomas.
       (2)   Warren Thomas.
f.   Estelle Fulks born March 1, 1910, married J. Hildebrand.
4. James Wesley Walker, born December 27, 1876; died July 13, 1877
5. Clara Eveline Walker, born 1878; married November 22, 1899 to Walter Marion Magruder, and had children:
a.   Marshall Magruder, married a King.
b.   John W. Magruder.
c.   Dorothy Magruder, married Merle Ferguson.
6. Dorsey Vernon Walker, born April 22, 1881; died July 17, 1882
7. John Walter Walker: August 12, 1888; died June 13, 1890

CHILD 2

George Edward Walker
1851-1910

This son of Nathan James Walker (1824) was born July 27, 1851, probably on the family farm known as *Rolling Knoll*, just north of the town of Gaithersburg, Montgomery County, Maryland, along Goshen Road, and died March 17, 1910. Married October 31, 1876 to Ella Smith Miles, born May 23, 1848; died February 27, 1939. Her parents were James Hanson Miles and Elvira Beall, who died at the home of her daughter, July 30, 1899, at the age of 90 years. George Edward's will, dated March 7, 1910, and probated April 19, 1910, is found in Liber HCA 8 at folio 274 in the will records of Montgomery County. Her will, dated December 17, 1931, and probated March 28, 1939, is found in Liber HGC 23 at folio 287. She names her two children, and several other family members, including grandchildren. The farm of George Edward Walker adjoined his father's farm to the west, and is today part of the new town of Montgomery Village. His wife's twin brother, Richard Henry Miles, was Mayor of the town of Gaithersburg from 1912 until his death in 1918. The children of George Edward were:

1. Carrie May Walker, born July 1, 1878; married December 31, 1903 to Harry C. Hoskinson, and had three children:
   a. Florence A. Hoskinson, born December 13, 1903, and married to Dr. Francis Hummer. They had children:
      (1) Francis L. Hummer.
      (2) Harry H. Hummer.
   b. Helen M. Hoskinson, born December 31, 1908; married Hugh Jones.
   c. John Henry Hoskinson, born May 22, 1919; married Jessie Kaufman and had one son:
      (1) John Henry Hoskinson, Jr.
2. Marshall Murray Walker, born October 19, 1880; died December 19, 1959. Married December 28, 1910 to Minnie Lee Briggs, born February 17, 1886; died February 25, 1967; daughter of Gideon D. Briggs and Ida Sparrow. Marshall M. Walker was a merchant in Gaithersburg for more than fifty

years, starting his first business with John A. Belt and later with a brother-in-law, Harry Hoskinson. They first conducted their business on the edge of Washington Grove, where the 7-11 Store now stands. Mr. Hoskinson left the business to become one of the founders of what was first known as the Sanitary Grocery Stores, later becoming Safeway. Marshall Walker continued the store at Washington Grove, but when the Sanitary Grocery opened in Gaithersburg, became its manager. He was for a while associated with James Forest Walker in the grocery business, but later went back into the business for himself. Later, he and his sons operated the family grocery business in the Belt Building on the corner of Diamond Avenue and Summit Avenue in the City of Gaithersburg, which is now a historic site. In the early 1950s, they moved the store across Diamond Avenue into what is now a part of the Diamond Drug store. As a personal aside, the author recalls fondly that when I first came to Gaithersburg in 1946, my family shopped in the Marshall Walker grocery in the old Belt Building. The Town Post Office was located in the other part of the building. He served everyone personally, and added the grocery bill with a short stub of pencil on the brown paper bag. He never needed an adding machine, and very seldom made an error, which would be quickly corrected. I recall also that Mr. Walker apparently did not like the steel pennies that were made during the second world war to save copper. He put those he received in a box under the counter. Another of the things I remember was the long pole he used to reach the higher shelves, with a clamp on the end operated at the handle, to pick out a box of cereal, or some can of food. Perhaps few of my readers have seen those, as part of the passing American scene. He had three children:

a. Murray Lee Walker, born April 27, 1913; died April 17, 1964. Married Cornelia H. "Bubbles" Grimm, born September 11, 1912 and died April 27, 1984; daughter of Frederick H. Grimm and Abbie Rebecca Hilleary. A son:

(1) Kimberly Lee Walker, born July 13, 1933, and married Constance Frye. One child:

(a) Mark Alan Walker, a doctor

b. Margaret Belle Walker, born August 20, 1916; married Reverend Frank Hoadley, and lived in Binghampton, New York, and Wayne, Pennsylvania. Two children:
    (1) John F. Hoadley.
    (2) Kenneth W. Hoadley.
c. Milton Miles Walker, born May 23, 1919. Married October 1, 1940 to Julia Ward, born November 20, 1916, daughter of George Sprigg Ward and Daisy Belle Benson. Milton worked with his father in the family grocery, and after his father's death, sold the business in 1966. In 1958 he opened Walker's Laundry and Dry Cleaning on Diamond Avenue, across the street from the present Great China Restaurant, and later added the Apartment Laundry Route Service, and a second laundry on Frederick Avenue. Milton was a member of the City Council of the City of Gaithersburg from 1956 to 1974, at which time he was appointed Mayor, and served in that capacity until 1976. Two children:
    (1) Katherine Elaine Walker, born February 21, 1949; married to Gregory Hand and had children:
         (a) Patricia Hand.
         (b) Brian Hand.
    (2) Barbara Ann Walker, born January 8, 1951

CHILD 3

James King Walker
1852-1934

This son of Nathan James Walker (1824) was born November 24, 1852 on *Rolling Knoll Farm* north of Gaithersburg, Maryland, and died November 20, 1934. Married March 18, 1879 at the Clarksburg Methodist Church, to Emma M. Waters of Potomac, Maryland, born September 24, 1853 and died June 10, 1900, daughter of Andrew Jackson Waters (March 6, 1825 to February 15, 1897) and Keturah Ann Windsor (1824 to 1907). Married second to Anna Myers, born May 12, 1857 and died February 14, 1940. There were eight children born to the first marriage, and none to the second. The will of Anna Myers Walker, dated April 24, 1937, is found in Liber HGC 33 at folio 164 in will records of Montgomery County, Maryland. She mentions her late husband and his daughter, Grace Maude Walker *"for all she has done for me"* and her Executor is Russell King Walker.

At the time of her death, she was living with Mrs. Evelyn Bessie Darby, one of her stepdaughters. James King Walker lived on a dairy farm on the east side of Goshen Road, north of the town of Gaithersburg, which he had purchased from the Saffell family. After the death of their father, James King and his brother, McKendree Walker (1870), purchased the grist mill site and operated the Spring Valley Mill until it was sold in the early 1900s. Children from the first marriage were:

1. Grace Maude Walker, born February 21, 1880; died January 14, 1947 single. Her will was dated May 1, 1945 and probated March 19, 1947, and recorded in Liber OWR 21 at folio 209 in the will records of Montgomery County, Maryland. She left to her sister, Evelyn Bessie Walker Darby, the ten acres of land on Frederick Pike, which she had purchased from Clay and Rosabelle Plummer. She also provided for the installation of a window in Grace Methodist Church to read *"In Loving Memory of James King Walker."* She mentions other members of her family, and her lifelong friend, Elizabeth Kingsley Sterrick.

2. Harry Waters Walker, born April 24, 1882; died November 3, 1952, single.

3. James Forest Walker, born April 28, 1884, and died February 20, 1964. Married November 3, 1917 Marie Louise McCabe, born July 4, 1892 in Washington, D. C. and died April 22, 1975, daughter of Harry Robert McCabe and Rosa Belle Wills. The book, *Gaithersburg, A History*, published by the City in 1978 as part of their Charter Centennial, contains a lengthy biography of James Forest Walker, as well as much of the basis for some of the Walker genealogy presented here. The reader is urged to read the entire book referred to in order to gain a better insight into the history of the region, and the part that the Walker family has played.

Known as J. Forest to all his friends and associates, he was often referred to as "Mr. Democrat" because of his vast knowledge of, and involvement in, the workings of the party in Montgomery County, and the state of Maryland. I remember him well, and consider it a privilege to have known him, and his lovely and gracious wife. He began his working career clerking in various stores in the area until about 1915, when he and Clay Plummer purchased the store of George Linthicum, which was then located in the Belt Building on the corner of Summit Avenue and Diamond Avenue, in the heart of Gaithersburg. He soon purchased the interest of Mr. Plummer, and took in as partner his cousin, Marshall Murray Walker (1880), who ultimately took over the business on his own. James Forest was also a partner with Clay Plummer in the Forest Oak Hotel, and in a livery stable.

In 1926, he began his political career, being elected to the County Board of Commissioners. After just six weeks, he was appointed Treasurer of the County, a position he held until 1938. He served in a number of capacities over the years; finally as chief appraiser of the Orphan's Court from 1953 until his retirement in 1963. His civic and social activities are too numerous to catalogue; his worth is best expressed by a Resolution of the Maryland House of Delegates at the time of his death, which states, in part:

"He took an active part in the political, civic, religious, fraternal and community life of his city, county and State; Gaithersburg, Montgomery County, and the State of Maryland have lost a foremost citizen and servant who will be long remembered for his many activities."

James Forest and his wife, Marie, were parents of three children, born at Gaithersburg:

a. James Forest Walker, Jr., born July 21, 1918; died February 6, 1987. Married first to Blanche Colbert, and second December 26, 1946 to Grace Barbara Fisher, the mother of his two children. For twenty years, Jimmy was Vice President, Sales and Marketing, with Kettler Brothers, Inc., a family owned building and development firm organized by the Kettler family, including Milton E. Ket-

344

tler, who married Jimmy's sister, Barbara Elizabeth. He was instrumental in acquiring for the company the various farms which were to become the new town called Montgomery Village, adjacent to the City of Gaithersburg, including *Rolling Knoll Farm*, belonging to his uncles, William Ralph Walker and Grover King Walker. When he retired in 1982, he was sales executive with the Cathedral Corporation, based in Arlington, Virginia. He was a Mason, and a founding member of St. Andrew's Methodist Church in Bethesda, and of Faith Methodist Church in Rockville. His children were:

(1)　James Forest Walker, III, born May 20, 1950

(2)　Allen Windsor Walker, born January 16, 1954

b.　Robert McCabe Walker, born July 9, 1922; died May 10, 1981 at a military hospital in San Diego, California. He was Lieutenant Colonel, USAF, retired in 1968. He had served in the second World War, and in Korea, as a navigation officer, receiving various medals and commendations. He served on one of the first Air Force planes to recover in flight an object that had been sent into space by the United States. Upon retirement, he moved to California, where he lived until his death. Married first to Connie Slicer, and second December 20, 1950 to Estelle Joselyn Oliver of Solana Beach, California. Children:

(1)　Robin Marie Walker, born November 26, 1951; married Enlow and had a child:

(a)　Jessica Enlow.

(2)　Patricia Joyce Walker, born March 11, 1954; married Tirona.

(3)　Forest Clayton Walker, born September 16, 1955

c.　Barbara Elizabeth Walker, born September 2, 1924; married October 4, 1947 to Milton E. Kettler, born 1921 and died 1982. After Milton's death, she married second James Mills, and currently lives at their home on Kent Island, Maryland. On a personal note, in my position as a Vice President of Kettler Brothers, Inc., for most of my twenty years there, I reported directly to Milton Kettler.

He was a gentleman, a fair golfer, filled with wit and generosity, and a wonderful person to have known. Milton, together with his brothers, Clarence E. Kettler and Charles L. Kettler, their brother-in-law, William F. Forlines, and family friend, Frank M. Ewing, were the owners of the development firm, Kettler Brothers, Inc., builders of major residential communities in Maryland, Virginia and the District of Columbia, including their signature project, the new town of Montgomery Village. The nucleus of that project was *Rolling Knoll Farm*, purchased by the company in 1963 from William Ralph and Grover King Walker, Barbara's uncles. Barbara and Milton had children:

(1) Ellen Luise Kettler, born July 25, 1950; married to Scott Paseltiner, a builder and stock broker; she is an attorney. At last report, they lived in Chicago.

(2) Robert Charles Kettler, born July 18, 1952; married first to Eleanor Anderson. He is most recently managing owner of Kettler-Scott, a building and development firm formed with his brother-in-law.

(3) Martha Belle Kettler, born November 19, 1954; lived seven days.

(4) Peter Brookes Kettler, born December 17, 1963

4. Roland Nathan Walker, born April 23, 1886; died August 6, 1934. He was married May 18, 1917 to Laura Cecil, born March 17, 1895 and died November 25, 1962. By deed dated 1927, and recorded in Liber 438 at folio 384 in Montgomery County, he and his wife obtained from his father and his stepmother, a lot on Frederick Avenue in Gaithersburg, containing 54 square perches, and being part of *Valentine's Garden Enlarged.* They had children:

a. Charles Roland Walker, born February 16, 1919 in Gaithersburg, in the house that originally stood at 106 North Frederick Avenue, and died March 14, 1989 at his home on Brookes Avenue in the City. Married to Doris Talbert, born 1923. Known to all as "Boots" he was a real estate broker and executive with the H. L. Rust Company for many years. He served the City of Gaithersburg for more than thirty years as Chairman of the Board of Appeals, was a Trustee of Asbury Methodist Home, a member of the Epworth United Methodist Church, and a Director on the Board of GEICO Insurance. In 1987, he received *The Gazette* newspaper Community Service Award. He and Doris had children:

    (1)   Philip Hughes Walker, born November 28, 1947; married Marcia McCully, and lived in Manassas, Virginia

    (2)   Linda Cecil Walker, born March 17, 1949, and married to Robert L. Robbins. Lived in Falmouth, Massachusetts.

    (3)   Elizabeth Ann Walker, born May 18, 1952, and married to Donegan. Lived in Gaithersburg.

  b. Mary Louise Walker, born November 10, 1920, and married to Thomas E. Robertson. They had children:

    (1)   Thomas Patrick Robertson, born August 26, 1946

    (2)   James Roland Robertson, born May 21, 1949

    (3)   Judith Claire Robertson, married David Beach.

  c. Elizabeth Cecil Walker, born September 20, 1927; died October 14, 1932.

5. Jesse Windsor Walker, born July 16, 1888; died October 24, 1957. He was first married April 26, 1911 to Ethel Louise Ingalls, born 1891 and died 1929. In 1923, in a deed recorded in Liber 340 at folio 82, he and his wife conveyed a one-half acre lot on the Rockville to Great Falls Road, being part of the tract known as *Williamsborough Resurveyed*. He married second in 1932 to Alice Grace Bruff, born 1903. There were two children to the first marriage, and one to the second:

  a. Dorothy Bell Walker, born 1912; married William Lynch and had children:

    (1)   June Marie Lynch, born 1932

    (2)   William Hartley Lynch, born 1933; married in 1953 to Frances Latham.

  b. Margaret Waters Walker, born 1916; married October 26, 1942 Michael Douglas Howes, and had children:

    (1)   Michael Howes, born 1943

    (2)   Gary Windsor Howes, born 1947

c.   Gertrude DeLisle Walker, born 1934; married to Harry N. Leizear.

6.   Russell King Walker, born July 8, 1890; died October 26, 1950. In 1924, he married Agnes Frissell (or Frizzell), born 1893 and died 1978. They had children:

a.   Elaine Walker, married Benjamin Rockman.

b.   Louise Lindsay Walker, born 1925; died 1939

7.   Franklin Carroll Walker, born Janury 15, 1893 and died June 18, 1970. Married at Grace Methodist Church, Gaithersburg, Maryland, September 8, 1921 to Marjorie St. Clair Plummer, born December 18, 1896, and died September 28, 1948. She was the daughter of Samuel Robert Plummer, born August 23, 1854; died December 20, 1924; and his wife, Ellen Roberta Pope, born September 1, 1853; died August 1, 1920. Marjorie had siblings: Katie M. Plummer, born April 16, 1891, died December 21, 1897; George Pope Plummer, born 1888, died 1953, and married to Virginia Rebecca Walker (1893), daughter of Crittenden Henning Walker (1857); and Ella Roberta Plummer, born 1882 and died 1962. Miss Ella was single, member of the Daughters of the American Revolution, and for many years, Judge of the Orphans Court of Montgomery County, Maryland, loved and respected by all who had the privilege of knowing her. Franklin Carroll Walker was a builder of custom homes in Montgomery County, widely known and respected in the industry. The author knew him rather well, having provided land surveying services for him in connection with his construction activities. He was the father of three children:

a.   Helen Adair Walker, born June 29, 1922; married to Edward Boone Talbott, born May 29, 1920, and had two daughters:

    (1)   Roberta "Robin" St. Clair Talbott, born July 1, 1952; married to Mark Irving Swope, born October 14, 1948. They have two children:

        (a)   Bretton Mark Swope, born October 22, 1979

        (b)   Alexander Walker Swope, born July 21, 1988

(2) Leigh Adair Talbott, born July 7, 1955. Married Christopher Edward Grover, born September 4, 1953. Two children:
    (a) Nathan Talbott Grover, born August 5, 1985
    (b) Jane Adair Grover, born August 29, 1987
b. Frances Carol Walker, born April 5, 1925, and married to Ivor Henry Gehrman, born December, 1922. Two daughters:
    (1) Diane Carol Gehrman, born January 19, 1953; married first to Roy DiVincenti, and divorced. She married second to Robert O'Halloran. A daughter was born to the first marriage:
        (a) Kristen Carol DiVincenti: December 19, 1983
    (2) Nancy Ellen Gehrman, born February 21, 1955; married to Donald Harden, and divorced. Married second Stuart Davis, and had one daughter from the second marriage:
        (a) Shannon Leigh Davis: September 3, 1987
c. Jack Waters Walker, born September 7, 1926; married first to Ruby Johnson, and divorced. He married second to Jean West, born November 20, 1925. One daughter:
    (1) Susan Lynn Walker, born September 5, 1951; married Russell Eddie Mull and had three children:
        (a) Joseph Zachary Mull: November 3, 1983
        (b) Lauren Ashley Mull: September 23, 1987
        (c) Melissa Ashley Mull: July 11, 1991
8. Evelyn Bessie Walker, born May 23, 1895; died October 15, 1980. Married George Washington Darby, born August 11, 1891 and died August 3, 1947. They had children:
a. George Walker Darby, born October 17, 1916; married to Ruth Davis, and had children:
    (1) George Walker Darby, Jr., born 1947
    (2) Scott Davis Darby, born 1950
b. Grace Priscilla Darby, born May 31, 1923; married to Alvin Donald Foster, and had children:
    (1) Grace Priscilla Foster, born 1947
    (2) Deborah Joan Foster, born 1949

CHILD 4

Amanda E. Walker
1854-

This daughter of Nathan James Walker (1824) was born March 19, 1854, and died February 25, 1925. Married November 26, 1878 to Nathan H. Darby, born c.1842 and died June 10, 1910. Children:

1. Minnie Estelle Darby, born November 18, 1879; died May 1, 1909. Married November 12, 1902 Herbert Nolan Adamson, born August 25, 1869; died September 10, 1958. They had children:
   a. Irene Anderson.
   b. Consuelo Anderson.
2. Ira Darby, born June 6, 1884; died June 14, 1961. Married Kathryn V. Bottomly, born December 28, 1891, and died November 19, 1952. At least one son:
   a. John H. Darby, died December 20, 1924, an infant

CHILD 5

Charles William Waters Walker
1855-1921

This son of Nathan James Walker (1824) was born December 1, 1855, and died December 21, 1921. He was living in Conley, Georgia, at the time of his father's death, and was later killed there. There is a marker in Forest Oak Cemetery with his name, but no dates. His one known child was:

1. Mary Virginia Walker, married to Joseph McCarthy.

CHILD 6

Crittenden Henning Walker
1857-1930

This son of Nathan James Walker (1824) was born November 19, 1857 and died December 22, 1930. Married January 22, 1884 to Rebecca Virginia Coomes, born March 9, 1858; died May 20, 1933, daughter of William Henry Coomes (1833) and Mary Ellen Darby (1834). Crittenden served in the Maryland House of Delegates from Montgomery County during the 1920 session. His will, dated January 31, 1920 and probated January 15, 1931 is found in Liber PEW 20 at folio 50 in the will records of the county. There were seven children:

1. Cleveland Walker, born November 4, 1884; died December 19, 1901
2. Nathan Walter Walker, born March 9, 1886; died October 15, 1939. He married first June 11, 1910 to Virginia Bell Ray, born July 7, 1886, and they had four children. She died at their home near Colesville, Maryland, February 5, 1920. In 1916, by deed recorded in Liber 254 at folio 274, they sold two parts of *Beall's Manor*, containing 105 acres, and 19 acres. He married second in November, 1921 at Baltimore, Maryland, to Mary Antoinette Carr of Laurel, Maryland, born December 4, 1890, and had one child. He and Mary purchased the home farm of 177.9 acres on the Laytonsville Road from his brother, Crittenden Henning Walker, Jr. (1896) and his wife, by deed dated 1924 and recorded in Liber 362 at folio 473. Mary died March 17, 1927; and he married third Marie Margaret Maggio; no children. His children were:
    a. Nathan Walter Walker, Jr., married Eva Stotler and had children:
        (1) Donald Jerry Walker, married Jane Barton.
        (2) Nathan Walter Walker, III.
        (3) Constance M. Walker, married Edward Wettengel.
        (4) Dwight Eugene Walker, married Linda Day.
    b. Alice Virginia Walker, married June 22, 1934 to Edmund Russell Gloyd, born February 14, 1911, son of Edmund

Alexander Gloyd (1863). Russell was widely known in his home town of Gaithersburg, and throughout Montgomery County, as an expert photographer; many of his photographs were published in local papers, journals and reports. From 1954 to 1959, he served as a member of the City Council, and also served on the City Planning Commission, and the Board of Appeals. For many years, he was employed by the National Geographic Society. Known affectionately to his friends as "Moonie", he was a member of the Gaithersburg Lions Club for more than thirty years. They had six children:

(1)　Sylvia Ann Gloyd, born April 26, 1935; married May 9, 1953 to Orin Foster Burdette, Jr., son of Orin Foster Burdette, Sr. (1904), and Margaret A. Burdette (1913); and had children:

    (a)　Deborah Kay Burdette: December 11, 1953

    (b)　Jill Diane Burdette: October 5, 1955

    (c)　Lori Ann Burdette: January 30, 1957

    (d)　Teresa Lynn Burdette: October 3, 1960

    (e)　Jeffrey Wayne Burdette, born November 4, 1962, and died January 30, 1963

    (f)　Jacqueline Marie Burdette: April 1, 1964

    (g)　Karen Michelle Burdette: November 28, 1965

(2)　Janet Carol Gloyd, born February 24, 1943, and married first October 1, 1959 to Raymond Kenneth Hunt, born April 1, 1941; and had two children listed. Married second September 28, 1969 to Richard Emanuel Thayer, born December 26, 1935. No children. The Hunt children:

    (a)　Debra Lynne Hunt: June 11, 1960

    (b)　Raymond Kenneth Hunt: August 30, 1964

(3)　John Walker Gloyd, born December 2, 1944; married October 23, 1965 to Lynn Yvonne Newcomer, born November 12, 1945. One child:

    (a)　John Michael Gloyd: August 16, 1971

(4)　Rita Elaine Gloyd, born June 8, 1948; married May 2, 1970 to Jack Edward Blomquist. One son:

    (a)　Josh Blomquist: January 16, 1974

(5) Joan Marie Gloyd, born June 9, 1951; married October 23, 1973 to William Carroll Kearns, born November 3, 1950. One son:

    (a) Gary Alan Kearns, born February 16, 1978

(6) Linda Jean Gloyd, born October 2, 1956

c. Annie Mae Walker, married Herbert Butts and had a son:

    (1) John Walker Butts, married Betsy Behringer.

d. Hilda Rebecca Walker, born February 6, 1917; married April 17, 1937 to James Schaeffer King, who was born c.1913 and died February 20, 1987 at his home in Snow Hill, Maryland, to which he had retired. He was the only son of James Deets King (1889 to 1958) and Macie Schaeffer (1893 to 1992). They had children:

    (1) Faith Virginia King, born November 7, 1946; married to Paul Duvall and had a son:

        (a) Paul Duvall, Jr.

    (2) Sara Rebecca King, born November 14, 1949; married to William Stark and had a son:

        (a) James William Stark.

e. Lorraine Walker, married Donald Hall and had children:

    (1) Donald Hall, Jr.

    (2) Steve Hall.

    (3) Debbie Hall.

    (4) Chris Hall.

    (5) Rick Hall.

    (6) Bryon Hall.

3. William Augusta Cooke Walker, born July 12, 1887; died July 14, 1967. Married June 6, 1910 to Hester M. Kimble, born c.1890 and died March 31, 1974 in Wilmington, Delaware. Children:

a. Janet Walker, married Thomas Strange and had a child:

    (1) Joyce Kinser Strange, married Mossburg; children:

        (1) Gregg Thomas Mossburg.

        (2) Keith Richard Mossburg.

b. William Augusta Cooke Walker, Jr., born February 11, 1918; died November 9, 1951. Staff sergeant, USA; perhaps killed in Korea, the time frame being correct.

4. Mary Ellen Coomes Walker, born January 26, 1891; died August 22, 1892.
5. Virginia Rebecca Walker, born August 14, 1893; died March 13, 1966. Married November 7, 1913 George Pope Plummer, born 1888; died 1953, a son of Samuel Robert Plummer (1854) and Ellen Roberta Pope Plummer (1853).
6. Crittenden Henning Walker, Jr., born April 27, 1896; died August 2, 1969. Married first in Rockville, April 5, 1916 to Bessie Priscilla Bussard, daughter of Thaddeus T. Bussard of Redland, Maryland, and had one child. Married second Lena Geisbert, and had nine children. The obituary of his son, Gary Ronald, tends to indicate, however, that there were a total of thirteen children in this family, as reported following. In 1919, by deed recorded in Liber 290 at folio 36, he obtained from his parents a farm containing 177.9 acres, located on what was then called the Mechanicsville to Laytonsville Road, being part of the tract of land called *Addition to Brooke Grove*. By deed dated 1924, and recorded in Liber 362 at folio 473, he and his wife Bessie conveyed the farm to his brother, Nathan Walter Walker, who took over the full operation, and Crittenden purchased property on Walker Avenue in Gaithersburg. He served in the Maryland House of Delegates in 1919 and 1920. Children:
   a. Roy Walker, married Marian Mann. Lived at Solomon's Island
   b. Jane Walker, married Francis May, lived in Frederick, and had children:
      (1) Michael May.
      (2) Crittenden May.
      (3) James May.
      (4) Francis May, Jr.
      (5) Susan May.
   c. Barbara Walker; married John Knoblock, lived in Germantown and had children:
      (1) John Knoblock, Jr.
      (2) Tammy Knoblock.
      (3) Kimberly Knoblock.

d. Mary Walker, married Hugh Neal, lived in Rockville, and had children:
   (1) Gladys Neal.
   (2) Susan Neal.
   (3) Linda Anne Neal.
e. Sally Walker, married to Gilbert Bolton and lived in Germantown. Children:
   (1) Gilbert Bolton, Jr.
   (2) Ruth Anne Bolton.
   (3) Darlene Bolton.
f. Beverly Walker, married Michael Bland, lived in Germantown, and had children:
   (1) Jimmie Jo Bland.
   (2) Tina Elizabeth Bland.
g. Crittenden Henning Walker, III, married Phyllis Burgess, lived in Rockville, and had children:
   (1) Mark Walker.
   (2) Crittenden Henning Walker, IV.
   (3) Trina Renee Walker.
h. Harry R. Walker, married to Joyce Littural, lived in Damascus, and had children:
   (1) Mary Jo Walker.
   (2) Darlene Walker.
   (3) Harry R. Walker, Jr.
   (4) William Crittenden Walker.
   (5) Robert Thomas Walker.
   (6) Teresa Anne Walker.
   (7) Jerry Dwayne Walker.
i. William Wayne Walker, lived in Germantown.
j. Gary Ronald Walker, died by drowning July 1, 1977. Married to Virginia Gullion, and had a son:
   (1) Gary Ronald Walker, Jr.
k. Phyllis A. Walker, married to Deny. Lived in Baltimore
l. Helen Wallker, married to Brill and lived in Germantown
m. Kathleen Walker, married to Shepherd; lived in Havre de Grace
7. Sarah Marion Walker, born August 18, 1897; died February 8, 1899

CHILD 7

Margaret Jemima Walker
1860-1862

This daughter of Nathan James Walker (1824) was born May 6, 1860; died June 17, 1862.

CHILD 8

Eveline Rebecca Walker
1864-1943

This daughter of Nathan James Walker (1824) was born May 6, 1864, and died October 30, 1943. Married November 25, 1890 to Cornelius H. Browning, born June 28, 1861; died January 28, 1935, son of Charles T. Browning (1827). They lived at Germantown, Montgomery County, Maryland, and their children are discussed under their father's name in Chapter 4, devoted to the descendants of Elizabeth Miles King (1802), which see.

CHILD 9

Nathan Asbury Walker
1865-1935

This son of Nathan James Walker (1824) was born January 12, 1865 and died September 28, 1935. Married January 21, 1890 to Frances Willard Hughes, born April 21, 1866 and died May 5, 1933; the daughter of William D. Hughes and Elizabeth Conley. Nathan worked at the family grist mill west of Goshen Road, and north of the town of Gaithersburg; and then moved to the Silver Spring area of Montgomery County, Maryland, where he operated a farm. In 1905, he and Fannie (as the deed reads) purchased a farm of 162 acres from Jesse L. Burns, a widower. He returned to Gaithersburg, where he made his home on Frederick Avenue, adjacent to the Forest Oak Cemetery. His home site is now the location of Executive House Garden Apartments, built a number of years ago by William Lawson King (1897). At one time, he also worked with the Post Office. His children were:

1. Lena Helen Walker, born September 6, 1891; died March 10, 1947. Married to William Henry Gartner, born September 5, 1885 and died December 20, 1945. Children:

   a. William Edgar Gartner, born September 13, 1912; died December 7, 1977. Married Marietta Crawford and had children:

      (1) William Edgar Gartner, Jr., born July 31, 1944

      (2) Joan Gartner, born May 10, 1947

   b. James Oliver Gartner, born August 10, 1913, and married Thelma Allnut, born September, 1920; died January 14, 1978.

   c. Margaret Dorothy Gartner, born June 25, 1915; married William F. Magers and had children:

      (1) Carole Lynn Magers, born May 22, 1950

      (2) Charles Edward Magers, born February 5, 1953

      (3) Jeanmaire Magers, born April 5, 1954

      (4) James Allen Magers, born February 18, 1956

   d. Frances Irene Gartner, born August 8, 1916; married to James Oliver Monard, and had children:

      (1) Judith Ann Monard, born February 22, 1939

      (2) James Oliver Monard, Jr., born January 27, 1944

      (3) Richard Alan Monard, born August 14, 1949

   e. Helen Lucille Gartner, born September 7, 1919; died April 17, 1977. Married to William Ward Shipe.

   f. Nathan Stanley Gartner, born October 7, 1926; died September 29, 1968. Married to Joclaire Campbell, born 1932, and had children:

      (1) David Campbell Gartner, born February 4, 1953

      (2) Linda Dawn Gartner, born 1957

      (3) Jacquelyn Gartner, born February, 1958

      (4) Patricia Ann Gartner, born 1959

   g. Catherine Rosalie Gartner, born June 5, 1928; married first to Clifard Llewelyn Howard, born February 15, 1924; died May 25, 1959. They had four children, and after his death, Catherine was married second to Anthony

Thomas Mocarsky, born November 6, 1917, and had one child, all listed following:

    (1)   Sharon Lee Howard, born May 3, 1948

    (2)   Patricia Lynn Howard, born November 30, 1950

    (3)   Linda Sue Howard, born November 12, 1955

    (4)   Catherine Ann Howard, born March 16, 1959

    (5)   Tracy Adam Mocarsky, born November 27, 1968

h.   Lois Jeneiva Gartner, born June 2, 1932; married David Leonard Crown, born December 1, 1926. Children:

    (1)   Timothy David Crown, born October 2, 1955

    (2)   Debra Sue Crown, born April 13, 1958

2.   Mary Elizabeth Walker, born November 16, 1892; married to William Rodney White, who died September, 1953. Seven children:

a.   Joseph Rodney White, born September 14, 1914; married first Violet Stinnett; one son. Married second Catherine I. Becraft, born October 10, 1913, and had three children. Married third Mariam M. Cramer, born September 8, 1926; no children. His children were:

    (1)   Joseph Rodney White, Jr.

    (2)   Joyce D. White, born May 28, 1944

    (3)   Karla Kay White, born August 21, 1946

    (4)   Joseph Michael White, born August 10, 1947

b.   Dorothy Elizabeth White, born November 17, 1915; married Charles E. Welty, born December 14, 1904. A son:

    (1)   Douglas MacArthur Welty, born February 14, 1943

c.   Charles LeRoy White, born August 13, 1917; died February 13, 1962. Married Kate H. Deiorka (or Detrick) born October 4, 1925 and had a son:

    (1)   Charles Stephen White, born December 14, 1953, and married June 4, 1977 to Susan Diane Adams, born October 8, 1957; daughter of Jesse Adams (1928) and Ruth Diane Fulks Adams (1933).

d.   William Earl White, born August 18, 1920; married to Barbara L. Kirby, born February 6, 1923. Children:

    (1)   Cheryl Lynn White, born March 25, 1944

    (2)   Charlotte Marie White, born September 18, 1947

(3)   Dana L. White, born April 20, 1959
e.   Betty Lee White, born November 10, 1925; married first George E. Viers, born April 20, 1921, and had one daughter. Married second Robert Eugene Viers, born September 26, 1926, and had three children:
(1)   Deborah Jene Viers, born November 23, 1949
(2)   Vickie Lee Viers, born September 23, 1954
(3)   Robert B. Viers, born October 26, 1955
(4)   Nancy Jene Viers, born November 12, 1957
f.   Alvin White, born 1928; died 1930
g.   William Rodney White, Jr., born October 4, 1930; married to Margaret E. Swann, born December 24, 1935. Children:
(1)   Mary Margaret White, born April 3, 1956
(2)   William Rodney White, III, born August 1, 1964
3.   Eleanor Walker, born March 2, 1896; died September 19, 1967. She married first Byron H. Miller, born August 11, 1881, and died October 22, 1932. They had the five children listed. Married second to Leslie L. Mullineaux, born September 26, 1897; died September 19, 1967. He and his wife died together on an auto trip to the west. Miller children were:
a.   William Kenneth Miller, born September 16, 1914; married to Frances Bohrer and had a daughter:
(1)   Janet Irene Miller, born March 4, 1939; married Wilson Dove.
b.   Byron Headly Miller, born April 19, 1916; married to Charlotte Mullineaux, a daughter of Leslie L. Mullineaux from his first marriage. Known to his friends as Popeye, he worked with the gas company for years, and was widely known as one of the top duckpin bowlers in the area. They had children:
(1)   Karlene Yvonne Miller, born May 2, 1940; married to Carroll Burke Bestpitch.
(2)   Byron Headly Miller, Jr., born June 2, 1947, and married Linda Reed.
c.   Eleanor Rebecca Miller, born July 1, 1917, and married Ernest B. Lipford.

d. Nathan Myrell Miller, born August 25, 1918; married Madeline Elkins and had children:
  (1) Thomas Nathan Miller, born November 25, 1943; married to Sue.
  (2) Michael Miller, born February 23, 1948
  (3) Catherine Miller, born March 7, 1959; married to Jerry Doroshenko.
e. Margaret Ellen Miller, born October 8, 1919, and married first to Clark Windsor; no children. She was married second to Norman Elwood Duvall; a son:
  (1) Norman Elwood Duvall, Jr., born August 21, 1952
4. William Hughes Walker, born August 27, 1901, and died January 24, 1962. Married first about April 8, 1921 to Mabel V. Poole, daughter of Oscar Poole of Barnesville, Maryland, and had one son. He married second Hallie Gott, born March 13, 1910; died August 29, 1969. His son was:
a. William Oscar Walker, born July 5, 1923; married to Florence Aiken and had a son:
  (1) William Edward Walker, born February 16, 1949; died at age 15 about 1964.
5. Frances Walker, born 1905; died 1927

CHILD 10

Miriam W. Walker
1867-

This daughter of Nathan James Walker (1824) was born October 16, 1867, and died May 2, 1927. Married November 20, 1889 to William M. Carlisle, born July 1, 1867 and died September 22, 1894 of typhoid; son of David Carlisle. Under her father's will, she received lots 5 and 6, in Block 2, *Russell and Brooke's Addition to Gaithersburg*, as well as "my new two-seat carriage, the harness and my driving horse." They had children:
1. Roger Carlisle, born September 27, 1890, and died September 8, 1956. Married Lulu McBain, born March 30, 1900.

2. Marjorie Carlisle, born July 27, 1892; died June 4, 1955. Married William S. Mackall, born February 24, 1884; died April 6, 1953.

CHILD 11

McKendree Bond Walker
1870-1954

This son of Nathan James Walker (1824) was born October 17, 1870, and died June 11, 1954. Married June 15, 1904 Rachel Corrine Holland, born August 23, 1878; died October 30, 1967; daughter of Samuel B. Holland and Marian Hoy. He remained on the family homeplace, *Rolling Knoll Farm*, on Goshen Road. With his two sons, he developed a nationally and internationally recognized herd of Holstein Friesien cattle. He was very active in 4-H Club work and Future Farmers of America. He was the father of three children:

1. William Ralph Walker, born September 16, 1905; died February 13, 1995. Married Lorraine Elizabeth Watkins, born September 30, 1906; died March 19, 1972; no children. Ralph was widely known and respected in agricultural circles in Montgomery County and the region. After he and his brother sold the family farm, he retired from active farming, but for many years, was associated with the management functions of the Montgomery County Agricultural Center in Gaithersburg, site of the annual Fair. He was a charter member of Montgomery County Farmers Club.

2. Grover King Walker, born September 18, 1907; died April 6, 1981. Married June 18, 1929 to Marian Eleanor West, born September 28, 1908 at Darnestown, Maryland and died April 4, 1995; daughter of Edwin M. West. In 1950, Grover was elected as a Democrat to the Montgomery County Council, serving in that capacity for sixteen years. He was active in the local Lions Club, the Farm Bureau, the Maryland State Fair Board, the Montgomery County Coop Agricultural Center, and was a bank director. He was a supervisor of the Montgomery Soil Conservation District when the author was

Chairman of that Board. In 1961, he and his brother, Ralph, sold *Rolling Knoll Farm* to Kettler Brothers, Inc., and it became the nucleus of the new town called Montgomery Village. Within the Village can be found the high-rise apartment building called *The Walker House*, communities known as *Grover's Forge* and *Walker's Choice*, and Lake Walker, keeping alive the family name in a new urban setting. One daughter:

a. Gloria Mae Walker, born December 6, 1930; married Curtis Gordon Keesee, and had children:

    (1) Cheryl Ann Keesee, born October 20, 1957

    (2) Charlene Elizabeth Keesee, born February 15, 1960 and married to Lacy.

    (3) Charlotte Elaine Keesee, born December 5, 1961 and married to Gillespie.

3. Pearl Marian Walker, born July 24, 1913; died February 12, 1945. Married to Henry Corens.

CHAPTER 16

Frederick County Records

Numerous references to members of the King family are found in records of Frederick County, Maryland. As mentioned earlier, residents of the upper northwest section of Montgomery County have, for generations, used services available in Frederick rather than in Montgomery, simply due to accessibility. The King families with which we are primarily concerned, lived in the early years in that part of Montgomery which is almost immediately adjacent to the Frederick County line. Thus, many records of related families are to be found there.

It should be noted, however, that several members of the King family living in Frederick County, were found in Middletown, members of the German Reformed Church, or the Evangelical Lutheran Church, and often bearing Germanic given names. Early Frederick County was rather heavily populated by German families moving across southern Pennsylvania, and south into the valleys of Maryland. Many of these Frederick County families are probably not related to those in our basic study, but will be included.

A check of the land records of Frederick County reveals entries for members of the family during the mid to late 1700s, including the period prior to 1776 when Montgomery County was formed from part of Frederick. Entries during that period could have covered land transactions in what is now Montgomery, although we did not find the name of any recognized members of the immediate family under study, as for example, Edward King of 1740 and his wife Rebecca Duckett (1742).

There were several entries for land transactions involving Abraham King, Christopher King, Francis King, and Robert King. There were no will record entries prior to 1800, although there were administrative accounts dated February 19, 1779 for Philip King; August 13, 1781 for Andrew King; and December 1, 1784 for the estate of Abraham King, by his wife, Madelena King.

Herman Allen King

This individual was married to Mary V. and lived in Mt. Airy, Maryland. Several children, not necessarily in the order following:
1. Herman Allen King, Jr., born December 28, 1942; died July 20, 1975 and buried at Friendship Methodist Church. He was married to Joan Dorsey, and had one son, one daughter, and a stepson:
   a. Charles Dorsey.
   b. Herman Allen King, III
   c. Malissa Lynn King.
2. Gloria King, married to Dove
3. Agnes King, married to Dorsey
4. Mary Louise King, married to Spencer
5. Betty Jean King, married to Spencer
6. Anna Mae King, married to Gray
7. Darlene Virginia King.
8. Alma Susie King, married to Diggs
9. Albert King.
10. Michael King.
11. Woodrow King.
12. Charles Henry King.

Charles F. R. King
m/1856

Charles lived in the Middletown area of Frederick County, and was married there September 25, 1856, in the German Reformed Church, to Louisa E. Mix. They had at least three children:
1. John William King, christened August 2, 1857
2. Charles Lewis King, christened May 27, 1860
3. Robert Arthur King, christened April 22, 1862

Christian King
1835-1893

This son of Lewis King was born c.1835, and died August 17, 1893; buried Mount Olivet Cemetery, Frederick, Maryland. Married May 13, 1860 to Mary Margaret Fross (last name spelling questionable), born November 25, 1841 and died November 28, 1909; buried with her husband. They lived in or near Middletown, and were apparently members of the Evangelical Lutheran Church. At least ten children, four of whom are buried with their parents:

1. Joseph Franklin King, christened June 8, 1862; died 1871
2. James Albert King, christened November 15, 1863. Probably same individual buried at Mount Olivet Cemetery, born December 2, 1862; died June 10, 1920. His wife, Rosa M., born August 27, 1870; died June 1, 1949; buried with him. Also an infant daughter:
   a. Edna M. King, died February 4, 1889 at 3 months, 23 days old
3. Jacob Samuel King, christened July 15, 1866. Probably same individual buried at Mount Olivet Cemetery, who died 1933. His wife, Jessie E., born 1867; died 1934; buried with him.
4. John Thomas King, christened July 15, 1866; died 1869
5. Calvin Luther King, christened 10/27/1867. Probable the same whose tombstone reads 1867 to 1937; with a wife, Mary S., born 1868 and died 1944. Three daughters, who died quite young:
   a. Mary J. King, died April 1, 1903; 3 years, 4 months and 18 days of age.
   b. Annie V. King, died April 15, 1903; 3 months, two days.
   c. Clara N. King, died August 29, 1904; perhaps stillbirth
6. Laura Elizabeth King, christened November 15, 1871
7. Oscar Ritchie King, born February 22, 1869; died February 7, 1934. Christened November 15, 1871. Married to Annie E., born June 16, 1871, and died May 21, 1936. At least two children, all buried at Mount Olivet Cemetery:
   a. Clara C. King; died March 16, 1901; three days old
   b. Franklin E. King, born January 26, 1905; lived 7 months
8. Lillie May King, christened July 1, 1873
9. Minnie V. King, born 1879; died 1881, perhaps a twin
10. Mary H. King, born 1879; died 1881, perhaps a twin

Nicholas King

Married to Elizabeth, (probably Elizabeth Gaunt, on July 17, 1797), he lived in the Middletown area of Frederick County, and had children:
1. Anna Eliza King, born August 11, 1809 at Woodsboro
2. Hyrum King, born October 15, 1810
3. Charles James King, christened October 23, 1812 at Middletown
4. Susanna Rebecca King, christened July 24, 1817

John E. King

The obituary of his wife appeared in the Montgomery County Courier of March 1, 1978. She was born c.1933 and died February 21, 1978 at Montgomery General Hospital in Montgomery County. They were then living at Monrovia, in Frederick County. She was Nancy M. Johnson, daughter of Luther S. Johnson and Grace Pugh Johnson of Boyds. One son survived his mother:
1. John E. King, Jr., of Monrovia

Charles Clayton King
1856-1933

This is probably the same individual who was born March 19, 1856 and christened May 31, 1856, son of John and Mary Elizabeth King. He died November 3, 1933 and is buried at Mount Olivet Cemetery in Frederick County. His wife is buried with him, Rosie M., born March 15, 1854 and died February 23, 1927. There is also one son there:
1. Columbus R. King, died March 11, 1886; aged 12 days.

Charles W. King
1832-1917

Probably the same individual reported as born to John King in IGI records of the Mormon Church, Charles was born about June 6, 1832, and died September 10, 1917 at the age of 85 years, 3 months and 4 days. Buried at the Ellerton Brethren Cemetery in Frederick County, with his wife, Mary E., born about April 3, 1830, and died August 25, 1892 at the age of 62 years, 4 months and 22 days. Buried with them are two daughters, who died young:

1. Anna C. King, died February 19, 1884, aged 16-7-9
2. Mary J. King, died October 29, 1888; aged 19-11-8

Jesse King
1795-1821

Buried at the Jefferson Methodist Church in Frederick County, Jesse was born February 26, 1795 and died January 20, 1851. His wife, Lydia, born 1798 and died August 2, 1883 at 85 years, 4 months and 10 days, is buried with him. They are apparently the parents of:

1. Jesse King, Jr., born c.1822
2. John M. Vanburen King, born October 29, 1838; died April 11, 1857.

John H. King
1858-1906

Buried at Feagaville, Frederick County, John was born c.1857 and died April 25, 1906 at age of 48 years, 8 months and 1 day. He was perhaps married twice, one wife being Martha B., by whom he had at least two sons, both buried with him:

1. Jacob F. King, died January 5, 1899; aged 7-11-0
2. Abraham T. King, died August 3, 1893; aged 0-3-15

John W. King
1858-1931

Buried at Ellerton Brethren Church, Frederick County, this individual was born August 24, 1858, and died February 26, 1931. Married to Susanna V., born c.1856; died May 29, 1883. At least two children, buried with their parents:

1. Daniel B. King, died August 9, 1894; age 15-10-2
2. Mary E. King, died May 22, 1882; age 0-10-0

Elizabeth Louise King

The parentage of this individual is not now known, but she was married May 3, 1843 in Frederick County, Maryland, to George W. Angelberger. He was born c.1814 and died 1862 on the old family homestead, which he then owned, located in the Tuscarora District, containing about 80 acres. He and his wife were Lutherans, parents of nine children; six of whom grew to maturity:

1. Mary S. Angelberger, married to Lewis Heffner
2. Philip J. Angelberger.
3. Harriet A. Angelberger; married L. W. Williams of York, Pa.
4. William D. Angelberger.
5. Julia J. Angelberger; married Luther Shankle
6. Edward I. Angelberger, born June 22, 1860. As a young man, he purchased a 110-acre farm about four miles northwest of Frederick, where he was well-known as a breeder of fine Holstein cattle. Married Annie M. E. Michael, daughter of Abraham and Caroline Houck Michael. Six children:
   a. Worthington R. Angelberger.
   b. Ada May Angelberger, and married to Heber Summers of Thurmont
   c. Lola B. Angelberger.
   d. Rhoda E. Angelberger.
   e. Arthur O. Angelberger.
   f. Edith M. Angelberger.

William H. King
1857-1929

Buried at Mount Olivet in Frederick, this individual was born 1857 and died 1929. His wife and two sons are buried with him. She was Annie, born 1866 and died 1932:

1. William Ellsworth King, born 1888; died September 10, 1956
2. Charles L. King, born 1889; died 1958

All individuals appearing in the left column bear the surname of King. Most events occurred in Frederick County, Maryland; some in nearby counties as noted.

Individual	Information
Alice Maria	Christened 1858; daughter of Ann
Ann	Married 01/03/1795 to Thomas Barnes.
Ann	Married 07/25/1815 to John Gross.
Ann R.	06/19/1829 to 07/24/1909. Jefferson Cemetery
Anna	04/04/1762 to 01/29/1819. Union Bridge Cem.
Anthony	Chr. 1858; son of Ann
Caroline	Born 12/16/1824 to Joseph and Peggy
Caroline	12/17/1829 to 07/21/1811. Mt. Olivet Cemetery
Carrie Alice	04/03/1875 to 06/18/1956. Mt. Olivet Cemetery
Catharine L.	Born c.1841 to Jesse
Catherine A.	02/22/1823 to 10/04/1879. Mt. Olivet Cemetery
Charles	Born c.1833 to Lewis
Charles	Married 04/17/1879 to Rosanna Monroades
Charles	Married 03/30/1779 to Elizabeth Risener
Charles	Married 04/03/1779 to Mary Middagh
Charles E.	Born October 5, 1880; buried at Jefferson Union; husband of Lillie G. (1883)
Charles F., Jr.	1943 to 1944; Mount Olivet Cemetery
Charles Wesley	Died 01/07/1954, aged 63-08-28. Woodsboro.
Charles William	Died 05/05/1853; aged 1-0-23. Son of Henry and Caroline. Mount Olivet Cemetery.
David	Married 12/10/1807 to Rachel Phelps
Elba J.	1879 to 1962. Frederick Mem. Park. Husband of Mary E., born 1886.
Eleanor	Born 05/21/1734; daughter of Rufus
Elizabeth	Married 07/08/1792 to George Cox
Elizabeth	Married 05/20/1780 to William Adkins
Elizabeth	Married 09/18/1780 to Peter Cile
Elizabeth	Married 11/30/1843 to Jesse Roberts
Elizabeth	Christened 06/02/1824; daughter of Joseph and Margaret
Elizabeth	1803 to 01/31/1881. Emmitsburg Catholic

Elizabeth	1827 to 1894. Mount Olivet Cemetery.
Ellen C.	Born c.1836; daughter of Jesse
Ennis D.	Born 06/28/1816; son of James & Elizabeth
Ellen R.	1871 to 1954. Frederick Memorial Park
Fannie M.	1899 to 1931. Daughter of George W. and Mary E. Montgomery King. Mount Olivet Cemetery.
Florence E.	Born 01/31/1910. Mount Olivet Cemetery.
Francis	Born c.1849; son of Henry
Francis E.	1881 to 02/20/1919. Mt. Airy Methodist
George	Married 12/06/1788 to Rachel Perry
George I.	06/13/1905 to 07/29/1929. Mt. Tabor.
Harriet	Born c.1829
Harriet	Married c.1846 to Aquilla A. Fortney
Henry	Married 02/18/1868 to Elizabeth Fleshman
Henry	10/01/1821 to 05/04/1897. Mount Olivet Cem.
Henry	Born 10/06/1903. Mount Olivet Cemetery. Son of Henry and Fannie King.
James	Born 04/23/1730; son of Cyrus
James Lawrence	1892 to 03/14/1957. Mount Olivet Cemetery.
Jennie	Married 05/13/1880 to Noah Hill
Jesse Peyton	1865 to 1951. Mt. Airy Methodist. Married December 6, 1888 at Laytonsville to Jennie M. Kimble, 1866 to 1953.
Jesse W.	1826 to 01/05/1895. Jefferson Methodist Church
Johannes	Chr. 09/27/1786; son of Martin and Maria
John	Married 06/23/1798 to Margaret Toup
John	Married 07/21/1853 to Mary E. Cissel
John	1791 to 06/13/1851. Emmetsburg Catholic
John B.	10/04/1921 to 10/13/1937. Mount Olivet
John E.	11/18/1845 to 06/19/1908. Kemptown Methodist His wife: Martha E.; 02/18/1844 to 03/14/1916
John E.	1895 to 1945. Frederick Memorial Park, and his wife, A. Pearl, born 1897.
John Henry	Chr. 05/08/1858; son of John & Mary Elizabeth
John Lewis	04/25/1792 to 11/09/1863. Mount Olivet. His wife, Anna Maria: 07/26/1794 to 02/09/1882
John W.	1866 to 1946. Jefferson Union Cemetery; and his wife, Matilda C.: 1868 to 1943

John W.	05/09/1887 to 03/21/1892. Walkersville. Son of Joseph I. and Annie E. King.
Joseph	Married 08/28/1823 to Margaret Houck
Julia Virginia	05/30/1855 to 06/18/1857. Daughter of Henry & Caroline. Frederick Catholic Cemetery.
Lewis	Born c.1848 to Henry
Lewis	Born c.1846 to Frederick
Lewis E.	12/15/1857 to 03/10/1926; husband of Mary E., 01/29/1858 to 11/03/1933. Children: Charles O., 03/10/1878 to 02/08/1952; Flora E., an infant death c.1892. Mt. Airy Methodist Church.
Lewis Henry	Chr. 07/20/1847; son of Henry and Caroline
Lillie G.	01/29/1883 to 07/08/1942. Jefferson Union Cem. Wife of Charles E. King (1880)
Lottie (Burke)	05/30/1879 to 03/16/1956. Jefferson Union.
Lucretia	Married 01/06/1868 to Charles Baumgartner
Luesitia	Born c.1846; daughter of Henry
Margareth A.	Married 04/25/1833 to Jacob Sullivan
Martha	Born c.1836; daughter of John
Martha A. R.	1858 to 05/04/1893; wife of John H. Middletown Lutheran
Mary	Chr. 10/28/1786; daughter of Wm and Elizabeth
Mary	Born c.1839; daughter of Lewis
Mary A.	Born c.1839; daughter of John
Mary E.	Born 1886; Frederick Memorial Park. Wife of Elba J. King (1879)
Mary Virginia	Christened 06/04/1854, daughter of John and Mary Elizabeth
Nancy	Born c.1847; daughter of John
Nicholas	Married 07/17/1797 to Peggy Gaunt
Philip Edward	Chr. 03/30/1851; son of Henry and Caroline
Samuel	Chr. 01/11/1788; son of Charles and Mary
Sarah	Chr. 05/14/1780; daughter of Charles and Mary
Sarah	Married 08/17/1857 to John L. Wilhide
Sarah A.	Born c.1840; daughter of John
Sarah J.	Born c.1834; daughter of Jesse
Sarilla	Born c.1840; daughter of William
Susanna T.	Born 05/11/1812; daughter of James & Elizabeth

371

Thomas Franklin	Born c.1858; son of Ann
William	Married 06/29/1780 to Elizabeth Wright
William	Married 02/01/1882 to Annie Castle
William	Born c.1837; son of John
William	Born c.1844; son of Frederick

CHAPTER 17

Montgomery County Records

Numerous individuals have been found in records pertaining to Montgomery County, and the District of Columbia, where wills were filed in the county. They have not been identified within the framework of the principal genealogy under study, but many of them are probably related. Many are not, there being a number of individuals bearing the King name who moved to the Washington area from other locations. All such references are included here, however, for further evaluation.

The land records of the county contain hundreds of references to family members from 1777 to the present date, in the grantor and grantee indexes. There are several dated prior to 1800, although most of them are for lots in what was then the most recent addition to Georgetown, then in Montgomery County. They included Adam King, Benjamin King, George King, Grace King and William King.

Adam King was the only entry prior to 1800 who purchased land in upper areas of Montgomery County. On September 5, 1796 by deed recorded in liber G at folio 278, for the sum of two thousand pounds, he purchased lands from Ignatius Pigman and his wife Susanna Pigman. It included 50 acres of the land known as part of *Charley Forrest*, later called *Pigman Inheritance*. That land grant name places the land in the general area of Olney and Sandy Spring. There was a second tract, containing 513 and 3/4 acres, being part of *Land of Goshen*, and part of *Pigman Purchase*, adjoining the land known as *Mill Seat*. The Goshen reference suggests that this larger property was near to and north of the village of Gaithersburg. A third part of the conveyance was for a one-acre lot out of *Water's Forrest*, "whereon the meeting house now stands."

By deed dated November 21, 1796 and recorded in liber G at folio 363, Adam King also purchased from William Bernard, for six hundred pounds, two parcels of ten acres each, out of *Owen's Resurvey*. Also, 234 acres of *Philenia and Sara*, which adjoined the *Resurvey of Brooke Park* as patented to Richard Brooke of

James. Reference to the Brooke family suggests the property was located in the Olney and Sandy Spring area. We have yet to identify Adam King within the framework of the family principally under study.

There is also a deed recorded July 15, 1800 in liber I at folio 214, Montgomery County, in which Upton and Matilda Beall convey lot 28 in the town of Williamsburg, to Thomas King, for the sum of thirty pounds. Rockville, the county seat of Montgomery, was then called Williamsburg.

Francis King

The King family can rightly lay claim to numerous family members who have achieved some measure of greatness, and who have contributed heavily to the success of their county and state. Every family, however, has one member (or more) who does not quite measure up to the norms of the society in which he finds himself. I include this individual simply due to the unusual report that was found concerning him. On March 5, 1774, Francis King was excommunicated from the Seneca Primitive Baptist Church of Dawsonville, Maryland. It was reported that he was "*excluded publickly from Union or Communion until we can have Reason to Hope that the Lord Hath given him repentance for the following Crimes Viz: for getting Drunk Several times and Conforming to the Ways of the World and Misbehavior & In his family threatning to Kill Himself and others and for Doing So He would Dye a true Martyr of Jesus Christ. Secondly for Speaking Disrespectfully of his Brethren and Denying of His Behaviour In Acting the Above Crimes.*"

Warren King
1794-1871

This individual appears as head of household in the 1850 census for Medley District, now Poolesville, Montgomery County, Maryland, at the age of 54, and a farmer. His obituary states that he was born in Prince George's County and in early manhood moved to the western part of Montgomery. His wife, Mary Ann

Belt, was born c.1807, according to the census, and they had two children. He is buried at Monocacy Cemetery, where it is stated that he was born January 31, 1794 and died January 12, 1871. His wife is also buried there, born May 13, 1805 and died July 9, 1885. Married December 21, 1824 to Mary Ann Belt. His will, dated October 4, 1870, was entered for record August 7, 1871 in Liber OWR 6 at folio 153 in the will records of Montgomery County. He named his wife, and three children. The will of his wife is dated February 2, 1882 and entered October 23, 1885 in Liber RWC 15 at folio 50. The children were:

1. James E. King; probably married June 20, 1844 Amanda S. Norris in Georgetown, D. C.; at least an infant daughter:
   a. Emily Amanda King, born October 10, 1845, and died June 14, 1846.
2. Elizabeth Isabella King, born October 14, 1830, of whom more.
3. Margaret Ann King, born c.1840, of whom more

Elizabeth Isabella King
1830-1916

This daughter of Warren King (1794) and Mary Ann Belt (1805) was born October 14, 1830 and died November 7, 1916. Buried at Monocacy Cemetery in Beallsville, Maryland. She was married March 1, 1853 to Leonidas Jones, born January 18, 1827 and died April 26, 1902, son of William and Alma Newton Jones. They had eleven children:

1. Joseph Warren Jones, born February 18, 1853; died 1921.
2. Helen Newton Jones, born September 22, 1855; died July 20, 1955; single.
3. William Edward Jones, born October 25, 1857; died May 13, 1884
4. Edgar Hartley Jones, born October 25, 1859; died April 2, 1862
5. Mary Isabel Jones, born November 1, 1861; died June 10, 1954. Married April 4, 1889 to Richard E. Sellman.

6. Margaret Sumner Jones, born January 28, 1864; died June 24, 1955. Married first William T. Mockbee, and second to Buckey.
7. Ann Mildred Jones, born April 2, 1866; died January 19, 1944. Married first August 22, 1900 Joseph M. Johannes, and second to Henry.
8. Sarah Elizabeth Jones, born July 19, 1868; died June 16, 1960. She married James F. Byrne and had a daughter:
   a. Gertrude Byrne, married Moler.
9. John Augustus Jones, a twin, born October 14, 1870. Married July 6, 1896 to Edna Mannakee.
10. Leonidas Jones, Jr., a twin, born October 14, 1870; died October 22, 1870
11. Susan Emma Jones, born September 30, 1873; died 1946. Married April 29, 1909 to Albert Veikmeyer.

Margaret Ann King
1840-

This daughter of Warren King (1794) and Mary Ann Belt (1805) was born 1840, and died May 2, 1908 in Washington, D. C. Married March 27, 1860 John Thomas Norris. They had eleven children:
1. Anna Mable Norris, born January 2, 1861, at Woodstock, Maryland. Married October 30, 1889 to William Whitney Christmas and had children:
   a. Norris Whitney Christmas, born October 20, 1899; died July 13, 1940 and buried at Arlington Cemetery. Married August, 1932 to Ocia Webb in Washington, D. C.
2. Lutie Norris, born December 24, 1862 in Poolesville, Maryland, and died February 28, 1944. Married there June 1, 1887 to William H. Hempstone, born 1855, died July 3, 1929. Both are buried in the Hempstone lot at Monocacy Cemetery near Beallsville, Maryland. No children.
3. Warren Norris, born July 13, 1864 at Poolesville; died Mary 26, 1909 at Ashville, North Carolina; single.
4. Francis Marion Norris, born August 26, 1866 at Poolesville; died August, 1906 in St. Louis, Missouri; single.

5. Clinton Norris, born October 14, 1868 at Poolesville; died May 16, 1892; single.
6. Cora Elizabeth Norris, born February 1, 1871 at Poolesville; died October 8, 1950 in Washington, D. C. She attended Brierly Hall Academy in Poolesville and moved with the family to Washington in the 1890s. Married there June 28, 1899 to Howard Seymour Gott, born January 22, 1868 in Spencerport, New York; died June 24, 1952, buried Rock Creek Cemetery. One child:
   a. Mildred Seymour Gott, born October 20, 1904
7. John Thomas Norris, a twin, born November 8, 1872 in Poolesville. Married January 25, 1911 in Washington Florence Ritter, born 1877; died January 6, 1945, buried Oak Hill Cemetery in Georgetown, D. C. No children.
8. Margaret Ann Norris, a twin, born November 8, 1872 at Poolesville. Married November 15, 1902 to Julius Crawford Forrest, born 1872 in Washington; died October 21, 1966. One child:
   a. Julius Forrest, born March 1, 1908; died August 20, 1966
9. Reginald Heber Norris, born May 13, 1875 at Poolesville; died October 19, 1918; single. Buried Arlington National.
10. James Almer Norris, born May 3, 1877 in Poolesville; died July 2, 1928; single. Buried Monocacy Cemetery, Beallsville.
11. Charles Olin Norris, born March 14, 1879 at Poolesville; died February 9, 1931; single. Buried at Monocacy Cemetery.

David King
1777-

David is listed as head of household in the 1850 census of the Berry District, now Colesville District, Montgomery County. He is said to be a shoemaker, and a pauper, who can not read or write. In the household is one Jane Powell, born c.1795, and five persons bearing the King name, apparently related to David, although the relationship is not clear:
1. Elizabeth King, born c.1824
2. Francis M. King, born c.1841

3. Susanna King, born c.1844
4. Elizabeth F. King, born c.1846
5. Mary Ann King, born c.1850

George T. King
1793-

Head of household in the 1850 census of Medley District, now Poolesville District, George was listed as a miller, born c.1793. His wife was Sarah, born c.1810. Also in the household was Elizabeth Johnson, born c.1788, who may be Sarah's mother. Three children:
1. Elizabeth King, born c.1834
2. Mary E. King, born c.1836
3. Lydia King, born c.1839

John J. King

The obituary of his wife states that this individual was the founder of the Equitable Purchasing Company of Washington, and that they lived on Colesville Road in Silver Spring, Maryland. His wife, Clara B.; born c.1867, died August 16, 1959. Her will, dated October 17, 1944, was filed in liber VMB 118 at folio 155 in Montgomery County, naming three grandsons as heirs. At least:
1. A son, married Gertrude E., and had three children:
   a. John J. King.
   b. William W. King.
   c. James R. King.

James Autie King
died 1965

The will of this individual, dated August 13, 1963, was filed January 25, 1966, in liber VMB 199 at folio 439 in the will records of Montgomery County. He died December 29, 1965, leaving a wife, Jane M. King. He also mentions one daughter and Mrs. Fannye W. King of Atlanta, Georgia, not otherwise identified. The daughter was:
1. Susan West King, of Atlanta

Ira Leroy King
1909-1984

Ira was born c.1906 and died October 9, 1984 at Shady Grove Hospital near Gaithersburg, Maryland. He was a native of Clarksburg, and a farmer, and was survived by one brother, Herbert C. King (1911) of Damascus, as well as his wife and children. Married April 15, 1937 to Laura E. Davis, born January 21, 1909 and died July 3, 1992, daughter of Edgar W. and Maude Watkins Davis. Ira and Laura are buried at Salem United Methodist Church in Cedar Grove, as was their infant son. They had children:

1. Ira Leroy King, Jr., born June 9, 1938; died September 13, 1938
2. Sterling T. King, who had two children:
   a. Anthony King.
   b. Brandy King.
3. Arlene D. King, married to Carlton and had children:
   a. Sherri Carlton.
   b. Eric Carlton.

Charles Herbert King
1911-1985

As mentioned just above, Herbert was a brother of Ira Leroy King (1909), and lived in the Boyds area of Montgomery County, Maryland. Born c.1911 in Cedar Grove, he died July 21, 1985 at Shady Grove Hospital near Gaithersburg, and has been found in some records as Herbert C. King (with his two given names reversed), although marriage records clearly carry them as we have shown. He was a farmer, and had operated a milk transport business and a general store at Germantown. He was married March 20, 1934 at Germantown, to Eleanor A. L. Bowman, born there March 8, 1912, and died July 17, 1978, daughter of Charles R. Bowman and Clara Jane Crawford. Two daughters:

1. Jean King, married to Phillips.
2. Carol Ann King, married to Mumma.

Conrad King
1817-1910

This individual appears as head of household in the 1870 census for Clarksburg District of Montgomery County, Maryland, at the age of 51 (born c.1819). He is buried at the Mt. Airy Methodist Cemetery in Frederick County, where his stone reads that he died May 25, 1910 at the age of 93 years (born c.1817). In other records, he appears to have lived in the Middletown area of Frederick County, at least for a time, where several of his children were born. Further, the family is perhaps German, and therefore unrelated to those studied in the main body of the text, some of the children having been christened in the Evangelical Lutheran Church, and the German Reformed Church; although, as noted, they are buried in a Methodist cemetery. He was married to Ann Elizabeth, born c.1814, and died April 6, 1900; buried with her husband. They had a large family:

1. David Henry King, born January 8, 1843
2. Ann Mary King, born October 3, 1847
3. Sarah King, born c.1848
4. Sophia Catharine King, born November 21, 1849
5. Clara Virginia King, born June 6, 1853
6. Julia Ann E. King, born c.1857; married December 24, 1870 to J. S. Curtis at Clarksburg, Maryland
7. Louis E. King, born c.1859
8. Ida Emma G. King, born February 7, 1864

Melvin Leroy King
1913-1972

Born c.1913, Melvin Leroy King, Sr. died July 18, 1972. At the time of death, he was living on Muncaster Mill Road, Gaithersburg, Montgomery County, Maryland. He was survived by four sisters and three brothers: Mrs. Doris Boyd; Mrs Theresa Kinder; Mrs. Esther Tarlton; Mrs. Mary Thompson; Harvey King; Carlton C. King; and Willard W. King. Survived by his wife, Mildred C. Trigger King, born July 21, 1920 in Virginia; died February 16,

1992; daughter of John and Lillian Trigger. Four daughters and five sons:

1. Ruby M. King, married to Howell
2. Nancy L. King, married to Stokes
3. Peggy A. King, married to Daufeldt
4. Debbie L. King, married Bennett
5. Melvin Leroy King, Jr.
6. Carlton R. King, known as "Pookie"
7. William R. King.
8. John Robert "Bobbie" King.
9. Ronnie King.

Preston Cloud King
died 1953

Preston was an executive with the C & P Telephone Company and died November 28, 1953. Married in 1903 to Sallie Maury Myers, born March 31, 1875 in Georgetown, and died September 2, 1974, daughter of John Parsons Myers and Annie Myers. Soon after their marriage, they moved to Takoma Park where they lived for the next thirty years, then moved to Bethesda, and later to Potomac, where they lived on their estate, Rexholm Farm. His will, dated August 24, 1933, was entered December 10, 1953 in Liber WCC 47 at folio 150 in the will records of Montgomery County. Prominent in the Potomac Hunt, and social circles of the area, she was presented to President Grover Cleveland as a young lady, and graduated in the class of 1892 from Mt. Vernon Seminary. Survived by a son, a granddaughter, and two great grandchildren:

1. Preston Cloud King, Jr., born c.1904; died November 15, 1991 at his home, *Rexholm Farm*, at Potomac, Maryland. He formerly served as president of the D. C. Bar Association and other positions in the legal profession. Member of the Potomac Hunt, Chevy Chase Club and the Metropolitan Club. Married 1929 to Kathryn M. Larcombe, and had a child:
   a. Barbara Ellen King, died 1980. Married June 7, 1952 to Bruce Allen Reichelderfer and had two children:
      (1) Kathryn Reichelderfer.
      (2) Bruce A. Reichelderfer, Jr.

James Richard King
died c.1916

The will of this individual, dated October 17, 1916, was entered for record January 16, 1917 in the will records of Montgomery County, Maryland, in liber HCA 19 at folio 230. His wife, Anna Elizabeth Walker King, two sons and four daughters appear in the will. He is quite possibly the same James R. King found in cemetery records, who was born April 19, 1841; died November 20, 1916, and is buried at St. John's in Forest Glen. His wife's will, dated October 15, 1925, was entered for record March 7, 1933, and recorded in liber HGC 5 at folio 49. It names two of the daughters and one son, as well as a grandson. The children included:
1. James William King.
2. John Richard King.
3. Mary Katharine Carroll King, born December 3, 1893; who received the family home in Takoma Park under her mother's will. She may have been married to a King, since she is specifically called that in her mother's will. Cemetery records report one John R. King, born 1889 and died 1942; with a wife, Katharine Carroll, born 1893 and died 1957.
4. Grace Harriet King; married to Trail, and deceased by 1925, when her mother wrote her will. At least one son:
   a. Charles Richard Trail, born c.1918
5. Olive Teresa King, born June 23, 1897; married to Dunn
6. Sarah M. King; married to Rabbitt

Cora E. King
1879-1960

Her husband has not yet been identified, but Cora E. was born March 27, 1879 and died April 19, 1960. Her stone at Clarksburg United Methodist Church cemetery reads "mother" and buried near her are apparently her two sons:
1. Henry E. King, (or Henry L.), born November 18, 1900; died May 26, 1933 in an auto accident. Married to Edna May.
2. Larry M. King, born December 9, 1933; died December 15, 1941

Porter Jay King

The wife of Porter was Mary E. Bowles, born 1927 and died August 27, 1984 at Shady Grove Hospital. Her husband survived her, as did several children:
1. Robert A. Hubbard King, suggesting an earlier marriage
2. Porter Jay King, Jr.
3. Joann King.

Emma King
died 1914

The will of this individual is found in Liber HCA 14 at folio 362 in the will records of Montgomery County, Maryland. It is dated November 6, 1909 and entered for record July 14, 1914. She died July 7, 1914. In the will, she mentions her sister, Florence M. Wetherel, and two sons, a daughter in law and a granddaughter:
1. Lawrence A. King, born July, 1879; married October 24, 1900 Katharine C. Burriss; divorced in April, 1912. Father of:
   a. Martha C. T. King.
2. William J. King.

John C. King
died 1945

Said to be of the District of Columbia, his will, dated August 10, 1925, was entered for record May 29, 1945 in the will records of Montgomery County, Maryland. Filed in liber OWR 6 at folio 480. Names wife, Irene A.; brother, Thomas P. King; reference to two un-named sisters. Also names Carl Allen King and Edith E. Lipphard Joyce, as the "boy and girl raised by us."

James King

The obituary of the daughter of this individual states that he was married to Joanna, and that his father was Quesselin King. The parents of Joanna were apparently Joseph and Anna Richter. The children of James were:

1. Deanna Elizabeth King, born August 1, 1971; died October 8, 1980 at her home in Comus and buried at St. Mary's at Barnesville.
2. James D. King.

Ellen A. King
died 1935

Said to be of Chevy Chase, her will dated April 15, 1931, was entered November 30, 1935 in liber HGC 11 at folio 211. There, she names two daughters and a son, as well as a daughter-in-law and a granddaughter. She appears to have been rather well-to-do, mentioning in her will a cottage at York Harbor; house and lots in the District of Columbia; land in Nokesville, Virginia; and the family home in Chevy Chase. The three children were:
1. Albert F. A. King, married to Elizabeth Logan. A daughter:
   a. Elizabeth Dexter King.
2. Louise Freeman King.
3. Sarah Vincent King.

Melvin King
1901-1940

Born May 12, 1901 and died May 29, 1940, son of Henry and Fannie King, Melvin is buried at Bethesda United Methodist Church in Browningsville, Maryland. He was married to Margaret; at least a daughter, buried with him:
1. Grace Mae King, born December 27, 1927; died February 1, 1928

Ellen T. King
1922-1995

Born December 5, 1922 in Washington, D. C.; daughter of Harold C. and Eugenia King. Apparently married to a King, and died June 9, 1995 at Shady Grove Hospital, leaving two children:
1. Ann King, married to Lanier, of Nashua, New Hampshire
2. Stephen T. King, of Damascus

Andrew W. King

This individual and his family are named in the obituary of his son, John M. King. Married to Dorothy E., they lived on Summit Avenue in Gaithersburg, and had children:
1. John M. King, died August 5, 1966; buried at Arlington National Cemetery
2. Elva E. King, married to Atkins
3. Larry A. King.
4. Harry A. King.
5. Patsy A. King.
6. Tommy H. King.

James A. King

The obituary of his son, Larry Bruce, appearing in the Journal of December 18, 1992, provides information relative to this family. Married to Bessie, and had children:
1. Larry Bruce King, born c.1942 and died December 5, 1992. He had eight children:
   a. Colleen M. King.
   b. Jesse L. King.
   c. Trevor King.
   d. Shelsea M. King.
   e. Shalene D. King.
   f. Sarah D. King.
   g. Brittany A. King.
   h. Sandra Darlene King.
2. Irma King, married to Rollison
3. Norma King, married to Beall
4. Sarah King, married to Mitchell
5. Charles King.
6. Allan King.
7. William King.

Willard B. King
1921-1987

Born c.1921 in Maryland, Willard died October 14, 1987 at Shady Grove Hospital near Gaithersburg; buried at Flower Hill Cemetery in Redland, Montgomery County, Maryland. He was a crane operator for a construction company, and was survived by four sisters: Esther Tarlton of California; Doris Boyd of Morningside; Teresa Kinder of Gaithersburg; and Mary Thompson of Gaithersburg. He also left two sons, four daughters, thirteen grandchildren, and six great grandchildren. Children were:
1. Tommy King, of Rockville
2. Willard B. King, Jr. of Olney
3. Janet King, married Horton, of Germantown
4. Gloria King, married Cogan of Gaithersburg
5. Peggy King, of Mount Airy
6. Pauline King, married Michael of Boyds.

John M. King
died 1956

The will of this individual is dated April 22, 1955 and filed August 21, 1956 in liber EA 70 at folio 138 in the will records of Montgomery County. He died June 15, 1956, and was married to Pauline M. The will names three daughters, and his mother, Marie E. King. The daughters were:
1. Constance King, married to Holmead
2. Shirley King, married to Kreimeyer
3. Carolyn King, married to Scudder

David H. King
1846-1921

This individual was a shoemaker, born c.1846 and died April 28, 1921; buried at Bethesda United Methodist Church at Browningsville. Married second (a widower), December 13, 1899 to Fannie Redmon at Browningsville. At least a son:
1. David King, born September 17, 1900

Miscellaneous Montgomery County Records

During the process of research, a number of references were found to King family members, not otherwise identified in the main body of the text, primarily in cemetery records of Montgomery County. They are listed following; all given names in the left column carry the King surname. Obviously, some of the females listed have other maiden names, but married King men.

Does not include marriage records listed after 1935 in Montgomery County. Beginning with that date, only the names of the parties and the date of issuance of license are reported in the records. No ages, no place of residence or place of marriage, and no dates of marriage are listed.

Individual	Information
Addie Abell	08/05/1876 to 11/23/1965. Friends Meeting House
Albertis Ward	12/20/1883 to 03/24/1970. Upper Seneca Baptist
Amy Kirstin	04/01/1967 to 05/20/1967. Daughter of Donald King and Martha T. Thompson King. Rockville Cemetery.
Anna M.	Born c.1923; married 08/18/1944 to Arthur R. Johnson at Gaithersburg
Annie May	Born c.1889; married 10/13/1909 to Virgil M. Baker at Damascus
Arthur Charles	Born c.1876; married 03/31/1910 to Grace Lee Hobbs at Rockville.
Barbara Emaline	1973 to 1973. On stone with grandmother with the same name, following. Colesville Methodist Church.
Barbara Emaline	1929 to 1955. Colesville Methodist Church.
Bee	1921 to 1987 with wife Louise, 1926. Flower Hill Brethren.
Bertha Agnes	Born c.1887; married 06/29/1907 at Forest Glen to Maurice A. Umstead.
Bessie Ada	11/20/1901 to 10/24/1979. St. John's at Forest Glen

Birdie M.	Born c.1894; married 12/03/1912 to Thomas E. Knott at Germantown.
Catherine	1851 to 07/26/1885. Forest Glen
Cecilia F.	Died 02/02/1965; will in VMB 185, folio 819.
Charles, Jr.	Married 01/13/1937 Emily Edwards; Kemptown
Charles W.	Died 08/17/1895. St. John's at Forest Glen
Charles Wilson	Born 03/12/1894 to Charles Edward and Laura Ivin. St. Mary's Catholic Church register.
Charlie L.	04/24/1881 to 08/25/1905. Woodside
Charlie D.	01/13/1890 to 08/26/1962. His wife Augusta W., 11/10/1888 to 04/02/1922. Upper Seneca Baptist at Cedar Grove.
Columbus	07/10/1866 to 07/20/1886. Mt. Zion Cemetery
Cora B.	1868 to 1929. James W. Johnson plot at Clarksburg United Methodist Church
Cordelia	1831 to 04/25/1899. St. Mary's at Barnesville
Craven J.	Died 08/24/1960; will in VMB 127, folio 632
David	Married 08/20/1816 to Highley Crow
Dorothy Clagett	Born 08/18/1902. St. Mary's New at Rockville
Douglas W.	03/17/1891 to 01/09/1977. Mutual Memorial Cemetery
Dulcia	Christened 04/11/1911; father was J. M. King of Kemptown
Edmund Carlton	Married 01/29/1895 to Harriet May Dutrow.
Edward J.	1826 to 03/03/1885, died at age 59 years, 5 months and 17 days. Kingstead Farm Cemetery
Elias	Married 01/04/1819 to Elizabeth Thompson
Elias	Born 10/25/1841 to Charles and Mary E. King at Forest Glen
Elizabeth	Married 02/07/1779 to Thomas Miles.
Ella E.	Born c.1903; married 09/26/1921 at Colesville to Charles E. Hamilton.
Ellen Irene	Born c.1881; married 08/17/1909 to Arthur G. Noble at Rockville.
Ellen Thomas	Born 11/08/1837 to Thomas R. and Priscilla
Emeline	12/20/1837 to 06/18/1898. Wife of Walter King. Mt. Ephraim Cemetery, Dickerson, Maryland
Emma	02/27/1854 to 07/07/1914. Woodside

Emma J.	Born 03/12/1890
Ernest W.	10/28/1882 to 03/01/1962. Wife, Hattie G. King, 08/29/1881 to 06/06/1958, nee Watkins. They were married December 9, 1908 at Clarksburg. Both are buried at Bethesda United Methodist, Browningsville
Ena M.	Died 07/30/1899. St. John's at Forest Glen
Florence Mabel	Died 01/30/1935. Daughter of Samuel B. and Emma J. Haney King.
Fillie R.	04/24/1892 to 08/28/1892. Salem United Methodist at Cedar Grove
Frances E.	1892 to 1971. Bethesda United Methodist Church at Browningsville
Frederick Mason	04/22/1884 to 09/27/1968, and his wife Sarah Hallowell, 07/29/1889 to 08/17/1978. St. John's at Forest Glen. Married there 01/14/1908.
George Francis	Born 03/17/1836 to Charles and Mary at Forest Glen
Georgia Eleanor	Born c.1886; married 06/02/1904 at Rockville, to Bradley Winfield Warfield
Gertrude E.	Died 06/13/1960 at Gaithersburg; will in liber VMB 127, folio 326; names a foster daughter, Blanche Rice, of Mt. Airy; nieces, Dorothy Horner and Mildred Hronik; and her sister Anna Morningstar.
Gertrude Hargett	03/23/1887 to 06/13/1960. St. Rose Catholic Church at Rockville
Grace E.	Married 07/02/1927 to Lloyd R. Green.
Harry G.	01/17/1848 to 04/13/1932. Brooke Grove Cemetery
Howard H.	1912 to 1972. Damascus Methodist Church
Howard O.	09/17/1936 to 11/24/1941. Damascus Methodist
Hubert G.	Died 08/08/1959 at Potomac, Maryland
Ida A.	Born c.1887; married 06/13/1908 to Grover G. Lewis at Kings Valley
Iris I.	06/13/1934 to 12/14/1980. Lot owned by Robert H. King. Rockville Cemetery
Isaac N.	Married 05/09/1842 to Nancy O. Prather

James	Married 02/17/1801 to Kitty Caton
James H.	10/13/1872 to 11/12/1943. With son, Upton R., born 02/11/1916, died 05/10/1919. St. Mary's Church at Barnesville
James R.	04/19/1841 to 11/20/1916. St. John's at Forest Glen
Jesse	Married 12/24/1817 to Lydia Walker
Jemima	03/08/1782 to 10/30/1861. Kingstead Farm
John	Married 08/29/1829 to Susan Ray
John H.	Born 01/08/1841. Mutual Memorial Cemetery
John W.	1867 to 1932. St. John's at Forest Glen
Judson	Died 07/04/1958; wife Bertha Hale King; will in liber EA 98, folio 152.
Laura Lavinia	Born 05/18/1861 to William & Sarah Jones King
Lee M.	1884 to 1971; wife Jessie M., 1896 to 1959. Salem United Methodist at Cedar Grove
Lottie	Born 06/15/1884 to Charles & Sarah Ertter
Lucille Frances	Born c.1914; married 09/02/1932 to Joseph N. Shook at Rockville
Lucy Poole	11/17/1893 to 08/20/1943. Buried at Mountain View Cemetery
Luther Roland	1891 to 10/22/1945, husband of Esther Moore King Brown. Monocacy Cemetery.
Mabel Frances	Born 06/03/1907 to Charles King
Mahala J.	04/19/1863 to 02/19/1877. Buried Salem United Methodist at Cedar Grove
Margaret E.	04/18/1917 to 12/27/1995. Daughter of Charles Lee Watkins, Jr. & Rose Mae Johnson Watkins. A daughter: Margo of Colton, California in 1995.
Marietta Kinery	Born 03/16/1884 to Nathan and Jane K. King
Marion F.	Born c.1887; married 06/23/1910 at Rockville to Elmer E. Williams.
Mary Catherine	Born 02/20/1889 to Charles and Sarah Ertter
Mary F.	04/05/1805 to 09/05/1873. Kingstead Farm
Mary I.	1848 to 05/19/1922. Mutual Memorial Cemetery
Mary J.	Married 11/27/1926 to Zachariah T. Windsor

Mary Magdalene Born 11/25/1902 to John H. & Mary Magdalene Ganley

Mary Rebecca Born 03/16/1884 to William and Cora

May V. 1904 to 12/06/1907. Daughter of William and Bertie King. Brooke Grove Cemetery.

Mary Warner Widow, aged 58. Married 10/22/1925 to George Bancroft Sprague. Her parents were Willard and Eliza Woods Warner.

Maude Alverta Born c.1899; married 09/21/1921 to Walter M. Magruder at Gaithersburg

Merle V. 02/16/1925 to 01/12/1946; wife Lucy I., 06/19/1927. Buried Clarksburg United Methodist Church

Mildred Adele Born c.1907; married 07/29/1926 to John P. Thompson at Gaithersburg

Milton Thomas 1905 to 1966. Stone erected by the Fraley family at Brooke Grove Cemetery

Muriel Lucille Born c.1915; married 09/05/1934 Louis E. Platt at Silver Spring.

Myrtle Irene Born 04/03/1895 to John and Virginia

Nancy Margaret 04/10/1932 to 02/21/1978. Boyds Presbyterian

Nellie E. Born c.1901; married 1925 Clarence K. Duvall at Darnestown

Nettie Elizabeth Born c.1910; married 08/16/1930 Ledoux Elger Riggs, Jr., at Rockville

Nicholas Married 11/20/1865 to Eulalie Johnstone.

Noah Married 01/15/1938 at New Market, Virginia, to Mrs. Martha Hillery of Kemptown, Maryland

Patrick Allen Of Chevy Chase; married 12/17/1966 to Linda Lorraine Davis of Potomac

Rebecca Married 12/11/1798 to Charles Harvey

Ruth Married 01/09/1800 to Basil Poole.

Samuel P. Born 07/03/1855 to Wilson and Sarah Jones

Sarah Married 02/05/1799 to James Groomes.

Sarah A. 02/19/1866 to 05/09/1885. Daughter of John W. and Arubell King. Wildwood Baptist, Bethesda

Sarah Elizabeth Born 05/28/1888 to William and Virginia Crump

Sarah Estelle Born 08/05/1886 to Charles and Sarah Ertter

Sarah F.	1843 to 10/27/1907. Wife of John H. King. Mutual Memorial Cemetery
Selina G.	1855 to 03/14/1903. Wife of Albert B. King. Mutual Memorial Cemetery
Stanley D.	1907 to 1959. Wife, Rosalee, 1909 to 1951. Upper Seneca Baptist at Cedar Grove. She was Rosalee Flinn; married 08/25/1928.
Susan E.	1844 to 12/02/1873. Kingstead Farm cemetery
Theresa Virginia	Born 10/23/1883 to John and Mary Chaney King
Thomas E.	Died 01/30/1963; wife Catherine C.; will in liber VMB 162, folio 199
Thomas Gould	Died 05/21/1966; will in VMB 208, folio 871
Thomas Lee	Died 04/07/1947; Mountain View Cemetery
Thomas Matthew	06/27/1908 to 12/19/1978, wife Mary Magdalene, born 03/30/1906. Monocacy Cemetery.
Tommy Lee	Born 04/25/1936 to Woodrow Wilson & Gurvis Pauline Moxley King, married at Clarksburg 05/25/1935
Upton	Married 12/13/1817 to Polly Bates
Vinton G.	Married 09/26/1903 to Lillian Irene Kidwell
Virginia R.	12/30/1890 to 07/25/1973. Salem United Methodist at Cedar Grove
Walden V.	07/07/1894 to 02/20/1978, wife Violena, 10/27/1899 to 09/04/1979. Clarksburg United Methodist Church
Walter D.	Born 07/07/1894 to J. B. and Lavinia King
William	Married 08/04/1804 to Delilah Miles
William A.	Died July 6, 1935. Rockville
William R.	Died 04/17/1960; wife Ethel W.; will in VMB 127 at folio 298, Montgomery County
Wilma Fay	Died 03/07/1957, aged one hour. Forest Oak
William Warren	Born 05/13/1857 to Wilson and Sarah Jones

CHAPTER 18

Prince George's County Records

References to several families, and a number of individuals, have been found in various records of Prince George's, including:

James King

This James was married to Sarah, and some of their children are identified in the International Genealogical Index records of the Mormon Church, including:
1. Charles King, born October, 1763
2. Mary King, born January 19, 1766
3. Amelia King, born July 10, 1768; perhaps the same Amelia King who was married December 24, 1797 to George Upton.
4. Sabra King, born July 1, 1774.

Thomas King

Married to Eleanor, Thomas appears in the records of Prince George's County; the father of at least these children:
1. Ann King, born December 29, 1765
2. Susanna King, born October 26, 1769
3. Priscilla King, born February 23, 1772

Edward King

This Edward, of several to bear the name, was married to Ann, and had several children born in Prince George's County:
1. Susannah King, born January 8, 1764
2. Ann King, born September 28, 1766
3. Mary King, born December 23, 1773
4. James King, born April 23, 1776

Francis King
1695-

Born about 1695 in Prince George's County, Francis was perhaps the son of William and Elizabeth King. Married September 25, 1717 to Margaret Sprigg, and had children:
1. Margaret King, born August 28, 1718
2. Thomas King, born November 5, 1720
3. Cave King, or Cane King, born June 1, 1722. This could also be Cavie, a girl, married c.1740 to Thomas Williams.
4. Sarah King, born c.1723
5. Francis King, Jr., born January 19, 1724

Sylvester King
1822-

Married to Sabrina, born c.1824, he was the father of several children born in Prince George's County, some of whom appear in their parents household in the 1850 census of Spaldings District, including:
1. Richard Warren King, christened September 29, 1839
2. John Henry King, christened June 5, 1843
3. Alfred King, born c.1847
4. Thomas Warren King, christened May, 1849.

Richard King
1808-

Richard appears as head of household in the 1850 census of Queen Anne District of Prince George's County, at the age of 42, with a wife, Ann, born c.1818, and several children. The children appear in the listings in order of eldest to youngest, which is customary. However, at the end of the listing is yet another child, Ben, born c.1841, who may be their son, but for some reason is listed out of age sequence. In any event, the children listed were:
1. Mary King, born c.1840
2. E. King, a girl, born c.1843
3. Catherine King, born c.1845

4. Margaret King, born c.1847
5. William King, born c.1848
6. John King, born c.1850
7. Ben King, born c.1841

Elisha King

Elisha was born in Prince George's County, and married at Accokeek, in Piscataway Parish, December 11, 1775 to Lydia Webster. They had several children:
1. Ann King, born September 31, 1776
2. Sarah King, born September 11, 1778
3. James King, born February 3, 1782
4. John King, born December 11, 1783
5. Violender King, born August 6, 1786
6. Charles King, born August 25, 1787

John King

John was married to Eleanor, and they had children in Prince George's County, including these:
1. Ruth King, born July 4, 1762
2. Eleanor King, born February 19, 1764
3. Elizabeth King, born January 26, 1766
4. Mary King, born September 13, 1774

Vincent King
1802-

Head of household in the 1850 census of the Piscataway District of Prince George's; married November 1, 1828 Sarah White, born c.1805. Children:
1. John King, born c.1829
2. Letty King, born c.1830
3. Rebecca King, born c.1837
4. Benjamin King, born c.1839
5. Lucinda King, born c.1847
6. Elizabeth King, born c.1848

Thomas King
1798-

Head of household in the 1850 census for Spaldings District, Prince George's County, Thomas was born c.1798, and married to Capy, born c.1803. Several children:
1. E. King, a daughter, born c.1824
2. J. King, a son, born c.1826
3. James King, born c.1828
4. William King, born c.1832
5. John King, born c.1835

Henry King
1810-

Listed in the 1850 census of Piscataway District, Prince George's County, Henry was a farm manager. His wife listed only by the initial, M., born c.1816, and several children:
1. Thomas King, born c.1838
2. Henry King, born c.1841
3. Oscar King, born c.1843
4. M. King, a daughter, born c.1846
5. L. King, a son, born c.1849

Elizabeth King
1810-

Apparently a widow, Elizabeth is head of household in the 1850 census of Bladensburg District, in Prince George's County, Maryland. She was born c.1810 and had children:
1. Elizabeth King, born c.1835
2. Mary King, born c.1837
3. Henry King, born c.1841
4. William King, born c.1843
5. Otho King, born c.1845
6. Martha King, born c.1849

Elizabeth King
1793-

This Elizabeth appears as head of household in the 1850 census of Spalding District, Prince George's County, apparently a widow. There are others in the household, including at least a son and a daughter, living with her husband and two of her children in her mother's household:
1. James H. King, born c.1824
2. Mary E. King, born c.1822; married April 11, 1844 to Joseph N. Arnold, and had children:
   a. Thomas Arnold, born c.1845
   b. Mary Arnold, born c.1849

Ann King
1812-

Ann was married February 21, 1838 in Prince George's County, to Benjamin Mullikin, born c.1804. They appear in the 1850 census of Piscataway District for the county, with children:
1. Mary Mullikin, born c.1839
2. John S. Mullikin, born c.1841
3. Margaret Mullikin, born c.1843
4. James Mullikin, born c.1847

Mary King
1797-

Mary was married February 4, 1824 in Prince George's County, Maryland, to Henry Taymon, born c.1797. They appear in the 1850 census for Spaldings District, with several children:
1. William Taymon, born c.1825
2. E. Taymon, a daughter, born c.1830
3. Richard Taymon, born c.1831
4. Phillip Taymon, born c.1832

A number of King family individuals appear in records of Prince George's County, tabulated according to the event. All names in the left column bear the King surname:

Individual	Information
Alexander	Married 01/14/1798 to Anne Stonestreet.
Amelia	Married 12/24/1797 to George Upton.
Ann	Married 03/06/1779 to Zadock Moore.
Ann	Married 12/07/1794 to Charles Cox.
Ann	Married 02/21/1838 to Benjamin Mullikin.
Ann	Married 06/29/1841 to Richard S. Ridgeway.
Ann	Born 03/14/1794 to James and Eleanor.
Anne	Born 11/30/1775 to James and Eleanor.
Charles	Christened July 22, 1797; son of William King and Susannah King.
Charlotte Anne	Born 11/16/1808 to James Swean King & Sarah Lecrecey King. This is perhaps James Swann King and Sarah Lee Lanham, reported elsewhere.
Daniel	Married 03/07/1847 Elizabeth Mahala Goddard.
David	Born 05/19/1775 to Richard and Eleanor King
Eleanor	Married 08/24/1782 to John H. Wilson.
Elisha	Married 02/18/1800 to Elizabeth Spalding.
Elisha	Married 12/11/1775 to Lydia Webster
Elisha	Born 12/17/1798 to Elkanah and Anne.
Elizabeth	Married 01/05/1786 to Robert Simm.
Elizabeth	Married 02/21/1786 to Richard Pumphrey.
Elizabeth	Married 1789 to John Dorsey.
Elizabeth	Born 04/03/1800 to Thomas and Mary King.
Francis	Married 1726 to Margaret Keene.
Francis	Married 09/25/1717 Margaret Sprigg, daughter of Colonel Thomas Sprigg
George B.	Born 02/17/1787 to Jonathan and Verlinder.
Henrietta	Married 02/09/1803 to John Brightwell.
Hetty	Married 12/26/1794 to Zadoc Cooke.
Isaac	Married 03/16/1799 to Sarah Weaver.
Isaac	Born 1800 to Michael and Hannah King.

398

Jacob	Married 03/02/1802 Ann Soper. Two daughters: Elizabeth, born c.1803; Juliet Ann, born c.1805
James	Married 01/08/1819 to Elizabeth Gray.
James Swann	Married 12/22/1800 to Sarah Lee Lanham.
James Thomas	Born 08/14/1860 to John H. and Melvina.
Jane	Married 03/07/1799 to George Wise.
Jane	Married 11/07/1833 to Theodore Mitchell.
John	Married 11/-/1777 to Susan Lynch (see next)
John	Married 11/25/1777 to Susanna Leach
John	Married 06/23/1779 to Keziah Upton.
John	Married 08/02/1791 to Elizabeth McDarall.
John	Married 01/10/1794 to Ann Lewis.
John	Married 01/11/1831 to Mary Bayne.
John	Married 09/23/1847 to Catharine Davis.
John Duckett	Born 01/28/1772 to William and Letitia.
Joseph	Born 1796, son of Michael and Hannah.
Laura Jerusha	Born 07/02/1862 to John and Catharine.
Leonard	Married 11/15/1780 to Susannah Watson.
Lloyd	Born 10/23/1788 to Jonathan and Verlinder.
Margaret	Married 12/18/1735 to John Hilleary.
Maria Elizabeth	Born 05/16/1853 to Daniel and Sarah Ann.
Maria Elizabeth	Born 05/14/1854 to John H. and Malvina.
Martin	Married 06/09/1867 to Sarah A. Rowe.
Mary	Married 01/05/1799 to Thomas Mullican.
Mary	Married 10/31/1808 to John Parmer.
Mary	Married 02/04/1824 to Henry Taymon.
Mary	Born 10/11/1759 to Francis and Ann.
Mary Ann	Married 05/14/1818 to Zadock Riston.
Mary Eleanor	Born 06/13/1805 to ? and Nancy King.
Richard	Born 08/26/1764 to Richard and Eleanor.
Richard	Married 02/15/1795 to Elizabeth Brown.
Richard	Married 03/08/1795 to Annamaria Weaver.
Ruth	Married 04/10/1787 to Thomas Simpson.
Sabrat	Married 02/12/1793 to William Jones.
Samuel T.	Born 11/27/1798 to John and Elizabeth.
Sarah	Married 11/06/1834 to William H. Mitchell
Sarah	Married 01/03/1798 to John Grimes.
Sarah	Married 02/09/1802 to Jesse Wilcoxen.

Sarah	Married 11/22/1855 to William Sayman.
Susanna	Married 12/16/1779 to John Biggs.
Susannah	Married 02/28/1789 to John Watson.
Susannah	Married 04/14/1798 to Caleb Thomas.
Thomas	Married 10/16/1787 to Mary Mitchell.
Thomas	Married 02/26/1821 to Elizabeth Thompson.
Thomas	Married 03/29/1823 to Cassandra Riston.
Thomas M.	Married 01/18/1790 to Rebecca Gray.
Vinson	Married 11/01/1828 to Sarah White.
Walter Gustavus	Born 08/15/1869 to John H. and Susan.
William	Married 1727 to Susannah Price.
William	Born 05/24/1762 to Richard and Eleanor.
William	Married 10/22/1796 to Susanna Holland.
William	Born 04/20/1786 to James and Eleanor.
William Arthur	Born 08/15/1869 to John H. and Susan.
William Swan	Born 06/16/1805 to James S. and Alethia.

CHAPTER 19

Baltimore County Records

During the course of research, at least one rather large King family has been found in Baltimore County, with descendants elsewhere in later generations. Others have been identified from the various records, not necessarily associated with this major one, or with the others under study in earlier chapters of the text. As mentioned in other sections of the study, we have found present-day King families with apparent Germanic origins in other areas of the state. During the information gathering phase of the study, a letter was sent to randomly selected Kings from the local phone book, seeking data relative to their families, primarily as they might be associated with the Montgomery County families. Several phone calls were received in response, and at least two of them indicated German origins, with roots in America in New York and Pennsylvania. In any case, they are included here.

John Frederick King
1828-1904

This individual was born March 26, 1828 in Germany, with the original spelling of the surname being Koenig. The time of his arrival in America has not been determined, and he died November 6, 1904 in Baltimore, Maryland. He was married c.1853 to Anna Catherine Kirschner, born October 31, 1833 in Germany, suggesting that they may have been married before coming to America. However, it is noted that one of the children married a Kirschner also, indicating that both families had migrated to America. She died October 3, 1909 in Baltimore, and they had ten children, all born there:

1. Louisa Jane King, born September 26, 1854; died May 17, 1935. Married c.1874 Henry Albert Raycob, born January 10, 1847.

2. Henry King, born November 14, 1855; died December 27, 1926 in Chester Township, Eaton County, Michigan. He was married there June 28, 1883 to Ina Fuller, born December 23, 1867 in Hillsdale, Michigan. Nine children, born in Eaton County:

   a. Grace King, born January 6, 1886; married Edward Arnold, born January 18, 1873, and had three children.

   b. Franklin V. King, born July 13, 1887; married Etta Simpson, born August 8, 1884

   c. Luvern L. King, born April 22, 1889

   d. William H. King, born May 16, 1891; married to Anna M. Litchfield, born June 23, 1900

   e. Emma King, born October 12, 1893; married Alton Larabee, born February 9, 1894, and had two children.

   f. Myrtie King, born June 9, 1895; married Earl Cole, born June 9, 1897, and had three children. She apparently married second Herman Lentz, and third William Downey.

   g. Ida Lucy King, born June 22, 1901; married to Robert Ewing, born January 21, 1892 and had three children.

   h. Irvin King, born about 1903

   i. Nellie King, born February 7, 1912; married Robert Ewing, born January 21, 1892, and had four children. Note the report just above of the marriage of her sister to the same individual. Perhaps one of the girls died young, and he was married secondly to the sister.

3. William Louis King, born March 10, 1860; died January 25, 1931 in Eaton County, Michigan. Married there January 16, 1885 to Nellie Evalena Fuller, born October 27, 1866 in Michigan. Six children, born in Eaton County, Michigan:

   a. Charles Frederick King, born November 13, 1887; married to Beulah Mae Briggs, born July 28, 1889, and had six children.

   b. Zella Irene King, born August 15, 1891; married to Perry H. Wells, born September 10, 1887. Two children.

   c. Hazel Eliza King, born September 1, 1892; married Leon Arthur Bosworth, born January 11, 1885. Five children.

d. Mabel Eloise King, born May 2, 1896; married Otto Johnson, born December 23, 1893. Two children.

e. Albert Louis King, born July 9, 1902; two children.

f. William Harold King, born March 10, 1904; married.

4. Henrietta Catherine King, born March 26, 1862 and died June 12, 1937. Married March 24, 1880 George Hartung, born April 2, 1856.

5. John Frederick King, Jr., born December 6, 1863; married c.1885 to Louise Kirschner.

6. Christiana King, born October 8, 1865; died April 17, 1926. Married 1885 Charles Stocker Krebs, born October 21, 1860.

7. Mary Missouri King, born November 27, 1867; died February 9, 1957. Married March 21, 1889 George Fred Heintzman, born April 14, 1865.

8. Charles Edward King, born March 21, 1870; died August 18, 1945. Married May Henry. Married second 1897 in Maryland to Martha Ella Nolte, born February 6, 1863.

9. Thomas Franklin King, born June, 1873; married c.1896 to Mollie O. Kemp, born December, 1873.

10. Margaret Elizabeth King, born October 23, 1876; married 1911 to John Edward Kemp, born c.1876.

A number of individual records were found of King family members in Baltimore County. All names in the left column bear the King surname; male parents are also King:

Individual	Information
Abram	Born c.1847 to David
Adela	Born c.1849 to David
Agnes	Born c.1848 to William
Amelia	Married 01/10/1833 to Benjamin P. Lurby
Amos	Married 04/29/1833 to Elizabeth Tracy
Ann	Married 12/13/1779 to Peter Davis
Ann	Married 02/13/1789 to Rezin Hardesty
Ann	Married 01/15/1791 John Christian Louderman
Ann	Married 10/27/1834 to William Dimmitt
Ann Maria	Married 07/29/1817 to William P. Moore

Ann Maria	Born 12/24/1799 to Benjamin and Hannah
Anthony	Married 06/24/1802 to Doris Harttert
Benjamin, Jr.	Born 12/24/1802 to Benjamin and Hannah
Caroline	Born 1840 to Alfred C.
Catharine	Born 1840 to David
Catharine	Married 07/29/1806 to John Duncan
Catharine	Married 05/20/1809 to George Schleich
Cecilia	Born 1848 to Thomas
Charles	Married 03/29/1741 to Ann Green
Charles	Married 11/24/1803 to Elizabeth Hughes
Charles	Born 03/22/1907 to Charles and Elizabeth
Charles	Born 1831 to Alfred C.
Charles Allen	Chr. 12/17/1863; Charles and Ann R.
Charles Fisher	Married 06/14/1883 to Lizzie Bayles
Charles L.	Married 03/30/1859 to Anna R. Bean
Comfort	Married 10/29/1798 to Thomas Bennett
David	Married 02/03/1796 to Martha King
David	Married 05/05/1835 to Eliza Blair
Edward	Born 07/25/1741 to Charles and Ann
Edward	Married 05/10/1809 to Mary Williams
Elias P.	Married 10/17/1853 to Doris Palgemeyer
Eliza	Born 10/25/1804 to William and Eleanor
Eliza	Married 09/07/1809 to Robert Boggus
Eliza	Married 05/29/1818 to Samuel McFaddon
Elizabeth	Married 06/09/1772 to William Jones
Elizabeth	Married 11/30/1809 to Patrick Rooney
Elizabeth	Married 02/01/1810 to Joseph Reddy
Elizabeth	Married 05/09/1815 to Samuel Williams
Elizabeth	Born 1829 to Alfred C.
Ellen	Married 08/13/1833 to Peter Vails
Esther	Born 1841 to Isaac
Fanny	Married 02/01/1783 to Peter Martin
Francis	Married 11/13/1805 Elizabeth Ann Hardiston
Francis	Married 09/18/1835 to Eliza Ann Grindell
Frederick Wm	Chr. 01/18/1871 to John and Mary Frances
George	Married 06/13/1811 to Susanna Earing
George	Married 10/23/1813 to Juliana Benson
George	Married 06/28/1832 to Sarah Shipley

George	Married 12/17/1833 to Mary Jane Niemyer
George	Married 08/16/1837 to Eleanora Ellens
George	Born 1835 to Alfred C.
George H. C.	Married 10/29/1835 to Mary Inloes
George Wash.	Born 02/25/1827 to George and Elizabeth
Georgeann	Born 1846 to David
Georgeanna	Married 10/31/1836 to John M. Gardner
Gideon T.	Married 10/10/1816 to Louisa Bush
Hannah M.	Married 05/02/1835 to Luke D. Johnson
Harriet	Born 02/07/1798 to Ann King
Harriet Randolph	Married 05/24/1837 to Alpheus Hyatt
Helen	Born 07/28/1872 to John and Mary
Henry	Married 11/09/1808 to Nancy Coulson
Henry	Born 1849 to Thomas King
Honor	Married 12/24/1799 to James White
Jacob	Married 10/03/1832 to Emily Larman
James	Married 12/18/1804 to Elizabeth Jones
James	Born 1842, son of Alfred C. King
Jane P.	Born 06/30/1813 to Vincent & Phebe Trimble
Jarrett T.	Married 01/27/1835 to Eliza Finley
James	Chr. 11/03/1805, s/o James and Eliza
Jasper	Born 1837 to Alfred C. King
John	Married 12/02/1789 to Elizabeth Joyce
John	Married 11/02/1799 to Polly Butler
John	Married 03/27/1806 to Ann Blagdon
John	Born 10/05/1809 to John and Eleanor
John	Married 04/16/1818 to Katharine Baker
John	Married 04/15/1833 to Caroline Griffith
John	Married 05/31/1836 to Sarah Whealen
John	Married 12/10/1836 to Eliza Ann Fox
John Cincinnatus	Christened 05/07/1843
Joseph	Married 02/28/1835 to Rachel McKnew
Julianna	Married 1719 to William Meredith
Laura	Born 1842 to David
Lydia Ann	Born 09/06/1859 to Robert Allen & Mary Ann
Lydia Ann	Married 10/18/1882 Charles Henry Clay Curtis
Margaret	Born 03/17/1793 to Elias and Margaret
Margaret	Married 12/02/1794 to Neale McKinley

Margaret	Born 12/21/1805 to Charles and Eliza
Margaret	Married 11/30/1808 to Joseph Wallace
Margaret	Married 11/06/1811 to John Allen
Margaret	Born 1849 to William
Margaret	Md 11/26/1850 Alexander W. Goldsborough
Margaret A.	Married 07/25/1848 to John Holliday
Margaret Ann	Chr. 07/09/1848 to John and Hester
Martha	Married 02/03/1796 to David King
Martha	Born 1846 to Isaac
Martha	Born 1844 to Alfred C.
Mary	Born 1676 to Henry and Mary Haile
Mary	Married 1720 to Samuel Maxwell
Mary	Born 07/25/1741 to Charles and Ann
Mary	Married 06/04/1778 to Francis Garrish
Mary	Married 10/28/1780 to John Steward
Mary	Married 01/30/1781 to William Chambers
Mary	Married 05/07/1784 to John Lonigen
Mary	Married 12/27/1803 to John Summers
Mary	Married 06/16/1806 to John Reubaugh
Mary	Born 11/22/1807 to James and Elizabeth
Mary	Married 04/18/1809 to John Durian
Mary	Married 01/14/1816 to Zebulon Harmon
Mary	Married 04/05/1849 to Lewis Kalbfus
Mary	Born 1844 to Isaac
Mary	Born 1838 to David
Mary	Born 1873 to Wallace and Rebecca Wood Lanier
Mary	Married 11/14/1878 to Ralph Elliott
Mary	Married 1897 to Richard Emory
Mary Ann H.	Married 11/28/1846 to John M. Bailey
Mary Barbara	Chr. 07/09/1848 to John and Hester
Mary Cecilia	Chr. 02/11/1849 to Thomas and Sophia
Mary Elizabeth	Born 04/07/1842; John & Caroline Ash Griffith
Mary Elizabeth	Married 04/23/1863 Nicholas McCubbin Smith
Mary F.	Born 1849 to Alfred C.
Mattie Adelaide	Married 03/15/1910 Benjamin Sherman Abbott
Michael	Married 02/02/1781 to Biddy Eaton
Michael	Married 12/13/1787 to Mary Gordon
Nancy	Married 03/14/1786 to George Crowse

Nelly	Married 11/20/1801 to John Mitchell
Peggy	Married 10/21/1787 to Joseph Pew or Penn
Rachel	Born 1833 to Alfred C.
Rebecca	Born 1844 to David
Richard	Born 02/09/1773 to William and Dorothy
Richard	Married 02/08/1797 to Anne Gardiner
Richard	Married 03/28/1808 to Elizabeth Ostrander
Robert	Married 12/02/1783 to Susanna Hall
Robert Lanier	Born 08/27/1872 to Wallace and Rebecca Wood Lanier
Rose Ann	Married 07/13/1840 to Dennis McMahan
Rosina Fitz	Married 07/29/1837 to William Anderson
Rufus	Born 1836 to David
Ruth A.	Born 1846 to Alfred C.
Samuel	Married 10/09/1793 to Sarah Rea
Samuel	Married 02/20/1815 to Sarah Berry
Samuel Hayward	Chr. 02/25/1827 to George and Elizabeth
Sarah	Married 12/14/1797 to Thomas Carroll
Sarah	Married 11/05/1805 to Levi Mantle
Sarah	Married 07/03/1832 to Thomas S. Poteet
Sarah	Born 1842 to Isaac
Sarah Anne	Chr. 03/22/1807 to William and Eleanor
Stephen R.	Married 03/22/1836 to Rachel T. Allen
Thomas	Married 09/04/1783 to Ann Barnes
Thomas	Chr. 10/24/1790 to Elias and Margaret
Thomas	Married 11/14/1808 to Deborah Crawford
Thomas	Married 11/12/1832 to Lucy Ann Thomas
Thomas	Married 06/22/1780 to Sarah Gice
Thomas Henry	Born 07/29/1877 Thomas Harmon & Ann Booz
Thomas Riddell	Chr. 03/07/1803 to William and Eleanor
Wallace	Born 12/12/1834 to John and Hester Stoffer
Walter R.	Married 04/18/1936 to Ruth E. Conner
Whittington	Married 04/25/1833 to Elizabeth Kennard
William	Born 1675 to Henry and Mary Haile
William	Married 08/04/1784 to Elizabeth Ann Hammond
William	Married 01/11/1802 to Eleanor Wilson
William	Married 07/30/1808 to Mary Flaherty
William	Married 12/10/1808 to Martha Campbell

William	Married 09/19/1810 to Martha Green
William	Married 06/29/1876 to Emma A. Cook
William D.	Married 08/25/1835 to Almira Spencer
William G.	Married 09/22/1832 to Frances Ann Davis
William Henry	Married 10/10/1882 to Lillie Slothower
William McCrary	Chr. 09/16/1817 to Gideon T.
William Regnall	Chr. 10/25/1804 to Charles and Elizabeth

CHAPTER 20

Miscellaneous King Family Records

As mentioned in Chapter 1, the King families were found quite early in Prince George's County, Maryland. A number of them have been located there, and later in Montgomery and Frederick Counties, as well as other counties of the state, during the search process, who have not yet been placed within any of the particular family groups with which we are mainly concerned. They are included here, however, for further research.

Thomas King Carroll
1792-1873

Every family should have at least one very famous individual in their lineage; this person qualifies in the King family. There are numerous others, however, not quite as well positioned as this one, who perhaps contributed just as much to the growth of Maryland. In any event, this gentleman was born c.1792 in St. Mary's County, and died October 3, 1873. He was the son of Colonel James Carroll, and Elizabeth Barnes King, of Somerset. She was the only daughter, and sole heiress, of her father, Colonel Thomas King, of Somerset, and a descendant of Sir Robert King, Baronet, whose descendants built the first Presbyterian Church in America, in 1691 at Rehoboth, Delaware.

Thomas King graduated from Princeton at the age of seventeen, with the highest honors, and was married three years later to Juliana Stevenson, daughter of Dr. Henry Stevenson, of Baltimore. He studied law, and held many social beliefs somewhat advanced for his time. In 1824, he was appointed Inspector for Somerset County, and when he was barely of age, elected to the State Legislature, following which, he was selected as Governor of the State, serving in that capacity during 1829 and 1830. While governor, he proposed education, criminal and social reforms; advocated payment of pensions to Revolutionary veterans; recovery from Britain of American Revolutionary records; improvement of the University of Maryland; and many other progressive moves. He retired to his estate in Dorchester County, near Church Creek, where he died, and is buried in the churchyard of the Old Church. He had several children:

1. Thomas King Carroll, Jr., a doctor
2. Daughter Carroll, married to John E. Gibson
3. Daughter Carroll, married to Dr. Bowdle
4. Daughter Carroll, married to Thomas Caddock
5. Anna Ella Carroll, a campaign strategist during the Civil War.
6. Mary Carroll.

Calvert County Records

A few records of marriages and births were found in Calvert. All names in the left column bear the surname King.

Individual	Information
Charles G.	Born 06/28/1784
Francis	Married 1765 to Sarah Parker
Margaret	Married 1682 to John Golaish
Mary	Married 02/10/1777 to Alexander Parran
Milton Sinclair	Born 08/23/1869. Son of Walter Watt King and Elizabeth H. Trott King.
Nettie Blanche	Born 08/27/1871. Daughter of Walter Watt King and Elizabeth H. Trott King.
Richard	Married 1695 to Catharine Charlett
Richard	Married 12/17/1778 to Sarah Rawlings
Thomas B.	Born 02/01/1794 to Benjamin and Susanna
William	Married 1670 to Margaret Wright

Charles County Records

We have demonstrated that some of the earliest members of the King family had their origins in old Prince George's County. It was formed in 1695 from parts of Calvert and Charles, both of which were original counties of the Maryland Province. Members of the King family are found in those counties as well, and are perhaps related to the main body under discussion here.

Joseph King
1734-

References to this individual were found in the records of the Mormon Church, indicating that he had a very large family. He was born c.1734, apparently in Charles County, Maryland, and married there June 14, 1756 to Draden Johnson. The spelling of her name may be incorrect, but that is the most common spelling found in the records searched. They had children, born in Charles County:

1. Aquilla King, born April 9, 1757
2. Zephaniah King, born July 1, 1759
3. Basil King, born October 17, 1760, and perhaps married September 24, 1783 to Deborah Waters; at least one child:
   a.   Orpha King, born July 26, 1784
4. Cornelius King, born March 6, 1763, and perhaps married c.1786 to Sarah Barnes.
5. Elias King, born October 17, 1765
6. Walter King, born November 16, 1768
7. Vinson King, born June 18, 1769
8. James Carroll King, apparently a twin, born August 30, 1771
9. Frances Carol King, apparently a twin, born August 30, 1771
10. Anna King, born March 13, 1773
11. Millicent King, born November 2, 1774

Benjamin King

References to Benjamin and his wife, Elizabeth, were also found in Mormon Church records. They had several children, born in Charles County, Maryland:

1. Chloe King, born July 4, 1750
2. Barton King, born January 24, 1753
3. Cornelius King, born September 1, 1755
4. Dorcas King, born February 20, 1758

411

Basil King

Basil and his wife, Sarah, lived in Charles County, Maryland, where they had at least two children:
1. Anna King, born December 4, 1788
2. Elizabeth King, born August 26, 1790

Several references were found in Charles County to births and marriages. All names in the left column carry the surname of King.

Individual	Information
Ann	Married 1715 to Jesse Dayne
Ann	Married 1745 to Francis Gray
Ann	Married 12/23/1787 to John Smith
Catharine	Married 1783 to Pheusin Dye
Catharine	Married 1745 to James Muncaster
Draden	Married 09/17/1780 to James Waters
Elizabeth	Married 1677 to Philip Jones
Elizabeth	Married 1744 to Jeremiah Bowers
Elizabeth	Married 1788 to James Ritchie
Johanna	Married 1680 to Richard Hodgson
Mary Ann	Married 1765 to Joseph Hagen
Rebecca	Married 12/16/1782 to Townley King
Reuben	Married 02/03/1788 to Mary Ann Vincent
Richard	Married 1716 to Ann Cooper
Robert	Married 06/13/1777 to Judith Wood
Sarah	Married 1748 to Henry Moore
Sarah	Married 1775 to Richard Brett
Thomas	Married 1673 to Joanna Strand
Thomas	Married 1677 to Johanna Jones
Thomas	Married 1761 to Isabell Breeding
Townley	Married 12/16/1782 to Rebecca King
Walter	Born 1710 to Alfred and Sophia Burgess King
William	Married 1788 to Sarah Davis
William	Married 12/30/1781 to Ann Ware
Zephaniah	Born 1734 to Walter King

A number of references to King family members are found in records of St. Marys County; some of families, and some individual records, all listed following.

Gerard King
1834-

There were several individuals bearing the name, Gerard; this one was born c.1834 in St. Marys County, Maryland, and married c.1865 to Mary J. Stone, born c.1842. They had several children:
1. Jane Rebecca King, born c.1864
2. Ann E. King, or Annie M. King, born c.1866
3. Ellen C. King, born c.1867
4. William Francis King, born c.1871

Joshua King
1776-

Born about 1776, Joshua was married October 17, 1802 in St. Marys County, Maryland, to Eliza Ann Bohanan, and had children:
1. Judy King, born c.1803
2. Anna Maria King, born c.1809
3. James A. King, born c.1816
4. Mary M. King, born c.1820

There are numerous references to births and marriages in the county. Names in the left column carry the King surname:

Individual	Information
Adam	Born 10/17/1757 to Edward and Eleanor
Ann	Married 04/15/1807 to Job Smith
Ann M.	Born c.1809 to Josiah
Ann Maria	Born c.1838
Bennett	Born 07/14/1764 to Margaret King
Charles F.	Born c.1819

Cornelius	Born c.1789
Dorcas	Married 12/24/1778 to Bernard St. Clare
Edward	Married 1816 to Mary Villnor
Elizabeth	Married 12/28/1798 to Bennett Collison
Elizabeth	Married 1841 to William Mills
Elizabeth	Born 11/27/1820; John L. & Elizabeth Rinehart
Ellen C.	Married 08/23/1887 to John Wesley Tucker
George Stanley	Born 1835 to Jacob Doyle King (1803) and Marie Alphonso Slye (married c.1834)
Gerard	Born c.1779; married c.1824 Louisa Carpenter
Gerard	Married c.1865 to Mary J. Stone
Gerard	Born c.1839 to Gerard and Jane
Hannah	Married 02/13/1798 to Joseph Dorsey
Henry	Married 06/17/1784 to Catharine Watts
James	Chr. 05/21/1780; son of William
James A.	Born c.1847 to Josiah
James L.	Born c.1847 to Joseph E.
James T.	Born c.1847 to James E.
James T.	Married 1871 to Florence Oster
James Wright	Married 11/14/1926 to Rachel Melba Herbert
Jane	Born 01/29/1772 to Thomas and Eleanor
John F.	Born 10/10/1825 to Gerard and Louisa Carpenter
Joseph E.	Born 1843 to James E.
Joseph Oster	Born 05/31/1872 to James T. and Florence Oster
Julia	Married 11/10/1858 to Thomas R. Biscoe
Mary	Born 03/16/1800 to Stephen and Chloe
Mary M.	Born c.1820 to Josiah
Polly	Born 1786
Rachel	Married 02/11/1778 to Hezekiah Moran
Richard Barton	Chr. 06/23/1809; son of Edmund and Mary
Sarah	Married 01/07/1783 to Richard Hill
Susannah	Married 1718 to George Doffern
Susannah	Married 1736 to William Aisquith

BIBLIOGRAPHY

American Genealogical Research Institute. *Walker Family History,* Washington, D. C. 1972.

Barnes. *Maryland Marriages, 1634-1777*

_____. *Maryland Marriages, 1778-1800*

_____. *Marriages and Deaths From the Maryland Gazette*

Bowie. *Across The Years in Prince George's County*

Bowman, Tressie Nash. *Montgomery County Marriages, 1796-1850*

Brown, Ann Paxton. *Personal genealogical collection, family history, obituaries, official record copies.*

Brown. *Index of Marriage Licenses, Prince George's County, Maryland*

_____. *Index of Church Records, Maryland*

Brumbaugh. *Maryland Records.* 1915 and 1928 issues; Washington County Marriages.

_____. *Maryland Records, Colonial, Revolutionary, County and Church.* Volume 1.

_____. *Census of Maryland, 1776*

Burke. *Burke's Peerage and Baronetage.*

_____. *The General Armory*

Carr, Lois Green; Menard, Russell R.; Peddicord, Louis. *Maryland at the Beginning.*

Chapman. *Portrait and Biographical Record of the Sixth Congressional District, Maryland.* Chapman Publishing Company, New York. 1898

Church of Jesus Christ of Latter Day Saints. *Family group sheets, computerized ancestral files, International Genealogical Index, and other pertinent records.* Family History Center, Silver Spring, Maryland.

Coldham, Peter Wilson. *The Bristol Register of Servants Sent to Foreign Plantations 1654-1686,* 1988

_____. *Complete Book of Emigrants, 1607-1660*

Crozier. *The General Armory*

415

Day, Jackson H. *The Story of the Maryland Walker Family, Including the Descendants of George Bryan Walker and Elizabeth Walker Beall.* 1957, privately printed.

_____. *James Day of Browningsville and his descendants: A Maryland Family.* 1976, privately printed.

Ferrill, Matthew & Gilchrist, Robert. *Maryland Probate Records 1635-1777.* Volume 9.

Filby. *Passenger and Immigration Lists Index.*

Fry, Joshua & Jefferson, Peter. *Map of Virginia, North Carolina, Pennsylvania, Maryland, New Jersey 1751.* Montgomery County, Md Library, Atlas Archives.

Gaithersburg, Maryland, City. *Gaithersburg, The Heart of Montgomery County.* Privately printed. 1978

Gartner Funeral Home, Gaithersburg, Maryland. *Alphabetical computer print-out of funerals and dates.*

Goldsborough. *Maryland Line in the Confederacy.*

Hinke and Reinecke. *Evangelical Reformed Church, Frederick, Maryland*

Holdcraft, Jacob Mehrling. *Names in Stone, 75000 Tombstone Inscriptions from Frederick County, Maryland.* Volume II. Ann Arbor, Michigan. 1966

Hopkins, G. M. *Atlas of Montgomery County, Maryland.*

Hurley, William N., Jr. *Hurley Families in America, Volumes 1 and 2,* Bowie, Md., Heritage Books, Inc. 1995

_____. *The Ancestry of William Neal Hurley, III,* Chelsea, Michigan: BookCrafters, 1985

_____. *Maddox, A Southern Maryland Family.* Bowie, Md., Heritage Books, Inc. 1994

Jacobs, Elizabeth Jeanne King. *Personal papers and records.*

Lord, Elizabeth M. *Burtonsville, Maryland Heritage, Genealogically Speaking*

MacLysaght, Edward. *Irish Families, Their Names, Arms and Origins*

Malloy, Mary Gordon; Sween, Jane C.; Manuel, Janet D. *Abstract of Wills, Montgomery County, Maryland 1776-1825*

Malloy, Mary Gordon; Jacobs, Marian W. *Genealogical Abstracts, Montgomery County Sentinel, 1855-1899*

Manuel, Janet Thompson. *Montgomery County, Maryland Marriage Licenses, 1798-1898*

Maryland State. *Archives of Maryland*, all volumes.

Maryland Hall of Records. *Wills, estates, inventories, births, deaths, marriages, deeds and other reference works relative to counties of Maryland.*

_____. *Maryland Calendar of Wills.* Eight volumes.

_____. *Maryland Historical Society Magazine.*

_____. *Vestry Book of St. John's Episcopal Parish Church, 1689-1810.* Original.

Montgomery County Court Records. *Wills, inventories of estate, deeds.* Rockville, Maryland.

Montgomery County Historical Society, Rockville, Maryland. *Folder files; correspondence, newspaper records, library, and family records.*

_____. *Queen Anne Parish Records, 1686 - 1777*

_____. *King George Parish Records 1689 - 1801*

_____. *King George Parish Records 1797-1878*

_____. *St. Paul's at Baden, Parish Records*

_____. *Frederick County Maryland Marriage Licenses*

_____. *Montgomery County Marriages*

_____. *1850 Census, Montgomery County, Maryland*

_____. *1860 Census, Montgomery County, Maryland*

_____. *1850 Census, Prince George's County, Maryland*

_____. *Pioneers of Old Monocacy*

Newman. *Mareen Duvall of Middle Plantation*

Omans, Donald James and Nancy West. *Montgomery County Marriages 1798-1875.* Maryland.

Preston, Dickson J. *Talbott County, A History*, Centreville, Md., Tidewater Publishers, 1983

Prince George's County, Md Historical Society. *Index to the Probate Records of Prince George's County, Maryland, 1696-1900*

_____. *Prince George's County Land Records, Volume A, 1696-1702.* Bowie, Maryland, 1976

_____. *1850 Census, Prince George's County, Maryland.* Bowie, Maryland, 1978

_____. *1828 Tax List Prince George's County, Maryland.* Bowie, Maryland, 1985.

Ridgely. *Historic Graves of Maryland and District of Columbia*

Sargent. *Stones and Bones, Cemetery Records of Prince George's County, Maryland.*

Scharff. *History of Western Maryland*

Skordas, Gust. *Early Settlers of Maryland*

_____. **(Perhaps).** *Servants to Foreign Plantations*

Tepper, Michael. *Emigrants to the Middle Colonies*

_____. *Passengers to America*

Tombstone Records. *Bethesda United Methodist Church, Browningsville, Maryland. Forest Oak Cemetery, Gaithersburg, Maryland. Goshen United Methodist Church (now Goshen Mennonite Church), Laytonsville, Maryland. St. Paul's Methodist Church, Laytonsville, Maryland.*

VanHorn, R. Lee. *Out of the Past.*

Warfield, J. D. *Founders of Anne Arundel and Howard Counties, Maryland.* Kohn & Pollock, Baltimore. 1905

Williams, T. J. C. *History of Frederick County, Maryland.* Two volumes.

_____. *History of Washington County, Maryland*

Wright, F. Edward. *Maryland Militia, War of 1812.*

INDEX

All names appearing in the text appear in the index, with each page on which they can be found. In order to distinguish between family members with the same name, most names in the index will be followed by a date, in most cases the date of birth. Occasionally, a name will be followed by the date of marriage of death, as in m/1876 or d/1923. Entries without dates may be more than one individual; in the case of common names such as James, Sarah and the like, they are nearly always more than one person.

Allnutt, Ida, 273
Allnutt, Jacob M., 289
Allnutt, Lewis Philip, III 1944, 160
Allnutt, Lewis Philip, Jr. 1910, 160
Allnutt, No given name, 10
Allnutt, Walter, 273
Allport, Elizabeth Viola, 248
Allport, Helen Margaret, 248
Andelman, Albert E., 182
Anders, Matilda 1825, 33
Anderson, Alice 1917, 156
Anderson, David, 327
Anderson, Eleanor, 346
Anderson, George, 327
Anderson, Heide Lynn 1969, 95
Anderson, James William, 95
Anderson, Mary Alice, 327
Anderson, Perry, 301
Anderson, Robert Lee 1948, 95
Anderson, William, 327, 407
Andrews, Aileen, 242
Andrews, Beryl Alta 1947, 242
Andrews, Richard, 242
Angelberger, Ada May, 368
Angelberger, Arthur O., 368
Angelberger, Edith M., 368
Angelberger, Edward I. 1860, 368
Angelberger, George W. 1814, 368
Angelberger, Harriet A., 368
Angelberger, Julia J., 368
Angelberger, Lola B., 368
Angelberger, Mary S., 368
Angelberger, Philip J., 368
Angelberger, Rhoda E., 368
Angelberger, William D., 368
Angelberger, Worthington R., 368

Anthony, Florence Y., 242
Appleby, Charles Albert 1948, 229
Archbold, William Frederick, 41
Archibald, Sue 1944, 254
Arehart, Charles Michael 1962, 43
Arehart, Patricia Michelle 1957, 43
Arehart, Roy Charles 1905, 43
Arehart, Thomas Mitchell 1930, 43
Arehart, Tracey Ann 1963, 43
Armas, No given name, 328
Armstrong, Alice Pearl 1904, 70
Armstrong, Darryl, 181, 288
Armstrong, Hugh, 43
Armstrong, Janet Faville 1910, 43
Armstrong, Laban B., 70
Armstrong, Minnie, 70
Arnold, Edward 1873, 402
Arnold, Joseph N., 397
Arnold, Margaret Lavina 1876, 9, 312
Arnold, Mary 1849, 397
Arnold, No given name, 175
Arnold, Robin Kathleen, 20
Arnold, Thomas 1845, 397
Arnold, Walter Claude, 20
Arnot, Mary Joyce 1934, 229
Arntzen, Karen Lynn 1969, 103
Arntzen, Marcus Damaine 1976, 103
Arntzen, Martin C., Jr. 1942, 103
Arntzen, Michael David 1967, 103

Aschenbach, Brandon Victor 1992, 80
Aschenbach, Conrad Lawson 1959, 80
Aschenbach, Conrad Robert 1981, 80
Aschenbach, Conrad Victor 1932, 79
Aschenbach, Dustin Victor 1986, 80
Aschenbach, Elizabeth Anne 1961, 81
Aschenbach, Jason Robert 1985, 80
Aschenbach, Lois Marlene 1956, 80
Aschenbach, Robert Victor 1953, 80
Aschenbach, Ryan Conrad 1990, 80
Aschenbach, Shaun Michael 1986, 80
Aschenbach, William Henry 1955, 80
Aschenbach, William Lawson 1983, 80
Ashecroft, Charles T. 1919, 223
Ashecroft, Cynthia Lynn 1957, 223
Atkins, No given name, 385
Atwood, Kathryn Jo, 19
Aycock, Edna King 1919, 37
Aycock, Joseph Felix, 37
Aycock, Lillian Ruth 1921, 37
Ayton, Elizabeth 1871, 280
Ayton, George Edward 1881, 281
Ayton, James Edward 1847, 280
Ayton, Jane, 167
Ayton, Susie A. 1876, 281

—B—

Bacon, Charles, 146
Bailey, Christian Paul 1991, 272
Bailey, John M., 406
Bailey, Luke Henry 1993, 272
Bailey, Patricia Ann 1933, 50
Bailey, Richard Wager 1964, 272
Bailey, Richard Wager, Jr. 1989, 272
Baker, Aimee Elizabeth 1974, 242
Baker, Alice Roberta 1873, 135, 232
Baker, Alice Sardinia 1867, 138
Baker, Allen Dale 1931, 130
Baker, Amelia C., 166
Baker, Bernard, 135
Baker, Betty Jean 1926, 130
Baker, Bonnie Lee, 49
Baker, Carol Ann 1954, 129
Baker, Carson Remington 1985, 243
Baker, Charles Oscar 1922, 242
Baker, Darlene Dee 1952, 243
Baker, David William 1922, 129
Baker, Day, 135
Baker, Della Day 1884, 129
Baker, Dennis Raymond 1955, 243
Baker, Donald E. 1946, 73
Baker, Dorsey Lewis 1867, 135
Baker, Edna Elizabeth 1863, 132, 159
Baker, Edward Louis 1876, 182
Baker, Elva Muriel 1913, 130
Baker, Estelle, 182

421

Baker, Ethel Duvall 1910, 130
Baker, Eveline J. 1856, 132
Baker, Evelyn, 125
Baker, Frances A. 1864, 134
Baker, Franklin Lansdale 1891, 131
Baker, Glenn Charles 1948, 242
Baker, Harold Levering 1896, 131
Baker, Irene Elizabeth 1905, 146
Baker, Isla Lorraine 1909, 83, 128
Baker, J. Bradley 1877, 73
Baker, J. Bradley, Jr. 1931, 73
Baker, James Allen, 130
Baker, James Vernon 1886, 129
Baker, Jean Gibson 1923, 129
Baker, Jeffrey Lee 1975, 243
Baker, Jerry Wayne 1951, 242
Baker, John C. 1935, 73
Baker, John Morris 1960, 129
Baker, John T. 1851, 128
Baker, Katharine, 405
Baker, Lillian May 1888, 130
Baker, Mamie 1888, 127
Baker, Marilyn Jean 1951, 243
Baker, Martha W. 1860, 132
Baker, Mary Jane, 193
Baker, Mary W. 1853, 132
Baker, Matthew Aaron 1973, 242
Baker, Mollie W., 309
Baker, Norwood, 135
Baker, Oliver Lee 1927, 243
Baker, Oscar Lee, 242
Baker, Patrick Lee, 130
Baker, Robert Gilmer 1952, 129

Baker, Rudelle Brandenburg 1914, 129
Baker, Rufus E. 1870, 135
Baker, Russell Austin 1916, 130
Baker, Sarah A., 36, 126, 324
Baker, Seth Ashley 1977, 242
Baker, Stella Faring 1884, 129
Baker, Susan Farg, 130
Baker, Susan L. 1954, 129
Baker, Terry Lee 1949, 243
Baker, Thomas 1800, 128
Baker, Thomas Milton, 127, 138
Baker, Thomas R. 1933, 73
Baker, Valerie Jill 1973, 243
Baker, Virgil M., 387
Baker, Willard, 135
Baker, William Andrew 1880, 83, 128
Baker, William David 1956, 129
Baker, William H. 1826, 128
Baker, William H. D. 1854, 132
Baker, Winfred, 135
Ball, No given name, 68
Banda, Austin Dais 1937, 46
Bandy, No given name, 303
Bannon, Frank 1883, 72
Barber, Charles, 22, 23
Barber, Cheryl Pauline, 94
Barber, Diane Marie, 94
Barber, Eldridge Simpers 1916, 94
Barber, James Webster 1942, 94
Barber, Susan, 94
Barklay, Robyn, 238
Barnard, Teresa Catherine, 17
Barnes, Ann, 407
Barnes, Anna Louise 1920, 200

Beall, Edward Maurice 1870, 271
Beall, Elizabeth, 29
Beall, Elvira 1809, 340
Beall, Fred Parker 1930, 309
Beall, Heather Marie 1986, 237
Beall, Helena 1901, 88
Beall, Hilda L. 1901, 87, 114
Beall, James F. 1833, 258
Beall, Joan Elmon, 297
Beall, John Cronin, 236
Beall, John Cronin, Jr. 1949, 236
Beall, Joseph Asbury 1838, 151
Beall, Joy Julia 1957, 310
Beall, Joyce, 83
Beall, Kathleen Ann 1942, 272
Beall, Kevin 1967, 115
Beall, Laura Washington 1859, 197
Beall, Leathey P., 96
Beall, Lillie Mae, 187
Beall, Lindy N., 287
Beall, Luther T., 96
Beall, Mark Willis 1950, 206
Beall, Mary Ann, 306
Beall, Mary C. 1922, 300
Beall, Matilda, 374
Beall, Melanie Ann 1953, 206
Beall, No given name, 10, 82, 385
Beall, Patsy Lee, 236
Beall, Robert 1944, 114
Beall, Rudell, 114
Beall, Rudell C. 1918, 236
Beall, Sally Louise 1940, 83
Beall, Samuel Webster 1877, 87, 114
Beall, Sandra Ruth, 236
Beall, Sarah Wilson 1830, 114
Beall, Shirley Ann 1937, 83
Beall, Silas Cronin 1906, 83

Beall, Survila Ann 1831, 147, 159
Beall, Teresa Elizabeth 1983, 237
Beall, Upton, 374
Beall, Wendy Jeanine 1959, 206
Beall, William M., 179
Beall, Willis Webster 1927, 206
Bean, Anna R., 404
Beane, Forrest Chipman 1927, 192
Beard, Donna Jean 1959, 56
Beard, Garland Roland 1931, 56
Beard, William John 1957, 56
Beck, Beth Luella 1969, 145
Beck, Charles Franklin, II 1929, 145
Beck, Charles Franklin, III 1964, 145
Becraft, Catherine I. 1913, 358
Becraft, Cecilia 1871, 175
Becraft, Dolly, 336
Becraft, Milton, 175
Becraft, Susan Jane, 170, 171
Beglin, Joanne Irene, 257
Behn, Ida Elizabeth 1891, 303
Behn, John E., 303
Behringer, Betsy, 353
Bell, Barbara Alice 1950, 156
Bell, Bruce Charles 1948, 156
Bell, Catherine Marie 1945, 156
Bell, Catherine Roberta 1902, 153
Bell, Charlene Elizabeth 1939, 156
Bell, Charles Edward 1909, 155
Bell, Donald, 124, 329

Bowman, James Marlin 1945, 35
Bowman, John Sterling 1911, 35
Bowman, John Upton 1937, 35
Bowman, Julian U. 1907, 35
Bowman, Kenneth Edward, 130
Bowman, Kimberly Renee, 35
Bowman, Mary Elizabeth 1903, 163
Bowman, Mary Elizabeth 1949, 70
Bowman, McKendree, 165
Bowman, McKendree Boyer 1911, 163
Bowman, Sarah, 298
Bowman, Sarah 1819, 297
Bowman, Stephanie Ann 1988, 274
Bowman, Thomas Sterling 1941, 35
Bowman, Tyson Michael, 35
Bowman, W. Lafayette, 163
Bowman, William Craig, 35
Bowman, William H., 297
Bowman, William H. 1821, 297
Bowman, William Upton 1865, 34
Boyce, Della, 321
Boyd, Doris, 380
Boyd, No given name, 386
Boyden, Ernest, 308
Boyer, Alice Orlean 1881, 166
Boyer, Annie Mary 1916, 166
Boyer, Audry Virginia 1934, 162
Boyer, Bruce Alton 1960, 162
Boyer, Charles Donald 1944, 151

Boyer, Cora Elizabeth 1884, 160
Boyer, Donald Day 1925, 161
Boyer, Doris Addell 1899, 162
Boyer, Edna Maxine 1936, 163
Boyer, Eleanor Gleason 1929, 161
Boyer, Elizabeth Day, 159
Boyer, Emma Cassandra 1868, 123, 126, 163
Boyer, Ethel 1908, 166
Boyer, George, 165
Boyer, George Milton 1872, 165, 289
Boyer, George Milton, II, 289
Boyer, George Wesley 1911, 166
Boyer, Harry, 16
Boyer, Helen Amelia 1912, 166
Boyer, James Russell 1881, 302
Boyer, James Wellington 1859, 163
Boyer, Jemima Elizabeth 1864, 163
Boyer, Jesse Darby 1866, 163
Boyer, John, 16, 159
Boyer, John Alton 1926, 162
Boyer, John Henry 1959, 162
Boyer, John Milton 1902, 162
Boyer, John Spencer, 16
Boyer, John Wesley, 302
Boyer, John Wesley 1857, 132, 159
Boyer, Katherine Eleanor 1963, 161
Boyer, Lyndall Lewis 1895, 163
Boyer, Margaret 1805, 140, 335
Boyer, Mary Bird 1885, 163
Boyer, Mary Jo, 166

430

433

Burdette, Arthur 1881, 188
Burdette, Arthur Monroe 1880, 298
Burdette, Arthur Monroe, Jr. 1911, 299
Burdette, Arthur Russell 1905, 188
Burdette, Aubrey Wilson 1897, 338
Burdette, Audrey Marie 1915, 338
Burdette, Barbara 1940, 179
Burdette, Barbara Ann 1933, 250
Burdette, Barbara Ellen, 328
Burdette, Basil Boyer 1899, 292
Burdette, Basil Vernon 1887, 297
Burdette, Beatrice Ardean 1910, 188
Burdette, Bessie May, 137
Burdette, Betty, 64
Burdette, Betty Jane 1922, 85
Burdette, Betty Lou, 321
Burdette, Betty Lou 1936, 84
Burdette, Bonnie Jean, 329
Burdette, Bonnie June 1963, 293
Burdette, Brenda 1971, 86
Burdette, Brenda Ann 1952, 250
Burdette, Bruce Edward 1961, 294
Burdette, Caitlin 1987, 232
Burdette, Caleb 1825, 158
Burdette, Caleb J., 100
Burdette, Caleb Joshua 1849 Reverend, 325
Burdette, Calvin Kemp 1924, 306

Burdette, Carol Arlene 1940, 321
Burdette, Carol Baker 1942, 83, 129
Burdette, Carolyn, 124, 329
Burdette, Carolyn Lee 1944, 299
Burdette, Carroll Aubrey, 177
Burdette, Cassandra Elizabeth 1866, 179
Burdette, Catherine 1915, 295
Burdette, Charles 1885, 275, 297
Burdette, Charles F. 1898, 86, 326
Burdette, Charles King 1917, 22, 296, 308
Burdette, Charles King, Jr. 1947, 296
Burdette, Claude Edward 1905, 293, 330
Burdette, Claude H. 1872, 22, 166, 206, 243, 292, 308, 330
Burdette, Claude Michael 1943, 294
Burdette, Clifford Warren 1941, 294
Burdette, Cora Clark, 69
Burdette, Curtis Lee 1990, 232
Burdette, Dale Curtis 1959, 250
Burdette, Daniel Adam 1982, 232
Burdette, Danny Lee 1943, 321
Burdette, David Allen 1963, 294
Burdette, David L., 86
Burdette, David William 1960, 232
Burdette, Dawn Lora 1964, 294
Burdette, Dawn Michele 1958, 321

435

Burdette, Roger William 1909, 233, 289
Burdette, Roger William, Jr., 233, 289
Burdette, Ronald Monroe 1943, 299
Burdette, Rosalie Nadine, 124, 330
Burdette, Russell Lewis 1906, 248
Burdette, Ruth Ann, 306
Burdette, Ruth Ellen 1937, 250
Burdette, Sadie Roberta, 330
Burdette, Sarah E. 1836, 292
Burdette, Sarah Elizabeth 1904, 243, 294
Burdette, Sarah Ella, 327
Burdette, Sarah Evelyn 1915, 83
Burdette, Shane Marie 1974, 84
Burdette, Sherry 1967, 84
Burdette, Sheryl 1962, 84
Burdette, Shirley B. 1935, 306, 319
Burdette, Simpson 1884, 330
Burdette, Sophronia, 247, 330
Burdette, Steven, 326
Burdette, Steven Andrew 1958, 232
Burdette, Sue Ellen, 328
Burdette, Susan Clark 1956, 232
Burdette, Teresa Ann 1960, 326
Burdette, Teresa Lynn 1960, 352
Burdette, Theresa Wright 1956, 321
Burdette, Timothy Edward 1963, 250
Burdette, Tina Marie, 294

Burdette, Tina Marie 1965, 293
Burdette, Vera Regina 1919, 338
Burdette, Virginia Mae 1923, 247, 331
Burdette, Virginia Marie 1908, 329
Burdette, Vivian Dianne 1953, 250
Burdette, Wallace Franklin, 326
Burdette, Walter D., 328
Burdette, Webster V., 275
Burdette, William A. 1849, 181
Burdette, William Edwin 1917, 179
Burdette, William Hubert 1872, 135, 232, 289
Burdette, William Kent, 299
Burdette, William M. 1942, 179
Burdette, William W., 298
Burdette, Willie H., 237, 275, 326
Burdette, Willie Lloyd, 99
Burdette, Willis B. 1871, 338
Burdette, Woodrow W., 328
Burgess, Eleanor M., 299
Burgess, Joseph, 3
Burgess, Phyllis, 355
Burgess, Sophia, 412
Burkett, Shelley, 49
Burner, Gary W. 1950, 74
Burner, Kathleen M. 1953, 74
Burner, Paul F., Jr. 1926, 74
Burns, Anna Mae, 99
Burns, E. Minor 1901, 99
Burns, Edith C. 1877, 97
Burns, George William 1906, 100
Burns, Gertrude King, 97
Burns, Ida E. 1867, 215

441

442

Cohen, Shirley, 20
Colbert, Blanche, 344
Cole, Charles E., Jr. 1961, 237
Cole, Earl 1897, 402
Cole, Lorraine, 181
Collier, Beverly Diane 1944, 194
Collier, Janice Gayle 1946, 194
Collier, Jayne Blair 1953, 195
Collier, Joseph Bernard 1921, 194
Collier, Mabel Louise 1927, 129
Collins, Maurice Aloysius 1884, 38
Collins, Richard Harold 1945, 9, 99, 255
Collison, Bennett, 414
Coma, Angela, 333
Coma, Robert, 333
Condon, Mary Catherine, 124
Conklin, Jean Michele 1967, 320
Conklin, Richard, 320
Conklin, Richard Walter 1961, 320
Conley, Elizabeth, 356
Connelly, Arnold Lewis 1889, 47
Connelly, Caroline Delaware 1869, 41
Connelly, Clara, 46
Connelly, Dorsey Meshack 1891, 47
Connelly, Everett Paul 1892, 47
Connelly, Harry Elijah 1872, 41
Connelly, Jessie Ada 1887, 47
Connelly, Lucinda Roberta 1869, 38

Connelly, Martha Mary 1874, 41
Connelly, Mary Augusta 1878, 46
Connelly, Michael, 38
Connelly, Myrtle Louise 1907, 41
Connelly, Sarah Thomas 1877, 45
Connelly, Spencer Brown 1884, 46
Connelly, Thomas Jefferson 1846, 38
Connelly, Thomas Walter 1880, 46
Conner, AnnaMaria 1974, 25, 54
Conner, Deborah Sue 1978, 25, 54
Conner, Eben LaMonte, III 1955, 25, 54
Conner, Elisabeth Marie 1975, 25, 54
Conner, Joanna Ruth 1980, 25, 54
Conner, Rachel Jeannette 1984, 25, 54
Conner, Ruth E., 407
Conner, Sarah Grace 1982, 25, 54
Conway, Amanda Margaret 1984, 26, 55
Conway, James Owen 1960, 26, 55
Conway, James Paul 1982, 26, 55
Conway, Mathew Brian 1980, 26, 55
Cook, Elmira J. 1913, 110
Cook, Emma A., 408
Cook, Etta Mae 1927, 110
Cook, Lula May 1907, 174

445

Davis, Virginia Louise 1954, 309
Davis, Wilhelmina Gude 1956, 309
Davison, Frances Rebecca 1953, 96
Davison, Mary Louise 1950, 96
Davison, Stuart 1916, 96
Davison, Stuart 1948, 96
Davison, William Stuart, 96
Dawson, Janet, 339
Dawson, JoAnn, 339
Dawson, Joseph, 339
Day, Addison Singleton 1856, 197
Day, Alan Christopher 1962, 207
Day, Alice Marie 1922, 139
Day, Altona Bovincia Clintinchia 1857, 198
Day, Amanda Wilson 1857, 159
Day, Anna Lucille 1902, 203
Day, Annie Griffith 1896, 198
Day, Barbara Ann 1938, 206
Day, Barbara Loretta 1939, 196
Day, Basil Boyer 1936, 207
Day, Basil Boyer, Jr. 1958, 207
Day, Bonnie Jean 1958, 149
Day, Brenda Jean 1948, 205
Day, Brian Keith 1968, 207
Day, Carol Ann 1968, 205
Day, Carroll Davis 1944, 205
Day, Catherine Lynn 1966, 149
Day, Chapin Walker 1905, 147
Day, Chapin Walker, III 1968, 148
Day, Chapin Walker, Jr. 1936, 148
Day, Charles T. 1858, 147
Day, Cheryl Ann 1954, 206

Day, Christina Fredericka 1970, 148
Day, Christopher 1961, 115
Day, Cindy Lou 1957, 206
Day, Clara Lavinia 1913, 196
Day, Clarence Emory 1901, 203
Day, Claude Randolph 1906, 195
Day, Daisy May 1891, 198
Day, David Ellis 1943, 198
Day, David Franklin 1949, 197
Day, David Jeffrey 1959, 148
Day, Domini 1965, 115
Day, Doris Jane 1946, 209
Day, Dorothy Jean 1929, 206
Day, Douglas Edsel 1945, 198
Day, Douglas Robert 1961, 208
Day, Effie Madeline 1912, 208
Day, Elizabeth, 159
Day, Elizabeth J., 186
Day, Elizabeth M. 1826, 185, 186
Day, Emil Rodney 1921, 197
Day, Ethel Virginia 1897, 162, 202
Day, Evelyn Jane 1933, 207
Day, Evelyn Louise 1943, 209
Day, Evelyn May 1930, 234
Day, Franklin B. 1836, 285
Day, Gary Wayne 1952, 205
Day, Gayle Marie 1953, 207
Day, Gregory Robert 1966, 198
Day, H. Calvin, 173
Day, Hanford Perry 1916, 208
Day, Harold Lewis 1888, 199
Day, Harriet Emma 1863, 199
Day, Harrison Edward 1888, 198
Day, Helen Augusta 1878, 140, 142, 149

447

449

Finley, Pamela Marcel 1961,
63
Fisher, Allison, 44
Fisher, Andrew Geary 1904, 43
Fisher, Beatrice, 46
Fisher, Christine Lee 1951, 45
Fisher, Dorothy 1919, 73
Fisher, Douglas Vincent 1947,
44
Fisher, Elizabeth Catherine, 45
Fisher, Evelyn Aloysius 1902,
43
Fisher, Geary Aloysius 1873,
41
Fisher, Geary Lawrence 1940,
43
Fisher, Grace Barbara, 344
Fisher, Helen Agatha 1898, 42
Fisher, Jessie Theckla 1907, 44
Fisher, John Norman 1909, 44
Fisher, John Norman, Jr. 1941,
44
Fisher, John Warren, 44
Fisher, Joseph Milton 1905, 43
Fisher, Lawrence Gregory
1936, 43
Fisher, Lawrence Prescott
1903, 43
Fisher, Leslie Ann 1952, 44
Fisher, Linda Anne 1846, 44
Fisher, Lois Ann 1949, 45
Fisher, Mary Caroline 1900, 43
Fisher, Mary Constance 1949,
44
Fisher, Mary Edna 1913, 44
Fisher, Mary Elsa, 43
Fisher, Michael Alan 1954, 44
Fisher, Millard Clary, 42
Fisher, Nancy Lee, 44
Fisher, Patricia 1955, 247
Fisher, Patricia Marie 1955, 45
Fisher, Patrick Geary, 43

Fisher, Philip Adrian 1912, 44
Fisher, Robert Edward 1940,
43
Fisher, Stanley Albert 1944, 43
Fisher, Thomas Warren 1921,
44, 248
Fisher, William Michael, 43
Fitzwater, Wilma Elizabeth, 19
Flag Patch, 140, 159
Flaherty, Mary, 407
Flair, Glenrose Mary 1916, 192
Fleenor, Carla, 51
Fleming, Della, 211
Fleming, Elizabeth, 169
Fleming, John Edgar, Jr., 299
Fleming, Thomas W. 1956, 112
Fleshman, Elizabeth, 370
Flinn, Rosalee 1909, 392
Flook, Albert D., Jr., 89
Flook, Gerald Richard 1941, 89
Flook, Henry, 226
Flook, Jett Lorraine, 295
Flook, Sharon 1969, 89
Floyd, Lanier, 81
Flynn, David Curtis 1960, 321
Flynn, David Willis, 321
Flynn, Mary 1915, 177
Flynn, No given name, 270
Flynn, Robin Carol 1966, 321
Flynn, Thomas H. C., 310
Foard, Laura Belle 1887, 128
Ford, Wilma, 327
Forlines, William F., 346
Forrest, Julius 1908, 377
Forrest, Julius Crawford 1872,
377
Fort, Joan Pearl 1953, 232
Fortney, Aquilla A., 370
Foster, Alvin Donald, 349
Foster, Deborah Joan 1949, 349
Foster, Delmas, 217

Fulks, Thomas Iraneus 1870, 78
Fulks, Thomas Walker 1898, 339
Fuller, George Leonard 1903, 227
Fuller, Ina 1867, 402
Fuller, Nellie Evalena 1866, 402
Fullerton, Sandra, 35

—G—

Gadow, Brenda Jane, 235
Gaither, Eveline, 337
Ganine, Flora, 150
Ganley, Joseph Mackin 1927, 19
Ganley, Mary Magdalene, 391
Garber, C. Virginia 1927, 106
Gardescua, Janel, 141
Gardiner, Anna Edmonia 1891, 303
Gardiner, Anne, 407
Gardiner, David Carlson 1934, 56
Gardiner, David Wayne 1959, 56
Gardiner, Janet Sue 1960, 56
Gardiner, Randy Lee 1961, 56
Gardiner, Teresa Ann 1957, 56
Gardner, John, 108
Gardner, John M., 405
Garland, Dave W., 325
Garland, Ruby Jo 1930, 325
Garrett, Julia Ann, 21
Garrett, Mary Margaret, 78
Garrett, Thomas Moore, 78
Garris, William E., 321
Garrish, Francis, 406
Garrott, Julia Ann, 34

Gartner, Catherine Rosalie 1928, 357
Gartner, David Campbell 1953, 357
Gartner, David Wayne, 10, 99
Gartner, Frances Irene 1916, 357
Gartner, Helen Lucille 1919, 357
Gartner, Jacquelyn 1958, 357
Gartner, James Oliver 1913, 357
Gartner, Jason Thomas 1987, 252
Gartner, Joan 1947, 357
Gartner, John, 108
Gartner, Kimberly Joyce 1964, 233
Gartner, Linda Dawn 1957, 357
Gartner, Lois Jeneiva 1932, 358
Gartner, Margaret Dorothy 1915, 357
Gartner, Nathan Stanley 1926, 357
Gartner, No given name, 10, 99
Gartner, Patricia Ann 1959, 357
Gartner, Robert Ernest 1918, 252
Gartner, William Edgar 1912, 357
Gartner, William Edgar, Jr. 1944, 357
Gartner, William Harry 1946, 252
Gartner, William Henry 1885, 357
Gartrall, Pearl, 287
Gary, No given name, 364
Gathright, Alan Joseph, 40

457

Hawkins, James Floyd 1950, 255
Hawkins, James Wilson 1916, 255
Hawkins, James Wilson, Jr. 1950, 255
Hawkins, Jessica Lynn 1984, 256
Hawkins, John Wesley 1967, 256
Hawkins, Joseph 1969, 256
Hawkins, Karl Benjamin 1968, 257
Hawkins, Laurie Marie 1964, 256
Hawkins, Leroy Bradley 1946, 256
Hawkins, Lucille V., 90
Hawkins, Mary Belle 1915, 9, 99, 255
Hawkins, Michael Lee 1985, 256
Hawkins, No given name, 10
Hawkins, Patricia Ann 1964, 256
Hawkins, Pearl Winstead 1896, 322
Hawkins, Richard William 1969, 256
Hawkins, Sharon Louise 1946, 255
Hawkins, Sterling Lewis 1921, 256
Hawkins, Sterling Lewis, Jr. 1945, 256
Hawkins, Teresa Ann 1964, 256
Hawkins, Thomas, 256
Hawkins, Travis, 256
Hawkins, Wayne Elder 1948, 256
Hayes, Angus, 108

Hayes, Catherine, 109
Hayes, Edward, 109
Heagy, Charles A., 36, 315
Heath, Nellie, 156
Hedinger, Joseph, 331
Heffner, Lewis, 368
Hefner, Clifford 1922, 139
Hefner, Richard Paul, 187
Heil, Dorothy, 244
Heintzman, George Fred 1865, 403
Heller, Barbara, 224
Heller, Caroline, 224
Heller, Jacqueline, 224
Heller, Lawrence, 224
Heltner, Diane, 94
Helwig, Amanda Lou 1951, 207
Hempstone, William H. 1855, 376
Hender, Joseph, 317
Henderson, George Otis, 12
Hennjes, Betty Carol 1940, 36
Henry and Elizabeth Enlarged, 159
Henry, May, 403
Henry, No given name, 376
Hentish, Daria Nadja, 322
Herbert, Rachel Melba, 414
Herbert, Wendy, 230
Herndon, No given name, 138
Hewitt, George 1815, 122
Hewitt, Laura Richard 1855, 122
Hickman, No given name, 108
Higgins, Dora 1862, 72
Higgins, Eric, 72
Hildebrand, Dorothy, 110
Hildebrand, J., 339
Hildebrand, Lewis, 110
Hildebrand, Mary Jane, 110
Hill, Dana, 51

Hockenberry, Susan Marie
1974, 272
Hodgson, Richard, 412
Hodtwalker, Anna June 1926,
39
Hodtwalker, Frederick Wilhelm
Theodor, 39
Hoffman, Darlene Frances
1946, 105
Hoffman, Denise Darcel 1953,
105
Hoffman, Diane Carol 1968,
105
Hoffman, Ruth Lee, 130
Hoffman, William Nelson
1921, 105
Hogg, Andrew, 230
Holland, Edward 1833, 315
Holland, Rachel Corrine 1878,
10, 361
Holland, Samuel B., 361
Holland, Susanna, 400
Holliday, John, 406
Holmead, No given name, 386
Holt, Lillian, 85
Holt, Margaret, 299
Home, Virginia, 134
Honeycutt, Christopher, 245
Honeycutt, Jason Tanner 1983,
245
Hood, Andrea Lee 1982, 270,
325
Hood, Archie O. 1919, 77
Hood, Clarence Ellis, 270, 325
Hood, Daryl Ellis 1986, 270,
325
Hood, Denis Rex 1952, 270,
325
Hood, Dixie, 270
Hood, Glenn, 270
Hood, Larry, 207

Hood, Margaret Elizabeth
1913, 161
Hook, Karen, 246
Hooper, Martha, 137
Hopkins, Nola Mae 1943, 52
Horman, Aaron 1978, 49
Horman, Adam, 310
Horman, Daniel, 310
Horman, Dawn Ellen, 310
Horman, Duane 1971, 49
Horman, Elmer Augustus, 48
Horman, Elmer Augustus, Jr.
1923, 48
Horman, George Washington,
310
Horman, Jerry Augustus 1949,
49
Horman, Louis Randolph, 310
Horman, Nancy Kay, 310
Horn, No given name, 186
Hornbuckle, Mary Elizabeth
1925, 197
Horner, Dorothy, 389
Horton, No given name, 386
Hoskinson, Florence A. 1903,
340
Hoskinson, Harry, 341
Hoskinson, Harry C., 340
Hoskinson, Helen M. 1908, 340
Hoskinson, John Henry 1919,
340
Hoskinson, John Henry, Jr.,
340
Houck, Caroline, 368
Houck, Margaret, 371
House, Gilbert Wayne 1942,
24, 54
Houser, Elizabeth Ann 1947,
39
Houser, Herbert Joseph 1941,
38

Houser, Herbert Lester 1917, 38

Houser, Richard Michael 1942, 38

Houser, Sally Irene 1944, 39

Houston, Nancy Estes, 248

Howard, Catherine Ann 1959, 358

Howard, Clifard Llewelyn 1924, 357

Howard, Ida R. 1914, 323

Howard, Linda Sue 1955, 358

Howard, Marian Norman, 165

Howard, No given name, 10

Howard, Patricia Lynn 1950, 358

Howard, Sharon Lee 1948, 358

Howe, Mary A. 1827, 315

Howe, William E., 316

Howell, No given name, 381

Howes, Catherine 1916, 75

Howes, Connie Dianne 1955, 186

Howes, Dorsey 1914, 75

Howes, Gary Windsor 1947, 347

Howes, Guy Kenneth 1916, 186

Howes, Guy Kenneth 1917, 134

Howes, Joseph G. 1880, 75

Howes, Michael 1943, 347

Howes, Michael Douglas, 347

Howes, No given name, 10

Hoy, Marian, 361

Hoyle, Gene 1928, 293

Hoyle, Kenneth Edward 1957, 294

Hoyle, Mark Joseph 1959, 294

Hoyle, Richard Eugene 1952, 294

Hoyle, Scott Warren 1960, 294

Hoyle, Steven Michael 1966, 294

Hranicky, George Joseph, 42

Hranicky, Justine Claire 1957, 42

Hranicky, Kenneth Bede 1961, 42

Hranicky, Teresa Anne 1956, 42

Hranicky, Thomas Jerome 1958, 42

Hronik, Mildred, 389

Hubbard, Milton, 187

Hubbard, Robert A., 383

Hubble, Brenda Lee 1961, 204

Hubble, Harry L., 327

Hubble, Keith Allen 1959, 204

Hubble, Kevin Richard 1957, 204

Hubble, Marvin W. 1932, 204

Hubble, Robert Lee 1952, 204

Huchingson, Velma, 240

Huddleston, No given name, 327

Hudlow, Jesse Thomas 1984, 235

Hudlow, Joel Thomas 1955, 235

Hughes, Alexander Evans 1986, 245

Hughes, Arnold Victor 1894, 245

Hughes, David Arnold 1964, 245

Hughes, Donna Lee 1956, 245

Hughes, Elizabeth, 404

Hughes, Eveline Gaither, 337

Hughes, Frances Willard 1866, 356

Hughes, George Edward, 262

Hughes, Kelsey Victoria 1989, 245

Hughes, Kenneth Allen 1935, 245

Hughes, Kenneth Allen, Jr.
1957, 245
Hughes, Mary A., 262
Hughes, Robin Marie 1960,
245
Hughes, William D., 356
Hughes, William Kenneth
1989, 245
Hull, Helen Elizabeth 1891, 64
Hull, Wendy, 300
Hummer, Francis L., 340
Hummer, Francis, Doctor, 340
Hummer, Harry H., 340
Hummer, J. Ellwood, 90
Hummer, Jan Elizabeth 1980,
90
Hummer, Joann, 231
Hummer, Robert Dennis, 90
Humrick, Phebe, 107
Hungerford, Virginia, 161
Hunt, Alma Jean, 302
Hunt, Daniel Robert 1982, 237
Hunt, Debra Lynne 1960, 352
Hunt, Erin Michelle 1980, 237
Hunt, Katherine 1978, 237
Hunt, Larry E. 1956, 237
Hunt, Nancy, 49
Hunt, Raymond Kenneth 1941,
352
Hunt, Raymond Kenneth 1964,
352
Hunt, Richard, 302
Hunt, Richard George, 302
Hunt, Robin Marie 1974, 237
Hunter, Carrol Don 1936, 240
Hunter, Donna Yvonne 1961,
240
Hunter, Gwynn Ellen 1965,
241
Hunter, Jennifer Jean 1963,
241
Hunter, John, 240

Hurley, Addie Cassandra 1859,
301
Hurley, Anna Braddock 1891,
78
Hurley, Christine Lynn 1972,
104
Hurley, Daniel 1658, 172
Hurley, Dorothy Mae 1954, 104
Hurley, Duane Edward 1968,
104
Hurley, Elizabeth Mae 1910,
172
Hurley, Emma Jane 1863, 308
Hurley, Harry Gilmore, 172
Hurley, Harry Mankin 1853,
281
Hurley, Helen A. 1867, 279
Hurley, James Eric 1971, 104
Hurley, James Thomas 1948,
104
Hurley, John W. 1831, 308
Hurley, Llewellyn Powell 1922,
103
Hurley, Llewellyn Powell, Jr.
1947, 103
Hurley, Mary Katherine 1915,
281
Hurley, Michael 1811, 172
Hurley, Obed 1800, 301
Hyatt, Alpheus, 405
Hyatt, Barbara Lou 1945, 132
Hyatt, Bernard 1923, 134
Hyatt, Charles 1922, 133
Hyatt, Charles Vester 1886,
133
Hyatt, Clifford Boyer 1915, 132
Hyatt, Edgar 1915, 133
Hyatt, Edna Wilson 1905, 132,
137
Hyatt, Eleanor, 292
Hyatt, Eli, III, 124
Hyatt, Gertrude 1912, 133

467

Kettler, Clarence E., 346
Kettler, Ellen Luise 1950, 346
Kettler, Martha Belle 1954,
346
Kettler, Milton E. 1921, 345,
346
Kettler, Peter Brookes 1963,
346
Kettler, Robert Charles 1952,
346
Kettner, Eric 1958, 152
Kettner, Eugene Charles 1895,
152
Kettner, Jeanette 1924, 152
Kettner, Jill 1967, 153
Kettner, Mariamne Jeanette
1900, 153
Kettner, Mark 1956, 152
Kettner, Michael 1952, 152
Kettner, Robert, 152
Kettner, Robert Eugene 1925,
152
Kettner, Ronald 1950, 152
Kettner, Susan 1928, 153
Khairghadam, Audrey, 333
Khairghadam, Reza, 333
Kidd, Byrd Butler 1889, 234
Kidd, Madeline 1906, 132
Kidd, Madlyn, 234
Kidwell, Lillian Irene, 392
Kimble, Hester M. 1890, 353
Kimble, Jennie M. 1866, 370
Kinder, No given name, 386
Kinder, Theresa, 380
Kindley, Charlotte 1805, 122,
123, 210
King, A. Pearl 1897, 370
King, Abraham, 363
King, Abraham T. 1893, 367
King, Abram 1847, 403
King, Adam, 373, 374
King, Adam 1757, 413

King, Addie Abell 1876, 387
King, Addie Maria 1893, 304
King, Adela 1849, 403
King, Adelain, 274
King, Agatha W. 1885, 301
King, Agnes, 364
King, Agnes 1848, 403
King, Albert, 364
King, Albert B., 392
King, Albert Essex 1876, 75,
226
King, Albert F. A., 384
King, Albert Louis 1902, 403
King, Albertis Ward 1883, 387
King, Alethia, 400
King, Alexander m/1798, 398
King, Alfred, 412
King, Alfred 1847, 394
King, Alfred C., 404, 405, 406,
407
King, Alice, 308
King, Alice Maria 1858, 369
King, Allan, 385
King, Allen, 308
King, Alma Susie, 364
King, Altie Everett 1876, 87,
114
King, Alyson Anita 1991, 257
King, Amanda Cornelius 1870,
8, 98, 292, 311
King, Amanda Marie 1902, 97,
311
King, Amber Nichole 1996,
272
King, Amelia, 403
King, Amelia 1768, 393, 398
King, Amos, 403
King, Amy Kirstin 1967, 387
King, Amy Matrona 1881, 253,
319
King, Andrew, 363
King, Andrew W., 385

472

King, Anita K., 224
King, Anita Mae 1941, 230
King, Anita Renee 1966, 57
King, Ann, 369, 372, 384, 393,
    398, 399, 403, 404, 405,
    406, 412, 413
King, Ann 1746, 2
King, Ann 1765, 393
King, Ann 1766, 393
King, Ann 1776, 395
King, Ann 1812, 397
King, Ann 1818, 394
King, Ann E. 1866, 413
King, Ann Elizabeth 1814, 380
King, Ann Lyn 1959, 271
King, Ann M. 1809, 413
King, Ann m/1779, 398
King, Ann m/1794, 398
King, Ann Maria, 403
King, Ann Maria 1799, 404
King, Ann Maria 1838, 413
King, Ann Mary 1847, 380
King, Ann R., 404
King, Ann R. 1829, 369
King, Anna 1762, 369
King, Anna 1773, 411
King, Anna 1788, 412
King, Anna C. 1867, 367
King, Anna Elizabeth 1809,
    366
King, Anna Ella, 410
King, Anna Frances Maryum
    1849, 38
King, Anna Gertrude 1856, 68,
    97, 279, 280, 281
King, Anna M. 1923, 387
King, Anna Mae, 364
King, Anna Maria 1794, 370
King, Anna Maria 1809, 413
King, Anne, 398
King, Anne Garrett 1945, 79
King, Annie 1866, 368

King, Annie E., 371
King, Annie E. 1871, 365
King, Annie G. 1855, 279
King, Annie M. 1866, 413
King, Annie M. 1869, 217
King, Annie May 1889, 387
King, Annie Temple 1864, 274
King, Annie V. 1903, 365
King, Anthony, 379, 404
King, Anthony 1858, 369
King, Aquilla 1757, 411
King, Archie C. 1897, 216
King, Ardella Mae 1882, 298
King, Arlene D., 379
King, Arnold, 300
King, Arnold Rufus Franklin
    1848, 37
King, Arthur Charles 1876,
    387
King, Arubell, 391
King, Ashley Nicole, 58
King, Audrey, 300
King, Augusta Mae 1936, 273
King, Augusta W. 1888, 388
King, Barbara Ellen, 381
King, Barbara Emaline 1929,
    387
King, Barbara Emaline 1973,
    387
King, Barbara J., 301
King, Barry J. 1889, 215
King, Barton 1753, 411
King, Basil, 412
King, Basil 1760, 411
King, Beda Cassandra 1873,
    135, 232, 289
King, Bee 1921, 387
King, Ben 1841, 395
King, Benjamin, 3, 4, 373, 404,
    410, 411
King, Benjamin 1772, 5
King, Benjamin 1839, 395

473

474

King, Charles Clayton 1856,
366
King, Charles Dow 1890, 273
King, Charles E. 1880, 369,
371
King, Charles Edward, 388
King, Charles Edward 1869,
224
King, Charles Edward 1870,
403
King, Charles Edward, Jr., 224
King, Charles F. 1819, 413
King, Charles F. R. m/1856,
364
King, Charles Fisher, 404
King, Charles Frederick 1887,
402
King, Charles G. 1784, 410
King, Charles Henry, 364
King, Charles Herbert 1911,
379
King, Charles James 1812, 366
King, Charles L., 404
King, Charles L. 1889, 368
King, Charles Lee 1946, 246
King, Charles Lewis 1860, 364
King, Charles Maury 1896,
180, 277
King, Charles Miles 1814, 8,
30, 180, 191, 267, 271, 274,
276, 277
King, Charles Miles, Jr. 1861,
268, 276
King, Charles O. 1878, 371
King, Charles W. 1832, 366
King, Charles W. d/1895, 388
King, Charles Wesley 1886,
369
King, Charles William 1852,
369
King, Charles Wilson 1894,
388

King, Charles, Jr., 388
King, Charlie D. 1890, 388
King, Charlie L. 1881, 388
King, Charlotte Anne 1808,
398
King, Chloe, 414
King, Chloe 1750, 411
King, Christian 1835, 364
King, Christian 1971, 246
King, Christiana 1865, 403
King, Christine Anne 1968,
322
King, Christopher, 363
King, Clara B. 1867, 378
King, Clara C. 1901, 365
King, Clara N. 1904, 365
King, Clara Virginia 1853, 380
King, Clarence E. 1878, 126,
324
King, Clarence Middleton
1901, 96
King, Clark Fout 1910, 289,
322
King, Claude H. 1901, 307
King, Claudia Estelle 1906, 55
King, Clinton C. 1898, 215
King, Colleen M., 385
King, Columbus 1866, 388
King, Columbus R. 1886, 366
King, Comfort, 404
King, Conrad 1817, 380
King, Constance, 386
King, Cora, 391
King, Cora B. 1868, 388
King, Cora E. 1879, 382
King, Cora Idella 1878, 247
King, Cordelia 1831, 388
King, Cordelia E. 1881, 226
King, Cornelius 1755, 411
King, Cornelius 1763, 411
King, Cornelius 1789, 414

King, Cramwell McKinley 1895, 257
King, Craven J., 388
King, Crittenden 1857, 8, 268, 271
King, Crystal Paulette 1952, 96
King, Cyrus, 370
King, Dale Edward 1969, 240
King, Daniel, 398, 399
King, Daniel B. 1878, 367
King, Daniel Clark 1939, 322
King, Darlene Virginia, 364
King, David, 369, 388, 398, 403, 404, 405, 406, 407
King, David 1777, 377
King, David 1900, 386
King, David Andrew 1966, 272
King, David Franklin 1947, 246
King, David H. 1846, 386
King, David Henry 1843, 380
King, David Henry 1975, 274
King, David Ray 1950, 96
King, David Wesley 1959, 276
King, Deanna Elizabeth 1971, 384
King, Debbie L., 381
King, Deborah Anita Clair 1975, 257
King, Delsie White 1895, 95
King, Diane, 323
King, Donald, 387
King, Donald Genoa 1917, 323
King, Donald John 1989, 228
King, Dora Sophronia 1884, 302
King, Dorcas, 414
King, Dorcas 1758, 411
King, Doris, 386
King, Doris Jane, 306
King, Dorothy, 303, 323, 407
King, Dorothy Ann 1949, 95

King, Dorothy Clagett 1902, 388
King, Dorothy E., 385
King, Dorothy May 1924, 307
King, Dorothy Olivia 1939, 240
King, Dorsey Edward 1909, 225
King, Dorsey Edwin 1909, 225
King, Douglas Edward 1929, 272
King, Douglas M. 1963, 199
King, Douglas W. 1891, 388
King, Draden, 412
King, Dulcia, 388
King, E. (fem) 1843, 394
King, E. 1824, 396
King, Earl Raymond 1934, 239
King, Earl Virginia 1904, 88, 93
King, Edith 1877, 97
King, Edith Pauline 1915, 231
King, Edmund, 414
King, Edmund Carlton, 388
King, Edmund Dorsey 1847, 221, 258
King, Edna Estelle 1905, 36, 316, 332
King, Edna M. 1888, 365
King, Edna Mae 1908, 306, 319
King, Edna Maude 1885, 37
King, Edna May, 382
King, Edward, 3, 393, 413
King, Edward 1728, 2
King, Edward 1740, 4, 5, 29, 118, 120, 363
King, Edward 1741, 404
King, Edward Carlton 1872, 215

King, Edward J. 1821, 6, 8, 30,
  86, 166, 287, 291, 292, 297,
  301, 305, 308, 310, 311, 330
King, Edward J. 1826, 388
King, Edward Ray 1914, 98
King, Edward T. 1842, 214
King, Edward Walter 1869, 97,
  311
King, Edward, Jr. 1774, 5
King, Effie Lee 1883, 298
King, Eileen M., 307
King, Elba J. 1879, 369, 371
King, Eleanor, 393, 395, 398,
  399, 400, 404, 405, 407,
  413, 414
King, Eleanor 1734, 369
King, Eleanor 1743, 2
King, Eleanor 1764, 395
King, Elias, 388, 405, 407
King, Elias 1765, 411
King, Elias 1841, 388
King, Elias Dorsey 1863, 69,
  75, 226
King, Elias P., 404
King, Elias Vinson 1869, 180,
  268, 277
King, Elisha, 395, 398
King, Eliza, 405, 406
King, Eliza 1804, 404
King, Elizabeth, 3, 4, 366, 369,
  371, 388, 394, 398, 399,
  404, 405, 406, 407, 408,
  411, 412, 414
King, Elizabeth 1763, 5
King, Elizabeth 1766, 395
King, Elizabeth 1790, 412
King, Elizabeth 1793, 397
King, Elizabeth 1800, 398
King, Elizabeth 1803, 369, 399
King, Elizabeth 1810, 396
King, Elizabeth 1820, 414
King, Elizabeth 1824, 369, 377

King, Elizabeth 1827, 370
King, Elizabeth 1829, 404
King, Elizabeth 1834, 378
King, Elizabeth 1835, 396
King, Elizabeth 1848, 395
King, Elizabeth Barnes, 409
King, Elizabeth Dexter, 384
King, Elizabeth F. 1846, 378
King, Elizabeth Isabella 1830,
  375
King, Elizabeth J. 1845, 166,
  292
King, Elizabeth Jean 1927, 243
King, Elizabeth Jeanne 1927,
  79, 253
King, Elizabeth Louise, 368
King, Elizabeth Miles 1802,
  30, 119, 222, 329
King, Elizabeth Morris 1711, 4
King, Elkanah, 398
King, Ella E. 1903, 388
King, Ellen, 404
King, Ellen A. d/1935, 384
King, Ellen C., 414
King, Ellen C. 1836, 370
King, Ellen C. 1867, 413
King, Ellen Irene 1881, 388
King, Ellen R. 1871, 370
King, Ellen T. 1922, 384
King, Ellen Thomas 1837, 388
King, Ellsworth McKinley
  1914, 257
King, Elva E., 385
King, Emeline 1837, 388
King, Emily Amanda 1845,
  375
King, Emily L. 1866, 269
King, Emma 1854, 388
King, Emma 1893, 402
King, Emma d/1914, 383
King, Emma Estelle 1880, 250
King, Emma J. 1890, 389

King, Emma J. Haney, 389
King, Ena M. d/1899, 389
King, Ennis D. 1816, 370
King, Ernest 1875, 87
King, Ernest W. 1882, 389
King, Estella B. 1875, 270
King, Esther, 386
King, Esther 1841, 404
King, Esther Mae 1948, 257
King, Esther Moore, 390
King, Ethel Lansdale 1886, 320
King, Ethel W., 392
King, Ettie May 1881, 302
King, Eugene McKinley 1936, 257
King, Eugenia, 384
King, Eva Lee 1864, 6, 292, 310
King, Eveline 1828, 30, 222, 335
King, Eveline L. 1849, 316
King, Eveline L. 1864, 97
King, Eveline Lee 1864, 6, 310
King, Eveline Louise 1849, 225, 317
King, Evelyn, 308
King, Everett J. 1883, 226
King, Fairy Fay 1949, 90
King, Faith Virginia 1946, 77, 353
King, Fannie, 370, 384
King, Fannie Lois 1935, 79
King, Fannie M. 1899, 370
King, Fannie Thelma 1899, 81
King, Fanny, 404
King, Fannye W., 378
King, Fillie R. 1892, 389
King, Filmore Clark 1890, 289, 322
King, Flora E. 1892, 371
King, Flora S. 1886, 305
King, Florence E., 224

King, Florence E. 1910, 370
King, Florence G. 1875, 218
King, Florence Mabel d/1935, 389
King, Forest 1894, 77
King, Forest Donald, 77
King, Forest, Jr. 1918, 77
King, Forrest Edward 1889, 303
King, Frances, 308
King, Frances Addie 1923, 276
King, Frances Belle 1892, 95
King, Frances Carol 1771, 411
King, Frances E. 1846, 279, 280
King, Frances E. 1892, 389
King, Frances Elizabeth 1944, 89
King, Frances L. 1856, 268, 270
King, Frances Lucille 1914, 307
King, Francis, 76, 226, 363, 374, 398, 399, 404, 410
King, Francis 1695, 394
King, Francis 1849, 370
King, Francis E. 1881, 370
King, Francis M. 1841, 377
King, Francis, Jr. 1724, 394
King, Frank Robert 1951, 95
King, Frank Singleton, 226
King, Franklin E. 1905, 365
King, Franklin Monroe 1876, 22, 239, 294
King, Franklin Scott 1852, 292, 301
King, Franklin V. 1887, 402
King, Franklin Webster 1927, 94, 287
King, Frederick, 371, 372
King, Frederick Mason 1884, 389

478

King, Hattie Mae 1893, 9, 99, 255
King, Hazel Eliza 1892, 402
King, Hazel Ethel 1912, 268
King, Helen, 308
King, Helen 1872, 405
King, Helen Gertrude, 77
King, Helen Irene, 225
King, Helen Jane 1908, 55
King, Henrietta, 398
King, Henrietta Catherine 1862, 403
King, Henry, 369, 370, 371, 384, 405, 406, 407, 414
King, Henry 1810, 396
King, Henry 1821, 370
King, Henry 1841, 396
King, Henry 1849, 405
King, Henry 1855, 402
King, Henry 1903, 370
King, Henry E. 1900, 382
King, Henry Franklin 1936, 239
King, Henry J. 1872, 215
King, Henry L. 1900, 382
King, Herbert C. 1911, 379
King, Herbert Charles 1932, 239
King, Herbert Thomas 1971, 241
King, Herman Allen, 364
King, Herman Allen, III, 364
King, Herman Allen, Jr. 1942, 364
King, Hester, 406
King, Hetty, 398
King, Hiram G. 1863, 215
King, Holady Hix 1857, 22, 86, 287, 292, 305
King, Holliday Hix 1857, 305
King, Holly Ann 1965, 199

King, Homer F. 1852, 126, 316, 324
King, Honor, 405
King, Howard H. 1912, 389
King, Howard James 1964, 57
King, Howard Monroe 1883, 308
King, Howard O. 1936, 389
King, Howard T., 215
King, Hubert G. d/1959, 389
King, Hugh Francis 1899, 87
King, Hyrum 1810, 366
King, Ida A. 1887, 389
King, Ida Emma G. 1864, 380
King, Ida Landella 1903, 216
King, Ida Lucy 1901, 402
King, Ida May 1942, 56
King, Ira 1902, 88, 268
King, Ira Leroy, 91
King, Ira Leroy 1909, 379
King, Ira Leroy, Jr. 1938, 379
King, Irene, 77
King, Irene A., 383
King, Iris I. 1934, 389
King, Irma, 385
King, Irma d/1916, 224
King, Irvin 1903, 402
King, Irvin Elmer 1939, 230
King, Isaac, 398, 404, 406, 407
King, Isaac 1800, 398
King, Isaac N., 389
King, Iva C. 1885, 75
King, Ivy C. 1885, 75
King, J. 1826, 396
King, J. B., 392
King, J. M., 388
King, Jacob, 399, 405
King, Jacob Doyle 1803, 414
King, Jacob F. 1891, 367
King, Jacob Samuel 1866, 365

King, James, 370, 371, 383, 390, 393, 398, 399, 400, 405, 406
King, James 1776, 393
King, James 1780, 414
King, James 1782, 395
King, James 1805, 405
King, James 1828, 396
King, James 1842, 405
King, James A., 385
King, James A. 1816, 413
King, James A. 1847, 414
King, James Albert 1862, 365
King, James Autie, 378
King, James Carroll 1771, 411
King, James D., 384
King, James Deets 1889, 76, 353
King, James E., 303, 375, 414
King, James Edward 1854, 292, 301
King, James Forrest 1916, 303
King, James Forrest, Jr. 1949, 303
King, James Franklin 1937, 272
King, James Franklin, Jr. 1968, 272
King, James H. 1824, 397
King, James H. 1872, 390
King, James Harrison 1841, 75, 221, 223, 318
King, James L. 1847, 414
King, James Lawrence 1892, 370
King, James M. 1871, 69, 87
King, James Obed 1878, 302
King, James Otis 1872, 225, 318
King, James R., 378
King, James R. 1841, 382, 390

King, James Raymond 1917, 303
King, James Richard d/1916, 382
King, James Rufus 1871, 227, 288
King, James S., 400
King, James Schaeffer 1913, 76, 353
King, James Swann, 398, 399
King, James Swean, 398
King, James T., 414
King, James T. 1847, 414
King, James Thomas 1860, 399
King, James Thomas 1943, 241
King, James Thomas, Jr. 1973, 241
King, James William, 382
King, James William 1913, 230
King, James Wright, 414
King, Jane, 323, 324, 399, 414
King, Jane 1708, 2
King, Jane 1772, 414
King, Jane K., 390
King, Jane M., 378
King, Jane Marie 1963, 272
King, Jane P. 1813, 405
King, Jane Rebecca 1864, 413
King, Janet, 386
King, Janet Elizabeth 1972, 230
King, Janet Louise 1937, 246
King, Jarrett T., 405
King, Jasper 1837, 405
King, Jay Michael 1963, 244
King, Jean, 38, 379
King, Jean Elizabeth 1943, 230
King, Jeffery Wayne, 96
King, Jeffrey McKinley 1964, 257
King, Jemima 1782, 157, 390

King, Luther Roland 1891, 390
King, Luvern L. 1889, 402
King, Lydia 1798, 367
King, Lydia 1839, 378
King, Lydia Ann, 405
King, Lyndall Victoria 1901, 227
King, M. 1816, 396
King, M. 1846, 396
King, Mabel, 224
King, Mabel Eloise 1896, 403
King, Mabel Frances 1907, 390
King, Mabel P., 301
King, Mabel Sharretts 1895, 259
King, Mabel Waters 1908, 229
King, Macie Schaeffer 1893, 353
King, Madelena, 363
King, Madeline Virginia, 309
King, Maggie M. 1877, 218
King, Mahala Ann Rebecca 1836, 33, 100
King, Mahala E. 1864, 96
King, Mahala J. 1863, 390
King, Mahala Jane Victory 1853, 47
King, Malcolm Elwood 1913, 323
King, Malissa Lynn, 364
King, Malvina, 399
King, Manzella L. 1845, 221, 258
King, Margaret, 76, 226, 369, 384, 399, 405, 407, 410, 413
King, Margaret 1718, 394
King, Margaret 1793, 405
King, Margaret 1805, 406
King, Margaret 1847, 395
King, Margaret 1849, 406
King, Margaret A., 406
King, Margaret Ann, 303

King, Margaret Ann 1840, 375, 376
King, Margaret Ann 1848, 406
King, Margaret Ann 1937, 240
King, Margaret E. Watkins 1917, 390
King, Margaret Elizabeth 1876, 403
King, Margaret Ellen 1968, 58
King, Margareth A., 371
King, Margo, 390
King, Maria, 370
King, Maria Elizabeth 1853, 399
King, Maria Elizabeth 1854, 399
King, Marian T., 308
King, Marie E., 386
King, Marietta Kinery 1884, 390
King, Marion F. 1887, 390
King, Marjorie Belle 1915, 94
King, Marjorie Lee 1907, 228
King, Marjorie Roberta 1908, 244
King, Mark Sheridan 1962, 323
King, Mark W., 77
King, Martha, 404, 406
King, Martha 1836, 371
King, Martha 1844, 406
King, Martha 1846, 406
King, Martha 1849, 396
King, Martha A. R. 1858, 371
King, Martha B., 367
King, Martha C. T., 383
King, Martha E. 1844, 370
King, Martha Rebecca 1874, 17, 233
King, Martha T. Thompson, 387
King, Martin, 370, 399

485

King, Olive Teresa 1897, 382
King, Olive W. 1869, 115
King, Oliver Henry 1941, 180, 277
King, Opal Elena 1940, 241
King, Ora Henning 1910, 180, 277
King, Orida Jane 1883, 273
King, Orin Woodrow 1912, 323
King, Orin Woodrow, Jr., 323
King, Orpha 1784, 411
King, Oscar 1843, 396
King, Oscar Ritchie 1869, 365
King, Otho 1845, 396
King, Pamela Beth 1988, 228
King, Pamela Denise 1953, 96
King, Parke Leo 1912, 82
King, Patrice Marie 1967, 274
King, Patricia, 77
King, Patricia Ann 1933, 244
King, Patricia Ann 1934, 228
King, Patricia Lou 1970, 230
King, Patricia Lucille, 307
King, Patrick Allen, 391
King, Patsy A., 385
King, Paul, 323
King, Paul Richard 1938, 272
King, Pauline, 386
King, Pauline Almabelle 1900, 304
King, Pauline M., 386
King, Pearl Clark 1879, 88, 268
King, Pearle Avondale 1933, 239
King, Peggy, 323, 369, 386, 407
King, Peggy A., 381
King, Perry M. 1867, 222
King, Pete 1917, 303
King, Peter Brandon 1963, 272

King, Philip, 363
King, Philip Edward 1851, 371
King, Porter Jay, 383
King, Porter Jay, Jr., 383
King, Preston Cloud d/1953, 381
King, Preston Cloud, Jr. 1904, 381
King, Priscilla, 388
King, Priscilla 1772, 393
King, Protes E. 1880, 305
King, Quesselin, 383
King, R. Delaney 1874, 87, 216
King, Rachel, 414
King, Rachel 1833, 407
King, Raymond 1886, 303
King, Raymond Singleton 1914, 254
King, Rebecca, 391, 412
King, Rebecca 1776, 5
King, Rebecca 1837, 395
King, Rebecca 1844, 407
King, Rebecca Duckett 1742, 5
King, Rebeccah, 3, 4
King, Reginald Windsor 1878, 24, 36, 47
King, Reginald Windsor 1934, 57
King, Reginald Windsor, Jr. 1962, 57
King, Reuben, 412
King, Richard, 398, 399, 400, 407, 410, 412
King, Richard 1691, 2
King, Richard 1764, 399
King, Richard 1773, 407
King, Richard 1808, 394
King, Richard B., 215
King, Richard Barton 1809, 414
King, Richard M., 199

King, Richard Warren 1839, 394
King, Richard Willett, 96
King, Richard William 1948, 275
King, Robert, 363, 407, 412
King, Robert A. 1940, 254
King, Robert Allen, 405
King, Robert Arthur 1862, 364
King, Robert Charles 1948, 275
King, Robert H., 389
King, Robert Hilton, 306
King, Robert Lanier 1872, 407
King, Robert Lee 1931, 272
King, Robert M., 307
King, Robert, Sir, 409
King, Roberta 1855, 316, 324, 325
King, Roberta Columbia 1885, 79, 252, 320
King, Roberta Isabell 1853, 221
King, Roberta Olivia 1931, 239
King, Robey F., 301
King, Roby, 258
King, Roby Harrison 1889, 255
King, Roger Hood 1940, 58
King, Roger Hood, Jr. 1967, 58
King, Ronald Edward 1945, 275
King, Ronald Irvin 1972, 230
King, Ronnie, 381
King, Rosa Belle 1867, 87, 114
King, Rosa M. 1870, 365
King, Rose Ann, 407
King, Rosie M. 1854, 366
King, Rosina Fitz, 407
King, Ruby M., 381
King, Rufus, 300, 369
King, Rufus 1816, 30, 68, 97, 279, 280, 281, 282
King, Rufus 1836, 407
King, Rufus 1869, 279, 282

King, Rufus B., 267
King, Rufus Filmore 1850, 74, 315, 316, 318
King, Rufus Kent 1850, 291, 292, 297, 298, 300
King, Rufus m/1867, 280, 282
King, Ruth, 391, 399
King, Ruth 1762, 395
King, Ruth A. 1846, 407
King, Ruth Ann 1946, 58
King, Ruth Ann 1947, 89
King, Ruth Carolyn 1938, 56
King, Ruth Selby 1904, 24, 53
King, S. Allen 1912, 254
King, S. Allen, Jr. 1935, 254
King, Sabra 1774, 393
King, Sabrat, 399
King, Sabrina 1824, 394
King, Sallie Behn 1952, 303
King, Sally Jane 1886, 299
King, Samantha Lynn 1979, 231
King, Samuel, 407
King, Samuel 1788, 371
King, Samuel B., 389
King, Samuel Hayward 1827, 407
King, Samuel P. 1855, 391
King, Samuel Rufus 1949, 231
King, Samuel T. 1798, 399
King, Sandra, 323
King, Sandra Darlene, 385
King, Sandra Gail 1958, 57
King, Sandra Jean 1964, 239
King, Sandra Lee 1940, 228
King, Sara Rebecca 1949, 77, 353
King, Sarah, 371, 385, 391, 393, 399, 407, 412, 414
King, Sarah 1723, 394
King, Sarah 1764, 4, 5
King, Sarah 1778, 395

489

King, Sarah 1780, 371
King, Sarah 1810, 378
King, Sarah 1842, 407
King, Sarah 1848, 380
King, Sarah 1990, 240
King, Sarah A. 1840, 371
King, Sarah A. 1866, 391
King, Sarah Ann, 399
King, Sarah Anne 1807, 407
King, Sarah D., 385
King, Sarah Elizabeth 1888, 88, 92, 191, 391
King, Sarah Elizabeth 1950, 58
King, Sarah Estelle 1886, 391
King, Sarah F. 1843, 392
King, Sarah Hallowell 1889, 389
King, Sarah J. 1834, 371
King, Sarah Jane 1916, 59, 164
King, Sarah L. 1922, 303
King, Sarah Lecrecey, 398
King, Sarah M., 382
King, Sarah N. 1831, 213, 214
King, Sarah Rebecca 1818, 30, 285, 286, 289
King, Sarah Vincent, 384
King, Sarilla 1840, 371
King, Selina G. 1855, 392
King, Shalene D., 385
King, Shane Scott 1964, 254
King, Shannon Sherelle 1968, 241
King, Sharon Lee 1941, 254
King, Shelsea M., 385
King, Sherwood C. 1885, 308
King, Shirley, 301, 386
King, Singleton 1810, 30, 119, 162, 221, 222, 223, 226, 258, 259, 288, 294, 318
King, Singleton Lewis 1843, 22, 221, 226

King, Somerville 1848, 292, 297
King, Sommerville W. 1848, 297
King, Sophia, 406
King, Sophia Catharine 1849, 380
King, Stanley D. 1907, 392
King, Stauzy Lewis 1887, 254
King, Stephen, 414
King, Stephen R., 407
King, Stephen T., 384
King, Sterling T., 379
King, Steven Todd 1964, 57
King, Steven Todd, Jr., 58
King, Stuart Allen 1969, 254
King, Susan, 400
King, Susan Burdette 1956, 244
King, Susan C. 1846, 279
King, Susan E. 1844, 392
King, Susan Elizabeth 1961, 239
King, Susan Lynn 1970, 274
King, Susan Virginia 1960, 57
King, Susan West, 378
King, Susanna, 400, 410
King, Susanna 1769, 393
King, Susanna 1844, 378
King, Susanna Rebecca 1817, 366
King, Susanna T. 1812, 371
King, Susanna V. 1856, 367
King, Susannah, 398, 400, 414
King, Susannah 1764, 393
King, Sylvester 1822, 394
King, Tayler Lynn 1992, 240
King, Tegan 1979, 246
King, Teresa, 386
King, Theresa Virginia 1883, 392

King, Thomas, 3, 4, 374, 393, 398, 400, 404, 405, 406, 407, 412, 414
King, Thomas 1720, 394
King, Thomas 1790, 407
King, Thomas 1798, 396
King, Thomas 1838, 396
King, Thomas B. 1794, 410
King, Thomas D. 1868, 268, 276
King, Thomas E., 392
King, Thomas Franklin 1858, 372
King, Thomas Franklin 1873, 403
King, Thomas Gilmore, 274
King, Thomas Gould, 392
King, Thomas Harmon, 407
King, Thomas Henry 1877, 407
King, Thomas Irving 1943, 79
King, Thomas Lee d/1947, 392
King, Thomas M., 215, 400
King, Thomas Matthew 1908, 392
King, Thomas O. 1864, 215
King, Thomas P., 383
King, Thomas Peter 1840, 213
King, Thomas R., 324, 388
King, Thomas Riddell 1803, 407
King, Thomas Warren 1849, 394
King, Thomas, Colonel, 409
King, Thurston B. 1889, 86, 305
King, Timothy Wade 1969, 254
King, Tina Louise 1969, 57
King, Tommy, 386
King, Tommy H., 385
King, Tommy Lee 1936, 392
King, Townley, 412
King, Tracey 1971, 255

King, Trevor, 385
King, Upton, 392
King, Upton R. 1916, 390
King, Ursula Mahala 1857, 74, 318
King, Verlinder, 398, 399
King, Vincent, 405
King, Vincent 1802, 395
King, Vinson, 400
King, Vinson 1769, 411
King, Vinton G., 392
King, Violena 1899, 392
King, Violender 1786, 395
King, Violet Elizabeth 1902, 52
King, Violet Louise 1919, 94
King, Virginia, 391
King, Virginia Gertrude 1904, 81
King, Virginia Lorenz 1911, 225
King, Virginia R. 1890, 392
King, Vivian, 297
King, Vivian M. 1888, 275
King, Walden V. 1894, 269, 392
King, Wallace, 406, 407
King, Wallace 1834, 407
King, Wallace C. 1903, 217
King, Walter, 388, 412
King, Walter 1710, 412
King, Walter 1768, 411
King, Walter D. 1894, 392
King, Walter Gustavus 1869, 400
King, Walter James 1823, 33, 34, 60, 65
King, Walter R., 407
King, Walter Ross 1941, 58
King, Walter Watt, 410
King, Warren 1794, 374, 375, 376

King, Wootie Lee 1877, 301
King, Zadoc Summers 1839, 33, 91, 92, 113
King, Zadock Henson Windsor 1844, 34
King, Zella Irene 1891, 402
King, Zephaniah 1734, 412
King, Zephaniah 1759, 411
Kingstead Farms, 271
Kinna, Betty, 248
Kinna, Ruth Ethel 1906, 227
Kinsey, Alice Elizabeth 1919, 167
Kinsey, Bun, 182
Kinsey, Dorothy, 167
Kinsey, Edwin Reese 1903, 167
Kinsey, Edwin Reese, Jr., 167
Kinsey, George Milton 1910, 167
Kinsey, Granville Eggleston 1880, 166
Kinsey, Howard Granville 1908, 167
Kinsey, Mary Columbia 1906, 167
Kinsey, Robert, 167
Kirby, Barbara L. 1923, 358
Kirchgassner, Patricia, 234
Kirkland, Rose Camille 1902, 43
Kirschner, Anna Catherine 1833, 401
Kirschner, Louise, 403
Kitterman, Fred Blaine, 163
Kitterman, John, 163
Kitterman, Richard, 163
Kline, Sherman Claude, 143
Kline, Teri, 240
Klinefelter, Margaret Rebecca 1874, 60, 65
Kling, Frances Edna 1941, 319
Kling, Jack 1933, 306, 319

Kling, Laurie Gayle 1964, 306, 319
Kling, Ronald Maynard 1958, 306, 319
Kling, Thomas, 319
Kling, Thomas Maynard 1908, 306, 319
Klix, Kathleen, 179
Klix, No given name, 179
Klix, Sharyn, 179
Klug, Margaret 1941, 192
Knight, Edward Franklin, 19
Knight, Edward Franklin 1948, 19
Knight, Steven Carson 1979, 19
Knoblock, John, 354
Knoblock, John, Jr., 354
Knoblock, Kimberly, 354
Knoblock, Tammy, 354
Knoll, Thomas, 217
Knott, Allen, 248
Knott, Ashley Elizabeth 1984, 248
Knott, Thomas E., 388
Knotts, Christopher Michael 1972, 132
Knotts, Donald Lynn 1943, 132
Koehler, Annie Gertrude 1900, 112
Koehler, Betsy, 113
Koehler, Diane Marie 1963, 113
Koehler, Ella Mahala 1898, 112
Koehler, Etta Amelia 1897, 112
Koehler, Frederick Herman 1864, 111
Koehler, Herman H., 112
Koehler, John G. 1899, 112

493

Lathrop, George Allan, Jr.
1930, 320
Lathrop, Marden Burdette
1932, 321
Lawson, Amy, 82
Lawson, Annie, 132
Lawson, Arthur, 136
Lawson, Cecil, 245
Lawson, Cleveland, 318
Lawson, Cleveland F., 82
Lawson, Daphne Carson, 19
Lawson, Darleen, 317
Lawson, Dianne Cecil 1941,
202
Lawson, Dorsey E., 82
Lawson, Eli, 132
Lawson, Emma Jane 1859, 298
Lawson, Evelyn Jeanette 1942,
192
Lawson, Evie, 82
Lawson, George, 308
Lawson, Grace 1882, 308
Lawson, Hanford, 136
Lawson, Hattie Gertrude 1865,
75
Lawson, Ivan 1886, 136
Lawson, James H., 146
Lawson, James Uriah, 87, 319
Lawson, John, 82
Lawson, John William 1912,
202
Lawson, John William Ran-
dolph 1950, 202
Lawson, Leslie, 317
Lawson, Lola May 1873, 87
Lawson, Maggie, 82
Lawson, Marie D., 82
Lawson, Mark 1957, 244
Lawson, Mary Wooten, 298
Lawson, Ola, 132
Lawson, Phillip, 82
Lawson, Richard, 244

Lawson, Robert, 317
Lawson, Sallie, 146
Lawson, Sally, 83
Lawson, Spencer, 82
Lawson, Sylvia Elaine 1939,
202
Lawson, Uriah, 82
Lawson, Vinnie Edna 1875,
319
Lawson, Wayne, 317
Lawson, William Filmore, 82
Layton, Catherine 1797, 214
Layton, Charles F., 82
Layton, Cora, 138
Layton, Emma, 15
Layton, Ettie 1858, 214
Layton, John, 69
Layton, John 1796, 214
Layton, Mary 1836, 92
Layton, Mary Keziah 1836, 69
Layton, Obediah Stillwell 1832,
214
Layton, Susie Elizabeth 1886,
82
Layton, William Kenneth 1908,
15
Layton, William Kenneth, Jr.,
15
Leach, Susanna, 399
Leakins, Ronnie, 176
Leaman, Hattie 1872, 262
Leamon, John, 16
Lear, Arthur John, 21
Leatherwood, Bradley Clifford
1886, 130
Leatherwood, Genevieve 1914,
131
Leatherwood, Guy E., 127
Leatherwood, Helen Baker
1917, 131
Leatherwood, John Francis
1920, 131

495

Lebowitz, Alan Harvey, 20
Lebowitz, Holly Joy 1962, 20
Leda, Catherine Marie 1924, 275
Ledford, Nora, 325
Lee, Ina Marie, 249
Lee, Keith, 77
Lee, Laura, 77
Lee, Nicie V., 124
Lee, No given name, 77
Lee, Rowena Jane, 205
Leese, David Watson 1970, 81
Leese, Howard Watson 1900, 81
Leese, Joan Olivia 1964, 81
Leese, Watson King 1933, 81
Leese, William Craig 1962, 81
Leftwich, Rebecca 1815, 122
Lehr, Alvin Ambrose 1933, 189
Lehr, Ann Marie 1965, 189
Lehr, Lenard Harry, 189
Leishear, Mary, 175
Leizear, Franklin Vernon 1927, 70
Leizear, Harry N., 348
Leizear, Sharon Patricia 1952, 70
Leland, Margaret, 153
Lentz, Herman, 402
Leslie, Frank, 177
Lester, Sallie Caskie 1882, 194
Lewicki, Walter, 196
Lewis, Ann Eliza, 149
Lewis, Anna Mary, 127, 138
Lewis, Annie Elizabeth 1857, 263
Lewis, Arnold T., 167
Lewis, Augusta, 262
Lewis, Bessie, 262
Lewis, Bettie 1857, 261
Lewis, Caroline 1835, 221

Lewis, Catherine, 6
Lewis, Catherine 1806, 267
Lewis, Deborah Lynn, 98
Lewis, Dorsey, 88
Lewis, Editha 1815, 115
Lewis, Edward, 262
Lewis, Edward King 1808, 261, 263, 264
Lewis, Elizabeth A. 1837, 261, 264
Lewis, Elva, 7, 8
Lewis, Emma Jane 1857, 6
Lewis, Ethel 1902, 110
Lewis, Georgianna, 124, 263
Lewis, Grover, 8
Lewis, Grover G., 389
Lewis, Harriet Ann, 6
Lewis, Harriet Ann 1805, 5
Lewis, Harriett, 262
Lewis, Iraneus 1849, 261
Lewis, J. Frank, 263
Lewis, Jane Rebecca, 119, 221, 223
Lewis, Jeremiah, 221, 261
Lewis, Jerome C. 1851, 261
Lewis, John, 262, 399
Lewis, John A. 1832, 261
Lewis, John R., 258
Lewis, John Robert, 262
Lewis, John Robert 1880, 332
Lewis, Lawrence, 262
Lewis, Leonard Leo 1894, 174
Lewis, Linwood, 262
Lewis, Mahlon T. 1834, 261, 263
Lewis, Margaret Vernona 1926, 262
Lewis, Mary Ann 1820, 221
Lewis, Mary Catherine 1839, 261, 264
Lewis, Mary E. 1843, 167
Lewis, Mary E. 1854, 113

498

Lucke, Jennifer Estelle 1951, 132
Luhn, Bessie, 317
Luhn, Beulah, 317
Luhn, Esther Pearl, 22
Luhn, Randolph, 22
Luhn, Sarah Elizabeth, 22
Luhn, Stonestreet Wilson 1908, 66
Luhn, Teresa Diane 1954, 67
Luhn, William, 317
Luhn, Wilson Stonestreet 1930, 67
Lunsford, Bertha, 108
Lurby, Benjamin P., 403
Lusby, David Franklin 1958, 61
Lusby, No given name, 226
Lusby, Sharon Willett 1963, 61
Lusby, Walter Franklin, Jr. 1932, 61
Lusby, Walter Kevin 1957, 61
Lydard, Emma Jane 1890, 289, 322
Lydard, John C. 1850, 322
Lydard, Nonie M. 1881, 216
Lydia Ann 1859, 405
Lyle, Dorothy 1913, 107
Lynch, Emily Roberta 1901, 40
Lynch, Ethel Catherine 1908, 41
Lynch, Evelyn Rita 1920, 38
Lynch, James Mackin 1889, 39
Lynch, John Edgar 1911, 41
Lynch, John William 1863, 38
Lynch, John William, Jr. 1886, 38
Lynch, June Marie 1932, 347
Lynch, Laura Elizabeth 1898, 40
Lynch, Martha Agnes 1896, 40
Lynch, Mary Frances 1891, 39

Lynch, Mary Roberta 1915, 38
Lynch, Oley Irene 1888, 38
Lynch, Susan, 399
Lynch, Urban, 320
Lynch, William, 347
Lynch, William Hartley 1933, 347
Lynch, William Thomas, 38

—M—

Mabry, Dean Caldwell 1920, 157
Mabry, John Nance, 157
Mabry, Letha Bell 1947, 157
Mabry, Patricia Dean 1951, 157
Mabry, Sarah Jane 1941, 157
MacIntyre, Judy Ann 1946, 138
Mack, Mary Elizabeth, 21
Mackall, William S. 1884, 361
MacKenzie, Elaine Agnes 1920, 299
MacKenzie, Joseph Stanislaus, 299
MacKusick, Elizabeth Ann 1974, 200
MacKusick, Meredith Hall, 200
MacLeay, Andrew Cameron, 253
MacLeay, Anna Marion 1990, 253
MacLeay, Benjamin Samuel 1983, 253
MacLeay, Daniel Gregory 1979, 253
MacLeay, Mark Robert 1981, 253
MacLeay, Richard C. 1950, 253
MacLeay, Steven Joseph 1987, 253

499

502

Mounce, James Robert 1964, 196
Mounce, Lloyd Michael 1942, 196
Mounce, Tammara Lynn 1967, 196
Mount, Fanny Gertrude, 162
Mount, John, 140
Moxley, Allison 1888, 123
Moxley, Cornelius Edward, 82, 325
Moxley, Donna Jeanne 1948, 208
Moxley, Elvira 1896, 124
Moxley, Emily Lorraine 1903, 292
Moxley, Emory Dorsey 1888, 82
Moxley, Ernest Walter 1882, 123
Moxley, Esther Leith, 136
Moxley, Ethel, 134
Moxley, Exie E. 1878, 318
Moxley, Floyd 1895, 325
Moxley, Floyd Keen Maloy 1926, 270, 325
Moxley, Glenn Floyd 1953, 325
Moxley, Gloria Alvin 1930, 208
Moxley, Harry B., 292
Moxley, Jesse Herman 1893, 124
Moxley, Jesse William 1855, 123
Moxley, Kelly Wayne 1969, 208
Moxley, Kevin Harold 1961, 208
Moxley, Kristen Leon 1964, 208
Moxley, Leonard Wayne 1941, 208

Moxley, Lester 1886, 123
Moxley, Lillie May 1890, 123
Moxley, Lucinda 1840, 126
Moxley, Nancy Lee 1957, 270, 325
Moxley, Raymond Merson 1909, 208
Moxley, Reuben M., 126
Moxley, Risdon, 123
Moxley, Vivy 1900, 124
Moyer, Carl Elmer 1912, 58
Moyer, George D., 58
Mull, Joseph Zachary 1983, 349
Mull, Lauren Ashley 1987, 349
Mull, Melissa Ashley 1991, 349
Mull, Russell Eddie, 349
Mullen, Jacqueline Elaine 1954, 231
Mullen, Janette Frances 1956, 232
Mullen, Jennifer Lee 1960, 232
Mullen, Joan Marie 1949, 231
Mullen, Judith Ann 1947, 231
Mullen, Juliet Maureen 1961, 232
Mullen, Thomas Joseph 1926, 231
Mullen, Timothy 1956, 240
Mullican, Archibald, 72
Mullican, Bertie 1919, 73
Mullican, Blanche 1911, 72
Mullican, Carl Oscar 1906, 64, 207
Mullican, Carroll Lee 1943, 64
Mullican, Charles 1913, 73
Mullican, Charles Thomas 1943, 73
Mullican, Clarence Mayfield 1876, 60, 65

507

Nicholson, Frances Helen 1904, 62
Nicholson, Harry L., 273
Nicholson, James Kenneth 1931, 227
Nicholson, Jessie Randolph, 15
Nicholson, John Wilson 1957, 227
Nicholson, Lizzie, 106
Nicholson, Marjorie Jane 1908, 293
Nicholson, No given name, 307
Nicholson, Reuben M., 15
Nicholson, Walter Wilson, 15
Nicholson, Walter Wilson 1896, 227
Nicklas, Mary Vandevort 1910, 146
Niemyer, Mary Jane, 405
Nivert, Edward Joseph 1947, 44
Nivert, Frank John 1915, 44
Nivert, Frank John, Jr. 1942, 44
Nivert, Mary Catherine 1944, 44
Nix, Sarah Beatrice 1922, 191
Noble, Arthur G., 388
Nolte, Martha Ella 1863, 403
Noonan, Edward Joseph, 124
Norman, Alma Anne 1931, 41
Norman, Doris Louise 1926, 41
Norman, Helen Ruth 1933, 41
Norman, Lynn David 1942, 41
Norman, Lynn Eugene 1900, 41
Norris, Adrian Stout, 160
Norris, Amanda S., 375
Norris, Anna Mable 1861, 376
Norris, Brett 1960, 152
Norris, Charles Lansdale 1942, 161

Norris, Charles Olin 1879, 377
Norris, Clinton 1868, 377
Norris, Cora Elizabeth 1871, 377
Norris, Francis Marion 1866, 376
Norris, James Almer 1877, 377
Norris, John Thomas 1872, 377
Norris, Lutie 1862, 376
Norris, Margaret Ann 1872, 377
Norris, Mary Ellen 1939, 160
Norris, Mitchell 1961, 152
Norris, No given name, 152
Norris, Patricia Ann 1940, 160
Norris, Reginald Heber 1875, 377
Norris, Wallace, 108
Norris, Walter, 263
Norris, Warren 1864, 376
Norson, Sandra 1936, 238
Norton, No given name, 17
Norton, Wayne, 17
Norwood, Annie Belle 1871, 60
Norwood, Elizabeth 1805, 213
Norwood, Julia, 74
Norwood, Lillie Mabel, 135
Norwood, Linda Dianne 1951, 133
Noyes, Cheryl Lynn 1950, 187
Noyes, No given name, 187
Nuber, Jacob Louis 1863, 46

—O—

O'Halloran, Robert, 349
O'Hara, Edith, 317
O'Neal, Lucille Yvonne 1936, 43
O'Quinn, No given name, 323
Oagle, Ada, 136
Oden, William T., 327

511

514

515

517

Redmond, Trudy Ann 1950, 134
Reece, Linda Sue 1943, 249
Reed, Allen Elon 1939, 85
Reed, Betty Jane 1946, 85
Reed, Charles Elon 1919, 85
Reed, Charles Francis 1942, 85
Reed, Chymer, 189
Reed, Fidelia, 170
Reed, James Edward 1944, 85
Reed, Linda, 359
Reed, Martha Eloise 1932, 189
Reed, Thomas, 109
Reed, William Lloyd 1940, 85
Reeder, Della Irene, 298
Reichard, Gloria Thomisina 1933, 244
Reichelderfer, Bruce Allen, 381
Reichelderfer, Kathryn, 381
Reid, Anthony Eugene 1959, 49
Reid, Barbara Jean, 73
Reid, Harrington 1918, 73
Reid, Jacquelyn 1982, 49
Reid, John Franklin 1920, 73
Reid, Linda L. 1949, 73
Reid, Lisa 1981, 49
Reid, N. Eugene 1917, 73
Reid, Paul Xavier, III 1963, 49
Reid, Paul Xavier, Jr. 1940, 48
Reid, Robert Earl 1923, 73
Reid, Samuel E. 1858, 73
Reilly, No given name, 296
Remsburg, Doris Lorraine 1932, 190
Remsburg, Mary C. 1877, 224
Renn, M. Luther, 125
Renn, Tillie 1871, 125
Repass, Helen Elizabeth 1942, 57
Resurvey of Brooke Park, 373
Reubaugh, John, 406

Rexholm Farm, 381
Rhoderick, Vernon L. 1901, 108
Rhodes, Ashley Elizabeth 1985, 233
Rhodes, Edmond Hamilton, Jr., 233
Rhodes, Kenneth David 1963, 233
Rhodes, Margaret Ann 1952, 79
Rhodes, Mark Hamilton 1960, 233
Rhodes, Matthew Hamilton 1987, 233
Rhodes, Timothy Wayne 1990, 233
Rhodes, Wayne Patrick 1968, 233
Rice, Blanche, 389
Rice, Douglas Dutrow 1882, 61, 65
Rice, Lillian Glenda 1912, 65
Rice, Maxine Clara 1913, 61, 65
Rice, Millard Fillmore, 88
Rice, Olive Elizabeth 1937, 64
Richards, David, 19
Richards, Lawrence L., 328
Richardson, Frances M. 1838, 308
Richardson, Julian Leigh, 196
Richter, Anna, 383
Richter, Burnette E. 1909, 98
Richter, Joanna, 383
Richter, Joseph, 383
Richter, Philip, 98
Ricketts, Audrey 1927, 71
Ricketts, Elizabeth, 337
Riddle, Beulah Fay, 101
Riddle, Constance Eileen, 102
Riddle, Cynthia Louise, 102

522

Sibley, Hettie, 17
Sibley, James E. L. 1866, 16
Sibley, Jonathan 1797, 114
Sibley, Joseph Russell 1901,
16, 235
Sibley, Joshua, 337
Sibley, Mary, 17
Sibley, Nora 1872, 337
Sickmen, Matthew, 56
Sickmen, No given name, 56
Sickmen, Stephen, 56
Sikken, Christa 1946, 146
Silance, John Richard, 47
Silance, Nannye Mae 1887, 47
Silance, William Walter 1881,
47
Sileck, Joseph, 147
Sileck, Joseph Snyder, 147
Simm, Robert, 398
Simmons, George James, 148
Simmons, George James, III
1971, 149
Simmons, Heather Joy 1972,
149
Simonds, Delora, 246
Simone, Guiseppe 1903, 58
Simpson, David Vernon 1956,
131
Simpson, Etta 1884, 402
Simpson, Helen Dianne 1942,
131
Simpson, John Reynolds 1949,
131
Simpson, Thomas, 399
Simpson, Vernon Ray 1915,
131
Skinner, Margie June, 173
Slagle, Cora Virginia 1866,
172
Slaughter, Dell Pemberton
1892, 199
Slave, Ignatius Green, 29

Slave, Jeremiah Mason, 30
Slave, Matilda Green, 29
Slave, Samuel Mason, 30
Slayton, Ruth Lydia 1903, 149
Slicer, Connie, 345
Slothower, Lillie, 408
Slye, Marie Alphonso, 414
Small, Debra Jean 1952, 130
Small, John Alan 1958, 130
Small, John Scott 1925, 130
Smiley, Anne, 60, 270
Smith, Allison Leigh 1976, 37
Smith, Ceara Rene 1975, 37
Smith, Charles Rosensteel
1905, 46
Smith, Christina S., 187
Smith, Diane Lynn 1947, 37
Smith, Doris Rene, 193
Smith, Douglas Edwin 1968,
36
Smith, Edward, 305
Smith, Edward H., 305
Smith, Edwin Townsend 1940,
36
Smith, Eugene Orrie, 94
Smith, Evelyn Virginia 1938,
57
Smith, Gordon David 1961, 39
Smith, Helen 1906, 107
Smith, Herbert Clayton 1886,
36, 315
Smith, Horace Michael 1965,
94
Smith, Horace Washington,
317
Smith, Job, 413
Smith, John, 412
Smith, John Woodrow 1915, 36
Smith, Katherine June 1991, 39
Smith, Kenneth Eugene 1931,
62
Smith, King W., 305

525

Soper, Mary 1911, 73
Soper, Mary Helen 1902, 70
Soper, Robert Armstrong 1934, 70
Soper, Robert Donald Marcus 1943, 71
Soper, Robert Leese 1888, 106
Soper, Robert Percy 1873, 70
Soper, Robert Percy, Jr. 1900, 70
Soper, Roy Roger 1911, 107
Soper, Sharon 1947, 107
Soper, Spencer Jones 1878, 72
Soper, Susan E., 119
Soper, Thomas Llewellyn 1917, 74
Soper, W. Franklin 1905, 71
Soper, W. Franklin, Jr. 1934, 71
Soper, William L. 1938, 71
Soper, William Oscar 1877, 71
Soper, William Wooten 1850, 23, 69
Souder, Archie W. 1884, 165, 233, 288, 322
Souder, Beulah 1889, 133
Souder, Dorothy Laurene 1912, 233, 289
Souder, Eleanor Day 1921, 161
Souder, Evelyn Elizabeth 1911, 160
Souder, Grace Wilson 1913, 289, 322
Souder, Hazel Eileen 1927, 161
Souder, Helen, 288
Souder, Helen Warfield, 165
Souder, Jane, 288
Souder, Mary Wilson 1918, 160
Souder, Philip Boyer 1920, 161
Souder, Ruth, 288

Souder, Willard Lansdale 1885, 160
Souder, Willard Lansdale, Jr. 1908, 160
Spalding, Elizabeth, 398
Sparrow, Ida, 340
Spates, Dorothy Ann 1971, 90
Spates, George Edward, 89
Spates, Joseph Edward 1948, 89
Spaulding, Debora Jean 1970, 189
Spaulding, John Frederick 1941, 189
Spaur, Gladys, 40
Speace, Brandon King 1972, 228
Speace, Stanley Coulson 1968, 228
Speace, Willard Coulson 1937, 228
Specht, Isaac Jacob, 282
Specht, Mary 1908, 281
Speier, David Torrance 1956, 251
Speier, Georgia Mae 1989, 251
Speier, William Farren 1930, 251
Spencer, Almira, 408
Spencer, No given name, 364
Spooner, Margaret Louise 1936, 245
Spooner, Marvin Louis, 244
Sprague, George Bancroft, 391
Sprigg, Margaret, 394, 398
Sprigg, Thomas, Colonel, 398
Spurrier, Clarence, 211
Spurrier, Everett, 211
Spurrier, Franklin E., 211
Spurrier, Margaret, 211
Spurrier, Stella, 211

St. Clair, Louise Frances 1939, 190
St. Clare, Bernard, 414
Staley, Merhle, 82
Stanley, Doris Eleanor 1916, 162, 249
Stanley, Estelle, 288
Stanley, Esther, 288
Stanley, George Anthony 1915, 58
Stanley, Gertrude Wilson 1914, 162
Stanley, Grover Mount 1892, 143, 162, 249
Stanley, Hazel Margaret 1922, 162
Stanley, Jeanne, 288
Stanley, Louise, 288
Stanley, Mary, 286
Stanley, Mary Lee, 228, 288
Stanley, Phyllis Ethel 1928, 143, 162
Stanley, Richard Harry, 162
Stanley, Robert L., 228
Stanley, Robert L. 1874, 288
Stanley, Roland, 288
Stanley, Roy 1953, 205
Stanley, Ruth A. 1903, 99
Stark, James William, 77, 353
Stark, William, 77, 353
Start, Teresa, 274
Station, Dorothy 1961, 238
Staub, Eunice Elaine 1945, 294
Staub, Luther Franklin II, 62
Steeley, Linda Low 1950, 150
Steely, Charles, 150
Sterling, Patricia Marie 1948, 275
Sterrick, Elizabeth Kingsley, 343
Stevenson, Henry, Dr., 409
Stevenson, Juliana, 409

Steward, John, 406
Stewart, George 1834, 261
Stewart, Katharine, 302
Stier, Una Estelle, 174
Stine, Ethel A. 1901, 111
Stinnett, Violet, 358
Stitley, Gary Wayne 1944, 139
Stockman, Cheryl Ann 1973, 105
Stockman, Cindy Lynn 1971, 105
Stockman, Richard E. 1942, 105
Stoffer, Hester, 407
Stokes, No given name, 381
Stone, Daniel Evan 1990, 20
Stone, Jena Renee 1993, 20
Stone, Mary J. 1842, 413, 414
Stone, Robert Jay 1962, 20
Stone, William, 20
Stone, William 1938, 20
Stonestreet, Anne, 398
Storm, Charles, 108
Stotler, Eva, 351
Stotler, Helen 1918, 73
Stout, Cecelia Agnes 1955, 293
Strait, Anita Joyce, 257
Strand, Joanna, 412
Strange, Joyce Kinser, 353
Strange, Thomas, 353
Stroud, Elizabeth Randall 1955, 154
Stroud, John Allen 1921, 153
Stroud, John Allen, Jr., 153
Stroud, Sally Palmer 1949, 153
Stroud, Thomas Whitney 1951, 154
Strunk, Carrie, 250
Strunk, Steven Wayne, 250
Strunk, Steven Wayne, Jr. 1981, 250
Stull, Arnold Raymond, 167

535

Walker, Nancy Lou 1961, 46
Walker, Nathan Asbury 1865,
336, 356
Walker, Nathan James 1824,
30, 222, 335, 336, 337, 340,
342, 350, 351, 356, 360, 361
Walker, Nathan Walter 1886,
76, 351, 354
Walker, Nathan Walter, III,
351
Walker, Nathan Walter, Jr.,
351
Walker, Parepa Wesley Wood
1872, 147
Walker, Patricia Alana 1957,
46
Walker, Patricia Joyce 1954,
345
Walker, Pearl Marian 1913,
362
Walker, Philip Hughes 1947,
347
Walker, Phyllis A., 355
Walker, Rachel Vivia Cochel
1874, 147
Walker, Robert Louis 1947,
151
Walker, Robert McCabe 1922,
345
Walker, Robert Muller 1909,
150
Walker, Robert Thomas, 355
Walker, Robin Marie 1951, 345
Walker, Roland Nathan 1886,
346
Walker, Rosabelle 1870, 146
Walker, Roy, 354
Walker, Rufus Wesley 1902,
145
Walker, Russell King 1890,
343, 348
Walker, Sally, 355

Walker, Samuel Wesley 1892,
202
Walker, Sarah Marion 1897,
355
Walker, Stewart Eugene 1944,
140, 142
Walker, Stewart Eugene Day
1918, 142
Walker, Stewart Eugene, III
1971, 142
Walker, Susan Lynn 1951, 349
Walker, Teresa Anne, 355
Walker, Thomas Addison
1925, 45
Walker, Trina Renee, 355
Walker, Virginia Rebecca
1893, 348, 354
Walker, Wava Jane 1934, 145
Walker, Wesley Day 1900, 145
Walker, Wilbur Bryan 1908,
146
Walker, Wilfred Taft 1908, 146
Walker, William Alfred Baker
1867, 143, 209
Walker, William Augusta
Cooke 1887, 353
Walker, William Augusta
Cooke, Jr. 1918, 353
Walker, William Crittenden,
355
Walker, William Edward 1949,
360
Walker, William F. 1942, 145
Walker, William Hughes 1901,
360
Walker, William Oscar 1923,
360
Walker, William Paul 1898,
145
Walker, William Ralph 1905,
10, 345, 346, 361, 362

Walker, William Randolph
  Mettauer 1944, 150
Walker, William Richard 1940,
  146
Walker, William Wayne, 355
Walker, Willing Wendell 1910,
  146
Wallace, Joseph, 406
Wallace, Miriam Winifred, 141
Wallach, Bessie T. 1892, 22
Walter, Agnes Jeanette 1930,
  24, 53
Walter, Edna Lorraine 1923,
  49
Walter, George Cloudsley, 49
Walter, No given name, 173
Wamsley, Gary Lee, 131
Wamsley, Jonathan Asbury
  1973, 131
Wandishin, John, 239
Ward, Albertis 1883, 273
Ward, Augusta 1888, 273
Ward, Carleton Wendell 1935,
  238
Ward, Carolyn Elizabeth 1975,
  252
Ward, Cherrie Lynn 1957, 252
Ward, David Irvin 1907, 238
Ward, David Lloyd 1957, 238
Ward, Eli Granberry 1877, 251
Ward, Enoch George, 251
Ward, George Sprigg, 342
Ward, Harrison Gilmore 1853,
  273
Ward, J. Garnet, 273
Ward, James Edgar Harold
  1944, 252
Ward, James Roland 1909, 251
Ward, Jennifer 1986, 238
Ward, Jennifer Lee 1970, 252
Ward, John Wesley 1883, 66
Ward, Julia 1916, 342

Ward, Lloyd Irvin 1931, 238
Ward, Martha 1821, 292
Ward, Mary Ann 1933, 251
Ward, Mary Lewis 1917, 257
Ward, Mary Rebecca, 251
Ward, Mary Sybil 1880, 87,
  216
Ward, Pauline Estelle 1947,
  249
Ward, Robert Christopher
  1983, 238
Ward, Steven Craig 1967, 238
Ward, Susanna Rebecca 1973,
  252
Ward, Terrie Lee 1959, 252
Ward, Thomas Carleton 1958,
  238
Ward, Thomas Jeffry 1963, 252
Ward, Thomas Roland 1938,
  252
Ward, Tracey 1974, 249
Ward, Vickie Sue 1964, 252
Ward, Woodrow Wilson 1912,
  249
Ward, Woodrow Wilson, Jr.
  1944, 249
Ware, Ann, 412
Ware, Dorothy, 94
Warfield, Charles Edwin 1884,
  263
Warfield, Amanda 1849, 285,
  286
Warfield, Basil T. 1859, 14,
  174
Warfield, Bessie C. 1895, 175
Warfield, Bradley 1855, 289
Warfield, Bradley Winfield,
  389
Warfield, Clyde G., 174
Warfield, Diane Louise 1948,
  242

537

543

Watson, Nancy Ellen 1923, 300
Watson, Susannah, 399
Watt, Viola, 108
Watts, Catharine, 414
Waugh, Elizabeth, 5
Wayne, Cynthia Louise 1957, 274
Wayne, Donald, 273
Wayne, Donna Marie 1960, 274
Wayne, Mary Beth 1968, 274
Weaver, Annamaria, 399
Weaver, Sarah, 398
Webb, Laura, 62
Webb, Linda, 256
Webb, Ocia, 376
Weber, Eleanor Marie 1939, 239
Weber, Kimberly, 49
Webster, Lydia, 395, 398
Weed, Clifford, 77
Welch, Pearl, 98
Weller, Jeanne, 231
Wells, Edward Graham 1944, 141
Wells, Edward Henry, 141
Wells, Mary Alice 1935, 141
Wells, Mason, 141
Wells, Perry H. 1887, 402
Wells, Ralph Scanlon 1940, 141
Welsh, Charlotte Lee, 299
Welsh, Elbert 1904, 188
Welsh, Elbert, Jr. 1930, 189
Welsh, Michael Stevens 1957, 189
Welsh, Terry Lee 1953, 189
Welsh, William Thomas, 188
Welty, Carol, 331
Welty, Charles E. 1904, 358
Welty, Douglas MacArthur 1943, 358

Wentz, Cora 1902, 72
West, Edwin M., 361
West, Jean, 349
West, Marian Eleanor 1908, 361
Westerfield, Edythe Giraud 1909, 155
Westerfield, George Sumner, 155
Wettengel, Edward, 351
Wetzel, Gary 1950, 106
Wetzel, Renee 1972, 106
Whalen, Alice E., 19
Whatman, Lawrence Edward, 52
Whatman, Stephanie Leigh 1982, 52
Whatman, Wesley Ryan 1979, 52
Whelan, Brandon Dalton 1977, 40
Whelan, Charles Nicholas, 39
Whelan, Charles Nicholas, III 1923, 39
Whelan, Charles Nicholas, IV 1955, 39
Whelan, Charles Nicholas, Jr. 1891, 39
Whelan, John Theodore 1961, 39
Whelan, Lauren Kimberley 1955, 40
Whelan, Lynn Alexandria 1979, 40
Whelan, Mary Catherine 1961, 39
Whelan, Robert Dalton 1926, 39
Whelan, Sarah, 405
Whelan, Thomas Dalton 1949, 40
Whipp, Edward F., 49

Whipp, Erica Lorraine 1977,
50
White, Alvin 1928, 359
White, Anne Riggs 1931, 271
White, Betty Lee 1925, 359
White, Carolyn Maye 1942,
205
White, Charles, 127, 324
White, Charles LeRoy 1917,
358
White, Charles Stephen 1953,
358
White, Charlotte Marie 1947,
358
White, Cheryl Lynn 1944, 358
White, Dana L. 1959, 359
White, Dorothy, 127, 324
White, Dorothy Elizabeth 1915,
358
White, Edward Blake 1940,
172
White, Frances, 127, 324
White, James, 405
White, John P. 1873, 110
White, Joseph Michael 1947,
358
White, Joseph Rodney 1914,
358
White, Joseph Rodney, Jr., 358
White, Joyce D. 1944, 358
White, Karla Kay 1946, 358
White, Kay 1924, 72
White, Lewis, 211
White, Lillian, 171, 211
White, Louisa, 127, 324
White, Mary Margaret 1956,
359
White, Murr, 211
White, Myrtle, 127, 324
White, Paul, 211
White, Richard Edward 1964,
172

White, Sarah, 400
White, Sarah 1805, 395
White, Susan Elaine 1965, 172
White, Washington, 127, 324
White, William Earl 1920, 358
White, William Rodney
d/1953, 358
White, William Rodney, III
1964, 359
White, William Rodney, Jr.
1930, 359
Whitworth, Brenda Lee 1964,
19
Whitworth, George Irwin, 19
Wiggins, Lillian Wanda 1930,
150
Wilbur, Elizabeth Fitch 1940,
131
Wilbur, John Mason 1911, 131
Wilbur, Susan Bradley 1942,
131
Wilcox, Shirley, 64
Wilcoxen, Jesse, 399
Wilhide, John L., 371
Wilkes, Jo Ann, 238
Wilkinson, Marilyn Paige
1948, 195
Willett, Clifford 1874, 61, 66
Willett, Clifford Mazenar 1910,
66
Willett, Cynthia 1961, 66
Willett, Donald Bruce 1963, 66
Willett, Elizabeth Naomi 1914,
61, 66
Willett, Elton Clifford 1906, 66
Willett, Nancy Joan 1931, 66
Willett, Richard Bruce 1944,
66
Willett, Thomas Elton 1937, 66
Williams, Carl, 328
Williams, Carol 1953, 236
Williams, Charlotte J., 23, 74

520463

Made in the USA